AUTHORITAS

INTERBOOK™

*Every Interbook features an extensive companion web site
just for owners of the print edition.*

*To view source materials and more for this Interbook,
follow along on-line at*

http://www.thinkpress.com/authoritas

*and look for the Interbook logo when making your next
book purchase.*

VERITAS
VEHRITAS
VETHRITAS
VETHIRITAS
VETHORITAS
VUTHORITAS
AUTHORITAS

One Student's Harvard Admissions and the Founding of the Facebook Era

Aaron Greenspan

Think Press

Palo Alto

Think Press
A Division of Think Computer Corporation
Palo Alto, CA
http://www.thinkpress.com

Think Press, Interbook and the Smiling Logo are trademarks of Think Computer Corporation.

For information about special promotions and premiums, please contact Think Press Sales at sales@thinkpress.com or +1 888 815 8599.

First Edition 2008

DESIGNED BY AARON GREENSPAN

Library of Congress Control Number: 2008903570

ISBN-13: 978-1-60669-000-0
ISBN-10: 1-60669-000-0

Printed in the United States of America on 30% PCW Recycled Paper

20 19 18 17 16 15 14 13 12 11 10 9 8 7 6 5 4 3 2 1

To honor my father and mother

To hope for my brother

To thank my friends

Contents

"We are a community that is committed to the authority of ideas,
rather than to the idea of authority."

—HARVARD UNIVERSITY PRESIDENT LAWRENCE H. SUMMERS
REMARKS AT OPENING EXERCISES
CAMBRIDGE, MASSACHUSETTS
SEPTEMBER 15, 2005

"Were she able to feel, she thought as she walked through the concourse of the Terminal, she would know that the heavy indifference she felt for her railroad was hatred. She could not get rid of the feeling that she was running nothing but freight trains: the passengers, to her, were not living or human. It seemed senseless to waste such enormous effort on preventing catastrophes, on protecting the safety of trains carrying nothing but inanimate objects. She looked at the faces in the Terminal: if he were to die, she thought, to be murdered by the rulers of their system, that these might continue to eat, sleep and travel, would she work to provide them with trains? If she were to scream for help, would one of them rise to his defense? Did they want him to live, they who had heard him?"

—AYN RAND
ATLAS SHRUGGED

Author's Note

It is almost guaranteed that every few years, another book will be published about Harvard University. You might think this is one of those books. However, Harvard is a big place, and trying to write a book about it is a bit like trying to fit World History into fifty pages or less. A lot goes on from many different viewpoints. So, for those hoping to find a compendium of every detail about the Ivy League, I'm afraid I will disappoint you. The book that you are presently reading is not really about Harvard University, though it certainly plays an important role in the following pages.

This book is about the strange events that have unfolded in my life, limited as it has been, and specifically, it is an attempt to answer a question that troubled me for some time after I completed my education. It would be a gross understatement to say that a lot of people aspire to attend schools like Harvard, and I was incredibly lucky to have the opportunity to actually study there. Yet my experience was overwhelmingly negative, with the notable exception of making real friends for the first time. My question is, how was it possible for such a wonderful education to be so horrible?

At this point, you may already be wondering if perhaps the real problem was not so much the education I received, as it was me. Surely, my own personality accounts for a large degree of the story you are about to read. (It takes two to tango.) For that reason, I chose to write about my life from an early age. There were aspects of my behavior as a very young child that gave telling clues to what I would be like later on. I also find it interesting that the curious and energetic personality I used to possess has largely vanished in favor of a guarded and skeptical persona that I feel society has forced me to assume. Mental scar tissue is difficult to shed, and the impact it has in social situations is very real, as you will see. Starting the story from early on also allows me to tell the complete tale, which I believe to be important. For without all of the facts of any story, it is impossible to truly understand its meaning, and even then, facts can fall victim to misinterpretation.

This is not a fairy tale. Those people who I have met who deserve to know shame will find their due portions here. Inevitably, some people will be offended. Specifically, parents, those of you who will do anything to gain entrance for your children to elite private colleges: read closely. High school students, and those in particular who dream of going to Harvard one day: you too. And to all of the politicians out there, blissfully unaware of the consequences of your harebrained policies: may you come to understand why I take a deep and personal offense at the phrase "no child left behind."

I am not ashamed to admit that I've benefited greatly from the therapy of writing in as much detail as I can recall. This book is partly a search for justice. Since our judicial system can't possibly know about all that surrounds us—and it would be even more overwhelmed if it did—it is my hope that the pages of this book will serve as an adequate, if less severe, substitute.

After considerable debate, I have chosen not to change the names of individuals in this book to preserve the accuracy of the tale. In some cases, I have simply omitted names partially or completely. Select paragraphs of correspondence, such as address blocks, signatures or other content irrelevant to the story at hand, have also been removed for the sake of legibility.

I have attempted to recollect dialog to the best of my ability, but as is the case with all memories that have been dormant for years, perfection is often elusive. I have consulted with others to ensure that even if the precise wording of a quotation is not always correct, then at least its general sentiment is.

Lastly, I will make an attempt to answer my critics, since there are always some, from the outset. Some will inevitably call me arrogant. That's not unreasonable—I too would be quick to assert that anyone writing a memoir right out of college must be completely full of himself. Read closely, though, and you will see that I make no claims to greatness. Like many high school students who found themselves suddenly labeled "Harvard" at one point during senior year, I've spent some time worrying about arrogance—both what it means and how to avoid it. By my own definition, arrogance is the difference between supposition and actual fact that may, or may not, be designed to inflict damage. Since I do not mean to harm anyone by telling my story, only the supposed and actual facts remain. In other words, if I am careful not to exaggerate anything, at least according to my own theory, I should be safe. Therefore, I have done my best to tell my tale as accurately as I know how.

By the end, you may be tempted to exclaim (as many have), "Well, you certainly got an education!"

While this is true, and I was lucky to get it, my education affected my health in profound ways. As the tale unfolds, you may want to ask yourself the following: would you wish my education upon your own children?

Take the rest how you will. I have done all that I can.

This is my story.

AUTHORITAS

One Student's Harvard Admissions and the Founding of the Facebook Era

Prologue

"What can I do for you?" he said.

From the moment the sound of the first word left his mouth and entered my ear, I knew that our meeting would be nothing less than a verbal train wreck. His tone indicated that I was already being ridiculed.

I was sitting on a plush beige sofa in an office in Massachusetts Hall, a small rectangular building lodged snugly next to Harvard Yard's Johnston Gate. There was a computer with a sleek flat screen on a desk on the other side of the room, and the dark African masks resting on the shelves to my left were silently watching me think. The walls were painted a deep shade of red, which by virtue of their location in Harvard's inner sanctum defined the word crimson. There was a woman sitting across from me, notebook in hand, ready to record my thoughts and emotional state so that in ten or twenty or a hundred years, someone might dig them out of a dusty filing cabinet. Sitting next to her, in an oversized chair, was the man who I had come to see and who had asked the question. His name was Lawrence Summers, he was the President of Harvard University, and this was his office.

I strived to ensconce my voice in the same formality that made the President sound so serious and dry. Yet when I heard myself speak, tinny and verbose by comparison, I knew that I would be perceived the same as every other overzealous undergraduate. I launched into the answer to his question.

"Well, I'm here because it was a pretty miserable month of August for myself and my entire family. I was forced to deal with the Office of the General Counsel for making a web site, called houseSYSTEM, with perfectly reasonable aims. To make a long story short, I feel as though College violated the guidelines in its own Handbook for Students, and it has certainly not allowed for due process. I guess my question for you really is, 'How was it possible for the College administration to react in such a way to student initiative?'"

"I can't answer for the behavior of other people," the President said. "The Office of the General Counsel was not being disrespectful by enforcing Harvard's trademark. Rob Iuliano wouldn't be doing his job if they had not contacted you. And 'due process' only begins after disciplinary action is brought upon someone." It seemed as though the President had been briefed. It didn't matter. I began my defense.

"Nevertheless, we were allowed to use Harvard's trademark as an officially recognized student group," I countered. "Regarding due process, aside from the timeline, I think it is inconsistent for an institution that prides itself on freedom of expression to prohibit voicing one's own side of things." There was a tinge of irritation growing in my voice, and I was sure he was going to notice. I couldn't stop it, though.

"I do not see the instance of disrespect here," the President said flatly. I was shocked.

"In that case, what would constitute disrespect?"

"Someone being generally hostile, someone hanging up on you..."

"Dean Kidd *did* hang up on me, and then didn't allow me to know anything about a meeting that had been held specifically about me." I kicked myself for not saying what I meant. I had intended to say that I didn't even know what crime I was being accused of. Sure enough, President Summers pounced.

"If there was a meeting about you, then it was perfectly acceptable for you not to be in the meeting. I want to make that clear. That was perfectly acceptable."

I did my best to recover. "I mentioned it only as a fact: I was not in the meeting. Even if that was acceptable, I was not even allowed to know the outcome of the meeting. I was told that I would see the outcome in a letter."

The assistant chimed in. "Was the letter sent?"

"No," I answered. My strategy of not wasting the President's time with details I guessed he didn't care about was failing miserably. He had missed the big picture: Harvard had tried to shut down a web site that thousands of students had signed up for because it was consistent with his goal of centralizing functions within the University. It made life easier. Neither of us knew it would start something of a revolution among college students nationwide in a matter of months. On house-SYSTEM, students reviewed courses, bought and sold books, uploaded digital post-ers, electronically RSVPed to campus events, found those events on the Harvard map with a single click, and uploaded their own color photographs to a part of the site the administration had specifically warned me about creating: The Universal Face Book, which I also called "The Facebook." I went on, hoping to convince him of my innocence with some hard evidence I had brought along in a thin binder.

"I don't want to bog you down in details, but it seems relevant to mention some now. Aside from issues of disrespect, the administration used false pretenses to gain access to houseSYSTEM even when I presented them with the opportunity to see how it worked. Then, the administration forced me to turn over confidential student records under duress, threatening me with 'disciplinary action' if I didn't comply."

"How was the 'disciplinary action' conveyed?" President Summers asked.

"I don't know, it was never specified."

"HOW was it conveyed?" he almost shouted.

"*He really is obnoxious!*" I thought, recalling everything I had read about him, but knowing that having such thoughts in the middle of our conversation could not possibly be helping.

"Jay Ellison e-mailed me on behalf of the Office of the General Counsel."

"Who?"

"Jay Ellison."

"Yes, who is Jay Ellison?" he asked, much to my surprise, with an intonation that clearly implied I was an idiot for not knowing who he did and did not know.

"My Lowell House Senior Tutor, who was the contact person for all of my dealings with the Administration."

"What was to be turned over?"

"Information about each student who had signed up for houseSYSTEM, which included personal details such as cell phone numbers, and whether or not the student wanted others to know that they had signed up."

"Oh, I read about that in *The Crimson*!" I had triggered some recollection of the issue in his mind, finally. "It said you were using their Harvard IDs against College rules. Of course you're going to get in trouble if you ask for their Harvard IDs!"

"Actually, we didn't use Harvard IDs. We just asked for their FAS passwords so that they could check their e-mail on the site. I was very careful to make sure that the way my server handled the requests did not violate College rules."

The President rolled his eyes and emitted a loud grimacing noise. Unsure of what to do, I kept talking.

"In fact, I informed Dr. Franklin Steen, who runs FAS Computer Services, about the system two years ago, and he did not seem to have a problem with it then."

The President paused to think, tapping his foot under the table. I had never observed such palpable impatience before. After a short but pronounced delay, he uttered a clear signal of dismissal. "I do not see how your description of the actual events that took place lives up to the seriousness of the allegations that you are making."

At this, I became truly alarmed that I had misrepresented something, or everything. Was I being too *calm*? Should I have come in screaming, with arms flailing? Did he realize the true potential of my work, as I did? Did he understand that this was about more than my vacation, or a web site, but the course of my entire life? I felt myself merely raising my eyebrows. "What would you consider serious, then?"

"Well, if there actually had been some sort of...disciplinary action...taken, or if someone had harassed you in an 'abusive' manner..." He trailed off. I tried to remain diplomatic.

"While I agree that those are certainly serious matters, I probably would not be able to talk to you today if disciplinary action had taken place. Personally, I consider several weeks of e-mail from the Office of the General Counsel accusing me of crimes I did not commit to be at least on the verge of abusive." The Administration had made it quite plain that they would have been happy to see me leave.

The President's mouth twisted into a smile. "Well, Aaron, what do you want me to do?"

"That's the tough part. I don't really know what to ask you to do. I don't know what is supposed to happen when the College violates its own rules, since that probably doesn't take place very often."

"It sounds to me like you were just trying to skirt around the rules...which entrepreneurially-minded people tend to do." It was a snide remark, and I took offense. I was proud to consider myself an entrepreneur. "You should have expected resistance for not going through the proper channels. You got quite a bit of it—but rightly so!"

"Do you really think it is fair for the entire Office of the General Counsel to take on a single student? I had to involve outside attorneys to defend myself!"

The President shot back. "First of all, it was not the 'entire' Office of the General Counsel. Harvard employs many lawyers, and I am sure just a fraction were concerned with your case. But absolutely! If you hired outside attorneys you should doubly expect the Office of General Counsel to get involved."

"I wasn't paying them—hiring attorneys to fight the Office of the General Counsel is not something I can really afford as a student."

"It doesn't really matter. If you were trying to be a rebel, then that is what you would get."

"I'm not trying to be a rebel! It's not like I'm doing this just to cause troub—" President Summers cut me off and spoke rapidly.

"Yes you are."

I sat, dumbfounded. After five very long seconds, sitting like a pigeon on his couch, I regained my composure. "Well, I don't know how to respond to that because it sounds like you've already made up your mind."

The President became more animated. "Oh, I haven't made up my mind. You have taken all of these actions, but really, you are just enjoying the fight." Suddenly, the third voice in the room manifested itself once more.

"What President Summers means is not that you are 'enjoying' the fight," his assistant said looking at President Summers, and then at me. There was an awkward silence.

"What he means is that...you've entangled yourself...in a complex situation." She was trying hard to erase what her boss had said from my memory. I just stared.

"*I know what the man said,*" I snapped in my mind. Outwardly, I swallowed.

"I disagree that I am enjoying what I am presently doing." It was true. There wasn't a smile anywhere close to my face. The President continued his analysis of my wrongs.

"You should have expected so much resistance after you had hired lawyers.

After that, it was basically all over."

"Perhaps so, but Harvard's lawyers made the first move! How is a student supposed to respond to the Office of the General Counsel? *Not* hire lawyers?" My tone of voice carried a mixture of disgust and disbelief, but my fate was already sealed.

"If I were you, I would write a letter trying to clarify the situation, explaining my point of view, saying that I was not trying to harm anything, that these are the steps I had taken..." the President said.

"I have written almost the exact letter you just described in an e-mail, sent to Jay Ellison."

"'I'm sorry.' Did it say that in it?" The conversation was going about as bad as it could go.

"I don't know what to apologize for, because I haven't done anything wrong!"

"I disagree with this legalistic approach that you've decided to take," the President remarked. "It's really a counterproductive approach to the whole 'venture,'—but if you want to do it that way, it's alright. I think you should have gone to the Deans and the Office of the General Counsel before making the site."

"There are no real channels to go through at Harvard to make a site like this. The Technology and Entrepreneurship Center at Harvard is the only possible channel, and once it heard about houseSYSTEM, it withdrew its support from my club completely."

"Well... my advice, as someone who has seen a lot of complex situations, is to not take the aggressive approach, and to work with people. If you want to write me a letter with 'serious allegations' against a faculty member, I will look at it—well, I'm sure you understand that I have a lot going on, and so someone on my staff would actually look at it—but they will look at it, and respond to it with details of how your concerns have already been addressed." It sounded like something a Stalinist court might have offered in the way of a compromise.

"I already wrote that letter," I said, taking it out of my note pad and holding it up for him to see. "I even CCed it to your e-mail address, but I can re-send it if you would like."

"I want a *letter*. If you really want to send it, that is, and it's really your decision. It would be better to just move on, though."

"I'm happy to move on! The reason I'm here is that I am relatively uncomfortable with the notion that another student could find themselves in a similar situation, and this could all happen just as easily to someone else! This seems to me to be a pretty clear violation of the Faculty's 1970 Resolution in the College's Handbook for Students on how to treat people with dignity and respect."

President Summers had had enough. He stretched in his chair slightly. "Well, Aaron, you're right. You're right. We do take the Handbook for Students very seriously, and you are absolutely right about the College needing to treat students with respect. Thanks for coming by."

I felt positively sickened. The President believed *The Harvard Crimson*—the same newspaper that had insinuated that he was fat, chubby and slow—more than he believed an undergraduate who had taken the time to share a real concern at his office hours. I even agreed with him on most matters of administrative policy. The entire point of houseSYSTEM had been to centralize College functions in one place, reducing inefficiency, improving undergraduate life.

"I appreciate you taking the time to talk with me," I said. Then I got up, and began to exit out the door I had entered from.

"Nope, other door," the assistant motioned, pointing behind me, and setting my cheeks on fire. She went out into the hallway right afterward. I could only smirk at everything I had just heard.

"Are you alright?" she asked, pretending to be genuinely concerned.

"Oh, I'm fine," I said. "Just disappointed is all."

"*So much for innocent until proven guilty,*" I thought.

As soon as I got back to my room in Lowell House, I wrote the entire conversation down, knowing full well that Harvard's notes, written by the assistant, would be forever locked away in my file.

Facing two more long, miserable years at Harvard College, going to President Summers was my last chance at closure. I had failed to achieve it, utterly and completely. There was only one thing to do.

"*I have got to get out of here.*"

CHAPTER 1

The Robot Problem

If you were to visit the Cleveland suburb of Shaker Heights, Ohio, you might notice the people or the homes, but it's almost certain that you would notice the trees. They line every street, they are next to every house, and they comprise the majority of the parks scattered throughout the suburb. The city's logo is a picture of a tree, as is the local public library's. Tens of thousands of dollars of tax revenues annually go toward the process of finding those trees with Dutch Elm Disease, cutting them down, and ensuring that the disease hasn't spread, in order to enable the growth of future trees.

Indeed, Shaker Heights loves its trees, and rightly so: along with the surrounding suburbs, "Shaker," as its residents refer to it, stands in stark contrast to the rest of Ohio. Southern Ohio is yellow with corn and red with Republicans. On the shores of Lake Erie, Northern Ohio is for all intents and purposes its own blue state under a veneer of green. Even long after the hotly-contested 2004 presidential election, Shaker residents kept Kerry-Edwards bumper stickers on their Volvo station wagons and Mercedes sport utility vehicles. With a City Hall that could only be characterized as obsessive-compulsive about zoning regulations, the suburb is almost entirely residential, with agriculture and industry both strictly *verboten*. In 1986, my father was offered a position as an assistant professor at Case Western Reserve University nearby, and as a result, Shaker Heights is where I grew up.

In those days and perhaps still, families moved to Shaker primarily because of its well-known school system. Aside from being well-funded (though it seemed poor compared to neighboring suburbs, which taxed their shopping malls), Shaker was remarkably diverse, both racially and socioeconomically. The District's marketing department had a clear favorite statistic: the racial composition of the student body, which was approximately 52% Black, 36% White, 9% "Other," and 3% apparently too diverse to even classify. While Al Lerner, the former owner of the Cleveland Browns football team, kept a multi-million dollar estate on South Park Boulevard amidst many other mansions, there were plenty of multi-family homes only a few blocks away. A number of private schools also had their homes in Shaker: Hathaway Brown and Laurel were all-girls schools, and University School, or "U.S.," was only for boys.

My family first lived in an apartment building called the Oliver House. My younger brother Simon and I were small enough to completely squish inside the plastic bins where we kept our toys, and so we did, because it was funny. Sometimes I'd sit on the floor in my room and speak to myself in what I imagined to be Hebrew—a stream of gibberish interspersed with the word "shalom" every so often. I also served as a translator for my brother, whom everyone else found impossible to understand. Eventually, my mother carted us both to Dana, a speech therapist, on a regular basis. While Simon repeated words and phrases, I played with the limited supply of electronic gadgets and toys she kept around the house. Simon had a lot of trouble with "R" and "Th."

Unbeknownst to me, my parents had saved up enough money to buy a house, so I had the dubious honor of accompanying them on the search for some afford-able, quality real estate. My intense boredom quickly dissipated when, standing on the porch of what our realtor assured us was The Model Home, I was stung on the chest by a bee. My parents sensibly kept looking, as the hive was under The Model Patio.

The house that we did buy was two stories tall, and had an attic and a basement. It was located on Shelburne Road, right around the corner from University School, where there was a fairly new, giant wooden playground.

The first thing that I did was go down to the basement where our new, silver, twenty-seven inch Sony Trinitron television sat on the same counter where my mother's answering machine had once been in St. Louis. I had watched television plenty of times before, but never in Cleveland. I was suddenly overcome by a fear that the shows might be different. Two inexplicable devices sat next to our TV: one was black; the other, a faux wood box which rested on top of the first, with a numeric keypad on top.

Though I was curious about the new devices, I did not hesitate to tear open a third box sitting nearby, which prominently featured Mickey Mouse. The black, boxy object inside fit perfectly into the slot of the larger black box on the counter. I guessed at which button would make it work: the biggest one. Luckily, instead of exploding into flames, the VCR whirred to life, and I welcomed Walt Disney's creation into my basement.

•

My parents, happy with my pre-kindergarten experience at Hathaway Brown down the street, decided to send me to another private school, Hawken, for kinder-garten. On the first day as I walked into our classroom, there was a list of students and their assigned chores on the far-left side of the massive chalkboard, which spanned the entire width of the room. The first chore was simultaneously the best and the easiest: line leader. I had magically been assigned to it before anyone else in the class.

"How did they know I wanted to be line leader?" I wondered. A few years later, I

learned about the properties of alphabetical order by first name.

There were different stations set up all around our classroom, which was very large, each corresponding to different activities that we were required to complete on a regular cycle. I dreaded the Listening Center most, because I found it almost impossible to follow along. I was already an expert at using tape players, but on the part where I had to answer questions about what I was listening to, I always got everything wrong.

Hawken placed a lot of emphasis on physical education. With the exception of dodgeball, I hated gym. There was a giant, fierce-looking hawk always staring down at me. I felt dwarfed by the abilities of the other boys in the class. They instinctively knew what to do when a ball sailed their way; if I didn't duck in time, the ball usually toppled me over. I caught things only by mistake.

By the end of the year, my perplexed teachers finally figured out why I was repeatedly failing the Listening Center. I was waiting until the ten-minute stories were over before I started answering questions, instead of answering them as I listened. To me, answering in real-time seemed like cheating. I also felt that the tape player was better suited to playing Bobby McFerrin's "Don't Worry, Be Happy." It was, after all, 1988.

Our cutting-edge classroom had an Apple IIe personal computer, which I recognized from my days at Hathaway-Brown, but the software was completely different. While I was accustomed to "Sticky Bear Math," Hawken's software had confusing, colored dots and bold white lines everywhere on the screen. I desperately wanted to know how to play, but none of the other children would tell me, let alone permit me to use the computer.

I complained so loudly about Hawken to my parents that they arranged for me to meet with the principal of the school, but conditions did not improve. There was still an invisible perimeter around the computer, I still had no athletic ability, and other children were often mean. My parents intervened. When it came time to go to first grade, I was going to Mercer School, a public school in Shaker.

My friends at Mercer let me use the Apple IIe we had in our classroom, and school was fun again. Relatively quickly, I made a friend who put forth a convincing case that he was much smarter than I was, since he already knew that $12 \times 12 = 144$. When I arrived home from school that day, I announced to my mother, "I made a friend today!" and told her all about Philip's ability to solve complex arithmetic.

For my seventh birthday, my uncle in Boston, Michael Keene, bought me a present that my parents had refused to even consider: the Nintendo Entertainment System. I wasted no time hooking it up to the television in the basement.

Before long, Nintendo of America, Inc. had accomplished its goal of turning one more child into an addict. When I came home from school (after reading *Nintendo Power* with friends on the school bus), I headed straight for our Nintendo in the basement. Whenever my mother protested that I should be doing something outside, I would always respond, "It improves my hand-eye coordination!" After a while, I started to believe it, though I still couldn't throw a football.

In school, I utilized my box of Crayola crayons to its fullest, drawing a new Boeing 737 or Concorde on tabloid-sized paper almost every day. I had conclusively settled on airplane pilot as the greatest career ever, mostly because pilots pushed buttons. Eventually, Miss Dunlap gave my hobby some structure when she assigned our class worksheets with pictures of Teddy bears on them. We were instructed to color them in, and then, according to directions on a cassette tape that was played to the entire class, we were told to arrange the nine bears on a 3 x 3 grid in a particular order. It seemed easy. Before I knew it, I was hooked on logic.

•

In second grade, my father, immersed in his research on cystic fibrosis at Case Western, ordered his first personal computer for home use so that he could take his work back and forth from the lab. Upon its arrival, there was no question that my father's Compaq DeskPro 386s easily beat out my aunt's CD player, my mother's answering machine and my old tape recorder as the most amazing gadget I'd ever seen. Best of all, there weren't any other children who could prevent me from using it. It even had a "hard drive."

"Are these also hard drives?" I asked, pointing to a 3.5" diskette with a hard plastic casing.

"No, those are floppy disks," my father said as my eyebrows furrowed, looking at the distinctly un-floppy disks in front of me. He told me what he knew about the computer, but warned me to be very careful and to always follow a specific routine when using it. Letting his children near his computer made him extremely nervous.

When I learned that unlike piloting, going into a career in computers didn't require intense physical training, the confusing jargon became peripheral. Then and there, I decided that airplanes were out; computers were in.

Soon, Simon and I had our own games, such as "OutNumbered!", which (naturally) involved maneuvering a boy in a floppy red hat around a TV station haunted by a mad scientist whose only weakness was elementary arithmetic. The music, a series of square waves that the machine's speaker blared at the player, was actually Mozart's Symphony No. 40. The first time I heard the music played by a real orchestra on my father's CD player, I thought the orchestra had stolen it from the game's manufacturer.

Making my games work at all on the 386 usually involved a small miracle. The machine had two megabytes of Random Access Memory, or RAM. (Today's

computers routinely ship with a thousand times more.) Even printing greeting
cards on our powerful laser printer was doomed to failure. Only half of the card
would print out each time, because only half of the card could fit in memory. We
had purchased an expensive add-on for the printer called QMS JetScript, but since
my father didn't know what it did, QMS JetScript went up to the attic with the
empty computer boxes.

Only a year or so after we set it up, the computer was in such bad shape that
my father asked a technician from the university to come and take a look. Using
our mouse pad as a coaster for his Heineken—which I gazed at wide-eyed since
I had been warned never to eat or drink near the computer, let alone *drink*—the
scruffy, fat man pulled up bizarre screens full of cryptic data that I had never seen
before. He told my dad that he had installed a program called "kill" that I had to
run before I played my games. My father simply nodded in agreement, while I sat
in amazement. After that, every time one of my friends came over to play, I would
ask, "Guess what I have to type in to make the game work?"

"What?" they'd say. I would type the "kill" command, leaving them open-
mouthed. It made up for all of the violence that my games lacked.

My father showed me how to use WordPerfect 5.1 for DOS, which he used to
type his letters, manuscripts and grants. When he and my mother went to Paris in
1991 for their only vacation away from their children, my maternal grandmother,
whom we called Nana, and her daughter, Aunt Leila, came to babysit, and my skill
became relevant.

Nana was not good with children. When my friend Peter came over to play,
Peter and I cleaned the basement for two hours, and then Peter went home. When
Nana attempted to show off her baking skills (as Simon especially enjoyed baking),
everything was going well—until she mistakenly added twice as much flour as the
recipe required.

"Did it say one-and-a-half cups or three cups?" I asked after the damage was
done while staring into the bowl. Nana pored over the recipe.

"Bah, humbug!" she muttered, eyeing the line that called for only one-and-a-
half. "We can just put in some more milk." Before I could even think, in it went,
the batter bubbling in acceptance. I lodged my protest.

"Are you sure you can do that? Why don't we just double the whole recipe?"

"It'll be fine!" was the answer, and it was final. The brownies came out of the
oven a few hours later, and since Nana was diabetic, it was my job to do the taste
testing. What should have been moist and delicious was slightly dry and bitter. It
didn't pass the test.

"These are awful," I muttered with Simon in earshot. Doubtful of my analysis,
Nana asked him to taste one.

"No!" he said from the doorway. Then he bolted, acting peculiar as usual, as if the brownies might eat him. From that lesson, any other child would have learned to keep his mouth shut, but I had her genes. Nana had been a reporter for *The Boston Globe*.

Later, as Nana sped down Fairmount Boulevard to take me to Hebrew school, the carefully-crafted schedule that my father had typed in WordPerfect flew out of her hands, and out the car window. Nana refused to call my parents across the Atlantic, who were there to free themselves from our schedules.

When we returned home, I went straight to the computer. With some guess-work, I began to get the hang of the abbreviations my father used for his files and directories. Finally, I found what I was looking for: the schedule. We all breathed a sigh of relief—until we started noticing that real life events were not matching up with the ones written down. My father, used to writing research grants upwards of seventy pages long, made compulsive backups of his files. Each document was saved at work, at home, and on dual sets of meticulously labeled floppy disks at each location.

"This isn't it!" I finally realized. "It's a backup, and a really old one..."

I sat down at the computer once more, started WordPerfect, pressed F5, and searched through directory after directory until I found another similar schedule.

With the scheduling crisis resolved, I could play games again, but our newest one required more memory, which was by then a familiar problem. Aunt Leila, who had recently been hired by Oracle Corporation, quickly typed in some MS-DOS commands that copied the game to a blank floppy disk, and after that, it magically worked. I had never realized that it was so easy to tell the computer to work with files—only that one could "kill" them.

I started to get curious. I found out about batch files, which could run several commands at once. After my father returned home, he was confronted with a no-ticeable change: a numbered menu system that appeared whenever you turned on the computer., making it unnecessary to memorize commands. Judging from his immediate reaction, he didn't find my innovation as brilliant as I did, especially when I switched the numbers around from time to time. He used my system, though, because reverting to the old setup would have required another change.

After receiving a postcard in the mail from the Marriott hotel chain, we went on a "trial" vacation to Hilton Head Island, South Carolina to learn about the Mar-riott timeshare system. In contrast to our previous voyages to Cape Cod and New Hampshire, the weather was actually nice. Always working, my father brought his new laptop.

One of Hilton Head's many advantages was that it was surrounded by beauti-ful beaches with hard-packed sand. I took some shells from the beach back to our small villa, and set them down on a table.

"Dad!" I called out, laughing. "Look!" I put one of the shells on top of his laptop's keyboard, just in front of the screen. "PC-Shell!"

Indeed, Central Point Software's PC-Shell utility handled MS-DOS file management, and came with my father's computer. I thought my joke was hilarious. The shell remained perched on top of the keyboard.

The next day, Simon was in a less-than-cheerful mood. He was the victim of relentless ear infections, and even when he was healthy he seemed to have frequent tantrums. So, as he bawled and screamed at the top of his lungs, my little brother slammed down the laptop screen, the seashell wedging itself tightly between the keyboard and the liquid crystal display. When we opened up the screen, there was a psychedelic ring pattern radiating out of the bottom right corner. The glass had shattered and the liquid crystals underneath had been smashed. I had never seen my father so angry in my life. The screen cost more than the price of the laptop to replace, and it was a while before either of us touched a computer again.

•

It was in third grade that I could no longer run from the fact that I wasn't as good at logic problems as I had originally thought. The previous year, I had admitted defeat at the hands of the Robot Problem, another logic assignment, when Mrs. Martin grew tired of watching me squirm and told me to give up. Now, once more I was completely unable to devise a solution.

It all started when Miss Eppich announced that we would be reading *My Robot Buddy*, an aptly named book about a futuristic boy who received a robot as a gift. As our first assignment, we had to think of futuristic projects of our own, and then make a prototype out of household materials. Using an Entenmann's cookie box, I created a machine you could place in banks that would dispense money on a smaller box that everyone would carry in place of cash.

"That way, you don't need to worry about losing money!" I said, beaming.

"It's called a credit card, Aaron," my father replied.

The second assignment, in keeping with the theme, was the dreaded Robot Problem once again. Not being able to figure out the problem, trivial as it was, did not help my self-esteem. For the second year in a row, I worked on it for weeks, and emerged with no solution.

So far as I could tell, in the minds of my peers I had always been one of the "smart kids," but at home I had a habit of slamming my head against the wall in my room, calling myself "stupid." When I walked by my parents' mirror, I repeated *"you're ugly!"* to myself. Not surprisingly, my parents were pleased to learn of Miss Eppich's "Positive Mental Attitude" program, in which we were forced to write our happy thoughts daily in a small notebook. It was a well-timed effort on Miss

Eppich's part, but an idealistic one. My inner pessimist remained, and the Robot Problem remained unsolved.

Perhaps to mitigate my behavior, my parents thought that it would be fun if they offered Simon and me a special treat: our Chanukah present was a trip to Disney World in Florida for winter vacation. My father showed me colorful maps of the park, travel guides and pictures, all of which made me even more anxious to go.

At the park, my mother formulated a plan to maximize the value of our trip. While I admired the Epcot Center, oblivious to the complexities of the corporate charade that had overtaken so much of Orlando, Simon liked the monorail, but understood even less than I did about what surrounded him. When he got lost near the bustling entrance to the Magic Kingdom for three hours, we therefore assumed that the monorail was where he had gone.

"The monorail's stuck, ma'am," a Disney employee at the lost-persons desk informed the panicked woman who was my mother. "He's not goin' anywhere."

My mother grew somewhat hysterical. Simon couldn't read, write, remember his telephone number, or speak clearly enough for most people to understand. We thought we would never see him again. There were people everywhere, and a surprising number of them were less than four feet tall.

As it turned out, Simon was just being his usual eerily independent six-year-old self. He hated ice cream, loved carrots, and was usually the only student able to sleep over at anyone's house without getting homesick. Now, he had decided to go for a walk around Disney World, alone, and after he got tired of that, he walked back, where he found us all conferring with Disney park officials about his mysterious absence and screaming his name. It was just what Simon did.

By the time we got back to our villa, I wasn't feeling very well. We took our family vacation to the emergency room, where a black-haired doctor whispered his diagnosis to my parents so that I couldn't hear. Unfortunately for the doctor, he was a loud whisperer: I had pneumonia, and I was sure that death would arrive at any moment. We had read about it in school.

We hadn't read as much about antibiotics. I promptly received a prescription for giant, yellow pills that my father had to break in half for me at every meal.

I was glad to return home, until Miss Eppich made an announcement. The Robot Problem would be put on display at the upcoming Open House, when all of our parents would be invited to school to see our work.

"*I have to figure out how to solve that problem,*" I thought, staring down the robots I had colored in green, blue, purple and orange crayon on my desk. I set to work yet again, trying as hard as I could, but once more, I was the only one in my class with no solution.

When Open House came, my parents were curious as to why my robot drawing was missing from the bulletin board. My work was conspicuously absent.

Then, as my parents talked, it struck me. When the directions had said that no two robots of the same color could be next to each other "diagonally," I had interpreted the word to mean that they could not be adjacent to one another in any diagonal direction. I had learned the rules of chess not long before, and I knew that a knight could move in an L-shape, up or down two squares and then over one—a position that I considered to be diagonal relative to the piece's original position. The grid of robots looked just like the grid on a chessboard, so I figured that the directions applied accordingly.

"Miss Eppich," I asked as my parents were staring at everyone else's work. "Does 'diagonal' mean that they can't be next to each other like this," I said, showing her a 45 degree angle, "or this?" I laid out the robots in the L-shape, at about 60 degrees.

"Only the first one," she said, with a confused look on her face.

Everything was crystal clear now. I had been thinking about the problem correctly all along; it was just the way that I interpreted the directions that was incorrect. I explained what I had been doing to Miss Eppich.

"Of course they can go that way!" she exclaimed after hearing my explanation. "Otherwise, it's probably impossible!"

As my parents were inspecting other areas of the classroom, I pounced on my blank 8.5" x 11" sheet of paper with as much force as my Elmer's glue and scissors would allow, and solved the Robot Problem from start to finish in less than five minutes.

•

Simon perplexed everyone. When my friends came over to my house, they were always taken aback. He would behave in weird ways, and it was hard to tell if he was deliberately trying to catch people's attention, annoy them, or if he was just in his own little world, completely oblivious to others. For months he had been singing a mixed-up version of a song on one of my records about the potential of each and every child.

"Oh noooo, see what you can dooooo!" Simon sang loudly.

"What does that *mean*?" I'd ask him, not really expecting an intelligible response.

"Oh noooo, see what you can dooooo!" he continued, ignoring me and singing the exact same phrase again and again. He knew it well. Sometimes, he would sing it for twenty minutes straight.

His repertoire was not restricted to one song alone. Simon took a special liking to some of the songs that we were taught at Sunday school. Since his grasp of the Hebrew language was not very good, he just substituted "doo-doo-doo" for the words, instead.

When Simon started to learn how to write, we quickly recognized that he was left-handed, but were fairly amazed when he began producing inverted images of everything he scribbled, so that they looked correct only when held up to a mirror. For a long time he called me "Ennen," unable to pronounce my name. He also took a while to master "oink-oink," which for years he replaced with "ink-ink" whenever pigs came up in books. His lisp remained, making it immediately clear to anyone who met him that something was slightly wrong.

Whenever I built something with Legos, Simon would copy me and build something with Legos too, but his creations were vastly different. Mine were colorful and symmetric, usually in the shape of airplanes or complex buildings. Simon built long, twisted, flat trucks out of black Lego slabs, with odd numbers of wheels and strange appendages, usually borrowing pieces heavily from my work and destroying whatever I had created in the process. It drove me crazy, and we sparred over Lego pieces regularly.

When Simon was angry or unhappy, which was almost always the case for one reason or another, he made the same strange face, contorting his muscles until his mouth was small and round and his teeth showed through like some sort of wild animal. I used to think it was hilarious and imitate him.

It took me years to decipher that face. While most people convey their mental state to others intuitively, Simon had no idea how. His expressions were poor copies of other people's. It was as if he had no ability to connect with individuals' emotions except as static images, which quickly became caricatures.

There was a time when Simon complained about his neck hurting, and my father took his word at face value. Yet there seemed to be nothing wrong with his neck.

"Check his throat," I said. Sure enough, when Simon and my mother came back from the pediatrician, they had already filled the prescription for penicillin. Simon had strep throat, but he hadn't known how to tell us what was really hurting him.

Already relegated to "special education" for part of the day and burdened by his speech impediment, Simon didn't need any additional flags to be singled out. That he had learning disabilities had long since been established, but I wasn't sure that anyone really knew what that meant.

Worst of all, Simon seemed to have trouble learning not only in an academic context, but in a behavioral one, as well. If he threw a tantrum one night because my parents wouldn't let him eat downstairs in the basement, he would demand to eat downstairs in the basement the next night as if he'd never been in the same situation before. If they punished him, it didn't matter. He'd do the same thing all over again.

My parents decided to let him repeat kindergarten. And so he began trailing me in school, three years behind, and worlds apart.

•

Fourth graders were the oldest students at Mercer. We were the first ones teachers went to for help, and we walked through the halls with our heads held high. There was essentially no one left to be afraid of.

Our fourth grade classroom was large, with blue carpeting and round, wooden tables for groups of students instead of individual desks. Philip, who now always beat me in chess, co-authored a story with me about a time-travelling weatherman. We hypothesized that by 2001, time travel would be the solution to one of the world's greatest problems: accurately predicting the weather.

I assumed that because of our inherently special fourth grade status, about five of my friends and I were introduced to Mr. Vossler. He was a tall, thin bespectacled man with short, spiky blond hair who made a point of signing his name as a capital letter "V" wearing glasses, which we all found moderately amusing. We were part of the W.A.R.P. program, an experimental curriculum for so-called "advanced students." So it was that Mr. V, as we called him, introduced us to the Apple Macintosh LC II computer and a program called HyperCard.

My immediate reaction to HyperCard was disappointment; it only worked in black and white. Using a stack of index cards as a metaphor for information display and retrieval, anyone could make a "stack" to be used as a game, a demonstration, a presentation, or a full-fledged software program. Clicking on buttons or words on one card would make another appear, which could link to another, and another, using a technology known as hyperlinking. A stack could be opened again on any computer with HyperCard, and since Apple shipped HyperCard on every Macintosh system that it sold for years, the software had universal appeal.

Later, Apple decided to start charging separately for the software, but it still shipped HyperCard Player with every Macintosh. The limited version allowed users to view, but not create, HyperCard stacks. The bait-and-switch was a brilliant marketing scheme, enticing new Macintosh owners to purchase HyperCard, while simultaneously protecting the existing owners of the product who still wanted to be able to use their intellectual property.

With Mr. V's help, my friends and I set about right away creating a spaceship game. The vast expanse of space was perfect for a development program that only worked in monochrome. On occasion, Mr. V would take us to the Mercer library to use the Macintosh there since his own room was only a bizarre sliver of space that was once a janitorial closet.

Word of my interest in computers spread around the school. I became so proficient at changing printer ribbons and clearing paper jams that our teacher referred students to me instead of trying to fix problems herself. Eventually, our music teacher also requested my assistance with creating overhead projector transparencies for her song lyrics. She mistook my computer savvy for musical talent, and suggested that I visit Dr. Miller, the band director at Woodbury, so that I could choose an instrument to play one year early. My mother thought this was a fabulous idea, and shuttled me to his office.

"If you're going to get braces, you know, you shouldn't really play the clarinet," he said as I made some ungodly sounds come out of the instrument. He proceeded to rule out trombone, tuba, percussion, and trumpet in a similar fashion. The French Horn caught my eye, though. Though it only had three buttons, it looked complicated.

"French Horn is a very difficult instrument to play, Aaron," he warned. I thought it sounded nicer than the other instruments, and it was a challenge. I was going to play the French Horn.

•

One day after school I went over to Peter's house, where I came across his father's desktop computer, made by a company called Gateway 2000. The front of the bezel slightly curved out on the left side, with elegant stripes and well-proportioned buttons. The metal case itself was huge, giving the components and cables inside plenty of room, and as I later learned, reducing the chance that you would cut your hands repairing the hardware inside. There was even a locking mechanism, just like the special keyhole on vending machines, which prevented the keyboard and mouse from functioning if you didn't want them to. Consequently, every Gateway 2000 desktop came with its own set of keys. Getting a new computer from Gateway was practically like getting a new car—if your car arrived in a box spotted like a cow.

Peter's computer wasn't the first I had taken note of. I had unintentionally started to keep track of the industry by going to my friends' houses to play. Almost everyone in Shaker owned a computer it seemed, and each person had a different type. Julie's father had a thirty-pound Compaq "laptop" shaped like a briefcase, much older than my father's Compaq. Philip had an Apple IIGS just like the computers at school. A few of my friends had Apple Macintoshes of various sorts. Billy's parents had a boxy NEC. It was that computer that got me into trouble.

Billy's mother ran a Mail Boxes, Etc. franchise, and she eventually took her computer with her to the office. Once, I got to visit her store, where Billy and I were told to stay in the back room. I had agreed ahead of time to bring my "Challenge of the Ancient Empires!" disks with me to the store so that we would have something to do in the back room, and I had them ready.

"Be very careful, Aaron, I need this computer for my business," his mother told me before letting me install the game.

"I will," I said, with the first floppy disk already halfway in the drive. "Don't worry." I typed in the commands to start installing the game. The disk drive started to whir, and I could see the little light underneath come on, which meant that it was working. Then, an unfamiliar message appeared.

```
Disk I/O error reading drive C:
Abort, retry, fail?
```

I pressed the "R" key until I realized that I had no choice but to press "A" for "Abort," though I had no idea what it meant.

"*If it's on drive C:,*" I thought, "*then there's something wrong with the hard drive, not my floppy disk.*" I decided to check the hard drive for problems.

"Arrghh," I said, catching Billy's attention for the first time in a couple of minutes. He almost jumped. Billy was afraid of his parents a lot more than I was of mine. I didn't blame him: his father was a very large person, and he could be pretty scary.

"It's nothing, I just forgot to change to the hard drive first, that's all," I said, hiding my latent fear that his mother's hard drive was damaged. If it was, though, it had already been that way when I'd arrived, because the game hadn't even been able to install itself. I kept typing:

```
A:\>C:
C:\>cd\dos
C:\DOS>chkdsk C:
```

The command worked. It spit out some numbers about the disk and a few other messages that I was accustomed to. Then, there were some new ones.

```
WARNING!  F parameter not specified.
Running CHKDSK in read-only mode.

File is cross linked on allocation unit 630

File is cross linked on allocation unit 631...
```

I didn't know what an "F parameter" was, or what I had to do to specify it, but I did know that the program had found bad sectors on the disk, which needed no further explanation. The list of cross linked files and allocation units went on and on. Worse yet, a cross linked file was like an animal with the head of a giraffe and the body of an elephant. There was no easy fix.

"I think there's something wrong with your computer."

"What? What did you do?" Billy's mother asked with a panicked look suddenly across her face. She squinted at the screen. "What does that mean?" she demanded.

"It looks like there's something wrong with your hard drive. But I think..." She didn't let me finish.

"Billy! I told you that I didn't want you to put any games on here, but no! You had to do it! Now look at this!" She was furious, and Billy looked like he was about to cry. "Aaron, come on, it's time to go home." There was no use in explaining to her that her computer had a pre-existing condition; she didn't want to hear it. Billy and I got our things and jumped back into their family's Jeep. Though the long ride out to Chagrin Falls had been fun, the long ride back was not.

"I'm going to have to call that computer guy now," she was muttering to herself. "He charges an absolute fortune...I just hope he can fix whatever it is you did to it." I offered to try to fix it, but neither she nor Billy was not very receptive to the idea. After what seemed like hours, we pulled into my driveway, and I got out of the car. They sped off. When I got inside, I told my mother what had happened.

"Billy's mom thinks I broke her computer by putting 'Challenge of the Ancient Empires!' on it, but I didn't. It wouldn't even install," I explained. My mother found the phone directory, and dialed. No one picked up. Later that night, Billy's mother called us, though. I could hear her arguing with my mother.

"Are you *sure* you didn't break their computer?" my mother asked furiously.

"Yes, I'm sure!" I said. And I was. The CHKDSK command output made it clear that there was physical damage to the disk, but it didn't matter how well I explained the situation. After that, I never talked to Billy or his family again. Billy was good friends with Philip, so he told Philip and everyone that he knew that I had broken his mother's computer. For a good part of the year, Philip and I had been angry at each other, so I didn't care. I didn't want to be friends with them anymore.

The school year came to an end. Mercer's "clap-out" graduation ceremony at the end of fourth grade worked just as it sounded: all of the younger students stood on the school's front lawn and clapped as the fourth graders walked out of the school. Parents and teachers were all smiles; their cheerful children beamed proudly as they walked past. We all looked forward to a hot summer vacation.

As I stood against one of the columns in front of the school building, my father snapped a photograph. I smiled for the camera a moment too late, leaving behind the image of a happy child.

CHAPTER 2

Tales of Woodbury Elementary

Woodbury Elementary School was situated parallel to South Woodland Road, one of the main east-west corridors in Shaker Heights, in a large brick building. All nine of Shaker's elementary schools, including Mercer, fed into Woodbury for grades five and six. Correspondingly, the school had a wing for each grade, with common facilities such as the library and gyms in the middle. The building had been expanded at least once for a swimming pool, as well as additional athletic facilities, which spun off of the back at a bizarre angle. Atop the center of the building stood a sizeable tower, which also served as the basis for the District's logo, but since there were no bells inside, it never rang.

On my first day at Woodbury, I was surrounded by hundreds of students who I had never met before. My friends from Mercer all seemed to be situated fairly close together in the fifth grade wing of the building, but as the school was stuffed to capacity, my classroom wasn't in its proper wing. Instead, I had been randomly assigned by the District's aging HP3000 mainframe to a classroom near the center of the building, where I was isolated from everyone I knew.

It wasn't just the first impression of the school that was bad. The transition from Mercer to Woodbury—a process that took several months—was about as graceful as being slammed into one of the light blue steel lockers lining the hallways. At Mercer, we had been given homework a couple of times each month, in large part to expose us to the very idea of homework in the first place. At Woodbury, our teachers assigned us homework every night. Any notion of free time vanished.

For students in the advanced English curriculum, called A.R.P. for "Accelerated Resource Program," and those in the advanced math track, the homework never stopped. At age ten, I found myself with at least three hours of homework each night. Mrs. Hess's weekly math problems were quite challenging, even for my college-educated parents. I mostly managed to avoid the bullying that I had feared, but it was still the case that every day after I came home from school I felt like I'd been beaten up.

Mrs. Fox, my A.R.P. teacher, was almost in her eighties. Her fluffy white hair made her seem perfectly harmless in person, yet her looks were deceiving. She took pride in her work, which involved teaching children with no prior English skills how to write. Her demeanor was strict, but only in the context of a classroom setting where everyone was permitted to work at their own (accelerated) pace. The other A.R.P. teacher, Diane Derrick, worked her students equally hard despite the fact that she was much further away from retirement. Most of my friends from Mercer were in her class down the hall.

In A.R.P., we sat at tables much like we had in fourth grade. The tables were supposed to encourage us to talk to our friends about the best way to work through problems. Mrs. Fox assigned us weekly "Orthography Club" lessons in which the goal was always to assemble a coherent paragraph using a slew of ten to twenty challenging vocabulary words.

The lessons were brutal at first. At Mercer, we had rarely been expected to write a paragraph of any sort, let alone a coherent one. The vocabulary words in our assignments were often completely unrelated. Fortunately, like most fifth graders, my writing style at the time was not especially formal, which gave me some leeway. My paragraphs were glued together by goofiness alone, and by the second quarter, I was able to assemble monstrosities for a passing grade.

Band, at least, provided a bit of comic relief. Everyone hated the elderly Dr. Miller, who appeared as though he had taken a drastically wrong turn at one of life's earlier junctures, ending up, much to his disbelief, in a room full of ten- and eleven-year-olds. During one particularly doomed rehearsal, he began to shout at the percussion section.

"No, Ethan, no! It's boom-boom-bam-bam-boom-boom-bam-bam-boom-boom-boom-boom-boom!" Dr. Miller's veins coursed dangerously. The room erupted into laughter when Ethan, unable to mimic the rhythm on the drums, caused our teacher to repeat himself several times. Dr. Miller lost control.

The overall strategy at Woodbury was to keep students so busy that their minds could not settle on any one aspect of their lives long enough to appreciate their miserable state. I waited anxiously for the year to end, but it dragged on. Mrs. Mahoney, my homeroom teacher, was alternately kind and unbearable. When the hard drive on her ancient computer (a Leading Edge 286) finally crashed, I offered to lend her the diagnostic and repair tools that were stored on some floppy disks sitting in my desk.

"Sit down at your desk and be quiet!" she yelled at me in a shrill voice. I did as I was told, trying to push down the lump in my throat that resulted from being simultaneously embarrassed and angry. I was not used to being scolded by teachers. While my eyes started to burn, Mrs. Mahoney returned to angrily muttering about her "Microsoft" not working. She referred to every software application as "Microsoft."

Mrs. Mahoney showed her true colors once again in late spring, when our class and the two others in our three-class "teaching group" went on a field trip to Hale Farm, located somewhere in the rural expanse of Ohio. We were made to dress up in ridiculous clothes that supposedly taught us what it would have been like to live on the Farm a hundred years prior. I wore knickers.

Mid-way through the field trip, I began to feel sick. Mrs. Mahoney was in her command-and-conquer mode to keep us all in line. When I told her I wasn't feeling well, rather than address my complaint directly, she dispatched the student teacher who happened to be with us at the time. During lunch, when I was relieved to be sitting, I overheard Mrs. Mahoney talking to the other two teachers in our group.

"That Aaron, whining that he couldn't walk. He can walk. There's nothing wrong with him at all. I really cannot stand his complaining!" she complained.

When I got home, my father confirmed that I had a high fever. I didn't return to school for several days, nor did I want to.

•

Our house sat at the bottom of a relatively large hill. One fall day, it began raining with alarming intensity, and our cleaning lady, Shirley, heard some gurgling coming from the emergency drainage pipes in our basement floor. We had never used the drainage system before, but the pipes were there as a precaution in case of a flood—an event that our realtor claimed happened in the area "once every one hundred years." When Shirley went to investigate the noise, water was already flowing through the drainage pipes the wrong way. The entire basement, furnished with commercial-grade carpeting and furniture (including my mother's desk), flooded with rainwater and raw sewage.

For weeks afterward, my mother found herself with the additional career of salvaging her business from the disaster, while trying to keep the house running as usual. It was a miserable experience, and my mother could never bring herself to hire a cleaning lady again.

Months later in December, a large check from the Royal Insurance Company finally arrived in the mail to cover what we had lost in the flood. For Chanukah, my parents decided to buy me a computer, as I had been nagging them about Apple and Gateway 2000 for months. While I dreamt of mountains of Apple System 7 boxes, my mother refused to buy a Macintosh on the grounds that Apple didn't have enough market share, and so I settled on a Gateway that was one step down from top-of-the-line: the 4DX2-50V, featuring Intel's 50MHz 486DX2 microprocessor. The computer had a sound card, an ATI Mach32 SVGA video card, Microsoft Office 4.3 Professional Edition, and all sorts of other features that I couldn't wait to try out. Much to my surprise, my father explained that even though this new computer was better and faster than his own, it only cost half as much.

When our UPS driver arrived with several cow-spotted boxes, I was thrilled. My parents had even bought me Prince of Persia, one of the hottest computer games on the market. I installed the software, started the game—and immediately noticed that something was wrong. The music played for about ten seconds before the entire computer froze. I tried starting the game again, but to no avail.

When starting up Windows, I encountered another problem: a cryptic error on a blue screen that seemed to somehow involve the sound card. I called Gateway 2000's toll-free technical support hotline, and listened to annoying music for more than an hour. Finally, I got through. I read the serial number off the back of the computer, which I soon memorized, and described the problem with the blue screen. I talked with the technician until it was late at night and I had to hang up in order to get enough sleep for school the next morning.

Later in the week, I tried a different tactic. I woke up at 6:00 A.M. to call technical support when there was barely any hold time. I couldn't talk for long before it was time to get ready for school, so I repeated the process for the entire week. With the technicians' help, I learned how to open a computer's case, how to check to see which slot an add-on card was placed in, and how to remove and insert the cards. I was instructed to move around "jumpers," the small black switches on the cards, re-seat different cables, find various files, and type in strange DOS commands. After about a week of troubleshooting, Gateway 2000 decided that my Aztech sound card was defective, and that they'd replace it. Sure enough, the new card worked.

My victory gave me enough confidence to dig QMS JetScript out of the attic, open my father's computer (much to his dismay), and install the necessary MS-DOS drivers. Once I snapped the case shut, I turned the machine back on, and watched. Within a minute, the boot sequence announced that the JetScript card had been found, and I realized that I knew how to fix computers.

•

I let out my frustration with Woodbury at Cleveland Hebrew Schools, also known as "CHS," where I became a complete goofball twice per week from 4:00 until 6:00 P.M. The teachers there were mostly Israelis who held other day jobs, usually teaching at Jewish day schools in the Cleveland area. At night, they taught public school students like myself who didn't have any other way of obtaining what my mother called "a good Jewish education."

I loved the fact that everything was laid back: we called our teacher "Malka," not "Mrs. Weil," and we never hesitated to shout out in class. When we did turn in tests, Malka reviewed them on the spot. Before we could sit down, she told us which questions to correct—and often, how to correct them. She would score them after they had been "revised," sometimes more than once. She wanted us to learn, and we did.

I got into the habit of spending my five-minute break between the first and second hour of class fixing the Hebrew school's aging lab of donated Apple II computers. Soon, my break time began carrying over the five-minute mark (which was already flexible thanks to Malka), and I began to skip parts of class. On many occasions, my only other friend from Shaker, Rachel, sped through all of the class material so fast that she helped me in the lab, as well. Malka didn't seem to care, since we were learning what she was teaching. Mrs. Shamir, the principal, didn't mind, as I was fixing her computers for free. (Many had been outfitted with Israeli add-on cards that were supposed to enable them to function in Hebrew, though the less well-designed cards sometimes had the side-effect of making software fail to function at all.)

After I had tested every 5.25" floppy disk that there was to test in the giant pile of Hebrew games that the school kept in the lab's metal cabinet, I needed something else to do to keep me occupied. I heard that the school was getting a new computer—a Macintosh LC III, the successor to the LC II that I had used at Mercer and Woodbury.

When I learned that CHS was also having trouble with the computer in the main office that was supposed to manage all of the class lists and frequent mailings, I decided that I had found my next project, at least until the new Macintosh arrived. My Gateway 2000 at home had shipped with version 2.0 of Microsoft Access, a newer version of the same kind of program that Mrs. Mahoney had used to track our grades, so I knew that Access could be used in schools.

Using code from Microsoft's example database, I started making my own program for CHS, adding screens and reports to keep track of students, teachers, and eventually, classes. I spent hours re-designing the school's report card in a digital format so that the program would have the capability of being used to track grades. Access wasn't designed to be used with languages that were written from right to left, so I had to type each Hebrew word backwards, letter by letter, without seeing the letters on my English keyboard.

More than once there were messages on my mother's answering machine from CHS during days when I wasn't even supposed to be at Hebrew school, urgently asking for a fix for the newest bug in my program that had caused the school's office to cease functioning. Eventually, though, the pain intrinsic to implementing Version 1.0 of my product, dubbed "Think! School," paid off: it drastically increased the office's efficiency.

I approached the computer teacher at Woodbury, Mrs. Geszler, about ways I could help her out, as well. Adrienne Geszler was in her late thirties, with curly black hair and large glasses. When she was happy, she bordered on kindness, but more often she snapped at her students. She felt no shame about choosing favorites. It was generally recognized that to become a candidate for favorite status, one had to join the Computer Club, which I did happily. That alone, however, was not enough. Complete loyalty to Apple Computer, Inc. was also a prerequisite, and as a self-proclaimed Gateway 2000 fanatic, I had rendered myself ineligible.

Luckily, Mrs. Geszler still had room in her universe for those of us who did not see Apple's light. "You could help me turn on the computers in the morning," she said, referring to the twenty or so Apple Macintosh LC II systems in the windowless lab, just like the one we had used in the Mercer library with Mr. Vossler. I didn't need to be asked twice. Power switches were buttons too.

Every morning, I would stop by the computer lab to flip the power switches on the back right corner of the computer systems. While I worked, with all of the enthusiasm of an eager fifth-grader, I asked Mrs. Geszler if she knew about Gateway 2000, or about the new version of PC-Shell that had been released for Windows, or about MacroMind Director, or about ways to write more complicated HyperCard stacks. Invariably, she always seemed to imply that she only cared about software that worked on Macintosh systems that all of her students would use. None of my interests were high on her list.

I was oblivious to the lukewarm response. In the spring, we were told about an upcoming contest called "Invent America." I knew that I wanted my invention to involve computers somehow, but initially, I wasn't sure what to do.

One of the few electronic devices I knew more about from school than I did from home was the modem. The librarians seemed very impressed by their ability to call CLEVNET, the central database of the Cleveland Public Library, to inquire about book listings via a terminal screen. I always thought that CLEVNET was about as boring as a program could get, but I was intrigued by the modem itself.

Something clicked. I wanted to use the modem to make a HyperCard stack that would let you shop for groceries. Newer modems could also send and receive faxes, and though she had never shown us how, Mrs. Geszler had also claimed that it was easy to make HyperCard control devices outside of the computer, such as LaserDisc players, and I assumed, modems. I set to work.

"Is there a way to make things in HyperCard show up only when you click on a button?" I asked Mrs. Geszler after school one day. She didn't even turn around from her workstation. All she did was point to the far end of the room, where there was a shelf full of manuals thicker than both of my arms combined.

"Over there," she said. "You can look it up in the manual."

I went to the back of the room, but there were so many huge manuals with almost identical titles that I was completely overwhelmed.

"Which one?" I asked.

Mrs. Geszler let out a sigh, got up from the scanner workstation at the far end of the room, walked over, and dropped one of the tomes into my hands.

"Thanks!" I said. I started reading. It seemed like what I was looking for was called an "event," supposedly called "onMouseDown." If you wrote a program within your HyperCard stack called a "script," and attached it to a specific button using the onMouseDown event, you could make something happen when the user pressed down on the mouse button. There was also an onMouseUp event, but I was having enough trouble just getting the down part to work.

I wanted to ask Mrs. Geszler for help again, but she made it clear that she was busy. I saved my HyperCard stack on one of my disks (we had been instructed to purchase several), and when we went on vacation over spring break to Palm Desert, California, I brought it with me. I showed our longtime family friends, the Golds, what I was working on using their Macintosh. I wasn't quite sure why our families were friends; something to do with "college," and my father being friends with their son, David. What mattered to me was that they had HyperCard, which I couldn't use at home.

Long after the Golds had lost interest, I kept on working, trying to make the buttons work the way that I wanted them to. I wanted different lists of food to appear when you clicked on different categories. I wanted users to be able to choose the items that they wanted to buy from the different lists, much like pulling boxes or cans off of a shelf at a real grocery store. At the end, I planned on having my program compile a list of everything that the user wanted, so that it could be automatically faxed to a grocery store, such as Stop 'n' Shop. At Stop 'n' Shop, a worker would receive the fax, put all of the user's desired items in a real shopping cart, and deliver the goods to the person's address.

I never got the shopping lists to work perfectly, but I did manage to scrape together a demo of the program suitable for display at Invent America. Whenever you clicked on the button to complete your order, I made the program show a giant screen that had a recorded clip of me saying "Demo Version!"

Mrs. Geszler seemed less than thrilled when she learned that I wanted to take a computer out of her lab to use in the gymnasium where Invent America was being held. All of the machines were set up with a program called At Ease, which Apple had designed to prevent curious users from changing system files or settings. Though it was easily disabled, Mrs. Geszler instead made a point of describing the trouble she would need to go to—essentially, walking to the gym—in order to type in the At Ease password every time I wanted to run my program. I thought it was worth the hassle; she relented.

"Yeah, did you see Aaron's program on the computer?" I heard one girl who I secretly liked mention on the school bus ride home. "It looked cool, but when you tried to buy anything it just said 'Demo Version.'" A few seats back, I smiled.

The final Invent America display was relatively uneventful, making America seem quite boring even in the midst of a flurry of innovation. Unlike other contests, we were not expected to present anything at our exhibits, so most of the students just walked around to the different tables to see what their peers had dreamt up. Out of the corner of my eye I noticed a few come around to my spot just to look at the computer, which was clearly out of place in the gym. Later that night, the judges visited, as well. They paid no special attention to my idea.

The 1994 awards went to other students and my software was quickly forgotten. Five years later, electronic commerce transformed the global economy.

•

I would have looked forward to the summer, except that my parents had decided that I should go to summer camp. Camp Ramah in Canada was a Jewish overnight camp four hours outside of Toronto, the closest major city. I feared the worst.

Swimming was a recurring nightmare, far worse than being homesick, or attending the mandatory prayer services, where I could at least muse over the meaning of the cryptic Hebrew we were taught to recite. The freezing cold water of the camp's lake triggered an asthma attack every time I stepped in. I became intimately familiar with my Ventolin Rotacaps inhaler, which I used so often that my counselors began to think that perhaps I was faking the symptoms to get my fix of albuterol.

The only thing worse than swimming was sailing, which we were also expected to do at least once each week. The counselor in charge of my sailboat told us that he had less experience than any of the other counselors, but that we'd have more fun as a result.

For the first five minutes, I tried to tell myself that sailing really wasn't so bad. The feeling of the wind hitting your face was pleasant enough, and the sight of a racing sailboat was always impressive to behold, though it really didn't do much for me when I was in the boat. By minute six, my rationalization attempt had failed, as my attention was drawn to ominously dark clouds beginning to form over the lake. Services had never done much to convince me that God existed, but when it rained at Ramah, the possibility seemed much more realistic.

"*The weather sure does change here more rapidly than it does in Ohio...*" I thought.

There was not even so much as the common courtesy of a light drizzle. Sheets of rain slammed onto the deck. Of all the places on Earth, I was in the middle of a lake in a tiny boat, trapped in a flash flood. I knew that if we tipped over, the second I plunged into the water, I wouldn't be able to breathe. I could picture my inhaler tucked away in my cabin, at least a mile away. I watched, horrified, as the number of sails visible on the lake started to drop, one by one. I could count the number of minutes that had elapsed on my fingers before I realized that we were the only boat with its sail above the surface.

By the time I stepped back on the beach, I was too scared to appreciate what had just happened. I added sailing to my mental blacklist, right after Disney World.

In my downtime at camp, even though Ramah was completely removed from the computer world, I managed to keep myself amused by reading old copies of *Byte* magazine. My friend Arieh liked computers as well, and he bet me that CD-ROM drives would eventually break the 600ms barrier, which would make them four times as fast as the original 150ms drives. I couldn't believe it and lost the bet.

Ramah made me appreciate Cleveland, Ohio in a way I never had before. Four weeks away in what seemed like the wilderness was plenty, until I returned home and found myself with little to do.

Then, on a miserable day in early August, I was standing near the countertop in the middle of our kitchen. Through the large window above the sink, I could see rain hammering down on the driveway outside, reminding me of the lake. I was distracted by a gurgling noise coming from the small sink next to me, which we almost never used.

"Uh-oh," I thought. I flew down the basement stairs, and my suspicions were confirmed: the basement was flooding again. It was the day before we were supposed to fly to Hilton Head, and the water was coming up through a different set of pipes, even closer to my mother's desk. Countless documents for her business that had been lying on the floor were ruined, and the carpet had to be pulled up again. Somehow, we still made it to Hilton Head.

On vacation, I had plenty of time to read through the September issues of *Byte* and *PC World*, including the advertisements. Gateway 2000, which designed all of its ads in-house, always used faux movie scenes featuring its CEO, Ted Waitt. In contrast, Dell liked to run ads on the back of magazines with giant bold type and images of squashed cows, targeting Gateway. I found Dell's ads obnoxious and their computers hideous. Gateway 2000 had secured its position as my favorite company in the world.

"Dad, I could get the 60MHz Pentium instead of the 90MHz and save $300!" I exclaimed after spending hours poring over the configurations in Gateway's latest ad. "I bet 30MHz doesn't matter that much, right?"

"Wonderful!" he said, irritated. "Can't you think about something else?"

"You really have a one-track mind," my mother scolded.

They didn't have to suffer for long, though. Less than three weeks later I was still on the same track, but I was back in school.

CHAPTER 3

A Hard Lesson

In sixth grade, it was my turn to have Mrs. Derrick for A.R.P. She ran her classroom with a calculated, authoritative tone that I didn't realize was the marker of a very high intellect trapped in an elementary teaching job. To my amazement, she had even memorized the last four digits of my house's ZIP+4 zip code. Fortunately, with a few exceptions involving outbursts of intense anger, she was very kind. Like Mrs. Fox, who had retired over the summer, she treated her students as adults while they were in her classroom, and expected them to act accordingly.

By the end of September, the grinding nature of school was beginning to get to me. In the realm of sixth-grade chaos, I found Mrs. Derrick's classroom to be a sanctuary for intellectual thought. All of the "smart kids" started eating lunch there.

Unfortunately, they weren't the only ones. A hockey player named Carson also happened to be in Mrs. Derrick's room when I went to eat lunch one day. I was looking up a word I didn't know in the dictionary, when I noticed that the table was moving. I looked up.

Carson was lifting the end of the table opposite from where I was standing high in the air. I thought about the best way to react. I knew that if I tried to do anything to him, he'd win, and my experience with Simon told me that he probably just wanted my attention. So, I did nothing, pretending to read the dictionary.

My strategy didn't work. The table kept rising.

I kept reading.

Carson lifted.

I read.

Finally, the table couldn't go any higher because Carson realized the finite reach of his arms. Aggravated that I hadn't responded in any way, and now faced with the prospect of having to carry the weight of the table, he let it crash down to the ground. I tried not to blink. There was an awkward silence.

"Do you put gel in your hair?" Carson seemed to have found a new topic of interest.

I had never given my hair much thought. It just sort of did whatever it wanted to once I got out of the shower each morning.

"No. I guess it must be grease!" I said with a smile.

"That's disgusting, man!" Without even intending to use it as a defense mechanism, my hair saved the day. Carson left and never paid any attention to me again.

One day, while I was sitting on the floor with all of my classmates in A.R.P., Mrs. Derrick's classroom telephone rang. Reflecting the unusual level of trust Mrs. Derrick placed in her students, a student nearby answered, speaking as professionally as any secretary. When she (unsurprisingly) handed the receiver off to our teacher, stretching the coiled light brown cord as far as it could go, we all watched and listened.

"Yes," she said. "I'll ask him." She turned to me, her hand covering the mouthpiece.

"Aaron, after class, during lunch, can you go to room 102? Mrs. Sandstrom would like you to set up her new computer." I was suddenly giddy. Apparently, word had gotten around once more that I was good with computers.

"Sure!" I said. After what seemed like hours, we finished our lesson for the day. I ate my lunch as quickly as I could, and then ran up the stairs to the sixth grade wing. Mrs. Sandstrom had a brand new Macintosh that was designed in the same style as the original Macintosh Classic, with its monitor and CPU integrated into one solid unit. I greeted Mrs. Sandstrom, who I had never met before, and went right to work plugging in cables. Then, she looked at me quizzically.

"Will I be able to type things on here now?" she asked.

"I'm not sure," I said, wondering if the machine had arrived pre-loaded with the school's software. I turned it on, and looked for Microsoft Works 3.0 on the hard drive. I couldn't find it anywhere.

"You'll need to get Microsoft Works," I told her, still looking at the screen to make sure that I hadn't missed something. "But I think everything else is set up."

She thanked me for setting up the computer, and I left to go back to Mrs. Derrick's room until the end of lunch. Just before I reached the staircase, I ran into Mrs. Geszler.

"Mrs. Geszler!" I said. "I just set up Mrs. Sandstrom's new Macintosh, and it looks really nice, but she needs Microsoft Works."

Her eyebrows furrowed, but I didn't understand why.

"Alright. I'm not sure when I'll get around to it," she said.

"OK. Thanks!" I sped back down the stairs.

At the bottom of the stairs, a few feet from Mrs. Derrick's room, I had an idea. Mrs. Derrick's Macintosh already had Microsoft Works on it. I could save Mrs. Geszler the trouble of installing it, especially if she was busy, by just copying it myself!

I already had my pile of floppy disks with me in my backpack. Yet, I still didn't want to risk getting in trouble, so I asked Mrs. Derrick for permission.

"Is it alright if I copy Microsoft Works from your computer to Mrs. Sandstrom's?" I asked as she was poring over students' papers. She looked up.

"Sure, go ahead." I had the green light.

Her computer's floppy drive made a satisfied click and hum as I put in the first disk, and it began copying files. Since Works had a tendency to save users' documents in the same place as the program itself, I did my best to make sure that Mrs. Derrick's documents didn't get copied—only the application software.

I hit a snag: the program didn't fit. Each disk could hold 1.44 megabytes of data, but it seemed like I would need to take multiple trips since I only had three disks. I ran down to the sixth grade wing and back again three times, depositing the contents of the disks that I had just copied. When I was finished, I started Works to make sure that it actually lived up to its name. The splash screen appeared, with the same irritating abbreviations I had noticed on Mrs. Derrick's computer:

Microsoft Works 3.0
Registered To: Shaker Hts. City Schl. Distr.

I silently wished that whoever had installed the program in the first place could have just spelled out the words completely. Mrs. Sandstrom didn't care, though; she seemed thrilled to have received such prompt service. It felt great to be doing something useful at school for once, other than homework.

The following week, Mrs. Matthias was teaching us about science from a textbook entitled "SCIENCE." Out of nowhere, Mrs. Geszler appeared in the doorway. I noticed, of course, only because it was Mrs. Geszler, which meant that something was going on related to computers. Mrs. Matthias went over to greet her, leaving us to our work. I saw them talk briefly. Mrs. Geszler left.

Mrs. Matthias walked over. "Aaron, Mrs. Geszler would like to see you in the computer lab."

"Wasn't she just here? Does she want me to go now or after school?" I asked. "Right now."

I left everything on my desk. This was the second unexpected event in two weeks. I thought that maybe I had done such a good job setting up Mrs. Sandstrom's computer that I might have the chance to work on another special assignment.

Behind her glasses, I could tell that Mrs. Geszler was indeed in a special state of mind. She was furious. Her lips were drawn into a perfectly straight line. She was sitting at the scanner workstation, right next to the entrance to the lab. It was deserted except for the two of us.

"I understand that you were asked to set up Mrs. Sandstrom's new Macintosh?" she began. I could only stare, terrified and unmoving. I couldn't tell if it was a rhetorical question. Either way, she answered it for me. "You saw me in the hallway, and asked me to install Microsoft Works on her computer." My silence implied confirmation.

"Mrs. Sandstrom *called* me to find out if I could set up her computer for her. I told her that I didn't have time, but I knew that you could easily do it, so I told her that she should try to find you. I *trusted* you, Aaron—and you discredited me in front of my colleagues." I gulped. "You saw fit to install Microsoft Works yourself. *Illegally.*"

She had come to the main point of the lecture.

"How did you transfer it?" she asked curtly. It wasn't as if I had many options. CD burners were not widely available, the World Wide Web barely existed, and wireless networking technology would not be around for about a decade. I stupidly answered her question.

"I put it on some floppy disks."

"That was illegal, Aaron. It broke the law. *You* may not understand, but there are actually *laws* that we have to follow here. You could have landed the entire school in loads of trouble, and you could have cost the district thousands of dollars in fines, just because *you* decided not to wait for me to install that software myself." She paused briefly.

"How many trips did it take to copy the entire program? Two? Three?"

"Three," I replied. The lecture went on.

"So you made *three, illegal* trips to Mrs. Sandstrom's room to install Microsoft Works, and in the end, you didn't even install it properly."

Now I was angry—she was insulting me.

"*I know how to install Microsoft Works,*" I fumed silently. She saw my jaw tighten.

"That's right, Aaron, you didn't just copy the program! You copied Mrs. Derrick's documents, as well!"

I cringed. I had tried to be so careful about selecting only the files relevant to the software, and yet Mrs. Derrick seemed to have saved her files in every possible folder, with no discernible method to the madness. At least on IBM/Compatible computers, it was clear what was a user's file and what wasn't. Programs always ended with the same characters: ".EXE."

"I thought I didn't..." I protested, but at approximately the same height standing as Mrs. Geszler was sitting, I was in no position to argue.

"I am *very* disappointed in you," she said. It came as a shock; she had never expressed much interest in me before, or at least none that I could discern. "I thought you would have known better than to make illegal copies of software."

She was right, I did know better. All of my friends did it, though, and they never got caught. I wasn't even sure that what I had done was illegal.

I then remembered what I had seen after making sure that the files had been copied properly: the abbreviations. I hated those stupid extra punctuation marks.

It was like I had received a physical blow. The software hadn't been registered to Dianne Derrick. It was registered to the District. That meant that the District had paid for it, and not just Mrs. Derrick's copy, because Works was installed all throughout the school. The District had a site license for Microsoft Works. What I had done was completely legal. My only real mistake was inadvertently copying one or two of Mrs. Derrick's documents, and that certainly didn't break any laws.

"*What the heck? What is this really about?*" I began thinking.

Standing, listening to the lecture, I did not want to believe what I knew deep down. Mrs. Geszler was the only computer teacher in the building. That meant that only she was knowledgeable enough to be listed as the primary contact for the Microsoft Works site license. Accordingly, she had to be aware of the legal arrangement. If she wasn't aware of how a site license worked, that would have meant that she was negligent in one of her duties as the computer teacher. On the other hand, if she was aware, then she was taking time out of her day to drum up charges against an eleven-year-old, because she knew that copying Works was actually legal within the building, if not the entire District, depending on the scope of the license. There was no possibility that I had exceeded some sort of quota specified in the license by installing Works on one additional machine, because Mrs. Geszler had already agreed to install it herself in the hallway. That brought me back to the second option. The charges were false.

Mrs. Geszler was talking, but I didn't hear. I just nodded my head, fighting back tears, and growing angrier at myself by the second because my throat was constricting.

"Promise me this won't happen again," she concluded. Mentally, I snapped back to the room. After a moment, I agreed.

"I won't do it again."

Finally, I returned to Mrs. Matthias's room. When I sat down at my desk again, I didn't want to talk. My arms and legs felt like putty. The other students could tell something was strange about my mood by the blank look on my face, but fortunately, my reputation for being "smart" allowed me to evade the jibes that I would surely have been subjected to had they known that I was in trouble. Even though I desperately wanted *someone* to ask what had happened, no one did.

Mrs. Matthias didn't mention it the next day, either. Neither did Mrs. Derrick. I didn't even hear anything the following day, or the day after that. The issue seemed as dead as I felt from it.

The incident moved to the back of my mind as the pace of work increased throughout the winter. Despite the protests of numerous parents including my own, students still received hours of homework that compounded nightly. I routinely stayed up until midnight, when at Mercer, I had often thought to myself that I might never live to see my alarm clock pass "11:00." More importantly, all of my friends from Mercer seemed to have banded together without me. A friend I had made the year before in Mrs. Mahoney's class had left Shaker immediately after fifth grade, and I never saw him again. My one remaining friend, Adam, was incredibly shy and barely ever talked. For all intents and purposes, I was alone with my work.

Though I could now write paragraphs without much of a problem thanks to Mrs. Fox and Mrs. Derrick, the unrelenting flow of busywork had the consequence of making me hate school, which I had loved only two years prior. I didn't even enjoy going to Mrs. Geszler's lab for computer class anymore. I dreaded what had once been the highlight of my week.

Luckily, I could still fly through the material that Mrs. Geszler assigned us in class. I simply didn't ask questions anymore, unless they involved asking her to check my finished assignment. I wasn't permitted to create anything outside of the curriculum on my own; since the Works incident, Mrs. Geszler refused to lift the At Ease restrictions for me, and I was locked out of everything but the software for our lesson. One day, when Mrs. Geszler planned to teach us how to use Copy and Paste, knowing the keyboard shortcuts ahead of time meant that, as was often the case, I finished the assignment in half the time allotted to our class. When she was in a good mood, she permitted me to spend the other half helping other students who were having trouble so that she didn't have to.

It had occurred to me in the weeks after the ordeal with Microsoft Works that maybe not all teachers were as protective of students as I had assumed them to be. My teachers had always been kind to me as long as I did my work. I had never caught a teacher lying before, though I thought Mrs. Mahoney had come close when she had complained about me being sick. I wasn't quite sure what to make of it.

I figured that the best way to solve the problem was to get on good terms with Mrs. Geszler again. Late in the fall, the computer lab was suddenly plagued by problems with the new server, which was kept in the adjacent hall closet that also doubled as Mrs. Geszler's office. My notion of the server's purpose was fuzzy, but based on the way Mrs. Geszler talked about it, it seemed very important. It made me wonder why she had purchased a better computer for herself than she had for the server, but I didn't say anything.

Yet the problems with the server were starting to affect our work in class. Whenever any student typed in a character on the keyboard, it took two to three full minutes for it to appear on the screen—a significant delay for a room full of impatient students trying to work in a fifty-minute class period. Using the mouse yielded only slightly better results. I figured that my Computer Club membership at least gave me some status to inquire about the difficulty.

"Mrs. Geszler, can I help with the server?" I asked. Hunched over a student while peering at the slowly-appearing letters he had typed minutes before, she turned to me.

"Stay in your seat," she hissed. "I'm working on it."

Indeed she was. Mrs. Geszler worked on the problem for three weeks, during which computer class was cancelled. I had long since stopped coming in to turn on the computers in the morning. Had she been willing to listen, I would have suggested swapping her own system with the server to eliminate that machine as the source of the problem.

Later, Mrs. Geszler told everyone that the problem was buggy software running on the server, designed to handle the network requests for the Asantè 10BaseT Thin Ethernet hubs scattered throughout the lab. I didn't know what any of that meant, so I didn't inquire further. The fact that she didn't try swapping anything for weeks gave me a hunch as to what was really wrong, though.

•

Mrs. Matthias often assigned group projects to our class with the hope that they would teach us how to work well with each other. The sad reality was that the smartest person in each group typically did all of the work while the other students slacked off.

One such project involved studying the different kinds of blood cells that flowed through our circulatory system. Mrs. Matthias took us all down to the library when it was time for each group to make its presentation, which crept up on us sooner than we would have liked. I used my new Gateway Pentium computer and Canon Bubble-Jet printer to print out a color transparency with photographs of red and white blood cells. Even the librarians seemed impressed; we rarely saw anything printed in color.

My partners and I went to the front of the room, and the main librarian turned off the lights so that everyone could see the screen. The spiky leukocytes showed up beautifully and the red blood cells looked like glowing jelly-filled donuts, with perfectly round edges.

It was all going smoothly until a large figure appeared in the doorway behind me and to my right. Mrs. Matthias stopped me mid-sentence.

"Mrs. Groves, how can I help you?" she asked.

"I'd like to see Aaron Greenspan," the principal said. "Now."

Mrs. Matthias gave the order. "Go with Mrs. Groves, Aaron." I didn't have far to go, since I was already standing in front of the class. Had it not been dark, my cheeks would have been the perfect demonstration of what happened to skin when it became flush with the cells being projected above me.

"But my group, and my presentation..." I thought, but I had no choice. I went.

The fluorescent lights in the hallway outside struck my eyes with their harsh glow. Mrs. Groves, a bulky, African-American woman with a low, rolling voice, walked two or three strides ahead of me, never stopping to let me catch up.

"Wait here," she said, motioning vaguely toward an empty seat across from a secretary's cubicle. There were four of them, all busily talking. I was almost sure they were gossiping about me. I had never gone to the principal's office for doing something bad in my life.

I was rarely hyperactive, but I did begin to get uncomfortable sitting outside Mrs. Groves's office. After five minutes, I thought that I had been idle for a lifetime. I saw another five minutes pass on my watch. What kind of deserter was I?

"Mrs. Matthias is going to fail me on this presentation for sure, and maybe even my entire group, or perhaps she'll fail all of us on the entire course, all because of me..." Ominous thoughts raced through my head.

I couldn't let it happen. Mrs. Groves had been in her office forever, and the secretaries weren't giving any signals—maybe she had forgotten about me. I glanced around the office frantically. She had definitely forgotten about me, and now I was going to fail my presentation. I had never failed before. As quietly as I could, I headed back to the library.

At least ten minutes passed before Mrs. Groves appeared in the library doorway again, making it readily apparent that of all the things in the universe she might have forgotten about, she had not forgotten about me. The library lights were back on, but I didn't even need to see her face to discern the anger radiating from the doorway.

"Is Aaron here?" she demanded. It was not a question; it was a statement. I knew where to go.

"I *told* you to wait! What did you not understand?" My head position defaulted downward, and I stared at my feet. Mrs. Groves was terrifying now that she was truly angry. Beyond that, I had special fear reserved for angering adults other than my parents, and at some deeper level, an even worse fear of angering the principal. Mrs. Mahoney had tripped the first switch only one year before, followed by Mrs. Geszler, and now, a short time later, I was about to face Mrs. Groves in her office.

"What is with me?" I wondered silently.

This time I was denied the chance to escape, as we went directly inside. Before I could absorb any of the drab décor, I noticed that two of my teachers were already there, waiting for me.

Facing Mrs. Groves's large wooden desk, Mrs. Derrick sat to the left. In the center sat Mrs. Geszler. She was casually perusing a MacWarehouse catalog that she had brought along to read while she waited. Behind her desk, looking quite formidable, Mrs. Groves settled herself into her chair.

My throat sealed itself off completely.

"Mrs. Geszler has brought it to my attention that you have been illegally copying computer software," Mrs. Groves commenced. Up until this point, I had thought the Microsoft Works issue for all intents and purposes dead. Yet she continued.

"You copied HyperCard Player, a program on Mrs. Derrick's computer, to a computer outside of the school using a floppy disk. Is that not correct?"

I looked at her, unblinking, totally confused.

"Mrs. Geszler has also told me that this is not the first time that you have copied computer programs illegally. Do you realize how serious this is, Aaron?"

Apparently, this was not about Works anymore. Finally, I remembered that I *had* copied HyperCard Player to a floppy disk, without even thinking about it. The Cleveland Hebrew Schools had finally received its Macintosh LC III, and I wanted to show one of my friends there a HyperCard stack that I had made at Woodbury. For some reason, the Hebrew School's Macintosh had arrived without any software installed, so there was no way to open the file. I didn't have a Macintosh at home, but I was always around the A.R.P. room.

Unlike the full version of HyperCard, the Player could only read files; it couldn't create them. I was almost positive that it was legal to copy HyperCard Player from one computer to another, but instead of voicing my logically reasoned argument, I assumed the look of a deer caught in headlights, and continued to stare straight ahead at the figure before me: my very unhappy, very large principal.

"Did you have permission to do this from Mrs. Derrick?" It was another question-statement, one which could only be answered correctly with whatever the interrogator was wanting to hear.

Missing the nuance in her tone, I thought back, trying to discern the answer that would actually have a factual basis for correctness. I always asked Mrs. Derrick before using her computer, and especially before changing any settings on it. I thought that I must have asked her, but now I wasn't sure.

I could no longer maintain the path of least resistance, which merely required staring. I forced the words out in choking gasps. "I thought..."

Mrs. Groves interrupted me. "Mrs. Derrick. Did you give Aaron permission to copy HyperCard Player to a computer outside of the school?" Her tone had risen slightly to a soft roar. I stole a glance to my left, and took in the sight of Mrs. Derrick looking pale. I was sure she would get me out of this mess. I was sure. Mrs. Derrick looked at her feet.

"No." She spoke softly, but it didn't matter. The pillars that had supported my mental picture of the world came crashing down. It was all a lie. The color drained from my cheeks, my blush of embarrassment long gone. I could feel my heart inside my chest. There was no way out.

"Aaron, this kind of behavior is not acceptable. I cannot let you go around the school copying whatever programs you like, especially when Mrs. Geszler has told you not to as many times as she already has. What, did you think you could just *ignore* her?"

Counting on my supposedly decent language skills to recognize the question as rhetorical in nature, I did not answer. Perhaps at this point Mrs. Groves realized just how scared I was, because her tone softened.

"I'm doing this for your own good, Aaron. Have you heard of a man named Kevin Mitnick?"

"No," I said.

"Kevin Mitnick is a hacker. He was in the newspapers a few weeks ago. He hacked into government computers—stole things. They say he started off in school learning about computers, just like you. I don't want you to turn into the next Kevin Mitnick, Aaron. Kevin Mitnick is in *jail*. And that's where you'll be headed soon if you're not careful. Do you want to be in jail?"

The comparison seemed like a bit of a stretch, but I was not given much time to go over it before sentencing began.

"This is what we're going to do. I've talked it over with Mrs. Geszler and Mrs. Derrick. You will not attend Computer Club meetings for the next three months." There was a pause. "You will not use any computers at school for the next two weeks." The softness was overcome by shrill barks. "You will not talk about, look at, or *think* about, computers, for the next two weeks! Do you understand me, young man?"

I nodded.

"If I hear your name and the word 'computer' in the same sentence *one more time* before then, you will be suspended from this school. You will be eliminated from the Student Council election—and there will be no going back."

I contemplated the length of a week, and then, a question sprang to mind.

"How did you know about the disk?" I asked. Eyes shifted across the desk.

"Mrs. Geszler received a note from a student," Mrs. Groves said.

"Who?" Now I wanted to know. Was it Carson getting back at me?

"That's none of *your* business," Mrs. Groves said.

The confusion returned, this time in waves. Who would have written a note telling on me? It would have to be someone who knew that Mrs. Geszler didn't like me. Or maybe it was someone who knew that I went to Hebrew school. Would the person have had to have been in the A.R.P. room when I copied the disk? Maybe it was someone else running for Student Council President...

"That is all."

I left quickly to get my things from the library, but it was deserted; everyone was already back in Mrs. Matthias's room. I wanted to go home more than ever before. The ugly beige floor tiles were a blur as tears started to sting my eyes. Before I knew it, I was facing the doors to go out to the lawn. I shoved them aside as hard as I could. I navigated on auto-pilot toward the buses lining the block, thinking in circles about what was shaping up to be some sort of weird conspiracy.

The tears came before I could hide them, and I got onto the bus looking sullen. This had happened before. It wasn't fair.

"*What is Mrs. Geszler's problem?*" I wanted to shout.

When I arrived home, my mother was unprepared for the storm of anger I unleashed upon her. The moment I walked through the front door, I was a monsoon, though of the type that preferred to consume a light snack of milk and cookies before doing anything else. As I wrenched the skim milk out of the refrigerator, I explained the technical and legal details of HyperCard Player to my mother, and then the saga at school from earlier that day, from start to finish. From past dinner table conversations, she was already familiar with what had happened with Microsoft Works. She noticed the pattern.

"Who the hell does this Geszler woman think she is!" she yelled. Then, she calmed down momentarily.

"What do you want me to do?" she asked, trying to comfort me.

"I don't know," I mumbled as I grabbed a tissue. "Call Apple."

To me, trying to call Apple Computer, Inc. was akin to trying to call God: they were everywhere, but they couldn't really respond if you started talking to them.

My mother was not so affected by the company's mythic status. She dealt with companies on the phone all day. She was already scanning through the yellow pages by the time I finished my glass of milk.

While I sat at the kitchen table, my mother expertly navigated Apple's corporate bureaucracy, extracting the telephone number of the national headquarters from the Cleveland-area regional office, and the telephone number of the technical support department from the national headquarters. I had said that I thought copying HyperCard Player was legal, and we were going to find out if I was right.

Since I could barely maintain a constant facial expression after the workout that I had given myself bawling, my mother did the talking. She asked the technician to fax her a written document stating what he had just told her on the phone. With its customary beep, I heard her press the "off" button on the gray AT&T cordless phone, concluding the conversation.

"Ha!" she triumphed. "You were absolutely right. It's not just legal. They *want* you to copy it."

"Well, yeah," I said. "It's good marketing for them."

A few minutes later, the fax machine sprang to life, and the Apple logo I had tried to draw on so many occasions appeared above a clip art picture of a call center representative on a headset. The transmission verified in writing everything I had just told my mother. She dialed another number: my father at work.

My father came home for dinner around 6:00 P.M. that night, as usual. Before he could even change out of his work clothes, he started to hear even more about the events that had transpired that day. The conversation continued throughout dinner, and by the time I was ready for dessert, the anger I had seen in Mrs. Groves seemed minuscule compared to what I was witnessing in my father.

"I am going to call that woman and set her straight!" he yelled amongst a slew of expletives. "I'd call her at home if I had her number, but I guess I'll just do it tomorrow when I'm at work."

The next day, Mrs. Groves received a telephone call. My father reported back that he had spoken to my principal for almost thirty minutes, during which time he relayed three main points: that I had done nothing wrong, that she had done something wrong, and that I was owed an apology by her, Mrs. Geszler and Mrs. Derrick. Mrs. Groves was incensed that a parent had the audacity to call her on the telephone and yell at her.

When my mother called Mrs. Derrick, my teacher was suddenly apologetic.

"I am *so* sorry, Judi," she said. "I did give Aaron permission to do that. I was afraid I'd lose my job if I said otherwise." I could forgive Mrs. Derrick, but neither Mrs. Groves nor Mrs. Geszler would apologize.

They were effective teachers in one sense. I stopped using illegal software, and I got a bitter glimpse of what was to come.

•

I lost the election for Student Council president, even after passing out pencils imprinted with my name—courtesy of my mother's position with Keene Advertising, Inc.—to every student in the school. While most students probably thought I was a stuck up kid with too much money to spend on imprinted pencils, it was actually more a matter of convenience. There happened to be a pencil factory who owed my mother a favor, and she had no other need for pencils at the time. They were all free.

Once again, I went home crying. A popular student in my grade had won, but Mrs. Groves refused to reveal the vote tally. The next day, a friend asked me if I had actually been crying.

"Why, who said that I was?" I asked.

"Oh, the secretaries in the main office were talking about you," she said, much to my horror.

For spring break, we went to Boston as a family to visit my mother's family. Along with Nana, her brother Michael ran the same family business that my mother worked for in Ohio. Keene Advertising had its offices at 137 South Street, in the Financial District of downtown Boston. My uncle had called before the trip to find out what kind of computer to order so that he could work with files from one of his clients. I recommended a Gateway, and spent two or three days in the office trying to set it up. Simon busied himself with the paper shredder. Before long, he managed to spill out the entire contents of the shredder's garbage bag all over the floor. With my mother screaming in the background about the company's broken vacuum cleaner, I tried to make the new computer work.

The Keene office ran on a strange program, which in turn ran on SCO XENIX, an operating system I had never heard of. In order to connect to the XENIX server from an IBM/Compatible machine, we needed a "gender changer" that physically changed the port on the back of the computer from one kind to another, and "terminal emulation software," I was told. Between the "bit rate," "parity," "port speed," and four other settings, there were several thousand possible permutations to try. Finally, through sheer luck, I was able to make the single word "login:" appear on the bottom of the screen. It was working.

Walking down the steps of Keene's office onto South Street that night, my mother made one of her typically ludicrous suggestions. "You should really start charging people. You're crazy to keep doing this for free," she said. I rolled my eyes.

"No one is going to pay an eleven-year-old to do anything," I said, trying to think of something that eleven-year-olds got paid to do. There was only one option, for which I had often felt guilty charging $4.00 per hour. "Except babysit."

My mom continued to harass me on the subject for a good five minutes. I tried to ignore her, but it was too late. The seed of the idea had been planted.

That spring, for Invent America, I went out of my way to avoid computers. I cut apart a "koozie" that had been designed for a Coke can and shrunk it down to the size needed for a medicine bottle. Nana had visited us in Hilton Head over the summer, and placed her insulin in the side of the refrigerator. When one of us swung open the door, the insulin went flying out, the glass bottle crashing to bits on the kitchen tile. The judges thought my insulin koozie no better than shopping with a computer.

Two months later, when I graduated from Woodbury, I had never been so glad to leave a place. Still, what I had endured was nothing compared to what Simon had gone through.

On a trial visit to Cleveland Hebrew Schools, which we all thought Simon might like because he enjoyed singing in semi-Hebrew so much, Simon's odd behavior attracted the attention of one of the boys in his class. The end result was a phone call at our home around 5:00 P.M. that made my mother blanch.

During the five minute break between the two hour-long periods, the boy had shoved Simon against the corner of a brick wall, which was sharp enough to pierce the skin on the back of his head, sending blood gushing everywhere. He needed stitches.

When my mother and I arrived at the hospital, we learned from the principal that from the time he fell to the ground to the time he arrived in the emergency room, Simon didn't even cry.

CHAPTER 4

Freedom to Conform

The District must have heard parents complaining about the transition from the elementary schools to Woodbury, because the administrators at Shaker Heights Middle School prepared an entire assembly for the incoming seventh grade class.

The first thing I noticed about the Middle School was its hideously ugly exterior. Voted the "most fenestrated building" in the United States in 1968 (or so I had been told), the outside was brick and cement, with cracking sidewalks and not a bit of symmetry anywhere in sight. The inside featured student murals every few feet on the yellowing walls, which I found repulsive compared to the clean, uniform walls of Mercer and Woodbury.

As bad as my transition to the Middle School was, Simon's parallel transition to Woodbury was worse. His peers were just starting to discover the meanest parts of their personalities, and without any understanding of social constructs whatsoever, Simon was a human dartboard. Eventually, my parents had had enough. They forced the Shaker Heights City School District to work with the neighboring suburb of Beachwood.

Simon ended up going to Hilltop Elementary School, where his new teachers had only one demand. Simon had to be on the prescription stimulant, Ritalin.

Their request boggled our minds. Simon was not hyperactive. He did seem to have more behavior problems than the average "learning disabled" child, but we figured that there was a broad range of problems that learning disabilities encompassed. Simon certainly wasn't the first child ever to act up at school.

The real problem was that Ritalin made Simon behave even worse at home. When he was off the medication, he was generally unhappy for one reason or another, but tolerable. On Ritalin, Simon was a holy terror. Yet, his teachers claimed, the opposite was true at school. It made no sense, but we had little choice. Woodbury was the wrong place for Simon, and despite the inter-district logistical labyrinth my mother had to navigate to get him to Beachwood each day, it clearly had more resources to help him.

The fact that my school would finally be within walking distance from my house did not give me any additional incentive to go. Nor did the rumor that in the event of a tornado—an event not entirely unlikely in Ohio—teachers were under instructions to move all of their students to the auditorium.

"That way," one student whispered, "when it collapses, everyone will be dead in one place." It seemed like it might be true; staying anywhere else in the building during a tornado was like asking to take a shower in a million shards of glass.

Once everyone had settled down for the assembly in the very same auditorium, I realized that my worries about the school being ugly, big and unfamiliar were nothing compared to what I was facing in front of me. Dr. Neil T. Glazer, who would apparently be our new principal, was speaking to us from a video screen.

"Hi! I'm Doctor Neil T. Glazer, principal of the Shaker Heights Middle *School!*"

From that first sentence alone, there was obviously something wrong. The balding, skinny man with thick, round tortoiseshell glasses spoke far too enthusiastically, and placed the emphasis on the last word of the sentence where it did not belong. His appearance was overtly bookish, yet he had an athletic side; there would eventually be reports of Dr. Glazer jogging around various streets in Shaker wearing tight spandex pants decorated with the stars and stripes.

After the taped speech, the Math and English department heads bored us all to tears, though in person. By 8:00 P.M., all of the parents were beginning to worry; most of them would have to stay up with their children to help them with homework.

Once I was officially a seventh-grader, I found out that the Middle School, unlike Woodbury, held lots of assemblies. The higher degree of freedom for students that the administration had designed into the school's environment came at a price. Everything, from the hallway to the vending machines in the cafeteria, was tightly regulated by Dr. Glazer's team of assistant principals. Over the first few weeks of our fall semester, Dr. Glazer himself repeatedly assumed his position at the front and center of the auditorium stage for various purposes: appraising us of the mandatory use of school-issued planners, the imperative need for "time-management" in our lives in general, or the "off-limits" status of the school's weed-infested gravel courtyard. Once, he called an assembly simply to berate the seventh grade class as a collective group. By October, I liked Dr. Glazer more as an overbearing nerd on the video screen than I did in person.

I decided that my locker, located outside of the seventh grade wing where all of my classes were held, was both inconvenient and useless. Getting anything from it required going out of the seventh grade wing simply to go back into the seventh grade wing. I accustomed myself to carrying around a backpack that weighed about one-quarter of my body weight.

As if the physical environment weren't enough to make me feel incarcerated between the hours of 8:30 A.M. and 3:00 P.M., the students were just plain mean. I had certainly never felt warm and fuzzy walking through the halls in fifth or sixth grade, but somehow, things had gotten worse. I was perplexed by the newfound hostility, since I was surrounded by the same people that I had been around for the previous two years. Almost everyone had something obnoxious to say to each other, except Adam, who still rarely said much. In the context of our chaotic middle school, however, I found this trait rather admirable, and tagged along with him whenever I could. It turned out that when Adam did have something to say, it was level-headed and kind.

On the polar opposite end of the spectrum, a popular girl named Gwen enjoyed making fun of me because I rode my bike to school. Whenever she saw the plastic guards on the front of my bike, she made it a point of laughing as loudly as she could.

"Aaron, can your bike *fly?*" she asked daily in her nasal, jeering voice, walking alongside her newest boyfriend. Even my own friend, John, who also played French Horn, said one day after school that he hadn't wanted to get a ride home in my mother's car because he didn't want to be seen next to me. He needed the ride, though, so he hopped in against his better judgment.

Philip, meanwhile, seemed to be nurturing an ego that was growing at a pace proportionally greater than the rest of ours. I had already noticed his tendency to adopt a new best friend each year, so that his clique always had someone to aspire to. His latest pick was a tall, lanky kid named James who loved football and liked to fantasize over lunch about "JamesWorld," a magical land where everyone else was his slave. JamesWorld wore on my nerves after a very short time, but at any other table I would have been a total outcast.

At my request, my mother arranged for my class schedule to be similar to Adam's, and I continued trying to talk to him every chance I could get, hoping to at least elicit a smile now and then. I began to worry that my efforts were backfiring. During the few minutes that we were actually allowed to talk in the hallway between classes, Adam still didn't open up. Our seventh-grade insecurities played off one another, with Adam's shy demeanor catalyzing my own eternal fear of being hated by my peers.

Luckily, there was a new computer teacher for me to meet, distracting me from my confusion over the rapidly changing rules surrounding the proper way to interact with other children my own age. I became acquainted with Mr. Kocian as soon as I had the chance to stop by the computer lab, right near the side entrance to the school. It was outfitted with the same Macintosh LC II computers that had been at Woodbury, but Mr. Kocian seemed much happier to see me than Mrs. Geszler ever had. I made a habit of coming by the computer lab after school to work on the Macintosh in the corner, which was slightly more powerful than the others.

When computer class was actually part of my schedule during the second semester as one of the rotating electives that every student was required to take, I didn't have to go. Mr. Kocian let me do what I wanted to, and we both decided that it would be a good idea for me to learn how to write web pages using something called Hypertext Markup Language: HTML.

The more I talked to people, though, the more it seemed like I was the only one who liked Mr. Kocian. A heavy-set man, his stomach jutted out in almost a right triangle, forming a perfect sixty-degree angle with his waist. He was a Vietnam War veteran, which manifested itself in his commandeering style of teaching. The War had taken the hearing in his left ear, he told us.

"I'm going to give you a lot of leeway," he said gruffly to me, the volume of his voice escalating steadily. "But if you screw up, I'm going to come down on you like a pile of bricks!" I decided not to screw up.

I named the project that I started "SMSnet One," because our school was often referred to as "Shaker Middle School." As far as I could tell, it was the school's first web site, but I added the "One" to the name just because I thought it sounded better. Every day, while I was supposed to be in computer class with another teacher, I went to Mr. Kocian's lab and worked on my own ideas for the allotted fifty minutes of class time.

Quickly, I came up against challenges. I wanted visitors to be able to click on an "image map," or picture, and depending on where they clicked, to be able to go to different pages. Using Netscape required programming your page one way, while using Microsoft Internet Explorer required another. I used a Macintosh at school, but IBM/Compatible computers at home, making things even more complicated. The computer that stored our web site wasn't a Macintosh or an IBM/Compatible—it ran UNIX, and I had no idea how it worked. There was a lot to learn.

A few other technologically-savvy students began making regular trips to the computer lab to help out with SMSnet One, serving dual roles as reporters and programmers. Penny, a tall Asian girl with a round face, and Greg, who I had once played Nintendo with until I realized that he rarely did anything else, both seemed to be looking to me for some direction on what to do.

I wasn't prepared to run a team, but I figured that we could start by trying to get some content about the school up on the site. I dispatched Penny and Greg to the various departments within the school in search of content. Surprisingly, the most responsive department of all was P.E.: the coaches wanted their teams' scores on-line.

I also wasn't sure what Mr. Kocian was talking about when he told me that he wanted me to help him with his "electronic archaeology" web site. It took several years for me to decipher the meaning of the phrase: using metal detectors to look for buried treasure.

One day at lunch, I told Philip, Adam, James and Peter about a new idea that I had come up with. I usually thought of businesses as having offices in giant buildings, but my mother ran a business out of our home, and she seemed to do just fine. Why couldn't I run a business to fix computers? I had already made up business cards that said "troubleShooting" on them, but I didn't like the name. Aside from conjuring mental imagery of guns and computers, it implied that when my work was done, you would have more trouble than what you started with.

"What should I call my company?" I asked after taking a bite of my sandwich. James responded immediately with "JamesCorp."

"*Cogitabit*," said Philip.

"What?" I replied. I thought I had misheard.

"*Cogitabit*," he repeated. "It's Latin for 'think,'" he explained. Though Adam and I were both taking Spanish, Philip was learning Latin. I thought the suggestion was actually pretty good.

"How about I just call it 'think,' then?" I said. "I'll be dealing with English-speaking customers."

"Whatever. I like *Cogitabit*."

I still needed a logo. My only idea stemmed from a trip I had made years before to Stride Rite, when my mother insisted that I needed a new pair of shoes. The store was decorated with a colorful, abstract drawing of a person, presumably one that was excited to be wearing Stride Rites. Strangely, all the man had for a head was a giant red dot.

I drew about twenty Stride Rite heads on a sheet of recycled paper with magic marker, using a Stride Rite shoe box that for several years had stored extra toothbrushes in my bathroom as a reference. All but one came out looking deformed, but one good logo was enough.

I brought the sheet of paper over to my new flatbed scanner that I normally used to help with Keene Advertising's client artwork, and within a few minutes I had a digitized version of the logo on my screen.

"Think! Technologies, World Headquarters," a sign on my door soon read. Though I wouldn't admit to myself that my mother had been right years before, I decided that from then on, I was going to charge people $25.00 per hour for computer help.

•

By the summer of 1996, in the middle of juggling her work, my brother, and myself, my mother had yet another idea I considered absurd: attending computer camp. It was being held at University School around the corner from our house, and she knew the director well since she had sold him T-shirts. His name was Bob Morgan.

"Go talk to Mr. Morgan and see if he needs any help. Maybe you'll meet some nice kids there," she prodded. By responding that I didn't want to go and meet a random teacher I had never met before, I communicated the fact that I was at least considering the idea. My mother knew how to push.

"Do you want me to call him?" she asked.

"Fine. I don't care," I replied, and within seconds, she had him on the phone. I had backed myself into a corner, but fortunately, it was the corner adjacent to my street.

Across Claythorne Road, I wandered around the University School buildings until I found what looked like a computer lab. Inside, I met Mr. Morgan, who had a large reddish-brown beard and a spark in his eye that I hadn't ever noticed before in Shaker's teachers—and certainly not its computer teachers. He didn't need any help, but the C++ counselor, a recent high school graduate named Carl did. Carl was working in one of the classrooms in the building's attic, assembling fifteen new computers that had just arrived. Not a single one was a Macintosh. I didn't have to be asked twice; I was there for the rest of the day.

Even though I still retained an instinctive fear of children older than me, Carl was amazingly tolerant of my presence. He was seventeen, and planned to attend Harvard in the fall. I figured that meant that Carl was smart.

In reality, Carl was very smart. He told me about the company that he had started, Shadow Software, which was an authorized reseller of the educational versions of commercial software products. He could get programs that everyone used, such as Microsoft Office, for 90% off of manufacturers' list prices, completely legally.

I tried my best to impress Carl. All of the new computers were custom-built to Mr. Morgan's specifications by Compaq, but each and every one seemed to be having trouble with its CD-ROM drive. I didn't know what was wrong, but I had a hunch that it was related to the sound cards that had been installed in all of the machines. After some testing, I turned out to be right. Mr. Morgan had them all replaced as soon as I described the problem to him.

"He actually took me seriously!" I was dumbstruck.

When I got back home, I asked my mother if I could take Carl's class on C++ programming.

"Ohh!" she exclaimed. "Now you want to go to U.S.!"

For the rest of the month until the official start of computer camp, I was at U.S. all day, every day, helping Carl and Mr. Morgan get everything set up for the other campers. Carl seemed sincerely interested in my ideas and ambitions, which made me giddy with excitement. He lent me a book called *StartUp: A Silicon Valley Adventure*, by Jerry Kaplan. I sped through it, and e-mailed the author a message chock full of exclamation points when I was done, asking for an internship. Mr. Kaplan responded quickly, but I was disappointed to learn that there wasn't anywhere for an eighth-grader to work at his company.

One of the other campers looked far too young to be there at all. He was probably a full foot shorter than me, and his huge, purple glasses reminded me of my father's, dwarfing the rest of his face. After Carl got us working on a number of small projects using a teaching toolkit called "Ootpik," our first major assignment was to write a tic-tac-toe program. Much to my dismay, Carl paired me up with the third-grader.

"*He'd better be bright,*" I mused silently.

The third grader, whose name was Tim, *was* bright—and he wasn't in third grade. Though he was short, he was going into eighth grade, just like me. We hit it off instantly. Everything I said seemed to make him laugh. At lunch, we collectively dubbed one of the squirrels "Boris," after the Russian President Boris Yeltsin. Shortly thereafter, I was inhaling 100% real lemonade through my nose, as Tim chided, "Here, Boris, Boris, Boris!" with a ridiculous grin.

When it came to programming, Tim ran circles around me. He understood everything Carl said instantly, while I struggled to catch up. I managed, on occasion, to come up with the proper algorithm to solve a problem, but Tim was always the one to translate it into code. On the other hand, I was much better at graphics. I spent hours making our Xs and Os look perfect for tic-tac-toe, and directed Tim as to how our checkers should be rendered once we started working on that program. It was a good partnership.

After I finished *StartUp*, I was enthralled by the idea of rubbing shoulders with the likes of Bill Gates, shifty IBM executives and devious venture capitalists. Yet I didn't want to give up control of my own company to anyone. I swore off venture capital with Carl and Tim as my witnesses, positive after one cursory reading that Kaplan's personal experience with venture capital was the rule, rather than the exception.

When the summer came to an end, we all had to go our separate ways. Tim was off to school at U.S., I was destined for Shaker once again, and Carl was on his way to Harvard Yard.

CHAPTER 5

The Technology Committee

As I sat in my room doing homework one night in March, the Omni Hotel's elegant sign glistened in the frigid air, overlooking the arrival of countless guests. It was located in the middle of the main campus of one of the foremost medical institutions in country, the Cleveland Clinic. The Omni, a floor of which the Saudi royals bought out in its entirety whenever the King needed back surgery, was also the location for the Shaker Heights City School District's annual fundraiser, the Night for the Red and White. The gala was held each March for the purpose of raising money for technology.

"They're setting up some sort of committee to decide what to do with all of the money from the Night for the Red and White," my mother reported back when she arrived home with my father.

Indeed, there was a lot of money to spend. With the funds from the previous year's event, the District had purchased more than thirty VGA-to-TV converters to let teachers project their computers' displays onto classroom televisions. It was an attempt to be "state-of-the-art" and a colossal waste. The school's televisions were so old that they could barely focus well enough to make anything legible, not to mention that the converters had to drop one-third to one-half of the information on the screen just to get it across. The other problem was that none of the teachers cared enough to project anything, anyway. The devices ended up sitting on a shelf in the library's A-V room in perpetuity, still in their shrink-wrapped boxes.

I didn't want the school to make the same mistake twice. "Can I be on it?" I asked, excited.

"I'll try to find out," my mother promised, and then I went back up to my room to do more homework.

True to her word, several weeks later my mother returned home from a community event at which she had dutifully sought out the Assistant Superintendent of the school system, Dr. James Paces. Dr. Paces had smooth gray hair and a chubby, red face. He oozed charm and happiness, features of which the superintendent had taken note. He was the point man for angry parents, and as the mother of a child with learning disabilities, my mother and Dr. Paces already knew each other well.

Ohio state law required our public school system to meet Simon's needs—even if it was fundamentally incapable of doing so. My parents had met with several lawyers to figure out how to best deal with Shaker when it refused to listen to their requests for additional assistance for Simon at school. I had heard them talking for months about my brother's Independent Educational Plan. In theory, the IEP was supposed to determine whether Simon would get what he needed or not, but the District had a tendency to diverge from what was written on the page.

Possibly sensing a public relations opportunity, Dr. Paces was delighted to entertain the notion of my being on the Technology Committee. Since he also happened to be the Committee chair, there was nothing more to it. I was invited to the next meeting, which conveniently took place in the Middle School library Audio-Visual Room. On October 23, 1996, I went to a committee meeting for the first time.

I never stayed at school until 7:00 P.M. except for when I lost track of time while trying to repair the high-end Quadra computer in the eighth grade lab. I actually preferred the Middle School at night when there wasn't anyone around to bother me except the occasional janitor.

The A-V Room on the first floor, with its weak fluorescent lighting and dark blue carpet, was even gloomier than usual at night, but for once there were more people present than machines. There was a portly African-American man talking to the equally stocky Caucasian man next to him, whose voice was so hoarse that he could speak no louder than a whisper. A teacher I didn't recognize was present, with oily black hair that slicked over his forehead used-car-salesman style. Dr. Paces was present, as was Mr. Kocian, who seemed glad to see me there, and Mrs. Strickler, a teacher who had recently begun sharing Mr. Kocian's room. A thin man sitting nearby would have escaped my notice entirely had it not been for his ponytail.

The meeting started off with Dr. Paces getting up from his seat and showering praise on everyone present. He asked everyone to introduce themselves, and passed out an agenda typeset in Palatino.

I soon learned the identities of the mysterious faces around the table: the oily-haired man was Mr. Boswell, the District's network administrator. The African-American man, who identified himself as Mr. Decatur, was a freelance IT consultant and Shaker parent who was offering his services to the District free of charge. His friend who spoke in a whisper, Mr. Forquer, was the father of a stocky, athletic girl in my grade, and worked for Cisco Systems.

Dr. Paces cut in after my neighbor's introduction with irrelevant-sounding pleasantries, presenting a convenient segue into my short self-introduction. I tried not to be nervous.

"My name is Aaron Greenspan. I'm a student here at the Middle School in eighth grade."

Smiles from around the table seemed to imply that many of the adults thought it was cute for a student to take such an active interest in the school's computers. Mrs. Geszler, who must have slipped in late since I hadn't noticed her before from across the table, wore a frown that seemed to indicate that she did not necessarily share the committee's view. The man with the ponytail introduced himself next as a former Microsoft employee.

The meeting was boring. Most of it concerned schedules for the contractors who would be drilling holes in the elementary schools' walls and the different types of wall jacks available that could support category 5 wiring, which would bring high-speed internet access to every classroom. Through a legislative program dubbed "SchoolNet," the State of Ohio was handing out grants to public school systems to put as many computers with internet access in classrooms as possible.

By the sound of things, Shaker was getting $1.5 million from the State. The money from the Night for the Red and White was dwarfed by comparison. I'd never thought of a practical use for so much money, but there they were, right in front of me: the spreadsheets and documents outlining how all of it could be spent in only a few weeks with a need for even more.

The Technology Committee met once each month, and even though the meetings tended to drag on, I found them to be infinitely more interesting than homework, even when they weren't. I was thus relieved when the main topic of conversation turned to more important things: computers.

I had already called Gateway for price quotes two days after the first meeting in October. As soon as I received one fax, I would think of another use for computers at school—and so I'd ask for another. Their salespeople never seemed to grow tired of sending them. They even faxed over copies of certifications that Gateway had earned for its factories, all of which I photocopied and highlighted in a fit of perfectionism.

A few days later, Mr. Kocian welcomed some new arrivals into his classroom: two beige IBM/Compatible computers made by a company called "Performance PC." They were thoroughly unimpressive. Their monitors weren't branded with a custom logo, as if the company had visited the nearest CompUSA or Micro Center and picked out the cheapest ones there. To make matters worse, they were made by LG Electronics, the parent company of GoldStar, a budget electronics giant with a horrible reputation in the computer industry. The fact that the monitors had speakers built into the sides disturbed me because I knew that if there were problems with either component, both would end up being useless.

The Trident video cards inside the machines were absolutely abysmal. From fixing other people's computers, I had noticed that if the drivers were confusing or lacking in features, the hardware was probably engineered just as poorly. From a business perspective, it made sense: few companies would spend all of their money on hiring expert electrical engineers, and none on software developers.

I pelted Mr. Kocian with questions. "Who is 'Performance PC?' Where are they even located?" I asked.

"They're a division of a company called ACE Software, in Columbus," he said.

The proximity of the company was supposed to be a huge plus since support techni-cians could respond to problems quickly. The company boasted a four-hour response time, but with a three-hour drive, a problem that arose at 2:00 P.M. wouldn't actually be solved until the next day. In other words, the service was roughly equivalent to what a major name brand could provide—and Gateway had promised to send spare systems to Shaker free of charge.

Performance PC didn't have much of a prior history selling to school districts. The serial number on the back of one of the systems read:

00001947

"This company has sold less than 2,000 machines in its entire history?" I asked, surprised. Given the tendency of school districts to order thousands of computers at a time, this meant that it had filled only one, perhaps two, major orders in its past.

I drafted a letter on my company's new letterhead, which now read "Think Computer," and sent it to Daniel Wilson, the Treasurer of the District, who was ultimately responsible for making the purchase. Not soon after, Treasurer Wilson sent back a critical response, arguing that the Performance PCs were much cheaper than the systems I had recommended—and that they came with sub-woofers. I had neglected to consider the vital role of loud bass in the learning environment.

Despite all of the problems, I thought maybe there were some redeeming qualities to the Performance PC machines that I was missing. I installed a program that ran benchmark tests to analyze the speed of Mr. Kocian's test systems. Then, I installed the same program at home, where my personal computer ran on a 100MHz Intel Pentium microprocessor, 33MHz slower than the ones at school. Yet the program seemed to show that my 100MHz Gateway 2000 was actually faster than either of the 133MHz Performance PCs. The trial computers were actually slower than computers that had been made two years before, and the district was proposing to spend $1.5 million on them.

Just to be safe, I decided to double-check the facts on Performance PC. Using AltaVista, the best search engine I knew of, I tried to find the web site of Performance PC on the World Wide Web, so that I could e-mail the company. Nothing turned up. I tried the parent company, ACE Software. There was a match.

What greeted me looked like the kind of illustration I had made in Microsoft Paintbrush when the mouse had first been a cutting-edge accessory. A spaceship labeled "ACE SOFT" with a slew of misspellings underneath appeared to be launch-ing from a moon-like terrace. I showed Mr. Kocian.

"Is this really the company we're going to get the computers from?" I asked, handing over the printed copy of ACE SOFT's home page, trying to conceal my glee. Mr. Kocian looked confused.

"I...I don't know," he said, brows furrowing. "It might be."

Dr. Paces strode into the room in his fancy topcoat just as I was showing Mr. Kocian my new aeronautic discovery. His pudgy face looked perplexed when I showed it to him.

"I'll have to check into this," he said, still managing a meek smile. "Do you mind if I take it with me?"

"Not at all," I said. If ACE Software really did manufacture systems slow enough to underperform two-year-old desktops and then hired web site designers without basic spelling skills, maybe there was a chance that the Technology Committee would consider another company after all.

•

When I came home from the Middle School after repairing the Quadra for what must have been the fourth time, it was a little after 8:00 P.M.

"Where were you? Why didn't you call!" my mother screamed.

"The Macintosh in the lab was screwed up again," I responded. "Someone's got to fix it. What should I do for dinner?"

"Make it yourself," she said. I took her suggestion to mean that I should use the microwave. My father came into the kitchen to help me prepare a fuller meal. At the kitchen table, which was too high relative to my chair, I crouched down with my chin in my hands, and I was angry that she was angry.

Of late, dinner had not been an event I looked forward to. It was a vicious cycle. Simon was always agitated, and fought with us because he couldn't make any friends at school. If the phone ever rang for me, which happened frequently thanks only to Think Computer, it just made things worse. If I had anything to say about my day, it usually came out in the form of a bitter complaint about homework or my teachers. My father was engaged in a constant battle with the hospital administration; many of his colleagues were leaving his department as they grew tired of the new hospital president's mandates. My mother was constantly exhausted thanks both to her own work and Simon—and so the proliferation of grief continued unabated.

For a while, we tried to get Simon to eat at the dinner table with the rest of us, even though he wanted to eat in the basement while watching television. The battles escalated night after night. They grew particularly bad whenever one of Simon's classmates had been mean to him at school, an occurrence that took place virtually every day.

Punishment did not even remotely phase him; he seemed to be unable to learn any sort of lesson at all. For years now, Simon had invariably repeated the exact same behavior nightly, screaming and yelling as if nothing of the sort had ever taken place before. The routine was exhausting. I took to locking myself in my bedroom, but it was still difficult to work while I could hear Simon's uncontrollable meltdowns.

He began to lose his voice on a regular basis. On particularly bad nights, he would throw things or scream outside, concerning our neighbors.

My father finally deduced that the least damaging way out of a conflict with Simon was simply to let him have his way. This typically led to my parents being criticized for being "too soft," or "not taking care of their child." Nothing in the world made me angrier than other sniveling parents (or doctors) pretending to know better. I didn't care how educated or distinguished they were. I hated them all.

My anger at having been "picked" to live in a family with a sibling like Simon was accompanied by an irrational but real jealousy of others who didn't have to deal with the various stresses of caring for someone with mental illness. Most of it was unfairly directed at Adam. With a large, loving family, including two siblings who also excelled in school, his situation appeared flawless to me. Like most boys, he also had some athletic ability, enjoyed sports, and had often told me about his family's sailboat that he loved to take out on the lake.

By comparison, I felt like I had been denied everything a normal child should have. Though I was fully aware that I was still better off than most of the children on the planet, Simon was still the living embodiment of a nightmare, leaving my family with only rare moments of peace. Yet when Adam was out on the lake with his brothers, he didn't even have asthma to worry about. Who gave a damn if his boat tipped over? Everyone would still be able to breathe. Everyone else thought it was enormous fun to get wet; I had flashbacks to the lake at Ramah. Why couldn't I enjoy what everyone else did? Was it really necessary for me to be doubly cursed? What had I, or my mother, or my father, or Simon, ever done to deserve such hell?

Whenever I tried to explain things from my perspective (though in less stark terms), Adam's blank response was never enough for me. It didn't matter that for a thirteen-year-old he was unusually empathetic, trying to understand my fears as best as anyone possibly could. I dismissed words of sympathy from him and others, assuming that people simply expected me to fix my family and stop complaining, after which I'd retreat back into my thoughts, more bitter still. As far as Simon was concerned, I knew words would change nothing.

My father, still standing nearby, snapped me out of my trance as I re-hashed the problems with the Quadra in my head. "Why can't Mr. Hendricks take care of his own computers? Or Mr. Kocian?"

"Yeah, right! As if Mr. Kocian knows what he's doing. The committee won't even think about looking at Gateways. They won't look at Dell. All they want are these cheap pieces of crap from Performance PC. My Pentium 100 from two years ago goes faster than their Pentium 133 from two weeks ago."

My mother looked up. She didn't understand much about computers, but she understood that.

"It's my money that's paying for these things!" she said. "What do you mean your computer goes faster? Does Mark Freeman know about this?" she asked, referring to the superintendent.

On top of her regular clashes with the administration building on Simon's behalf, my mother had another reason to be angry with Shaker. Whenever she tried to sell promotional products to the District, they required her to endure a competitive bidding process, even for the tiniest of orders.

"This is ridiculous. Why aren't the computers being bid out?" my father asked. I gave a blank stare.

"This is bullshit! I'm sure Gateway or Dell make a much better computer than whatever this junk is that they're getting," my mother said.

My father, as usual, was skeptical at first. "They're not looking at anything else at all?"

"No," I said between bites. "Just Performance PC." I kept chewing. "They keep giving me all these reasons, too, about why they can't look at anything else."

Now I had managed to enrage both of my parents, but I figured that if they were going to be angry, it would be better to have them angry at the District than at me.

"This is *my money* they're spending?" my father said loudly. "How much is this supposed to cost?"

"One point five million," I said, still eating. He nearly hit the roof.

"You know what, I am *sick* of them bullying you around!" he said. "Do you want me to go?"

At the next meeting of the Shaker Heights Technology Committee, there was a new participant: a concerned parent and an associate professor at Case Western Reserve University, Dr. Neil S. Greenspan.

•

ACE Software had nothing to do with the orthographically-challenged spaceship web site, Dr. Paces reported. It all came down to a hyphen in the web address.

Still unsure about the results of my benchmark test, I e-mailed the company at its Performance PC e-mail address asking about a plausible explanation.

I have a Gateway 2000 100MHz Pentium System that is two years old at home right now, and I'm interested in your product. At the Shaker Heights Middle School, I am involved with purchasing decisions, and noticed that according to benchmark testing, my computer is around 15% faster than your 133MHz Pentium systems. Currently, my computer has 16MB of RAM, and yours has 32MB. Your master hard drive is also 200MB larger, and reasonably faster. Please let me know why your system doesn't appear to be up to par. Thanks!

Despite the company's close proximity to Shaker Heights and its awareness of the District's interest in its machines, I still had to wait a couple of days before I received a response. Michael Uhrin, the President of ACE Software himself, wrote back.

I will only respond to such questions as proposed by the District Computer Coordinator, Treasurer, or Asst. Supt. as discussed with the Administration at my last meeting with these 3 people. My understanding is that you are a student and are not involved with any final decisions and this is a school administration matter.

Anyone can rig benchmark testing with any computer. If I bring my Senior Technician to benchmark he can make the Gateway look sick, but I will not spend the money for a student request, when I deal with the Administration.

"Who the hell does this guy think he is?" my father exploded.

"'Make the Gateway look sick!'" my mother mimicked, but my father was still carrying on.

"Aaron wasn't making his computer 'look sick!' It's a piece of junk!"

"I ran the same program on both machines," I thought aloud. "There isn't a whole lot you can change..." Yet even if there was, I didn't know how, let alone care to waste my time fudging benchmark results.

My mother sprung into action. She called Jerry Polster, a local advocate for taxpayers who was often seen as a thorn in the side of public school boards. He frequently questioned less-than-transparent spending decisions via his non-profit organization. Sure enough, Jerry Polster was present at the next Technology Committee meeting.

Dr. Paces looked somehow less thrilled than usual to see me when I approached him with the e-mail.

"I'll look into it," he promised once again.

Despite my skepticism that Dr. Paces was really just an expert actor, he did look into it. Within days I received a most apologetic letter on paper from a very different-sounding Michael Uhrin. There were all sorts of promotional materials about his company enclosed, but they looked very unprofessional, so I quickly threw them aside. According to Uhrin's letter, I was even invited on a tour of the company's factory in Columbus.

"*Yeah, I'll just ask Mom and Dad if I can go pay Mike Uhrin a visit. They'll be thrilled to drive me the two hours to Columbus,*" I laughed to myself. "*The committee has got to see this.*"

I had to tell all of the members what was going on, all at once. I had to make a presentation.

I had once watched my father give an immunology lecture at Case Western when I was in second grade. I thought it was hilarious that the medical students actually paid attention to him, as I could barely stand listening to my parents for ten minutes. I amused myself by coloring in the slide projection booth, talking to the student who was being paid to operate the projector, and who was also trying to take notes on the lecture.

Now, I needed slides of my own. Since the school already had more than enough overhead projectors, I designed my slides in Microsoft PowerPoint, and then printed them on my color printer. I would just need some more color transparencies. Fortunately, over the years, my mother had transported a sizable portion of the nearest Sam's Club to our basement via her inconspicuous Volvo station wagon.

In the next Technology Committee meeting on January 22, 1997, I spent less time observing and more time questioning. My father, as promised, had left work early to come along.

"I think we should look at name-brand computers, like Gateway 2000, or Dell, or Micron," I said at the meeting. "They have really good service, and if something goes wrong, you can just call a toll-free number."

The Committee wasn't impressed, but I wouldn't give up. Homework was as depressing as ever. I was thrilled to have yet another excuse to call Gateway 2000 and Dell, and ask their "major accounts" sales representatives for more quotations on computers. I amassed pages and pages of faxes, web site printouts, and direct promotional mailings.

Trying to find other sources of support, I went to Dr. Neil T. Glazer's office, hoping that my principal's inner nerd would comprehend the importance of the cause I was fighting for.

"Well, you can use the copy machine for your presentation," he offered, clearly missing the main thrust of my argument in favor of name brands. Still, it was something; students weren't normally allowed to use the copy machine.

"*God forbid we might...make copies,*" I thought as I thanked him.

The only other administrator I could think of appealing to was the superintendent, Dr. Mark Freeman. Not knowing precisely how to reach him, I left it to my mother to get in touch with him.

Their conversation was not productive. When pressed about the state law requiring large contracts to be bid out in writing, Dr. Freeman responded, "When the District wants to buy Post-It notes, does it send out a request for bids for Post-It notes? Of course not! Why would we bid these out?" He was under the impression that the law only required bidding out contracts under $1,000.

"Are you sure he doesn't have it backwards?" I asked.

Over President's Day weekend, I called Gateway 2000, Dell, and Micron with quote requests more urgent than ever. Then, I drew a chart with a column for each PC vendor, and rows for several relevant features of their computers, making a point-by-point comparison of each. I included a column for Performance PC at the end, as well, basing my data on invoices Jerry Polster had obtained from the administration. At the bottom of each column was the price, and the service contract that each vendor had promised.

I had papers spread out all over the floor of my room. I stood back for a second to survey the mess.

"These people are idiots," I thought aloud, reminding myself that not a single adult had bothered questioning anything the Committee was doing. So it was back to work, using my own trusty Gateway to make what I hoped was going to be a first-class presentation. I designed slides explicitly outlining the problems with Mr. Kocian's test systems. I photocopied the invoices labeled "ACE Software," pointing out that it was odd to buy hardware from a software company. Then, I designed a cover page with Think's logo on it, if only to give enhanced credibility to the whole project, as well as to Think.

When February 26th rolled around and the Committee gathered once more at the Middle School, Dr. Paces already knew that I had something to say. My slides were already photocopied and sitting on the table for each committee member. My personal copies, carefully printed on transparencies, were set. I knew my material, but I had never been so nervous.

"Just how dumb are you?" I thought to myself, the effects of Miss Eppich's Positive Mental Attitude program having worn off completely. *"These people aren't about to listen to a thirteen-year-old!"*

It was too late to turn back, though. With the lights in the room dim, I stumbled through the explanation of what was wrong with Performance PC as a company. I knew that I was doing a bad job presenting. I heard myself interspersing "um" between every other word, and there was a stutter to my voice that wasn't usually there. Everything seemed to go worse and worse in a feedback loop of self-consciousness.

I fumbled with my papers until I found the chart comparing all of the features, which should have been easy, because I had already arranged everything in order. I was certain that everyone listening looked bored.

Still, there was one issue that I was pretty sure would get everyone's attention. As I was speaking about the attributes of Creative Labs sound cards, I hadn't made up my mind as to whether I should say anything.

A few weeks earlier, Jerry Polster had made a key connection between Shaker Heights and ACE Software that I hadn't known about. When my mother passed the information along to me, I had been fairly surprised, but it made everything suddenly very clear: why Dr. Paces had always been all smiles, accommodating my every request with a sparkly grin; why Mr. Kocian's two new machines were a manufactured by a random off-brand, rather than Apple or Dell; why the Treasurer of the District had been so irritated by my letter; why Michael Uhrin was having such a bad day when I happened to e-mail him; why no one was talking about computers on the committee, except for me. It was all sickeningly clear, and I didn't want to believe that I had landed in the middle of it, but I knew it had to be true.

I had run back to my bed, where my papers were all spread out in piles to make the relationships between the data visible. There it was, in plain sight, right at the top of one of the badly-designed marketing materials that I had strewn aside from ACE Software. Michael Uhrin had unintentionally mailed me the final piece to the puzzle when he had sent his apology letter, and it fit perfectly.

I had to say something. After reviewing the last of the technical specifications, I took a deep breath.

"And Daniel Wilson, who's the treasurer of the District is an investor in ACE Software and the CEO of ACE Software is an ex-Shaker data-processing employee!" I spurted. It came out way too fast, but they had heard every word I said. The entire room froze. It was still dim, but I could see one thing very clearly. Dr. James Paces had turned bright red.

"Now Aaron! We don't want to jump to any conclusions!" he said quickly, and louder than usual. The chipper smile had been completely wiped from his face.

And then it was my turn to freeze. Two things had just become crystal clear.

The first was that Mrs. Derrick had been no aberration. Teachers lied, even when they told students not to.

The second was that I was in trouble—and this time there wasn't a fax in the world that could save me.

●

There was a delayed reaction.

I learned from Mr. Kocian that I would be going on a trip to the High School to evaluate new test computers from different vendors, including two of the three companies that I had championed, Gateway 2000 and Dell. The school wouldn't consider Micron. I had never been to the High School before, but based on my experience transitioning to Woodbury and the Middle School, I knew what to expect: a larger building, students taller than me, and my own sense of apprehensiveness.

"I don't know what I'll do when I leave the Middle School," I told Mr. Kocian. "I'm not looking forward to it."

"Oh, don't worry about it. You'll be fine," Mr. Kocian said. "It's not such a big deal."

As Mr. Kocian drove his tiny, blue Honda Civic into the High School parking lot, I took in my first impression. Hordes of students were all around, jumping on cars and screaming loudly, eyeing us as we pulled in. No one seemed to be in class. The scene was absolute mayhem. Teachers weren't even trying to stop the students who were running out of the building.

That afternoon, the school newspaper, *The Shakerite*, had just released its monthly issue. The lead article seemed to lend credence to the stereotype that African-American students performed less well on standardized tests than White students. Black students were outraged, and the school administration quickly lost control. Shaker's diverse student body was indeed in action, bordering on civil war.

Glad, for the only time in my life, to be seen walking next to the imposing figure of Joseph V. Kocian, I simply went into the building pretending that nothing abnormal was going on. Once we were inside, we were perfectly safe, for the hallways were empty. We found our way to the computer lab on the side of the building furthest from the commotion, and I immediately saw what we had come for.

Contrasting with the pure white of the Macintoshes dotting the lab's periphery, the giant beige Performance PC with its ugly multimedia monitor in the middle of the room was hard to miss. Next to it sat a more svelte-looking Gateway 2000 Pentium-class system, along with a system from Compaq. I didn't see the Dell that I had been expecting anywhere. There was, however, another generic brand that I hadn't heard of before: MTI.

After using each system for a few minutes, I decided that I liked MTI no better than Performance PC. It was essentially the same computer, with a marginally more attractive, but still generic, case. It seemed to me that I could build a better computer myself if I were given the money to buy the components. Gateway 2000 was still my pick.

Mr. Boswell's scratchy voice caught my attention. I marveled at the comb-over that actually was his real hair, and thanked him against my better judgment for the spreadsheet that he was handing out. It looked like my chart from the presentation, comparing the technical specifications of the different machines, and at the bottom of each column, it listed the respective company's prices.

I almost jumped. According to Mr. Boswell's spreadsheet, the price of the Gateway 2000 system, which I had quoted out again and again by fax and on the company's web site, had actually gone up in only a few days.

In fact, the spreadsheet very convincingly made the case for the district to choose either MTI or Performance PC. I felt a sinking feeling inside. I wasn't sure where the information was coming from, but I did begin to realize that I was the only one who really cared what kind of computers the district bought. The administration had better things to do than worry about computers. My friends certainly weren't interested. After fiddling around with the Compaq, which I decided was a certifiable piece of junk, I found my way out of the High School, depressed once more.

"They're really going to buy $1.5 million worth of crap. Unbelievable," I thought, kicking the ground. It wasn't the Committee members who would suffer; it was me. Students were going to have to use those computers. When they didn't work, I was going to have to fix them, whether I wanted to or not, because Mr. Boswell certainly wasn't going to be there to help. His previous title, I had discovered from

Mrs. Strickler, had been "Auditorium Manager." I wondered how long it would take before people would notice that nothing worked.

While I was walking through the hallway in the Middle School a few days later, I sensed Dr. Paces walking toward me. He stopped to exchange pleasantries, so that we met in the hall just outside Mr. Kocian's doorway.

"That was quite a job you did getting all that information," Dr. Paces said, referring to my outburst at the meeting. "But tell me, Aaron, why is it that you don't trust Mr. Forquer and Mr. Decatur with their suggestions? They don't seem to have a problem with Performance PC."

"I don't think they really deal with computers so much," I said, hands on my backpack straps to signal that I wanted to keep moving. I was trying to suppress my unease with the direction the conversation seemed to be headed. "They're networking people."

"Oh, really." Dr. Paces did not seem impressed. His voice started to rise, and I noticed that he had left his smile behind. "They seem to know what they're talking about to me."

"I'm just trying to make sure we get the best computers we can afford, and it seems like Gateway or Dell would be better," I tried to explain. Dr. Paces was tired of my insolence.

"You know, Aaron, what you're doing is a destructive force to the process!" he yelled.

Stunned, I froze yet again. He continued.

"What is it, do you think you know *more* than they do? They're parents, adults, working hard to donate their time to help this school system. Do you want to take their place? Do you want to be the one running this committee?" His shouting reverberated through the hallway. Detecting movement, I stole a glance at Mr. Kocian's doorway. Mrs. Strickler, at her desk in Mr. Kocian's room, had heard the commotion.

"Dr. Paces, I'm not sure I believe what I'm hearing," she said, stepping out into the hall. "Are you really standing out here in the hallway, yelling at a student—for doing more than anyone else around here to see that things work the way they should?"

She turned to me. "Aaron, you can go."

I took a few steps back, and then turned and walked as fast as I could, to the only telephone that I knew I could use without permission: the band's. Luckily, though the office looked deserted, it was open so that music teachers could get the keys out of the director's desk, in order to offer private lessons in the practice rooms. I picked up the phone and dialed my father at work.

"Is everything okay?" he asked. He was surprised to hear from me, since I never called him at work during the day. I described how Dr. Paces had accosted me in the hallway. Not surprisingly, my father was again furious.

"I'm going to call his office right now," he told me.

Somehow, Dr. Paces had already managed to return to his office on Parkland Drive, just in time to deny the whole thing.

●

I was crushed. It wasn't just anger; it was betrayal. The corruption that had been behind the Technology's Committee's every meeting became an obsession. It was all I could talk about with my friends, who just gave me weird looks. They didn't care how much money was being spent. Why did I?

Explaining that we were all being exploited by our teachers didn't seem to phase them. Yet that was exactly what was happening: the District was taking advantage of taxpayer money to line the Treasurer's pockets. The adults who my parents had entrusted with my care, and my education, were using me.

"Paces wanted me to be the poster boy. 'Look at us, we include our students so that they can support our decisions!'" Whenever I thought about it, I felt sick.

Now that I knew how things worked, I didn't care about advanced algebra, I didn't care about advanced English, and I wanted Spanish to go to hell and stay there. My thoughts ran in circles. I liked computers, I was good at computers, and we were guaranteed to have the worst computers manufactured in the great State of Ohio, or maybe the country for all I knew. We certainly wouldn't be getting any new cow-spotted boxes from South Dakota anytime in the near future. What a waste those quotes were, of paper, of time... What good did it do to learn about logical systems if nothing depended on logic, only personal connections?

No one seemed to get it. I kept explaining it to my friends: the conflict of interest, the sheer volume of money involved, the fact that it wasn't just anyone, but *our teachers and administrators* complicit in the plot. At the end of the day no one cared.

"What's the big deal?" one student me. "It's not your money. It's your parents'."

"It's your money, too!" I shot back. "Doesn't that matter to you?" It was no use. I couldn't convince anyone to care. We were all spoiled, but at least I knew it.

I stewed in my pool of anger alone. Dr. Paces had been in on the deal. Mr. Boswell knew, too. They were all slime. Disgusting, filthy, repulsive, slime. Worst of all, they weren't going anywhere; I would have to continue to see them around school, probably for years. My parents worked hard to make money to pay our taxes—just so they could be wasted on useless machines that didn't work; so that Daniel Wilson could make a few extra bucks.

My assessment of Jerry Kaplan's book, I decided, had been too conservative, if anything. It wasn't just venture capitalists who couldn't be trusted. It was everyone.

The phone was ringing. It was a Sunday, which meant it was probably family calling. I held my breath.

"Hello?" I picked up the phone in my room. My father picked up a moment later downstairs, staying on the line simply to see who it was.

"Hi, this is Jeff Sikorovsky from the *Sun Press* calling. I was wondering if I could speak with Aaron Greenspan?"

"That's me," I said, confused. We didn't need another subscription—we were already subscribers. Every Sunday another *Sun Press* made its way to our doorstep, and I could usually thumb through it in two minutes to confirm that there really wasn't any news. Apparently, people did read it, though, because they kept printing it.

"Hi, Aaron, I was wondering if you would be willing to be interviewed about the technology issues at Shaker. I heard you made a splash this past week," the reporter said.

I managed an "uhh" before my father chimed in. "This is Neil Greenspan, Aaron's father," he said, taking the pressure off of me temporarily. "What exactly would your interview consist of?" He spoke with an academic precision that I wasn't sure the reporter was accustomed to.

"I'd just like to ask him a few questions," he responded, not telling either of us anything we didn't already know.

"Well, if it's okay with Aaron, that's fine, I suppose," my father said.

"It's fine," I replied. The interview began.

"So, tell me about your involvement with the Technology Committee," the reporter queried, and for about five minutes, I tried to explain the situation as best I could, detailing the role of the administration, my research, my computer consulting company, and the presentation that I had given.

"Mmhmm," was all I got back. "And I hear that some administrators went to Perry, Ohio recently to see how they operate there, were you involved in that?"

"No, not really," I said. Mr. Kocian had mentioned something about going to Perry, where the revenue from the city's nuclear power plant was being funneled into technology for the schools. In Perry, students were apparently allowed to build their own computers. I wished I lived there, instead—except for the nuclear power plant. We had just watched a National Geographic video about Chernobyl in Mr. Alt's science class.

For the rest of the school year, I didn't visit Mr. Kocian's room anymore. I instead migrated to the band office after school, relentlessly trying to fix Mr. Pattie's Macintosh, which never seemed to work with the printer. I established a good relationship with Mr. Bohnert, as well, who led the band program for the entire district from his office at the High School. He stopped by the Middle School from time to time to see how things were going. Most of the other students didn't like him because he was severely overweight, and acted a little bit strange on occasion, but I didn't mind him. He was the best conductor I had ever seen.

Out of a sense of duty to all of Shaker's students, I continued to attend the Technology Committee meetings until May, at which point I grew so tired of them that I couldn't bear to sit through another minute. School was almost over, besides. I was already counting the days until that day in June, 2001, when I'd finally be done with it all.

The *Sun Press* article that ran on March 6, 1997 was a smorgasbord of factual error and misquotation. I had apparently traveled with the Shaker delegation to Perry, Ohio, to spend the $5 million dollars that the District had lying around. By the article's account, I also had a bad habit of speaking in short, ungrammatical snippets that were completely unrelated to each other. I couldn't believe that the press was actually allowed to publish articles without proofreading them first.

For about a day I was a small celebrity at the Middle School, with my friends coming up to me in the hallway with clippings from the *Sun Press* and huge grins on their faces. When I expressed my displeasure at the content of the article and the article itself, they were dismissive.

"No, it's great," Adam said, eliciting my shock, followed by considerable relief at his positive reaction to the article.

Some months later, Shaker's central administration ultimately decided not to use Performance PC computers in its thousands of classrooms, though the other members of the Technology Committee were never consulted on the matter, so far as I could tell. Our computers would be manufactured by MTI Computer Services, Inc., whose claim to fame was that it was an authorized service provider of Toshiba laptops.

When I questioned the decision, I was told that MTI was chosen over Gateway 2000, Dell, and Micron, to "keep the business local." I believed it for about a week, until I learned that MTI was headquartered not in Shaker Heights, but in neighboring Beachwood, where the company paid its local taxes.

Most of the teachers didn't know how the decision to use MTI had been reached, but when their computers began to break, word got around that it was all the fault of one pesky student who stuck his nose into other people's business.

CHAPTER 6

The Treadmill in Motion

Even before I walked through the doors of Shaker Heights High School, there was a plan in motion. The plan was drafted by the Guidance Department, and its main objective was to get us out. The name of the game was College.

The person assigned to help me through the ordeal of applying to college—and getting though my freshman, sophomore, and junior years before that—was Jasmine Corbitt. She referred to herself only as "Miss Corbitt," in the third-person. She was the sister of my former principal at Mercer Elementary School, but few people knew. Consequently, my parents switched my guidance counselor to Eileen Blattner, who was in charge of the Guidance Department.

For me, the year actually began one week early, on one of the two football fields at the Middle School. There, band program participants were forced to endure a week of "band camp" between the hours of 9:00 A.M. and 3:00 P.M. Our director, Mr. Deep, was new, and relied heavily on his military background when instructing his group of more than three hundred students. The new director of the Woodbury bands, replacing Dr. Miller, was also there to help out. Mr. Coelho, a professional clarinetist, had come to the United States from Brazil. Mr. Deep had all of his assistant directors learn how to issue commands to the band.

"Band! About—face!" Mr. Deep shouted, and the entire band reversed direction in a precise three-step routine.

"Band! Face—about!" Mr. Coelho screamed into a bullhorn with his Brazilian Portuguese accent, and we dropped our instruments, cracking up with laughter. We loved Mr. Coelho from that moment on.

Band camp was a fairly miserable experience. Mr. Deep warned everyone not to lock their knees when they stood at attention in the blazing August sun because they might faint. Some students either didn't take him seriously or simply forgot, and within twenty minutes, the first of many that week collapsed onto the grass. I wasn't used to carrying around a bulky instrument all day, and the soft tissue opposite my gums began to bleed when my braces dug in repeatedly. Fortunately, the directors were reluctant to criticize me too harshly. Their hard drives depended on me.

Once the semester began, my courses weren't actually that much different from those at the Middle School, though the teachers were. The instructors who cared about anything at all seemed to care about one thing in particular, however, which my Middle School teachers never had: extracurricular activities.

Mr. Dennis Hogue, or "Denny," as he also often referred to himself in third-person, was nuts. He taught Honors Geometry by shocking us into learning. When he reached the end of the chalkboard with his beloved pink chalk, he just kept on going, writing directly on the wall, or the door frame—whichever got in his way first. Rumor had it that if you misbehaved, he'd hang you out his third-story window over the courtyard, just as he had done to Abby's brother Josh, who later ended up at Harvard. We had to wonder if there was a connection.

Mr. Hogue assigned detentions to students he didn't like and also to those that he did like, just so he would get to see them after school. Often, students didn't know why they had been assigned a detention, because Mr. Hogue only conveyed the initial letter of each word constituting his reason. "DDWEOTE," for example, meant that you Didn't Do Well Enough On The Exam.

Grades were a non-issue for the thirty or so people in each one of his Honors classes. Mr. Hogue's theorem was simple: join JCWA and you got an "A" in math.

"JCWA" actually did stand for something sensible. The Junior Council on World Affairs was Shaker's Model United Nations club, and it was arguably the thing Dennis Hogue devoted his life to more than anything else outside his family. The club was huge: the second-largest at the school behind the Student Group on Race Relations (SGORR), the administration's official diversity-focused initiative, which had appeared on CBS's *60 Minutes* news documentary.

I had never thought about the United Nations much before ninth grade Geometry, let alone the idea of "modeling" it. Yet, like every other freshman, I was so captivated by the magic of Mr. Hogue and the semi-institutional nature of the club that I knew I had to get involved.

At my first JCWA meeting, I was thoroughly confused, thinking throughout the entire session that the "U.N." was the same as the "U.K." I tried to wrap my head around the idea that England's system of governance had endured an unprecedented sprawl to become one of the biggest bureaucracies ever created, coordinating world events. Then it dawned on me the United Kingdom was a member of the U.N. I was glad no one had heard my internal monologue.

Fortunately, I was surrounded by more than one hundred other similarly confused freshmen. Our number remained fairly strong even after we learned that joining the club would require enough commitment to come to school on a Sunday, for a simulation of a Model U.N. conference.

Since fifth grade, I had learned to sleep through as much of each weekend as humanly possible in order to compensate for the sleep deficit I built up during the week. That Sunday, feeling incredibly foolish, I put on a dress shirt, sport coat, khaki pants, navy socks and formal shoes, and asked my mother to drive me to school on the day of the simulation. I waited around for my assigned partner for twenty minutes, and then wandered in on my own when he didn't show up.

"The students just pretend to be countries, and then argue with each other? I can do that."

The bus ride to the first conference at the University of Virginia, which was considerably nicer than the decaying auditoriums at the High School, was in a sense no different than any other event, for the cliques were clearly defined. There was a group of sophomore guys who called themselves "The Amish Ninja Klan," or TANK. There were the "cool" girls, who prided themselves on what they wore, and spared no opportunity to demean those around them. There were also a fair number of nerds, who could never tell when they were behaving in a manner outside socially acceptable bounds. As a nerd who was too self-conscious to talk to other nerds, I didn't feel like I really belonged anywhere.

I slowly figured out what was going on. Robert's Rules were the set of protocols that made up "parliamentary procedure." As Mauritania, I figured that I really shouldn't have much to say about anything if the simulation were to be accurate, but I quickly distinguished the glaring discrepancy between the real U.N. and Model U.N.: the important countries in the Model United Nations were not the same as the important countries in the real United Nations. It completely depended on the students assigned to each country.

After we emerged from committee starved and exhausted, Jed, our club's Secretary-General, encouraged us to simply leap into the middle of groups of people and start taking charge by barking orders and yelling our opinions in an authoritative tone. It sounded totally obnoxious. He even told us to direct other people on when they were and were not allowed to talk. I thought he was crazy.

My committee session was becoming exceeding boring, though, so I reluctantly decided to try Jed's way of doing things. To my amazement, it worked. As long as I was talking, everyone else seemed afraid to. I knew that it wasn't because I was an imposing force at 5'8" and 130lbs. People just acted like sheep, as long as you pretended to know what you were doing.

Soon enough, the news came out that JCWA was going to Harvard, which from the name alone sounded like it had to be the best of all the conferences. It took place each December, and despite the steep price of $375.00, I wanted to go. Luckily, there was a spot on a committee devoted entirely to science and technology, and the topic was related to computers. I wrote my position paper at once, only to find out a few days later that the conference conflicted with a band concert that I was required to play in. Disappointed, I turned the position paper over to the senior who had quickly materialized off of the waiting list. When he returned, he told me that he had won the Best Delegate award for the committee, largely because the committee chairs had been impressed with his position paper. I grumbled my congratulations.

There wasn't very much time to be angry, because my every waking moment was spent involved with one activity or another. On Tuesdays and Thursdays after school, I went to Akiva, a Hebrew school for high school students. It never felt like I was actually learning much Hebrew, given that lessons were disorganized, textbooks were horrible, and most of the other students didn't want to be there. On Saturday mornings when I would have much preferred to sleep, I went to University Circle to play in the Cleveland Youth Wind Symphony. On Friday nights and Saturday afternoons during the fall, there were football games, and even though I hated football, I was required to attend every single game as a member of the Marching Band. On Wednesdays after school, there were JCWA meetings. Occasionally our temple would call to ask if I wanted to read from the Torah. Model U.N. conferences would eat up entire weekends every month or so. I was expected to play tennis for physical education credit, even though I was so bad that the only person who would even bother to play against me was my own father.

Running on so little sleep, waking up was a growing challenge. I routinely turned off my alarm clock unconsciously, forcing my father to check that I was actually awake five minutes later. Neither of my parents even brought up the issue of doing chores around the house; I simply had no time to do them. I tried to do my part by emptying trash cans, or vacuuming the stairs if guests were coming over.

I had already lost all motivation to work by November. Simon's tantrums were still unrelenting. By December, I was depressed. I relished my winter vacation, spending most of it asleep.

When school began once more, the slew of extracurricular engagements that I had committed myself to left Sunday as essentially the only day when I had any free time. I was rarely home, though. After reading the *New York Times Magazine* over breakfast, I would leave the house once more. Everyone in Shaker Heights seemed to have computer problems, and the telephone line we had installed for Think Computer would not stop ringing. I anxiously awaited learning how to drive.

During the week, I worked on my business from the time I arrived home until dinner. My choice of priorities never ceased to irritate my mother.

"Why don't you work on your business *later*," she said, "and get your homework done *now* so you can have some *fun*?"

"Are Gateway, Dell, Worldcom and everyone else I have to call, going to be open *later*?" I retorted. Dealing with customer service representatives was the bane of my existence. I found myself correcting other people's errors on invoices, in router configuration files, and on web sites almost non-stop.

Eventually, I wanted to do work on companies' computers, but my parents were afraid of what would happen if I got sued. After all, I still didn't talk to Billy.

We checked into insurance options, but there was nothing available. The only other option—according to a family friend who was also a lawyer—was incorporation. My father and I met with him over our kitchen table, and on April 29, 1998

I received a certificate by fax from his law firm informing me that I was the owner of Think Computer Corporation, an Ohio S Corporation, owning 100.00% of its stock. My father, Neil Greenspan, was its Vice-President and Statutory Agent. I was too young to sign legally binding contracts.

●

Being a perfectionist made school difficult. I felt compelled to design a different Microsoft Word template as a letterhead for each class, each semester—a practice I had started in seventh grade, and enjoyed because it gave me the opportunity to play with different graphic design elements and fonts. When Mr. Burry, our Global Studies teacher, assigned us his "GAP Notebook" project, designed to teach us to read the newspaper, mine ended up looking more like a corporate brochure than the tattered packets that some of the other students turned in. I was embarrassed by my creation as much as I was proud of it.

Similarly, when Mr. Burry assigned us the task of coloring in a map of the world, I used the most precise colored pencils I could find. When my father saw me coloring for hours, he grew furious that my homework included such inane, pointless tasks. It took me a minute to realize that he was right. I wasn't learning anything.

Throughout the spring, I became progressively more exhausted. The homework seemed overwhelming, and yet my friends gave me the impression that it barely phased them.

"I think it's just you," Philip said. "You work too hard."

"*Maybe I'm just not as smart as you,*" I wanted to sneer, but I didn't think it would help my case at all. I knew it was the truth, but I didn't think it gave him the right to be such a jerk.

Sophomore year, I was assigned to Honors English. My teacher, Mrs. Byrdsong, was a heavy-set African-American woman with a serious attitude problem. There was no doubt about it: she hated boys.

"Girls, if you marry an old man, you have to sleep with him. It's the only way to get his money!" she told our class. On rare occasions, she even threw barbs at members of her own gender.

"Not that you're a *heavy* little person, Jessica," she chided, "but if you jump on our chairs, they're bound to break."

To make matters worse, it always seemed that in particular, she hated me, even when she smiled as she said my name. Whenever I asked a question, she'd make a sarcastic remark.

"Aaron says a lot of things that I don't—uh, hmmm..." she trailed off, looking away. Still, I didn't have it as bad as some.

"Don't worry about Chris and the homosexuality. You guys are *so* homophobic," she sighed, referring to one of the louder (and also heterosexual) students in our class.

Mrs. Byrdsong graded English projects, such as creating African masks out of papier-mâché, on artistic merit alone. Her main grading system, however, worked on the basis of participation points, which she tallied in chalk on the blackboard. Since she preferred not to call on the fifty percent of the class to which I belonged, it was always an uphill battle.

Once, after reading a short story called "Addressee Unknown" about American and German pen-pals during the late 1930s, the latter of whom steadily became attached to Nazi ideals, Mrs. Byrdsong and I began debating the sequence of events in World War II. She wouldn't hear any of my arguments.

"Share your thoughts. And then I'll tell you why I'm right!" she encouraged us. "You have to do it my way!"

We also read "Catcher in the Rye." Our final quiz on the book posed the question, "Is Holden crazy?" but I didn't feel like I could answer it without knowing her definition of the word "crazy." Holden was in many ways the most sane person in the book, surrounded by people he considered "phony"—a topic we discussed many times in class. I was amazed at how she could think that suddenly there was a clear-cut answer to an obviously complex set of issues. Forced to fit as much of my explanation as I could into the one-and-a-half lines of space we had been given, I wrote that Holden was sane.

"Is Simon 'sane?'" I thought to myself. *"He's "learning disabled," but does that make him insane? Maybe he's reacting rationally to how he sees things..."* I sighed. *"I hate this freaking class."*

When we got the quiz back, I tried to defend my answer, which had been marked incorrect, by pointing out that I had a brother who might be called "crazy" by people who didn't know any better. Mrs. Byrdsong's response seemed less than heartfelt.

"I care what you think. But, of course, you can't think anything," she once said.

I also opted to take Honors Economics instead of the more prestigious Advanced Placement (A.P.) Modern European History, which most of my friends decided to take. My father was somewhat skeptical of my decision, but he knew why I did it. I already had a ton of work, and the class was known to be a killer.

"I don't know...European history is a good thing to know," he said. "A lot of our world today was influenced by it."

"I'll learn it later," I responded indifferently. I was too tired to care if I didn't know how to recite a list of the kings and queens of England. My father had always said how much he despised royalty, anyway.

I did start to feel left out, though, when Adam, Philip, and all of their friends seemed to be talking about European history all the time. I tried to pick up what I could from them, committing phrases such as "the defenestration of Prague" and "Let them eat cake!" to memory.

I signed up to take Honors Biology during second period from the husband of Mrs. Sak, my seventh grade Spanish teacher. Mr. Sak was a rugged and somewhat amusing teacher, but best of all, our class only had eight people in it. It was my smallest class ever.

When the JCWA Harvard conference came around for the second time, I decided to go in spite of my looming coursework. Our teachers always seemed to pile it on for long weekends and vacations. They simply didn't understand the concept of giving us a break, and the constant pressure wore on my nerves. I had had enough of being ordered around by adults.

We were destined for Boston's perpetually under-construction Logan International Airport. In the security line, at the gate, on the jetway, and finally in the plane, we all had our math textbooks and homework in tow. When the safety video on our flight began, I began my own running commentary.

"We know you have a lot of choices when choosing your flight..." the tape announced.

"Yeah, so many choices. Have you people ever heard of *price*?" I muttered. A nearby flight attendant, unwilling to allow me even a few seconds of humor, walked over to my row.

"They can't hear you, smart guy!" she said with an annoying smirk, and then laughed obnoxiously at her own joke. "Did you think they could hear you? 'Cause they're recorded."

I wanted to ask her if she knew how many polarizing filters were embedded in the liquid crystal display in front of her, but I figured it wasn't worth it.

"*No one actually 'chooses' airlines*," I reassured myself.

"Thanks," I responded aloud, trying to match her tone. "I noticed."

The Harvard conference was held at the posh Park Plaza Hotel in downtown Boston, whose aged conference rooms had been filled with close to 2,000 overambitious high school students and at least a few hundred power-hungry Harvard ones. Many of our club members wore T-shirts that I had designed with the words "NO FOOD / NO SLEEP" in the center, circling the Earth.

Due to space constraints at the Park Plaza, Shaker's delegation was relegated to the nearby Radisson Inn, where our request for non-smoking rooms went completely ignored. Paranoid about my lungs due to my asthma, I approached the front desk. An attendant re-assigned us to the nineteenth floor, much to the displeasure of my suitemates, who had to move their suitcases once more.

"Just use the elevators over there," the attendant said.

Our new room looked exactly like the old one, but it thankfully lacked the stench of smoke. We all dropped off our bags for the second time, and headed for the elevator bank. All we wanted was to meet the rest of the team in the lobby and get some food. After what seemed like an unusually long wait, the sudden absence of the orange glow on the down button indicated the arrival of the elevator car. The doors swung open.

There were already a few other people on their way down, so the "L" button had already been pressed. I started to retreat into my thoughts when in a flash all of the buttons on the front panel illuminated and held steady. Two seconds later, they all went dark. I barely had time to figure out what was going on when the elevator began to fall at several times its usual rate.

"What took you so long?" the rest of our team wanted to know once we landed in the lobby.

"Among other things, the elevator free-falling," I said bitterly.

As if that omen wasn't enough, the hotel chandelier suddenly came crashing down atop the Harvard students leading our committee during an afternoon session a short time later. It was apparent that not everything connected to Harvard always went smoothly—but I was too hungry and tired to notice.

●

Morning announcements always took place during the beginning of second period, during Mr. Sak's biology class. Throughout the entire Shaker Heights City School District, only the legendary Mr. Alt, my eighth grade science teacher, was able to silence the blaring speaker so many teachers loathed. He simply designed a switch.

On March 16, 1999, long after Mr. Sak had launched into his lesson and temporarily forgotten the resentment he harbored toward the students of the P.A. Crew who stole his class time each morning, there was an additional interruption. Broadcast by an assistant principal, this announcement was different.

"May I have your attention please," he said. "I have the regrettable role of informing you that an incident took place this morning that has left one of our students in the hospital. The incident involved gunshots, and the student is listed in critical condition. May I remind everyone that the High School is to be a safe learning environment, and no firearms of any sort will be tolerated. If you see any suspicious-looking activity, please make sure to report it immediately."

The announcement was vague, and I was glad I didn't know the student who had been shot. In the back of my mind, I guessed that one of the poorer, African-American students, who I thought would be more likely to have access to a gun at home, had been shot by a friend by mistake. I saw those kinds of stories on the local news about inner-city Cleveland all the time. Whoever it was, I hoped that they would be alright.

"*They would have told us if the person had been killed,*" I thought. I didn't hang around with any of the Black kids at Shaker, so beyond that I didn't think much of it.

I was as wrong about the facts as I had been about the racial stereotype. When I arrived home that afternoon, my mother told me that a girl named Penny had been shot to death by a man who had been stalking her. The man was Caucasian, and a graduate of Shaker Heights High School.

"Did you know her?"

"What!" I exclaimed, shocked. I had seen her in the hall just a few days before, and she had said hello to me. "Not well...but yeah. I did."

So did many of the people I played French Horn with in the band program. They had lost their best friend. Penny was one of the only people I knew who shared my interest in computers. I wished that I had spent more time talking to her, and I wondered if she thought I had brushed her off when we were working together on the SMSnet One site in middle school.

That night, I went to bed thinking that the world had actually gone mad.

"*I was right after all. Holden was sane.*"

●

Over the summer, I stayed with my grandmother in Boston so that I could work as an intern for Carl Sjogreen's company in Cambridge. The company made web-based programming software that centered around a new set of languages called XML and XSLT. My job was to test the software, and help with user interface issues.

Carl's employees, who were all Harvard students, were surprisingly nice. They didn't talk down to me, and Carl took many of my suggestions. I also got to watch and see how he handled different aspects of running his company, from contracts to coding.

Just before the school year started up again, as JCWA's Undersecretary of Finance I realized that not everyone in the club had been required to pay the full fee for the Harvard conference the year before, which had been set without anyone bothering to look at the costs. Crazy as he was, Mr. Hogue had been an extremely caring man, and had seen to it that those in need of financial aid could go to whichever conferences they chose. Sometimes this meant that he paid for students out of his own pocket. Other times, it meant that no one paid at all. Consequently, the club was very quickly sinking into debt.

Freshman year, I had run for Undersecretary of Finance, but just as in the sixth grade Student Council election, I lost to a more popular student. Unfortunately for the club, his popularity had not inclined him to record any of its financial transactions. It would not have been fair or accurate to say that the books were a mess;

the books really didn't exist.

Repeated, dire warnings from our advisor regarding JCWA's financial situation during my sophomore year played a large part in swaying the students to elect someone who they thought would be "responsible." I decided to run again, and for the first time ever I won an elected position. Once I had the title, I took the 2" binder containing my predecessor's incoherent scrawls, requested copies of the club's financial statements from the administration, and set to work.

By the fall of junior year, the central administration had begun to take note of JCWA. With a deficit of $6,700, the club finally had its check-writing privileges revoked, and we had our third club advisor in as many years, Mr. Parker. With a constant stream of incoming hotel bills, the club had a problem, and no one knew what to do about it.

Slowly, I compiled a phone directory of all of the club's members from the previous four years. After spending a few weekends writing a database application in the latest version of Microsoft Access, I began calling the parents of every student on my list, begging them to open their checkbooks dating back to 1997. I wasn't calling for donations—I wanted to re-create the club's records. Much to my surprise, the parents were usually happy to comply, as long as they knew where to look. In response to my queries, I received hundreds of check numbers, dates, and amounts.

There was still the issue of Mr. Hogue's generosity: even if my database was perfectly correlated to the checkbooks of the parents who had paid for the members' conferences, there were still instances where parents *should* have paid, but never knew that they had to. I designed a series of official-looking forms, one of which asked the students which conferences they had attended over the past several years. From the binder's chicken-scratch and vendor invoices, I deduced the approximate prices of each conference (there was always at least one student who paid for each, thankfully, though sometimes different students were charged different amounts), and then applied the total against each student's balance, based on his or her parents' checkbook records. At the end of the entire process, which lasted several months, each student was handed an Account Statement. Those with positive balances were expected to pay up.

For future conferences, I demanded that my specially-designed deposit slip, complete with fields "for internal use only," accompany each and every incoming check. That way, even after the checks had gone to the administration for the next bank run, I could still enter the payments into my database, keeping everyone's account balance up-to-date.

To make the database run at school, I informed Dr. Paces that the MTI computers the Technology Committee had decided to purchase would not be sufficient. The band department had similar "special needs." Within a few weeks, there were brand new Gateway workstations sitting in both classrooms, with enough RAM, disk space, and graphics processing power to last at least five years. The band's computer even had video editing equipment, per my request.

"There's only one explanation," I realized. *"He's afraid."*

●

By the time I was halfway through my A.P. U.S. History class on the first day of my junior year, well-versed in proper planner usage thanks to Dr. Glazer's seventh-grade assemblies, I tallied thirty-five assignments. I had yet to attend my afternoon classes.

None of my teachers individually were of the mindset that children should have no time to think, let alone time to enjoy themselves. They all presumably wanted the best for us. When combined, however, they each became a key component in a machine that reduced students to zombies and built stacks of completed assignments, rather than actual knowledge.

Mrs. Pessel, our A.P. U.S. History teacher, had a sarcastic wit like none other. She managed to tackle the subject with a truly special combination of dullness, overcritical zeal, and biting satire. I couldn't help but enjoy the last bit, as she flamed everyone from Abraham Lincoln to Hillary Clinton, but otherwise I hated her and her class with every fiber of my body. She gave us homework without pause, sometimes deliberately increasing the workload over holidays to "catch up." It was never the teacher's fault for assigning so much work—always the A.P. curriculum's. Our textbook was maddeningly boring, and I absorbed nothing from it. If a student wasn't excited about memorizing names, events and dates, then it was the student's problem. The idea that Mrs. Pessel would adapt her style of teaching to individual needs was laughable.

A.P. Chemistry had its own unique traits. Mr. Rankin insisted that his class last two periods with a four-minute break in-between, not because the class merited the extra time, but because Mr. Rankin just was not a very good teacher. H. Clair, as Philip liked to call him, was a pudgy, elderly man whose mental stability was constantly in question. He commonly wore a bright red sweater beneath a black sport coat. If asked, he claimed that his red Shaker baseball cap kept his ears warm, in what we could only assume was a miracle of modern chemistry. He accented the first syllable of people's names in a high-pitched voice, and then let the rest of the word trail off. Generally, I reacted to, "GREENspan!" Anyone caught talking during Mr. Rankin's interminable class was forced to stand in the corner for the remainder of both periods, and to take notes without a desk. He treated seventeen-year-olds like kindergartners.

A.P. Calculus with Mr. Tournoux was the class I enjoyed least, though Mr.

Tournoux was arguably the most reasonable of my instructors. I was constantly flummoxed by my own lousy mathematical ability. It seemed that I could work through the problems just as well as the next student, but it always took me forever to understand how. Whenever we took a test, I had an incredibly hard time parsing directions, usually deriving some alternate interpretation that led to the wrong answer. The Robot Problem and the Listening Center before it seemed to be mere parts of much longer legacy that unfolded each time a new type of problem arose, which was often.

A.P. English was fairly enjoyable in contrast to the year before, even if the books we were forced to digest were not. Mrs. Blair was an eccentric, thin woman who was truly passionate about the subject she taught, sometimes even acting out bizarre role-playing scenes for us when we least expected it. One day, Mrs. Blair began waddling like a penguin; the year before, we'd heard, she'd exclaimed, limbs flailing, "What am I? What am I! I'm a tree, I'm a tree!"

Meanwhile, I continued to attend the Cleveland Youth Wind Symphony every weekend until I could take it no more, and quit. Among the last songs I played with the orchestra was a track from *Indiana Jones and the Temple of Doom*, "Parade of the Slave Children." I was well on my way to college admissions success.

●

Amidst my mother's usual promotional products catalogs, bills, and one-time special offers, our mailman deposited an envelope with the Junior Achievement logo in our mailbox. I'd received a contest offer from the same organization the previous year, but the award had been given to a cancer survivor. This time, Junior Achievement was sponsoring a different sort of contest along with a company called BrightLane.com: the first annual Young IT Entrepreneur of the Year Award competition.

"*This, I can do,*" I thought to myself. I wasted no time writing the essay. To fit within the relatively small word limit it had to be short, and I felt confident reading it over a few hours later. Three finalists were promised that they would hear back the results by September 9, 1999.

The deadline came and went. For a moment, I found it hard to believe that there was another teenager somewhere out there who had started a company that was that much better than my own, and who knew about the contest. Then again, we were well into the dot-com era, and there was no telling what was happening in the "New Economy." It seemed like the inventors of the most important technologies were getting younger and younger. Even Mrs. Jones, my economics teacher, seemed uncertain sometimes.

For two days, when I walked into my room after school, my AT&T answering machine's light wasn't blinking and I had no new e-mail. The small part of my mind hoping for a late notice from Junior Achievement switched off. I had lost, and it was time to get back to work. It was then, of course, that the phone rang.

"This is Fredda McDonald from Meridian Management," the woman on the other end of the line started. "I'm looking for Aaron Greenspan."

"This is Aaron," I said. My heart dropped. It wasn't Junior Achievement, and it sounded like another survey I had absolutely no desire to participate in. I couldn't figure out how so many of these companies knew my name and phone number when Think Computer Corporation wasn't even listed in the yellow pages.

"Oh, great! I'm calling on behalf of Junior Achievement to let you know that you're one of the three finalists for the IT Entrepreneur of the Year contest, and we were wondering if you could come down to Atlanta."

My eyes lit up. Though I wanted to say, "Well, you're a little late!" I resisted the temptation.

"Sure!" I said, instead. "I'll have to check with my parents, too, of course..."

"We'll pay for one of them to come with you, actually. You just have to decide which one."

That night at dinner, it didn't take long to decide that my father would be the one to go with me. My mother had to stay at home to take care of Simon and her business. I was going to Atlanta.

On September 20th, Meridian Management sent an e-mail with all of the instructions for the contest, along with a rough outline of the schedule. In addition to paying for the plane ticket, they would also pay for my father and me to stay at the Ritz Carlton Buckhead, where we would have dinner with the sponsors and breakfast with Guy Kawasaki, an entrepreneur and a member of the original team that created the Apple Macintosh in 1984. At the contest, the judges would determine from among the three finalists who would be the grand prize winner.

Since the event was scheduled during the middle of the week, I had some explaining to do when I got to school the following day.

"¿Adonde vas, Señor Greenspan?" my Spanish teacher asked, wondering about my sudden request for a leave of absence.

"Voy a Atlanta por una competición sobre las computadoras," I responded, trying not to mangle my words.

"¡Ah! ¡Excelente! ¡Necesitas decirnos el resulto final!" I promised I would tell her, and the class, the end result.

I felt odd standing in Terminal B of Cleveland Hopkins International Airport on a Wednesday afternoon. There weren't very many people around, and the plane ticket I was holding in my hand had an astronomical price printed on it. So did my father's.

"I guess businesspeople pay a lot of money to fly whenever they want," I told

him. My father, always wary of the business world, nodded his head in agreement.
On the plane, I tried for at least part of the way to squeeze my binder, textbooks,
and paper all onto the tray table in front of me. The contest, however "excelente"
it was, did not exempt me from homework.

Upon arriving in Atlanta, my father and I found our luggage at the baggage
claim, and then began our search for the Delta Business Services Desk, where Meridian Management had told us to go. There was a tiny counter with a sign above
it that said "BUSINESS SERVICES," but it didn't have the Delta logo anywhere.
When I asked the man behind the counter if it was the Delta Business Services desk,
he said "no," and walked away.

Next we visited the Delta ticket counter. I asked an agent if she knew where
the Delta Business Services desk was. She had no idea. We wandered around the
terminal some more. Finally, I realized an hour had gone by. I found a pay phone
and pulled out the crumpled itinerary from Meridian. There was a phone number
on it. I dialed.

"Oh, you're standing right next to it," Fredda MacDonald told me when she
realized where we were in the airport.

"*That's funny,*" I thought, "*you think we might have seen it if we were right next to
it...*" The Delta Business Services Desk was, in fact, the Business Services desk, in
the Delta terminal. We went back. Going around to the rear entrance revealed a
small room—in which two fathers and their sons were patiently waiting.

"Are you here for the Junior Achievement thing?" I asked plaintively.

"Yes we are!" one of the fathers said with a thick southern accent. "I'm Bill
Johnson, and this is Cameron." We all shook hands, and I was also introduced to
Jeremy McGee and his father. Jeremy was also very clearly from the South.

Our mode of transportation was slightly classier than the maroon Volvo station
wagon I was accustomed to. A sleek, black Lincoln limousine with ample room
for our luggage whisked Jeremy, Cameron and me to the highways crisscrossing
Atlanta, until we finally rode up a slight hill to arrive at the Ritz. Our fathers got
to ride in their own limo.

Entering the lobby, I became acutely aware of the fact that I was the only one
wearing blue jeans. Most of the other men were wearing suits, or at the least, sport
jackets. My father and I approached the check-in counter, and the woman behind
the desk went to work at her terminal, which I surmised was running some sort
of UNIX variant.

"Will you be charging this on your credit card, sir?" she asked. My father
responded with a shocked look.

"I thought that this was all paid for..." he began.

"It is—but we still need your credit card as collateral for any potential damage
to the room." Reluctantly, my dad forked his card over.

Our room was beautiful, with small chocolates on the pillows that bestowed official "fancy" status on the hotel, in case there was any doubt. We were told to prepare quickly for dinner with the contest sponsors.

My father and I both arrived for dinner at the designated hotel conference room wearing jackets and ties. I did my best to shake the sponsors' hands with a firm grip, smiling all along. Once everyone sat down, dinner was served, and then the BrightLane management began to ask Jeremy, Cameron and me questions.

"Where do you see computing in twenty years?"

"Where do you see yourself by then?"

"Do you have plans to go to college?"

Jeremy, though quite nice, was not very talkative, and Cameron, despite looking harmless enough, came off as someone with a lot of training in acting slick. I talked mostly about my thoughts on voice recognition and three-dimensional technology impacting the future, until the sponsors asked another question.

"What are your thoughts on technology in education?"

They had pitched me an easy one, and JCWA had taught me all I needed to swing. I went off on a diatribe about the corruption in the Shaker schools, and how I thought it would affect students. When asked, Jeremy and Cameron didn't have much to add.

Dessert was even fancier than the chocolates on the pillows. The Ritz kitchen staff brought out liquid chocolate-filled bags of dough, which looked amazing but were a puzzle to eat. As I tried not to smear chocolate all over my face, I silently hoped that we were being judged on our industry knowledge rather than our table manners.

After dinner, Jeremy, Cameron and I went up to the lounge to talk without being judged. Jeremy seemed more hands-on than Cameron, having built hundreds of computer systems on his own in his basement. Cameron had simply hired someone to write a program for him that filtered out spam e-mail.

That night, I had just enough time to do some more homework before getting a good night's rest. We had been instructed to wake up early in order to get to the Carter Center on time.

Guy Kawasaki, who we learned would also be the keynote speaker at the award ceremony, turned out be very friendly. After chewing off part of my croissant, I only had one question that I wanted to ask.

"What was it like to work at Apple?"

"Apple is 10,000 people reporting directly to Steve Jobs. The guy is amazing," Kawasaki fired back. I gradually came to learn that Kawasaki hadn't been a Macintosh hardware or software engineer at all, as I had originally believed. Rather, he had been on the Macintosh marketing team.

After breakfast, the trip to the Carter Center was uneventful until the limousine pulled into the parking lot. There, we saw Jesse Jackson surrounded by several men with earpieces, walking toward a car. Clearly, this was a place for important people.

For the next hour or so, Cameron, Jeremy and I stood by tables with various promotional materials for our respective companies on them, speaking to the function guests as they arrived. I hadn't realized that the money for the contest's prizes probably came not only from BrightLane.com and Junior Achievement, but also from the high-priced tickets that they had purchased. Finally, it was time for the awards ceremony to begin. I walked by several cameras on my way into the auditorium. The whole event was being webcast, appropriately enough, on BrightLane.com.

The speech by the representative from Junior Achievement came as a shock. The woman at the podium had never spoken with any of us before, and yet felt comfortable disclosing my company's earnings to the audience, which I had been assured would be kept confidential. She never bothered to speak to any of us after her speech, either.

The CEO of BrightLane.com was a pathetic speaker, and I was sure that the applause at the end of his convoluted outburst was a signal of relief rather than appreciation. Lastly, Guy Kawasaki made his speech, which was at least entertaining and well-delivered. My father noted that it was simultaneously a promotion for his book.

At long last, Mr. Brannon assumed the podium once more to hand out the awards. Each of us would receive a check for $2,500 made out to the names of our enterprises. The grand prize winner would receive a glass trophy in the form of a majestic-looking eagle, along with a second $2,500 check made out to the individual's company, for a total of $5,000. I hadn't been nervous before, but now, my stomach was in knots.

"Third place!" Brannon announced. "Goes to...Cameron Johnson! For My-EZmail!" I was shocked. I felt sure that Cameron would have won, since he was without a doubt the most charming of the three of us. I was at least glad that I would get second, since I now knew that Jeremy's company had made about four times as much revenue as mine.

"Second place!" Brannon continued, after shaking Cameron's hand in front of various video and still cameras. A photographer in front of the stage was jockeying for the best angle.

"Jeremy McGee, for JM Enterprises, Inc.!" I began clapping autonomously, but I was shocked. I had won the contest, not by making the most money, and not by acting, but actually on technical merit. Jeremy went up to the podium to accept his award.

"And finally, the Junior Achievement Young IT Entrepreneur of the Year for 1999 grand prize winner... Aaron Greenspan, for Think Computer Corporation!"

Unable to help myself, I put on a giant stupid grin, and walked up to the stage, where an enormous eagle and two large checks were waiting to greet me.

●

"¿Entonces, Señor Greenspan, que pasó en Atlanta?" Doctora Guice, my Spanish teacher, was grilling me on the trip in front of the entire class. I knew of no better way to make enemies than to boast publicly about having won money. I tried to keep my response as short as possible so we could move on.

"Gané," I said, indicating that I had won. Doctora Guice pretended not to hear.

"*Damn her,*" I thought. She forced me to elaborate.

"Gané. El premio primero," I repeated. That did it—her face contorted with happiness, and she repeated it even louder so that no one could miss it.

"¡Señor Greenspan ganó el premio primero en Atlanta! ¿Era cada dinero con el premio?" she persisted.

"*I might as well just nail myself in a coffin now,*" I thought. I knew she'd get it out of me eventually no matter how long I tried to hold back.

"Cinco mil dolares," I said to partially to my desk, indicating the full amount.

"¡CINCO MIL DOLARES! ¡FELICITACIONES!" For once I wished Doctora Guice would just lapse into her normal obsession, Don Quijote. None of us understood why he traipsed around on a horse talking about windmills in English, let alone Spanish.

As a reward for my accomplishment, Doctora Guice gave us all some homework that night.

CHAPTER 7

Sudden Collapse

It started off just like any other October morning. My Sony alarm clock went off at 7:00 A.M., its digits angrily glowing red. I didn't care. It was frigid outside. My bed was the best place to be.

My father, knowing my routine all too well, knocked on my bedroom door five minutes later, chastising my hypocrisy.

"You want people to think you're grown-up enough to run a company," he said, "but you can't get yourself out of bed in the morning. It's pathetic." I took the insult because he spent far more time in aggregate lambasting the school system, which we both knew was the root cause of my inertia each morning.

After taking a shower, getting dressed, and eating breakfast, I grabbed the lunch my father had prepared for me the night before and waited for Zeke's father's car to appear in the driveway. With Zeke and his twin sister Chloé both more overpro-grammed than I, they were usually late.

I walked over to the band room, put on the dying tennis shoes I drowned in mud daily during marching band practice, grabbed my mellophone (since I couldn't march with an actual French Horn), and started out to the practice football field that the band used on Wednesdays. My friend John, who had apparently grown accustomed to being seen with me in public, walked alongside. Even though he was buddies with Philip, I liked John. He was frighteningly intense, but he had a great sense of humor.

We hadn't even reached the practice field when I was positive than an object approximately the size, shape and density of an iron had slammed directly into my chest. On top of my confusion surrounding the manner in which an iron might fly horizontally, or be outdoors in the first place, I hadn't even seen anything. I grimaced as quietly as I could, trying not to call any attention to myself. I glanced down again, thinking I might find an overweight bird on the ground. There was nothing there.

"What?" John asked. If he had seen anything, he wasn't showing it, either. John didn't seem like the type to play practical jokes.

"I don't know..." I started. "It feels like my lung just collapsed or something." Mr. Deep was waiting to begin the practice, though, so we kept walking.

The assistant band directors looked about as thrilled as the students to be out in the cold in the middle of October. After playing only a few bars of scales, I realized that I was out of breath. For a few minutes, I kept my mouthpiece to my lips, but didn't put any air through the instrument, pretending to be playing. When I thought I had rested enough, I tried again for real. I felt dizzy. Finally, I put down my instrument, risking the possibility of attracting the attention of everyone around me, including the ever-scrutinizing directors.

"*Screw it*," I thought. I walked over to one of the assistant directors, now knowing for sure that I had attracted everyone's gaze.

"Uhh...I can't breathe," I said. "It's probably just asthma. Can I sit down for a while?"

"Sure, sure, go ahead. Take all the time you need."

With permission to breathe granted, I sat down cross-legged under a tree and tried to focus on getting air into my lungs. I didn't have my inhaler; I practically never used it outside of gym. I tried sitting in a different position to see if it would help. The pain shifted slightly, but there was no question that it was still there. I thought that maybe if I coughed, whatever was lodged in my lungs would go away.

My voluntary coughing soon became involuntary. Within a minute, I couldn't stop. Each time, it just hurt more, and I seemed to be getting less and less air. I wanted to lie down, but the ground was muddy. I tried to hold my breath; that didn't work, either.

"Are you OK?" the director asked at the end of the period.

"Yeah, I'm fine," I responded, confident that I was despite my actual bewilderment. Practice finally ended, and I walked down the path back to the building, where I put my things away and went off to my second-period class. At least I wouldn't need to march around in the cold in Biology.

I coughed through U.S. History, where I took a Document-Based Question exam, I coughed through lunch, and I coughed through ninth-period Math until I began to wonder if something was wrong. At that point, the day was practically over. An hour later, I coerced my mother into picking me up and told her about the incident during band practice. When I got home, all I could do was lie down on my bed. Even in the comfort of my warm room, my chest still hurt. I called my father at work.

"Do you want to go to the E.R.?" my father asked over the phone.

"Not really," I said. I imagined that I'd need to be at least half-covered in blood to merit going there. "But it still hurts."

"I think I should take you, then," he said, sighing. He would have to drive home from work, and then drive right back to where he had been—a total waste of forty minutes. Meanwhile, I gathered all of my books into my backpack in preparation.

I spent the car ride to University Hospitals describing the exact sort of pain I felt to my father, but I knew that once I was there, it would be time to study. Even though we'd spent the entire period of U.S. History on the quiz without Mrs. Pessel saying a word, she had somehow still managed to assign us homework via the chalkboard.

Unfortunately for me, the E.R. nurses had a number of patients with more life-threatening cases to worry about. We arrived around 4:30 P.M. and quickly blended in with the muted chatter and a loud television that nobody watched. I tried to study: the exceedingly dry and boring chapter in my U.S. History textbook, a Chemistry assignment, chapters from Spanish that I didn't understand, and then some more U.S. History. All the while my hatred for my teachers grew. I was sitting in an emergency room, studying, not for me, but for them.

After about an hour, a triage nurse called my name.

"Green-span?"

Blood pressure, pulse, medical history...nothing seemed too outrageous. I mentioned my asthma. My father didn't say anything.

Seven hours later, there was finally a doctor who could see me. My watch read 12:30 A.M.

I described the symptoms as best I could all over again, though the most obvious problem by this point was hunger. The doctor listened to my chest with his stethoscope and immediately sent me off to have a chest X-ray. When I came back, I waited for another hour with my father until we had the final verdict. They were saying something that made it sound like I couldn't leave. My initial diagnosis the previous morning had been right on target: my right lung had actually collapsed.

At 2:00 A.M., lying in a hospital bed, I was vaguely aware of my father signing reams of legalese on a white, plastic clipboard. A nurse came by my room with a shrink-wrapped turkey sandwich.

"Spontaneous pneumothorax," they said, and not much more, except that each time I had coughed, I had made the pneumothorax worse. No one knew why it happened, except that it did happen to "tall thin males."

"Half the people in my school are 'tall thin males,' yet I don't see any of them here," I thought.

I was told that had the pneumothorax been any worse, around 50% or more, I would probably have required surgery to reinflate my lung. Instead, the nurses tied me to a gas tank and had me breathe pure oxygen for a few days. It had a distinctive smell that was slightly odd. Another doctor came by and explained something about O_2 displacing N_2, which was trapped in my chest.

"How does that work exactly?" I asked.

"No one really knows," he said.

"Oh, that's great," I thought, even more annoyed.

Hordes of medical students stopped by to watch me like an animal at the zoo: I was the "tall, thin male" exhibit. Everyone scribbled on their clipboards.

I turned on the television in my room at a most inopportune time: of all things,

NBC was showing a re-run of *E.R.* where a sixteen-year-old male was being wheeled into Cook County Hospital with a pneumothorax induced from a car accident. I flipped to CNN, where Congress was busy being stupid by failing to pass the Nuclear Test Ban Treaty.

"That's exactly what we need right now! More nuclear tests..." I said, before falling asleep, the mask covering my face.

When I awoke, I realized that for the first time in months, I had time to myself to sleep, think, and relax. I wondered if anyone at school would notice my absence.

Eventually, someone did. Three days after I was admitted, Adam called to find out where I was. It wasn't unusual for students to miss a day or two due to illness since everyone lacked sleep, but people rarely missed three days in a row.

When I got out of the hospital, there was more work to be done than ever before. On top of the usual mountain of assignments, I had to catch up with everything I had missed, but I entered the building with strings attached. My numerous doctors agreed that under no circumstances was I to carry around my forty-pound backpack. In addition, I could not play the French Horn. Not particularly saddened by either restriction, I offered my teachers the chance to negotiate the changes to my daily routine. Some acted as if leaving my textbooks in their respective classrooms somehow amounted to treason.

"*God forbid that I should negatively impact the 'learning environment,'*" I thought, realizing how much my teachers made me sick.

My clients weren't much better. One of them demanded to know why I hadn't been returning his calls, so I told him. He left me alone.

Over the next several months, I suffered from constant chest pain. Sometimes, it was dull and omnipresent. Other times, it hit like a lightning bolt out of the blue, such as one day during chemistry, when it was so severe that I again couldn't breathe. It gradually dawned on me that the severity was directly correlated to stress, which was particularly inconvenient, for I had five A.P. courses on my schedule until June, and several more planned for senior year.

Instead of playing my instrument during marching band, I stayed inside. I updated the band web site that I had created (boosting its ranking to #2 nationwide, only behind the site that produced the rankings, which called itself #1), finished homework that I hadn't had time to finish the night before, or talked to Mr. Bohnert, who would often churn through paperwork as the music department head, while an assistant conductor led his ensemble. He was very good about letting the student conductors have a chance to work, and everyone knew that it wasn't because he was trying to slack off. Despite the fact that he could be annoying in how he delegated tasks to students, picking on the same ones repeatedly, everyone knew that when Mr. Bohnert stood in front of an ensemble with a baton, he had nothing to prove.

Indeed, my condition had lifted a large weight from my shoulders. I at last had some of the extra time I had been wishing for—and all it had taken was a trip to University Hospitals of Cleveland.

●

National History Day was coming. With a choice between writing a paper and making a documentary film, having had my fill of papers, I opted for the latter.

I tried to use the band department's computer to produce our documentary, but its video editing system turned out to be more limited than I thought. Next, I tried using my father's new laptop, which was supposed to have video capabilities. Though this made him none too pleased, I finally gave up after discovering that the image quality was about as good as watching a television through a dirty fish tank.

The MTI systems in each classroom, which had video cards so bad, each and every icon displayed as a large black square, were out of the question. I decided to tap an old resource: Dr. Paces. I wanted another computer for Mrs. Pessel's room, specifically for high-end video production. Within weeks, a Dell workstation appeared, far more powerful than the Dimension line of desktops that Dell advertised in magazines and on TV. It ran on Windows NT and sported a full-length video capture card by Pinnacle Systems. Nevertheless, the school's high-speed internet connection was so unreliable, I had to download updates for the hardware at home. Bit by bit, my prophecies from the Technology Committee were coming true.

In November, I received an e-mail from a man named Akio Fujii, who said he was the Chief U.S. Correspondent for the *Nihon Keizai Shimbun*—otherwise known as the *Nikkei*, the largest newspaper in Japan. We set up an interview for the second week in December, when I would be on break. I had done plenty of interviews before about my company, but never with a reporter from another country.

He flew from Washington, D.C. to Cleveland to conduct the interview face-to-face in my bedroom "office," and was scheduled to arrive at 3:00 P.M. At 2:57, a red car appeared in my driveway which belonged neither to my father or my mother, but no one got out. For a moment I thought it was using our driveway to turn around, but it simply sat there, with the engine turned off. Then, I remembered what Mrs. Jones had taught us about Japanese business culture in our Economics class: in Japan, it was rude to be early, and it was rude to be late. One was only polite if one arrived precisely on-time.

Exactly three minutes later, the driver-side car door opened, and out stepped an impeccably dressed Japanese reporter carrying a briefcase. He walked up to our door and rang the doorbell, and I started to greet him when I realized that I had no idea what to say. Mrs. Jones had also told us that in Japan, people's names were inverted, so that the last name came first. I didn't know if I was talking to Mr. Akio, or Mr. Fujii. If I chose the wrong name, it was a grave insult, as it would imply that he was a personal friend.

"Hi!" I said. "Should I call you Mr. Fujii, or Mr. Akio?" The reporter looked confused.

"I'm sorry, our teacher at school taught us about business in Japan, and she said that the people's names are inverted relative to here—so I wasn't sure if you'd already inverted it for the U.S. or not..."

"Oh, it's alright," he said. "You can call me Mr. Fujii. Akio is my first name, Fujii is my last name." His distinct accent revealed that he was a Japanese native, but he smiled at my bumbling. The interview went pretty much like every other interview I'd ever had, until he asked a question I hadn't heard before.

"Are you working on projects now with anyone else?" he wanted to know.

I thought about it for a second and didn't see any harm in telling him about Cameron's spam-blocking service, MyEZmail, which I had just redesigned, so I mentioned the site and explained what it did.

"It's a spam filtering site. You give people your normal e-mail address, but it really forwards to a MyEZmail address, which is designed to filter out spam. I redesigned the web site after he had someone else do it initially." Mr. Fujii was intrigued.

"I see. Can you tell me the name of the person you are working with on... MyEZmail.com?" he asked, looking back to his notebook for the name.

"Cameron Johnson," I said.

"And where does...Cameron...Johnson...live?"

"Virginia, I think," I responded. I temporarily forgot that it was nearby where Mr. Fujii worked.

He snapped a few pictures with a small Nikon camera that he was carrying with him, and was gone. I was impressed that Japanese reporters took their own pictures instead of relying on professional photographers, who I had come to loathe. They had a tendency to turn my room red and purple with special lights and to make me look worse than I already thought I did.

With the interview over, it was time to get back to work, which meant History Day. Winter break, just on the horizon, would also be two weeks to prepare for History Day.

Until the judging took place in April, every day was History Day, and every day sucked.

CHAPTER 8

A New Economy

My hatred for the system—my teachers, my classes, my so-called friends, my activities—had reached new levels. Every day at lunch, I complained bitterly if there was anyone listening. Usually, I would just hear back that I was being too pessimistic, but I knew I wasn't. Things were every bit as bad as they seemed, if not worse. I knew, because I couldn't think for myself. There wasn't any time.

Think Computer Corporation was the only part of my life in which I consistently found some satisfaction. I alone determined the direction and magnitude of the company's success or failure.

"At least if I screw up, I know exactly who to blame," I told Adam. He laughed at my lame joke. Had I been smart, I would have put more stock in his reaction. Yet I remained convinced that absolute independence was the way to go, no matter the risks.

In January, just when I was forced to dive back into the swing of things, I was therefore ecstatic to receive a diversionary e-mail from Cameron Johnson, who wanted me to design a web site and a logo for a kind of prize referral network.

I had an opportunity to net my biggest contract ever, and it would be 100% profit. I wondered if everything I had read about the New Economy was actually coming true. It certainly seemed like it—Cameron had made a lot of money off of his MyEZmail system.

I quoted him $2,000 for the complete site, including graphic design services for the logo, which might have cost that much on its own from an ad agency. He signed the contract.

We went back and forth on the specifics of the site for a few days, but within a week he and his "business partner," another teenager in California named Tommy Kho who had met Cameron over the internet, had approved my proposed logo design. I started working on the graphic design for the web site. Tommy was responsible for the back-end programming using technologies called PHP and MySQL that I had never heard of.

In late January, I took a break from the site design for the University of Michigan Model U.N. conference in Ann Arbor. Our committee chair scared us all when she ran into the committee room after lunch one day, screaming and crying. We assumed the worst.

"I JUST MADE TWENTY-FIVE THOUSAND DOLLARS IN THE STOCK MARKET!" she yelled. There was a collective sigh of relief. By the end of the conference, I had earned my first mock award from the other high school students: Most Likely to go on a Third World Power Trip. I accepted it, wondering exactly what it meant.

A few weeks later, Cameron told me that Mr. Fujii had interviewed him, as well. He also sent a translated version of his article, which had already appeared in the *Nikkei*. It was about him, and him alone. My article, it seemed, had been cut.

I tried not to be jealous; there were, after all, plenty of other articles about Think, and they pretty much all had the same angle: "here's a normal teenager, but he's not normal, because he runs a business." Yet, the angle was always off. The real one was far less interesting: "here's a normal teenager, but he's not normal, because he does homework and extracurriculars non-stop. He started a business to replace his friends, who don't care. Wouldn't he look great on a college application?"

Progress on SurfingPrizes.com moved forward at a rapid pace. It was amazing to be working with other people who understood the potential of technology. I was used to customers who took forever to make decisions, but Cameron and Tommy were able to move as fast as I was—sometimes faster.

Instead of planning in advance, Cameron had a tendency to send a flurry of e-mails with curt instructions in each. Though he knew exactly what he wanted on his site no matter how trivial the detail, he was either too lazy to do it himself, or had no idea how. He delegated absolutely everything.

To handle the advertisements, Cameron contracted out to a company called L90, an on-line ad agency. It only took on high-traffic sites as clients, providing them with banner advertisements from large companies. On the SurfingPrizes.com "PrizeBox" software, which Tommy designed, Cameron eventually had ads for the Warner Brothers movie *Gladiator* and a number of other large brands.

I had never done something so cool in my life. I was helping run a *real* company, not my "company" with one employee who worked weekends. There were still problems—technical issues, e-mails bouncing, plans changing—that I had to dodge at a ferocious rate, but I was doing my part and doing it well.

Watching stocks such as Qualcomm, Inc. climb toward $600 per share, I invested the money that I made from the contract and some other consulting projects into the most promising technology and communications stocks on the market. *BusinessWeek* even included my choices in an article that it ran about teenagers who were investing for the future.

When SurfingPrizes.com launched on the evening of March 6, 2000, it was my responsibility to upload the finished files from my hard drive to the company's server. During those fleeting seconds, there were at least ten posts on internet bulletin boards from anxious people around the world.

"I see the files going on the server!"

"The upload has started! Looks like they're going live..."

There was no doubt in mind that a high proportion of our user base would be kids. The spelling on the bulletin boards was atrocious.

The next night, Cameron, Tommy and I met in an AOL Instant Messenger chat room to discuss the future of our new company. Earlier, Cameron had asked me to be President, and for at least a little while, I entertained the idea of running SurfingPrizes.com and Think Computer simultaneously.

Four days later, the NASDAQ composite index opened at 5,060.34. There was talk of Tommy and I receiving SurfingPrizes.com stock instead of a salary. Acting as the President of a such a start-up didn't seem like such a bad idea. I ran the idea past my father, explaining what Cameron had told me: we would pay people to look at ads on the desktops while they used their computers. I stressed that there were other companies in the sector, proving the validity of the business model.

"Cameron asked me to be the President of the company, but I'm not sure if it's a good idea or not..."

"Uhhh..." My dad and I had both been skeptical when Cameron's elite private school had sent its own public relations guru with him to spin his story to the press. "Yeah...well, I don't think that sounds like a very good idea. Don't you have enough on your plate?"

I took on the title of Chief Information Officer, instead. Tommy became the Chief Technology Officer. Strangely, our three-person company had a CEO, a CIO and a CTO, and all three of them still had to worry about turning in homework on time.

●

For the next several weeks, as I was trying to catch up on school, Cameron kept sending me an unending stream of minor changes that needed to be made to the site. He began posting messages on bulletin boards himself to respond to various customer inquiries and complaints. Tommy and I rarely posted anything.

Cameron had received a lot of attention from his article in Japan. A Japanese company called "FutureKids," a joint venture of Apple Japan and Microsoft Japan, invited him to be on its Board of Directors. It also invited him to go on a speaking tour. The jealousy I had tried so hard to temper flared once more, but I tried not to let it show in my conversations with him.

By late March, the number of people visiting SurfingPrizes.com on a daily basis was starting to have a crippling effect on the servers. Cameron fired off a series of furious e-mails. Our hosting company's sales representative assured Cameron that everything would be fine, but I was less enthused. I was the one who had to call every time there was a problem, and the technical support staff always referred me, for some reason, to sales.

On March 29th, Cameron forwarded a draft press release to Tommy and myself for approval. It was slated to be released over the wire on my birthday, two days later. The headline was "3 Teenagers Pact Together to Launch Internet Company." In an e-mail back to Cameron, I re-wrote much of the release for him. He was still disclosing information on the bulletin boards frequented by customers, revealing confidential data that made it harder for Tommy and me to do our jobs. People trying to earn extra money by hacking Tommy's software only had to ask the right questions in order to spur Cameron into action.

At long last, I left with my family for spring vacation in Florida. I found myself spending more time than I would have liked sitting idle in a lawn chair listening to a Dave Matthews Band CD that I wasn't quite sure if I was enjoying. At night, I worked on problems with the SurfingPrizes.com server.

I'd never seen a computer behave quite like Cameron's server was behaving: it was always out of memory from the moment it turned on. Then, I realized that it wasn't a problem with the server at all. The site was completely overwhelmed with traffic. By the time the Linux operating system had decided how to best allocate memory, another twenty page requests had piled up, waiting to be served. I tried tweaking settings, but that ended up pushing the operating system itself out of memory, freezing the server completely.

Cameron also sent me login information for the advertising revenue reporting tool, which outlined everything we needed to know about the ads running on the site. I took a quick glance out of curiosity, since the numbers Cameron were throwing around seemed exceptionally high for a company that had only been in business for two to three weeks. Surprised by what I found, I sent him a short e-mail.

> Just wondering...why, under the Finance Report for L90, does it say "$0.00" for our actual revenue for all of the advertisers? Everything seems to be "projected," and our numbers are not going up.

And then I went to sleep.

●

It was only a matter of time before the stress made me ill. It was probably just an ordinary virus that I contracted in mid-March, the kind that keeps you in bed for a couple of days. With my plethora of commitments, however, I was faced with an extraordinary workload. The virus kept coming back.

As I lay in bed, my muscles aching, body temperature miscalibrated, and energy completely sapped, I was incredibly thankful to be doing nothing. Yet I was also dreading every minute that I spent at home, missing assignments.

The pile of catch-up work started small, but then grew, and grew, and grew, until I finally felt good enough to go to school—and stayed up until 3:00 A.M. trying to cut it down to size. The following day I inevitably couldn't move again as my decimated immune system failed to do its job. This process repeated itself for three grueling weeks, as I counted the days until spring vacation, which would not really be a vacation, because we would still have homework to complete.

By the middle of the third week, I finally thought that I could make it to school for more than a day at a time, but I refused to get out of bed. My physical ailments had been replaced by a depression so deep that I saw no point in attending school any longer, ever. Beyond that, I saw no point in living. Not when learning was equivalent to forced labor, entirely detached from understanding. Not when I didn't have a single true friend in the world. Not when I couldn't even enjoy a few minutes at a restaurant with my family, without worrying that Simon's oppositional behavior might get us kicked out of the establishment. Not when every night meant hearing a screaming match. Not when I had to run Cameron's company for him. It just wasn't worth it.

That day in March was the first time that I made a serious attempt at suicide. It didn't work very well, as I discovered after repeated attempts that the brain will, in fact, make you start breathing again, even when you don't want to, and even when you obstruct your airway. The span of a few minutes after I gave up trying to kill myself felt even more hopeless than the few minutes before.

"Are you going to school today?" my mother asked, coming into my room.

"No," I said. "You can call Mrs. Blattner and tell her that I feel fine, but I don't have the energy to do a month of homework. So I'm not going to."

Much to my surprise, my mother did just that. She didn't even object to my rationale. She saw how miserable I was, and it made her sick, too. Mrs. Blattner didn't want me to be miserable, but unlike my teachers, she actually did something about it. She immediately made calls advocating on my behalf so that I could turn in my assignments whenever I felt like it. With the pressure partially relieved, I stayed home for the rest of the day. The following morning, I found myself at school, where I was sure that no one would have noticed had I never come back.

●

In April, WKYC Channel 3 News in Cleveland got wind of Think Computer Corporation and scheduled a time to interview me at my house. I had never been on television before. They gave me a lapel microphone to wear, and instructed me to act like I was working. The reporter even coaxed me into asking one of my best clients over to my house to pretend to pick me up for a consulting job.

"I can't believe how fake the news is!" I muttered under my breath, walking from my house to my client's car as the cameras were stopped.

"We heard that!" shouted the cameraman. I had forgotten—I was still wearing their microphone.

The next day during U.S. History, as Mrs. Pessel was lecturing, there was a knock on the door. A chipper Channel 3 reporter and his camera crew were waiting behind her large oak door with a horribly bright light.

"Aaron, I think there are some people here for you," Mrs. Pessel mocked. I was furious. Channel 3 had cleared the appearance at school with the principal, Mrs. Pessel, and my mother, but not with me.

"Hey, you, in front of Aaron," the reported ordered before I had time to react, pointing at my friend Josh. "Duck."

"Aaron, this is nuts! I have to duck for you!" Josh half-joked. I didn't think it was funny.

"*If they don't already, these kids are going to hate me for the rest of my life*," I thought. It wasn't the first clue I'd had. Without asking, the librarians had posted an article about me outside the library doors in the center of the school. Much to my dismay, my picture took up half the page. Fortunately, Channel 3 never aired the segment.

History Day for the Cleveland, Ohio region took place on the Case Western Reserve University campus, where the contest had originated. Hundreds of nerdy-looking kids swarmed the dilapidated campus carrying dioramas, papers, poster boards, and in our case, videotapes. Ours was the last documentary to present, so we had the chance to watch our competition's videos ahead of our own. They mostly looked like they had been put together by sixteen-year-olds. Some of them ran off of their creators' laptops.

Ours looked professional. I had no desire to see Windows NT crash in the middle of our presentation and I couldn't wheel Mrs. Pessel's workstation for miles, so I had worked for hours beforehand to write the video to a VHS tape.

The judges asked a few questions afterward, and Philip, James and I tried to split the answers evenly amongst ourselves. We passed the first round. Then, we repeated the process for the second. That was it: four months of work for ten minutes of video that we played twice.

The awards ceremony took place inside a nearby chapel at Case Western, where the judges cursed us with first place. The prize meant that we had to go to Ohio History Day in Columbus with three weeks to prepare. The only benefit was that Mrs. Pessel had to look more favorably upon our grades.

In late April, I wandered into Mrs. Blattner's office, which as usual made me feel strangely self-conscious since I was always the topic of conversation. The next two months were slated to be such nightmares, I didn't even know where to start. At random, I picked "standardized tests" as my first topic, and segued into Ohio History Day.

"Well, you can't do much about A.P. tests or the SATs, but you can talk to Mrs.

Pessel about Ohio History Day," Mrs. Blattner said objectively. I groaned, but agreed to go. "When is History Day?" she asked.

I recited the date that had been burnt into my skull. "Saturday, May 13th."

It seemed to ring a bell with Mrs. Blattner. She flipped through some pages on her desk.

"Oh, no. No, no. That won't work. The SAT is on May 13th. You have to take it then to get it to colleges in time."

"Oh, boy." I couldn't think of anything else to say. Now I *had* to talk to Mrs. Pessel.

"Where are you thinking of applying?" Mrs. Blattner went on.

"I don't know. What schools have good computer programs?" I asked. "Is Harvard any good?"

"Let's see," Mrs. Blattner responded. She re-arranged the papers on her desk until what looked like lists from my up-side down viewpoint emerged. She turned them around so I could see.

"MIT... Carnegie Mellon..." she said, scanning through the names. "Harvard doesn't look like it's on here, but that doesn't mean it's not a good school, of course. It's just more focused on liberal arts."

I assumed that the phrase "liberal arts" meant "not computers."

"I keep getting all this junk in the mail from colleges," I told her. I had been placing it all in a big stack on the floor in my room. Every college seemed to be trying to make its brochure glossier than the next. "I think I got one the other day from a place called Harvey, or Mud? What kind of name is that?"

"Harvey Mudd is actually a very good school," Mrs. Blattner responded to my jibe, setting me straight. "You should apply there." I didn't like the sound of it. By the end of our conversation, I added Stanford to my list and the University of Pennsylvania, too, for its undergraduate business program. I chose the University of Michigan as my backup. Mentally, though, my number-one choice was Harvard. I couldn't get past the name.

"*I doubt I'll get in, but why not try?*" I thought, walking through the bleak halls toward Mrs. Pessel's room for what I knew would be a lovely confrontation.

Mrs. Pessel was sitting in the small office that jutted off the corner of her room, with a picturesque view of the faculty parking lot. She was grading papers.

"Hi, Mrs. Pessel. I have a problem," I began.

"Okay..." she said, raising the pitch at the end of the word in her crackly voice, already suspicious.

"A.P. tests are coming up, and so are SATs, and History Day, and I'm way behind in my reading because I've been sick on and off for the past month. There's just no way I can finish everything, plain and simple. I have more homework for math than I know what to do with, and I've been having chest pain from my lung.

And, I just found out, Ohio History Day and the day we're all supposed to take the SAT are on the same day." Saying it out loud made it sound even worse. "So, I'm wondering what you think I should do."

"Well," she said curtly, and then hesitated. I thought she might actually be considering the idea of granting me some kind of reprieve. Then, she spoke.

"I'd panic. Yeah, I'd start panicking right now!" Her lips curled up into a smile, she let out a cackle, and then she turned back to the ungraded papers on her desk. I wanted to punch her, but instead I just stared. Then, she turned back to me—the only sign that she was human, and not actually a witch.

"I mean, I don't know what you want me to say. I can't postpone History Day, obviously. I'll have to talk to someone about the SAT date, that's definitely a problem. Aside from that, just do your best." My hatred for her increased tenfold, and yet in a way, she was right. There was nothing that could be done, except work. Lots of work.

Mrs. Blattner eventually arranged for everyone participating in Ohio History Day to take the SAT on Wednesday, May 10th, an alternate test date for Orthodox Jews who could not write on the Sabbath, when the test was normally offered. Our small group even got its own test proctor.

The state-wide Ohio History Day went much like the first event, only the quality of the work was slightly better on average, and we presented in a basement. Once again, our video came in first place. The curse continued unabated. We had to go to the National competition, which took place over the summer.

Soon after, an obituary appeared in *The Plain Dealer* that took us all by surprise. Dr. David Van Tassel, professor at Case Western Reserve University and founder of National History Day, had passed away. We had interviewed him for our documentary as a local civil war expert.

"Van Tassel founded History Day?" I asked Philip near his locker the next time I saw him in school. "Did you ever give him his copy of the interview tape, by the way?"

"I don't know. And no, I haven't had a chance yet. Why?" Philip asked.

"Because he just died."

●

At the annual JCWA dinner in May, just between the band dinner and the National Spanish Honors Society dinner that I was also expected to attend during the same week (on top of the usual piles of homework), I was expecting boos from the parents, of whom I'd demanded check after check to cover the club's past accounting errors. Instead, they applauded. I had gotten the club out of debt. In fact, we were making a profit on each conference, though I had had considerable difficulty convincing Mr. Parker that doing so was not morally destitute.

"What's the alternative?" I asked him. "We can either make a profit, break even, which is basically impossible in reality, or take a loss on each conference. I'd prefer the first one so that we have a cushion in case of an emergency."

"Well, I guess that's okay," he said. "But don't call it a 'profit,' call it a 'surplus.'" From then on, the price of each conference covered its own costs. The quality of the hotels I reserved increased, as well.

My relative success as a bookkeeper didn't do much for my social life unless I was away from school at a conference with other JCWA members. Adam, whose shyness had slowly given way to a personable and easy-going demeanor, had found a number of new friends whom he also wanted to spend time with. Consequently, every other day, he took the progressive step of breaking free from the lunch table we usually sat at to eat with his other friends, who I considered to be in the "cool" clique of smart kids.

I got used to eating by myself every other day, though once in a while I would have company from others. I tried to think about what was going on in the computer industry to keep my mind occupied, or I'd try to get caught up on homework, but usually the single thought that filled my brain like an echo chamber was that I had no real friends. I entertained the idea of going over and sitting with the cool kids, too, but even though some acted alright, there were one or two whom I absolutely couldn't stand. Besides which, when Adam was there, there wasn't any more room at their table.

To make matters even worse, I grew dependent on Adam to get home from school each day and felt awful about it. Even though I was in a carpool to get to the High School, my options for getting home were far less convenient. I could call my mother and ask her to pick me up, except for the fact that students were not officially allowed to use phones with outside lines. As long as the band office was open, I could always use their phone, but there was no telling when the door would be locked. In addition, picking me up required my mother to interrupt her work, which meant that she would be more inclined to ask for my help with it.

"If you want me to pick you up from school, you have to do this artwork," she would yell at me over the phone, under considerable stress from her business and my brother. In public, it never looked good to yell back, but often there was no other way to make her listen.

At first, I grudgingly agreed to help, but not for long. I soon asked to be paid at one-half of Think's hourly consulting rate, and Keene's bookkeeper in Boston agreed. Money wasn't the real issue, though; I just didn't have enough time. Day after day, my mother expected me to help her with each and every technical issue, and they were increasing in number.

Therefore, whenever I asked Adam to drive me home in his blue Chrysler minivan, it meant that he had to drive ten minutes out of his way to drop me off, but that I avoided hours of conflict at home—and so the burden of driving usually fell upon him. We usually had little to talk about aside from work, and that I constantly worried about his resenting me for asking him to go out of his way did little to help the dynamic of conversation. I did my best to thank him each time, but never felt that the words did my emotions justice.

Transportation home from school became a frequent source of conflict in our house. Keene Advertising employed two full-time artists in its Boston headquarters, but my mother didn't get along particularly well with either of them. She decided to handle all of her customers' artwork requests on her own—which meant that I had to repeatedly teach her how to use the Adobe suite of graphics software.

Weeks of serving as Keene's third artist turned into months. Dinner was a perpetually miserable experience. Simon's tantrums were escalating in magnitude and frequency, often lasting for five or six hours at a time. As he got stronger, he would throw things, not at anyone in particular, but with enough velocity that they became dangerous. I continued locking myself in my room after dinner, trying to drown out the chaos.

Sometimes, Simon would take a snow shovel and jam it into the ice on the driveway, making a horrific racket. Our neighbors eventually began calling the police, who got to know Simon well, but never well enough to react in an intelligent manner to each and every call.

When he entered my parents' bedroom, my mother and father did their best to get him to leave. It was their last refuge.

"COME WITH ME NOW!" he would shout in their doorway. It was 10:02 P.M. on a Friday night. In Simon's world, there was always someone on call waiting to help him, whether it was the doctor, or the Mayor, or the Governor, but sadly, it bore little resemblance to reality.

"Come with you now where?" my mother asked.

"COME WITH ME NOW!"

"Where? Where? Where!" my mother pleaded. The tantrum had already been going on for two hours.

"COME WITH ME NOW!"

"*Where* are you going?"

"STOPCOMEMENOOOOOW!" His words blended together into something totally unintelligible.

"Are you going to apologize to me I hope?"

"COME WITH ME NOW!"

"Are you going to apologize?"

"COME WITH ME NOW!"

The pattern was unending. "Are you going to apologize to me or I'll do nothing for you." Simon had just gone to a baseball game, thanks to my mother's resourcefulness. He clearly didn't understand the concept of reciprocity. He grabbed her arm.

"Leave me alone!" she warned.

"COME WITH ME NOW!"

"Are you going to apologize? Do you hear me?"

"COME WITH ME NOOOOOOW..." Simon wailed.

"Get out of here. Go away. Go—go away," my mother said. Simon grumbled something completely undecipherable, but very loudly.

"DONTELLMETHAT! DON'T MAKE ME MAD!"

"Don't make *me* mad? Get out of here," my mother said. "What do you want! What do you want from me, Simon?"

"I-NEED-TO-GET-OUTA-HEREEEE!" he screamed.

"Yeah, you do need to get out of here! We're sending you away!" my mother shouted. "Because you can't live here!"

"WELL IF YOU DON' CALL SOMEBODY TOMORROW, I AM GO-ING UP THERE! GOING UP THERE! I DON'T CARE GODDAMIT, I'M WALKING IN THERE TOMORROW! I'M WALKING IN THERE!"

We assumed he was talking about the doctor's office. He had little appreciation for the HMO referral process my parents had to go through each time he needed to be examined by a new physician or psychologist.

Simon had been seen by at least seven psychologists and psychiatrists, none of whom had done the least bit of good for him through their "talk therapy." He could barely express himself, let alone logically reflect on the advice he was given. The drugs he had been prescribed were useless.

In the short term, we were afraid Simon might permanently damage his vocal chords. Even if he had no voice left, it didn't stop him from trying to yell. My mother and father pleaded with him to comprehend that there weren't any doctors who could help him so late at night (every night), but he didn't understand.

I talked to Mrs. Blattner at school about the fact that I was having a hard time at home. She seemed sympathetic, but there was obviously nothing she could do. There was nothing anyone could do. Not the District, which fought my parents every step of the way, not the City, not the State, and certainly not the federal government. Simon slipped through every single crack. While everyone else progressed, including myself, it was Simon who was left behind, and what made it so bad was that he knew it.

Finally, I snapped. When I came home from school, expected to touch up a logo for a regional bank, I refused. The shouting match began, but I could not stop. I carried on, about my mother's artwork, about the fact that I thought she should be able to do her own job (even though I knew she couldn't), about the amount of homework I had to do, which was insane, about the fact that my only friend hardly ever talked to me. In tears, she called her brother Michael in Boston.

When she handed me the receiver, Michael embarrassed me enough to calm me down, but the residual effect of the episode had been set in stone. I didn't see how a mother who actually loved her son, as she claimed she loved me, could knowingly put her son in such a position.

"She damn well knows how much homework I have, and sales tax returns, and customer demands, and stress from JCWA..." I told Michael. "After all, she's the one who appears in my doorway at 1:30 A.M. to yell at me to go to sleep."

With my anger feeding off of my mother's frustration, and my father growing weary of serving as a mediator, the cycle never got the chance to enter the resolution stage. Simon went off like a time bomb, almost every day.

He had to go somewhere. He'd already been exported to the Beachwood school district after my parents insisted, correctly, that Shaker was unable to support his needs. Shaker had not given in until my parents threatened to sue.

Ohio state law apparently did not foresee the possibility that there might not be a single school in the entire state that could help a child like Simon. The nearest school able to meet his needs was in Carbondale, Illinois: the Brehm Preparatory School.

Brehm had been built specifically for children with learning disabilities. It was a two-hour drive through cornfields into the middle of nowhere from Lambert International Airport in St. Louis. Simon wasn't happy about going, but once he was out of the house, we all breathed a collective sigh of relief, and then waited to hear from Brehm.

●

SurfingPrizes.com was getting in my way. It wasn't that the office environment was unfriendly (I still worked out of my bedroom), or that the pay was too low (my position was still uncompensated). It was my boss.

Cameron refused to do anything on his own, and it was driving me insane. He kept nudging us along with quick one-liner messages such as, "This month's estimated revenue is up to $95,000." He hired a sycophantic teenager to write his newsletters for him. We had studied specialization of labor a fair amount in Mrs. Jones's economics class, but sometimes it seemed like it was possible to take it too far. When Cameron wanted to change a sentence on the site, instead of taking ten minutes to learn how to do it himself, he hounded Tommy or me for days. He seemed solely capable of issuing demands via e-mail and smiling for cameras.

The situation with fraudulent accounts was getting out of hand. Kids on chat room networks were creating more fake versions of Tommy's PrizeBox software than we could keep up with, and since I was the only one among the three of us who knew how to write a formal letter, it was my responsibility to follow up with internet service providers about legal matters.

It turned serious when members began using instant messages to send death threats aimed at Cameron to my personal AOL Instant Messenger screenname. I didn't know where the threats were coming from, or whether or not they were actually serious. My first call to the Shaker Heights police went nowhere, since Cameron lived in Virginia.

"If it's across state lines, it's a federal matter," the officer on duty told me. "Call the FBI."

When I followed through, a week after the death threats began, a six-foot-tall FBI agent showed up on my doorstep. I explained the bizarre situation to him, and he took down some notes in my family's living room. He concluded our meeting by handing me his card.

"I'll be out of the country on an undercover mission for the next three years," he said. "Call the main number if you need anything."

Meanwhile, I was tearing my hair out over a new server I had purchased to host SurfingPrizes.com in my basement, where our service provider's technical support team would no longer factor in. I finally had the ability to reboot the server on my own whenever I needed to, which was crucial because the site kept going down. It was connected to the internet via my DSL line, provided by a company called UUNET, which was eventually purchased by MCI, and then Worldcom after that. It seemed like SurfingPrizes.com was on the receiving end of a Denial of Service attack, where a connection was flooded with so much nonsense data that real traffic could not get through.

I called Worldcom's technical support hotline and found my way to the security department, where I talked to a representative named Neil. He was convinced that there was no problem at all, except that our site was merely jammed with traffic. He also claimed that he couldn't monitor the line to tell for sure.

"Get a bigger pipe!" he screamed in my ear. "That's the only solution to your 'problem!' I don't care what you say, but your DSL line is not good enough. Your current setup is just plain stupid!"

"How fast of a connection would I need?" I asked, humoring his attempts to up-sell me on a more expensive connection from Worldcom. T-1 lines typically cost $1,200 per month, while DSL lines were a tenth of the price.

"How should I know!" Neil responded. "Get a T-1, get a T-3, get something bigger for God's sake, just stop wasting my time!" His supervisor sounded much the same.

"*Unbelievable! This is 'customer service?'*" I yelled, slamming down the phone.

Unfortunately, Neil at Worldcom was right. We did need a faster connection, but until we could get one, I set to work making the site more efficient so that it required less bandwidth per visitor. All the while, complaints were pouring into my inbox.

By the end of May, I was genuinely worried about what I had gotten myself into. Cameron hadn't really discussed how he planned to handle the logistics of paying the members their earnings, and I had noticed that the advertisements typically on the PrizeBox had disappeared. I sent off an e-mail to one of our representatives at L90, our advertising provider, outlining my concerns. L90 wrote back, explaining that our traffic had surged so much they had been unable to keep up by recruiting new advertisers. In other words, we were out of luck. No one was going to use the PrizeBox if there wasn't anything on it.

Cameron asked me to make a graphic for Think Computer to use as the default advertisement, since we didn't have anything else to put in its place. Advertisers just weren't willing to pay L90 for any more impressions of their ad campaigns. I happily complied, hoping that at least Think would benefit from the mess.

Then, Cameron revealed that he had paid L90 a $2,000 fee simply to get set up with their system. I asked him if he had a copy of the contract so that I could read it over.

On May 31st, I sent out another e-mail to Cameron and Tommy concluding with the question, "Can we get it together?"

I never received a response.

●

As I was doing my calculus homework, it occurred to me that Cameron was overlooking a fundamental problem with his business plan. The system spread virally for marketing purposes, but there was no limit to the number of referrals each member could make. Since our payments to members were defined by a formula that involved a constant multiplied by the number of referrals at each level of the system (which increased toward infinity), our payments would increase to infinity for each member, with the rate of increase directly proportional to the number of members referred. Meanwhile, L90 was contracting with our advertisers for a fixed number of impressions, regardless of the size of our member base.

"*Holy Christ*," I thought. "*Our costs are increasing exponentially, and our revenues are increasing linearly!*" It was clear to me that my time with SurfingPrizes.com would be limited one way or another. My only choice was whether to quit before the company went bankrupt, or after.

On the last day of school in June, I ran into Mr. Tournoux in the main office. I threw my backpack onto the floor to rummage through it, pulling out a sheet of loose-leaf paper.

"Here's my last homework assignment," I told him. I was finally caught up with calculus from March.

My family and I left the next day for Boston to attend my father's twenty-fifth Harvard reunion. He didn't usually go, and I hadn't the faintest clue what they were all about. Still, I liked going to Boston, if only to help out with the Keene network.

For once, though, as I was pacing around Keene's conference room on South Street, I was more concerned with my network at home. Worldcom was supposed to have installed a T-1 line, but they never showed up during the six-week-long installation window. I asked our next-door neighbors to be on the lookout for any phone trucks. On the phone in Boston, Worldcom gave me the runaround, blaming everything on the local phone company, Ameritech.

"Can I talk to Ameritech?" I asked.

"No, we can't let customers do that," they said.

"Right. Can you talk to Ameritech?" I asked again.

"No, we can't." I was stymied.

"Well, is it just me, or does no one else see the problem here?" I said, exasperated. I spent several hours more arguing with Worldcom on the phone—all on Cameron's behalf. The Keene employees thought I had simply gone crazy.

At the Harvard reunion, our family was assigned to a dorm called Straus. It was very noisy with cars going past every minute. The floors were plain wooden planks, and everything looked exceptionally old. I wondered what they did with the building during the rest of the year. It didn't seem like much, the way it was kept up.

During the day, while my mother and father attended the numerous events scheduled for alumni, Simon and I went off with the other children, organized in groups according to age. Fortunately for me, Simon was in a different group, so I didn't have to worry about taking care of him. It looked weird when I was constantly worrying about everything my younger brother did, and Simon didn't like it, either.

I found a small group of temporary friends among the kids I was with, but they were mostly younger than me. I did enjoy talking to our counselors, who I learned were Harvard students. They seemed pretty normal and genuinely interested when I told them that I ran a business.

The reunion took us all to a concert by the Boston Pops, conducted by John Williams himself. The voyage to Symphony Hall was just as impressive as the concert. Harvard rented out a caravan of more than fifty yellow school buses, which stretched back along Memorial Drive as far as the eye could see. The Boston Police stopped traffic in a large portion of downtown so that the buses could wind their way to the Hall where we all disembarked to fill up the auditorium.

During one of the more rhythmic numbers, two small children next to each other on the left balcony, age six or seven, began bobbing their heads back and forth, and then pausing, in perfect unison with the beat. Entire rows of the balcony began chuckling, with people pointing out the kids to those sitting next to them. They had no idea that they were being watched more than the orchestra. I began wondering if I had ever been that oblivious.

The rest of the week was a blur of white tents and "Crimson Catering" food. Simon, constantly surrounded by other children who knew little of his past, managed to get through most of it without a fit. I also didn't mind meeting other people, for once. On the whole, it seemed as though the kids were more understanding than the kids I had grown used to from school or summer camp.

"*Maybe it's just me,*" I thought, dismissing the idea that Harvard alums' kids were different from kids on average.

The following week, I flew to Washington, D.C. to meet up with Philip and James for National History Day at the University of Maryland. Upon entering the main hall at the University, everyone received a small notice in their information packet notifying them of Professor Van Tassel's death. Consequently, our judges were quite surprised when they saw him come to life again before their very eyes. They grilled us harshly at the end of our videotape, and ultimately marked us down for not interviewing enough people, like some of our competitors had. We didn't have time to explain to them that unlike the other projects in our category, which somehow focused on recent historical events, everyone involved in the Trent Affair was dead.

We lost. The worst academic year of my life was finally over.

●

Cameron Johnson was certain of his company's success. Instead of focusing on the core business (riddled with problems), he had been talking to anyone who would listen about investors, venture capital, and IPOs. On his trip through Japan, he even spoke of opening a Tokyo office. I couldn't believe what I was hearing.

Later on, when he returned to the United States where his celebrity status was considerably diminished, Cameron and I finally had a chance to discuss the contracts he had signed with L90. Apparently, he had believed the terms "NET 30" and "NET 90" to mean that we would be doing business "over the net," not that he was agreeing to pay tens of thousands of people each and every month while taking in revenue every three months. Inherent in Cameron's brilliant scheme was a huge cash flow imbalance that also explained why L90 was so slow about paying us.

On June 19, 2000, Cameron wrote to say that he was going to be interviewed by CBS News with the head of YoungBiz, an organization that promoted young entrepreneurs. I was familiar with YoungBiz from Think Computer's inclusion in its Top 100 list, similar to the Fortune 500, but for teenagers. The reporters for YoungBiz didn't distinguish between profit and revenue, and when kids who didn't even know HTML fibbed, "I made $600,000 off of web site design," they didn't bother to question their claims.

When the T-1 line was finally installed so that SurfingPrizes.com could stay on-line, I forced Cameron to pay for it in advance, afraid that Think would get stuck with the bill. I simultaneously negotiated terms that allowed Think to use the line for its own web site hosting operations at no additional cost on a second identical server.

Check number 1077 eventually arrived from Cameron to pay for the new arrangement. It bounced. I made him send another. Fortunately, it went through.

On the seventeenth of July, I sent Cameron my resignation from SurfingPrizes. I bought his company's server so that Think owned both of the machines in my basement and forwarded on a refund from Worldcom that I had battled for months to win. I didn't intend to give Cameron any say in my company, and I wanted no part in his.

Over the next month, I checked in with Cameron and Tommy from time to time to see how things were going. I still owned stock, so I had an incentive to see the company succeed, but the possibility seemed remote. Even Tommy was beginning to agree.

"I'd be happy to get anything out of SurfingPrizes," he told me. "It's gone downhill for quite a while."

Four days later, a long and confused chat room conversation took place in which a desperate Cameron began lamenting his reputation. He claimed that the company had $225,000, but that it needed to pay members more than three times that amount—almost $700,000. I wasn't sure about his first number, but I easily believed the second. I had seen the 30,000 member database. On average, all we needed to owe each member was $25.00 to make Cameron's estimates work, and it sounded reasonable.

"This sucks." Cameron said.

"Welcome to the wonderful world of business," I replied, wondering if he finally understood what it meant to be an entrepreneur with actual responsibility—not just a kid who could win over the media with a cute smile.

On August 29th, though I had already resigned, Cameron asked me to design a notice for SurfingPrizes.com to announce that the site was closed. My skepticism about the company's financial state turned out to be correct.

"We won't even have enough to give every user $1.00," he told me.

"Pay people until our bank account reads 'zero.'" I demanded. Instead, he set up a web site where furious members filed claims for their earnings, to be filled on a first-come first-served basis. A single round of checks was mailed out to members for earnings from April and May. Then, on September 15, 2000, my new graphic appeared.

"SurfingPrizes.com is closed," it read.

Despite my insistance, Cameron didn't send out all of the company's money to its members, holding back $5,000 to pay "taxes." When I hinted that he should have a Certified Public Accountant take care of them, he told me what I should have been expecting.

"No, I dropped the CPA when we decided not to sell." His venture-capital-buyout-multi-million-dollar-IPO dreams were indeed long since past.

For months afterward, I kept on Cameron's case to make sure he sent out additional payments to the members. One man kept calling me from the Netherlands hoping to learn Cameron's home phone number, but after dealing with the FBI once on Cameron's behalf, I didn't feel like getting involved again.

The debacle didn't phase Cameron Johnson. Once the furor died down, he drained the funds from the company's checking account and used them to start another.

CHAPTER 9

The Envelope

In the fall, college was all Mrs. Blattner wanted to talk about. I knew I'd have to take it seriously eventually, but unlike many of my friends and their parents, I didn't think it was necessary to start wringing my hands until at least November. Most of them had already gone on massive college trips to nine campuses at a time, or more. Peter told me he was applying to eleven schools. All I knew was that eventually, I was expected to go.

"Still set on Harvard?" Mrs. Blattner asked during one of my visits.

"I guess..." I said. "It's a good school, isn't it?" She tilted her head.

"Sure it is, but I don't want you to think you're just going to get right in," she began. "There is a new person for our region this year and she seems very nice, so I'll get in touch with her and tell her about you. Tell me your list of other places, again?"

I went over the list, explaining that I had ruled out MIT because I hated math. Mrs. Blattner seemed certain that with my grades and a decent SAT score, I would get into one of the five I had mentioned.

At a night meeting held for the entire senior class, she outlined what we should expect from the admissions process. Everyone was, of course, pressed for time. Some students sent their parents as emissaries. Notebooks were out in spades.

"When it says 'Sex' on the form, I had one student write, 'yes, please.' Don't do that! You want to take these forms very seriously," Mrs. Blattner advised. "The essay is the most important part of all. There's no other way to distinguish yourself from the thousands of other applications that these people are going to be reading. SAT scores are important, but they don't say anything about *you*. It's much better to write something concise that says something about you, rather than a missive on world peace." Pens scribbled all around.

I did take the applications seriously, applying all of the perfectionist tendencies and technical skill that I could muster. I had taken an "Apply!" CD-ROM from Mrs. Blattner's office that purported to contain applications for most of the schools anyone would ever want to apply to. In my case, it turned out only to work for Harvard, since only Harvard used the ironically-named Common Application. All of the other schools had their own applications I had to complete separately.

On the CD, I found that the Common Application had been supplied in Adobe Acrobat PDF format, using fill-in technology so that you could type directly on the form and save your information for later use. Unfortunately, the technology was only in its beginning stages. The font was far too large to fit much of what I wanted to type, such as my name. I tried using Adobe Illustrator to open and edit the PDF directly. After hours of painstaking work, I had a professionally-completed application without using a typewriter. Now all I had to do was write the essay and then four more for other applications.

"At least I'm not applying to Brown like Chloé," I consoled myself. Brown made you fill out everything by hand so that they could analyze your handwriting, or so I'd heard.

I filled out most of Stanford's application on-line, but I still had to figure out what to write for the essays. I carried a printout of the Michigan application around with me in my binder for at least a month, never working up the resolve to actually begin writing on it. The one for Carnegie Mellon seemed very straightforward, and though I was able to finish it without much trouble, I decided not to pay the fee until I was sure that I was going to really try to get in.

Between essays for English and calculus assignments for Mr. Tournoux, I settled down one night to decide what to write about. Unless I did something drastic to alter my image, the college admissions offices would see me as just another computer nerd. For my Harvard essay, I decided to take the "well-rounded" approach, writing briefly about my experience at tennis camp, where my counselor called me "Bill Gates" since she had read about me in a magazine. I neglected to mention that my backhand consistently sent the ball sailing into the next court over. Instead, I made the case that Bill Gates was a lousy idol for a teenager and that Jim Henson was a much better role model.

Stanford wanted essays that touched on deep feelings. They also wanted a hypothetical e-mail to my future roommate, including proof that I had actively participated in extracurricular activities. I gave them a paragraph on JCWA and my company. The essay's only redeeming quality was that it had valid SMTP headers, making it look like a real, routable e-mail.

The University of Pennsylvania, meanwhile, wanted a laundry list of my defining characteristics. I never finished editing it.

Mrs. Blattner recommended that since Harvard was my first choice, I apply early. If I got in, I could rest easy; if not, I'd finish up all of the other applications by their respective deadlines, most of which were in January. I sent off my envelope to Garden Street in Cambridge, and waited. Harvard mailed its decisions for early applicants in mid-December.

In the meantime, I was required to attend an in-person interview with various Harvard alums in the Cleveland area. Discussions in the cafeteria and the senior lounge increasingly turned to which kinds of interviews were best. Some thought one-on-one interviews were better because the interviewer could really focus on you, and if you hit it off, then you were basically guaranteed admission. One of

Adam's friends believed this strongly, recounting his hour-long interview conversation about beer, which he believed had played a significant role in getting him into college. Whether true or not, had I been in the same situation, it would have been a fast track to rejection. I couldn't stand the smell of alcohol, let alone the taste.

For better or worse, my Harvard interview would be a group interview. I imagined that it would be sort of like kindergarten, with a bunch of overeager applicants all sitting in a circle around a smiling, deified alum, who would summarily decide our fates after a few words from each person. It turned out to be quite a bit different, mostly because I failed to comprehend that the "group" would be the group from Shaker. I knew each and every person there.

I never found out how the group interview actually started, because I was ten minutes late. By the time I actually pulled up next to the curb outside the interviewer's house in my father's Honda Accord, the sky was already pitch black.

Stumbling up the steps to the front door, I rang the doorbell, and was welcomed inside by Barry Gordon, the same alum who had been at a college fair representing Harvard one year before. At the time, I'd asked him hopefully if I could apply a full year early. He told me to take advantage of all the resources my school had to offer first. My father, who interviewed for the local Alumni Association himself, had told me that he was a psychologist.

I was not looking forward to being psychoanalyzed, but all of the other adults in the room were already engaged in one-on-one conversations with Billy, Chloé, Philip, and a few other students, all of whom I recognized. Dr. Gordon had been waiting for me to arrive. I managed a sheepish smile.

"Sorry I'm late," I started out, hoping it wouldn't be my biggest mistake ever. Like my mother, I was always just a few minutes late, no matter how hard I tried.

"Not a problem, glad you could make it." Dr. Gordon had one of those voices that seemed very pleasant, but I couldn't ever tell whether he was sincere. "Let's walk down to the basement—it's already pretty noisy up here," he suggested. I followed him into his kitchen and then down a staircase. We sat on a blue sofa, though my eyes darted for a moment to an Apple Macintosh LC II and a 12-inch color monitor that were lying on the gray carpet, disconnected, reminding me of Mrs. Geszler's lab at Woodbury.

"So, tell me," he began. "Why do you want to go to Harvard?"

I launched into my case: I liked doing things on my own, I had a lot of ideas, I was serious about school... I wasn't really sure which reason was the right one, so I did my best to cover them all.

"I've looked over your application," Dr. Gordon said, "and I'm curious if you could just go into some more detail on a couple of things. What did you do with Think Computer Foundation?"

"Well, actually, I'm trying to recycle old computers, like your Macintosh there, by shipping them to poorer countries like Jamaica. I have a contact there that I met at a conference at the Kennedy Space Center, and they're hopefully going to use the computers that I'm shipping them in schools."

He wanted to know about the company, too. It was pretty much the only thing that made me any different from the six other ridiculously smart students in his house. I hoped it was enough, because I felt like I was the stupidest of the bunch.

My next interview took place upstairs, where my next challenger introduced himself, though I failed to catch his name.

"So, do you follow current events?" I couldn't believe it—it was the perfect question.

"Actually, I don't know if you use the internet at all," I said, "but my home page is set to *The New York Times* site, so yes, I try to."

"So, let me give you a hypothetical scenario," he continued. "Let's say you're a school principal. And you have a student who is a Jehovah's Witness. But you've got a Halloween party coming up, and the student's parents don't want him to participate since it's against their religion. The student is going to feel left out, and isn't happy about it. Whaddya do?"

I had been trying to listen closely, but I was almost sure I had missed something, or drifted off in the middle. The question seemed totally out of left field. I had no idea what the man was even talking about. Jehovah's Witnesses? Halloween party?

"That's a tough situation...I really don't know," I stammered. "On the one hand, you can probably help the child socially by including him in activities with all of the other students, but then again, there is a constitutional right to freedom of religion; you'd almost be violating that if you were to force the student to participate."

The man kept on asking questions. After that, I just wanted to leave as fast as I could. Fortunately, there was no third interview. I had satisfied Harvard's social skills requirement—or at least I figured that's what it really was.

There was nothing left to do but wait.

●

On December 18, 2000, in the dead center of the bitterness that was winter break, I was sitting on the sofa in the living room of our house. The mailman always came at around 12:00 noon, and it was 1:15 P.M. My mother came in and sat down next to me.

"Do you think it will come today?" she asked.

"I don't know!" I said. Like many teenagers, I hated it when my mother asked me questions. "How should I know, I didn't send it."

I continued to wait nervously, indicating my true answer. The minute hand on my watch lurched forward. And then again. And then, there was a metallic clank as the United States Postal Service deposited the day's mail in the mailbox.

We always had a lot of mail thanks to Keene Advertising; factories sent their catalogs to our house, clogging our mailbox daily. The mailman took to leaving everything bigger than a standard envelope inside the screen door. And that's where it was.

It was big. People had been talking about which size was a good sign and which one was bad, but I couldn't remember. I figured that Harvard could afford all the 8.5" x 11" envelopes it wanted, and then some.

I brought it into the living room.

"It's here," I said to my mother. I opened it.

"What does it say?" she asked excitedly.

A smile lit up on my face as I scanned the page.

"I got in."

I had seen my mother happy before, but she was beyond happy. I found myself in the middle of a hug, almost a foot off the ground. Then, she rushed away to call my father at work. Not really having anyone to call myself, I updated the part of Think's web site that contained my short biography. It read that I would be attending Harvard College in the fall.

I received a giant packet of materials from the Admissions Office in the mail, with magazines, brochures, and advertisements from almost every club at the College. It took a full hour sitting on my bed just to sort out the papers. Someone in the Pops Orchestra had actually taken the time to cross out their form letter's greeting and write in my name. I was impressed.

One small slip of paper was a request for a photograph for the Class of 2005 Freshman Register. There was a $25.00 fee to have your photograph included. After thinking about it for a minute, I realized that I would probably feel left out if everyone else paid the $25.00 and I didn't, so I found a school photo and wrote a check. (Ever since I started Think, I had also started paying my own bills. It was a convenient way to quiet my mother's criticism that I didn't practice French Horn enough to merit her paying for my lessons.)

The Handbook for Students, a decent-sized book outlining the official rules of Harvard College, had also been sent along with the promotional materials. I looked through it, trying to find the page about running a business. I knew that Harvard had changed its policies on student-run businesses a few years prior; there had been a full-page spread in the *The New York Times* business section all about it.

"Student Business Activity" was on page 254, next to "Drugs and Alcohol."

From time to time, letters from the College also appeared in my mailbox. They never seemed to be from the same person, let alone the same office—the Freshman Dean's Office was separate from the Registrar, which was independent of the

Admission's Office, which wasn't the same as the Harvard Prefect Program, which was different than the Office of the Governing Boards. The amount there was to learn just about the institution was overwhelming.

The rest of my time at Shaker was much more relaxed, knowing that I didn't have to worry about college anymore. Carnegie Mellon called me during dinner one night to ask me if I would pay my fee. I said no. They sent me a letter of acceptance, much to my surprise.

I was somewhat embarrassed when Stanford eventually accepted me. It was a good situation to be in, but at the same time it felt unfair, knowing how many people wanted admission. Simultaneously, I wasn't sure which school to choose. My father said he'd try to find someone through the Harvard Alumni Association who knew about both.

My father eventually found Craig Silverstein through a friend of his at work. Craig had studied computer science during his undergraduate years at Harvard, and was a graduate student at Stanford researching such topics as "Scalable Techniques for Mining Causal Structures." I had no idea what it meant, but after working out a time to talk, I gave him a call one day. We spent forty-five minutes discussing the differences between computer science at each school. He seemed to believe pretty strongly that the undergraduate experience at Harvard was better overall. That was all I needed to hear.

There was a light at the end of the tunnel after all, and it was the Cambridge, Massachusetts sun.

CHAPTER 10

The Carrot

In mid-April, I packed my bags for Boston. Like many colleges, Harvard gave admitted high school students a sneak preview of a few days, which was useful if you had to decide between schools. In my case, the choice was strictly binary: Harvard on the east coast, or Stanford on the west.

The Admissions Office at 8 Garden Street was a squarish brick building offset from the road by a stately brick wall. An open gate led to the back, labeled "Byerly Hall," whose entrance comprising numerous steps had not been designed with travelers (or disabled students) in mind. Inside, there were hordes of brainy high school students, all vying for crimson folders containing their materials for the weekend.

"Your name?" a girl behind one of the tables asked.

"Aaron Greenspan," I said. She swept over to the "G"s and found my folder in a bin. The folder contained my itinerary for the weekend, a sheet listing the student I would be staying with, his dorm's location, and a map. Judging from the look of things, hardly anyone had arrived yet, even though the office was jam-packed with people.

It was chilly outside, but I had on my giant red and black puffy coat to shield me from the Boston weather. The Yard looked vaguely familiar from the reunion, but I couldn't place Straus, where I had stayed before. I flipped open my folder and learned that I would be staying in Grays Hall M on the Yard's southern edge. I started walking that way until I found myself facing a building clearly marked "Grays Hall – Middle." The red light near the key-swipe device indicated that the door was locked, so I dialed my host from the nearby telephone.

A minute later, the forest green door swung open, and a lanky freshman stood in the doorway. Once I ambled my way up to the door, I realized that there would be a lot more climbing to do. There was no elevator, and room M45 was on the fourth floor. My host for the weekend, Seth, offered to help me with my luggage. From that alone, he didn't seem like a bad guy.

Grays had been built over a hundred and fifty years before, but it had clearly been renovated in the recent past. The walls were brick and the floors were unpolished wood, giving the place a loft-like feel. Clustered around the common room were four desks, one for each person living there. The bedrooms, along with a bathroom for the suite, were in the back. There were pegs built into the wall to hang coats right across from the door. According to the Harvard Student Agencies Unofficial Guide to Prefrosh Weekend, which also came in our folder, Grays was referred to as the "Harvard Hilton." For once in my life, I felt like I had lucked out.

Neil Rudenstine, the outgoing Harvard president, gave a speech welcoming everyone that was remarkable neither for its content nor its presentation. He seemed like a nice old man, and my father had told me that generally speaking, people liked him. After all, he had raised a lot of money for Harvard University.

For dinner, Seth showed us the way to Annenberg, where all the freshmen ate their meals. It was enormous, almost like one of the cathedrals I had seen in Vienna on tour with the Wind Symphony, but made out of wood instead of stone. Next to Annenberg stood the Science Center, a metal and gravel mess that looked as if it had dropped out of the sky and landed next to the Yard by mistake. It was hideous.

Inside, a stern-faced woman in the corner of the hall swiped my temporary Harvard ID as we walked past. I noticed her name tag, which read "DOMNA." Each time a student slid an ID card through her machine, there was a series of five beeps: four short and one long. If you didn't swipe the card properly, the tones alternated rapidly to make a noise that was rather painful to listen to, alerting even the tone-deaf that something was wrong. A flexible barrier lining the wall closest to the entrance guided everyone toward Domna as they walked inside.

The inside of Annenberg was even more impressive than its exterior. There were stained-glass windows lining the sides, and rows upon rows of tables for students to eat at. Even so, there wasn't enough room—with the addition of the visiting high school students, long lines had already formed when we walked in the door.

Standing in line, I vaguely realized that I had been there before during the reunion. My memory felt muddled by months of sleep deprivation.

Though the food was displayed in a very attractive manner inside the kitchen, it seemed to lose some its luster once it was out of the reach of the infrared heat lamps. It was just good enough, on average, to be satisfying. The only exception was beef, which was awful. Fortunately, the soda machines with unlimited refills more than compensated. Harvard had free root beer—though as I later discovered, it lacked free dental care.

A quick trip to "Loker Commons" in the dining hall's basement put me face-to-face with students advising high-schoolers like myself on academic plans. It was the same place where I had checked my e-mail on the iMacs only a few months before.

"Have you thought about doing Advanced Standing?" a student asked me.

"Uhh... I don't really think I'd use it," I said.

"Yeah, most people here don't. It's really rare." There didn't seem to be much else going on, so I left.

That night, activities were planned for all of the visiting students to get to know one another. I went to a room in a dorm called Canaday, where students were split up regionally. One of the Harvard freshmen who hosted our group quietly boasted that he lived next door to Jonathan Taylor Thomas; the girls nearby immediately grew more interested. I met someone with a giant pimple on his cheek from Toledo, Ohio, who said he knew my cousins. He talked a lot about *The Crimson*, the school newspaper, which was having an introductory meeting for prospective students at some point over the weekend.

"I'll definitely check it out," I told him. After being rejected by the teacher who ran *The Shakerite* due to my lack of journalism experience, I thought it might be worth trying again.

There was also an A Capella concert in Sanders Theatre, where almost ten groups performed various musical arrangements to a packed audience. They were all surprisingly good, and some of them had been around for almost as long as the school itself. Each group made a point of noting its most recent tour destinations, which included such exotic locales as Egypt. If I'd had any vocal talent, I would have been sold.

I got the impression that I was being solicited to a lot over the weekend, but I didn't necessarily mind. It was fun, shopping for your interests. Everywhere you went, different student groups tried to get you to join their ranks, whether it was the Asian Baptist Student Koinonia ("No, thank you, I'm Jewish..."), or Hillel ("Well, actually, I'm not *that* Jewish..."), or the Glee Club ("Sorry, you really don't want to hear me sing..."), or the Objectivist Club ("How many members did you say you had?"). There were three groups that I ultimately decided I wanted to learn more about: the Harvard International Relations Council, which was commonly referred to as the "IRC," the Harvard Pops Orchestra, and the Technology and Entrepreneurship Center at Harvard, which had logically dubbed itself "TECH." *The Crimson* and the Harvard Band and Wind Ensemble were somewhere much lower on my list, even though my mother had pushed for me to try out for the latter.

Everywhere I went, everyone introduced themselves with the same four key pieces of information: their name, where they were from, what they were interested in, and where else they had applied. Almost the entire prospective Class of 2005, I learned, was choosing between Harvard and Stanford.

I could barely keep track of the people I met. I did manage to remember two: one who said he had some interest in technology, as did a really tall kid from Massachusetts named Nathan, who had started his own company. I was struck by the fact that I was having a really hard time finding anyone I didn't like.

When I got back to the room at Grays, I had a chance to talk to Seth for a little while. I had always thought of Harvard students as people who were so bright as to be obnoxious, citing their own intelligence in every other sentence. Yet, I hadn't met a single person like that all weekend. Harvard students, including Seth, seemed to be smart in an understated sort of way. You couldn't tell them apart from other people just by looking at them. You had to listen to what they said, and watch how they acted. Everyone seemed unbelievably relaxed.

"You like N64?" Seth asked. He revealed his Nintendo 64, and popped in a game that involved skateboarding. He was really good, so I inferred that he must have spent a lot of time playing.

"Last time I played Nintendo must have been second or third grade," I said. "I'm way out of touch. Way too much work lately."

"So what do you do outside of work for fun?" he asked, still playing.

"I run this company…" I started out, hesitating because I didn't have an answer. The truth was that I didn't do anything for fun. "It does software and consulting mostly. Takes up a lot of time."

"Whoa! That's awesome…so you run your own company?" I was taken aback by the positive reaction.

"Yep."

"Cool…so you like, design programs?"

"Web sites, and database software mostly."

"Cool."

I decided to change the subject. "So are you in any clubs or anything?" I asked.

"Yeah, actually, I'm in the Republican Club," he said.

"*Wow, this place really is diverse!*" I thought, accustomed to the Democratic stronghold that was my home town. Much to my surprise, Harvard had Republican Jews.

"So actually one of my roommates who you haven't met yet is CS, but he's never around. If he shows up, you might want to talk to him," Seth said. Indeed, I had no idea who he was talking about, but I did note that one of the desks had been vacant the entire time I had been there.

Seth went to check his e-mail and brought up "pine," a UNIX program that I was familiar with from my own servers. It reminded me that I needed to check my e-mail, too. After he was done, I asked Seth if I could borrow his computer for a few minutes.

"No problem, go ahead," he said. I sat down and added my server to the list on his computer. Oddly enough, there wasn't any e-mail in my mailbox. There wasn't any in the company's general mailbox, either. It seemed as if the server wasn't routing any mail at all. Something was wrong.

For the next several hours, I felt horribly embarrassed as I hogged Seth's computer to try to repair my server. At times, it wasn't responding at all to commands, so I had to borrow his phone to call home and ask my mother to reboot it, which was an ordeal in its own right. It wasn't how I wanted to spend my time, and I was infringing on Seth's space and property. I apologized profusely.

I made a point of visiting a computer science class, since there was one on the list of courses we could sample over the weekend. The history and literature ones didn't look quite as interesting, and all of the courses open to prospective students seemed to be fairly advanced, as opposed to the levels that freshmen would start out with. The course I went to took place in the new computer science building, which had been given the rather unintuitive name of Maxwell-Dworkin.

CS124, Data Structures and Algorithms, was taught by a professor named Michael Mitzenmacher. Based on his last name, I guessed he was of German-Jewish descent, but the person teaching the course was very clearly from the Indian subcontinent. My confusion about who was actually teaching was immediately compounded by the fact that I had absolutely no idea what the man was talking about. The course's content was purely mathematical, and it was abstract math at that. As I huddled in the back of the lecture hall, Nathan whispered what he had heard: they didn't touch a computer in the class the entire time. It made me wonder whether computer science was really what I wanted to study.

The meeting for TECH took place later in a different room in Maxwell-Dworkin. There were about twenty-five people at the meeting, most of them male, and enough pizza to go around four times over. The TECH Student Association, separate from TECH itself, was led by a surfer-dude named Arturo. He talked a lot about the club's funding: a venture capitalist alum named Rufus Lumry III had donated $3 million to create TECH, and apparently, the organization could do whatever it wanted with the money. Even though Arturo himself failed to impress, I took solace in the fact that the club seemed to have a stable budget and an actively involved staff advisor, a former patent attorney named Paul Bottino. I signed my name on the list of people who were interested in joining in the fall.

That night, I was a few minutes late to *The Crimson* meeting because I had no clue as to where it was being held. It took me a while to figure out that the news-paper had its own building outside of the Yard. Inside, there were tons of ebullient high-schoolers crowded into a tiny space on the second floor. The president of the newspaper introduced himself with a wave of his arm and a dripping tone of voice. Within a minute, I knew that I would not do well there. Once everyone broke up into smaller groups to ask questions about their main interests, I left. I had no desire to work in the IT department of an organization that considered itself, as my mother would have said, "God's gift to the world."

By the end of the weekend, there was no question at all about whether or not I wanted to go to Harvard. Stanford might have been prettier in brochures, but the other students who were going to be in Harvard's Class of 2005 were amazing. They were kind, they valued the discussion of abstract ideas, they had defined interests, they were funny, and by and large, they were all going to be in one, centralized location. Not to mention that there was a club specifically devoted to technology and entrepreneurship with $3 million in funding behind it.

I couldn't wait for September.

•

Knowing what was out there, going back to Shaker was torture. Everyone seemed completely dull. With the exception of Mrs. Jones, who let us go outside when the weather was warm, the teachers were insufferable.

Each May, JCWA, the National Spanish Honor Society, the band program, and a host of other extracurricular activities held their annual end-of-the-year dinner celebrations during the same exact week. The food was generally mediocre, it was stressful (with entire families expected to attend), and the awards were often not worth waiting for.

I also had the task of putting together the massive slide show for the band banquet. Two days beforehand, my mother delivered a piece of bad news. Hans Bohnert, the director of the band program, had died of a heart attack.

Mr. Bohnert had always been something of an enigma. Pictures that lined the walls of the band office showed a pudgy (but not obese) Mr. Bohnert, smiling next to ensemble after ensemble in the early 1990s. A lot had changed since then. Everyone had their guesses, but no one knew for sure. Since Mr. Bohnert joked about his weight, as he joked about everything, it was hard to get to the core issue. I could have sworn that once, as he was coming out of the band office at the Middle School, I smelled something awful on his breath. I could only guess that it was alcohol, so I never said anything. Years later, my suspicion was confirmed when someone else reported seeing a wine bottle. It explained why his cheeks were often flush, but I had never heard of someone putting on so much weight from drinking alone.

After my lung collapsed and I began spending more time in the band office, Mr. Bohnert was usually glad for the company. He would ask frequently how Simon was doing. Everyone in the band knew Simon; he pretended to conduct the marching band at football games in a bizarre routine that was indiscreet to say the least.

Eventually, Mr. Bohnert revealed the missing link that we all had been trying to figure out for so long. He had a young daughter with cerebral palsy, and I knew that on his salary he could scarcely afford to support her at home, let alone send her away to a private school like Simon's. He was stuck in the same quagmire as my family. There was nowhere to go, and no one to turn to, whether in government or otherwise. Our society decreed that mentally handicapped children were their parents' problems, and if the parents couldn't handle them, then it was just too bad.

With the help of the same Chris who had suffered through Mrs. Byrdsong's class, I hurriedly ported the band's slide show to Mrs. Pessel's video editing workstation over the weekend, and changed the last section to become a tribute to Mr. Bohnert. While I had had six months to work on the History Day project, there were only two days to put together a videotape of equal length. When the slide show finally aired at the band banquet, I evaluated its effectiveness based on the number of people crying at the end. It was effective.

Strangely, our other director, Mr. Deep, was nowhere to be seen. Rumor had it that he was angry that he had not been automatically promoted to head of the music department. I wasn't surprised. From my teachers, I had learned to expect nothing less.

By the time June came around a few weeks later, I was eating lunch outside every day, free from the segregated cafeteria, administrative politics, and most importantly, homework. No fan of roller coasters, I opted out of the senior trip to Cedar Point, choosing instead to revel in the joyous atmosphere on the front lawn.

Graduation took place on a hot, sunny day. Boys wore red robes; girls wore white. I had been out of the running to make the graduation speech for some time, but I had overcome my initial disappointment upon realizing that you couldn't say anything intellectually provocative in a high school graduation speech, and that even if you did, no one would remember it.

Sure enough, our class valedictorian spoke in a somewhat grating manner about impending global conflict and World War III. I chuckled to myself silently.

A short time later, I walked across the stage to receive the diploma I had worked so hard for. My public school education was over.

●

That summer, I had an agreement with Mr. Morgan. In exchange for working on a multimedia program to control the University School Space Camp shuttle simulator, I received the right to use the private school's library as my company's office. In short order, I hired Tim, who I'd met at U.S. years before, his friend Whitney, and Scott, the son of one of my mother's friends. Of the four of us, Scott, who had completed his freshman year at the University of Maryland, was the only one who had any formal computer science training.

My goal was to create a program to replace Keene Advertising's antiquated order management system, which was made by Quikey, Inc. The software, which had once run on XENIX, now ran on an equally esoteric operating system called SCO OpenServer. It was virtually impossible to connect to a web site, and just to change a printer setting, Quikey charged $100. It had taken me five years alone to figure out how to get the SCO server to function on a standard network, since Quikey had never been able to figure it out themselves. If Keene Advertising was ever going to catch up with the rest of the world, Quikey had to go.

I didn't even know where to begin. Quikey handled everything from Keene's sales commissions to the line items on each individual order. I had no idea how it worked, coupled with no background in accounting. I had taught myself a little bit of PHP in my free period at school, but not enough to be considered an expert.

Regardless, Tim, Whit, Scott and I set to work. I issued general instructions about what features needed to go where, and what they should look like. Tim, who had started multi-variable calculus in twelfth grade, did anything that looked difficult. Since none of us knew SQL, he invented his own syntax to take care of extracting the columns that we needed to have in our tables. I asked Whit to try his hand at making sales calls for our nonexistent product. Interested companies were faxed a Non-Disclosure Agreement that they had to sign in order to test our software. Unfortunately, we didn't have any access to a normal telephone or fax in the library. Everything had to be faxed to my house, and then brought back to the library where they were deposited in a green binder, just as Carl Sjogreen had done during my summer internship.

I had enough money to pay everyone for four weeks, but it quickly became apparent that we wouldn't be able to finish the product. Already, we all went home each day completely wiped out; it was impossible to work any harder.

On the first Tuesday in July, I was working on Think's web site just before lunchtime when I became aware of a gradual pressure building in my chest. After ten minutes, it hurt just to sit in place. There was definitely something wrong, but it didn't feel like my pneumothorax when the pain had been sudden and obvious.

For a few minutes, I didn't say anything, but the pain didn't go away. I walked out of the library as if I was headed toward the water fountain, but lied down on the floor outside, hoping my position would affect the pain. It didn't. We looked up the number for University Hospitals of Cleveland. After being transferred three times, I finally reached the emergency room.

"Hi, I have a history of spontaneous pneumothorax, and I'm having pain on the right side of my chest," I told the nurse who answered.

"Okay," she said. It was not the reaction I was hoping for.

"I'm not sure if it's another pneumothorax or just an asthma attack."

"Well, you can come into the E.R. if you want, but we can't do anything else for you," came the response.

"Well, I can't really get to the E.R. right now," I replied. I had no car, and my father was at work, where I had been unable to reach him. My mother was in Boston with Simon at a reading program for children with learning disabilities.

"There's nothing we can do for you then," the nurse said, and there was a click. She had hung up. I was incredulous.

Scott offered to take me home so I could try out my inhaler, and I took him up on the offer. The ride took no more than three minutes, and I made the painful trek up the stairs to my room, where my albuterol inhaler proved to be totally worthless. I went back to work.

The next day was July 4th, so there wasn't anyone at the hospital who was willing to see me. On July 5th, my father took me to the emergency room again, immediately informing the nurses of his status as a hospital physician. It was like magic: even though the waiting room was still crowded, instead of waiting for eight hours, we barely waited at all.

A chest CT scan showed that my right lung had indeed collapsed again. The doctors thought it would heal on its own, but if it happened again, I was warned, I would need surgery.

Fortunately, my pulmonary system did not preclude me from going on vacation. I spent more time than usual in front of the laptop, worrying about Harvard. I had already received the names of my randomly-assigned freshman year roommates in the mail. One of them, from California, was named Brian. Wentao was from a city in China called Guangzhou. The third was Nathan, one of the people I had met during the visiting weekend in April. Miraculously, I had been randomly assigned to room with another entrepreneur.

I combed the internet for information on all three of them, but all that I learned was that Brian played football. Wentao's name scarcely appeared, and Nathan was like a ghost, with no paper trail at all. It seemed odd for a teenager who said he ran a company.

I was determined to make friends in college. For years, I had attributed my lack of friends to something I had done wrong.

"Maybe it's my hair, or the company..." I mused. I decided to try a social experiment: I'd part my hair down the middle (a big change, I thought), and I wouldn't tell anyone at Harvard about Think for as long as possible.

Simon, meanwhile, couldn't have cared less about my hair or my company; he wanted to use the computer to visit ESPN.com. In a complete transformation, Simon had stumbled onto an obsession with sports. He had become one of the better players on the Brehm basketball team. From having no interest in anything whatsoever, he had started following all of Cleveland's sports teams, from the Indians down to their AAA minor league farm team, the Buffalo Bisons. He knew the statistics on every one of Cleveland's WNBA players, and he had taken to using the internet as a sports encyclopedia. It was impossible to get him to read anything in a library, but if my mother threw away the *Plain Dealer* sports sections that he accumulated when he came home for vacations, all hell broke loose.

Unfortunately for the rest of us, Simon liked to sing while he surfed. In addition to his usual collection of Hebrew prayer songs, his favorites now included the Star-Spangled Banner and America the Beautiful, which were sung at sports events.

I had an idea. I found "Fiddler on the Roof" among my collection of sound-tracks, put it in the laptop's CD-ROM drive, and plugged in some headphones. For a few minutes, Simon merely hummed the tune of "If I Were a Rich Man," instead of blaring the refrain to the national anthem. Then, he took off the headphones, and blared Tevye's lines instead.

"*Well, he's definitely capable of learning something,*" I thought, wishing I had picked a quieter melody.

When we arrived home, my mother transformed into a tornado of purchasing and packing. She bought boxes upon boxes of food at Sam's Club, which I refused to take.

"I don't need thirty packages of pretzels!" I finally screamed when she kept on pushing.

"Yes, you do! You don't understand!" she yelled.

"Correct! I don't understand why I need thirty things of pretzels when they have food in Massachusetts!" I yelled back. The battle went on this way for several days, as various items were added to and then removed from the duffle bags in our guest room.

A day or two before I left, Adam stopped by to say goodbye before I left for Harvard, and he for Princeton. I extended my hand to shake his, but he came back at me with a hug that caught me off-guard. With my arm in the wrong place to receive it, it ended up being yet another awkward moment, made worse because my parents were watching.

Since my mother had borne the brunt of the work up to that point, my father and I loaded up my mother's new silver Volvo station wagon. By the time we were done, there was just enough room for me to squeeze into the back seat.

The next day, the three of us began the drive east and then north to Boston. For twelve hours, I tried to amuse myself by reading, napping, and listening to music, though my parents didn't always share my taste. My mother managed to earn a speeding ticket on the Massachusetts Turnpike just before we arrived.

Finally, we arrived safely at my uncle's house in Wellesley, where we spent the night. The next morning, we woke up to complete the last leg of the journey: to Cambridge.

CHAPTER 11

The Cars of Harvard Yard

It was far too early in the morning, and the September air was brisk as we sped up Western Avenue. I was reading printed directions off of a bright red sheet of paper. Unlike most streets where you had to strain your eyes to read any addresses at all, the numbers here were larger than life, almost two feet tall and bold, so that they looked like they might hurt if they fell on you.

"Turn left at North Harvard Street," I said as we approached an intersection. The directions said where to go, but not really where, I realized, as we pulled into the Harvard University mail processing facility parking lot. The workers inside were sorting envelopes; the workers outside were sorting cars. My father rolled down the window.

"This is your parking pass," a student said. "You can park in the Yard for twenty minutes to unload, and then you have to go. Harvard Yard is straight that-a-way," he said pointing north, "and then you will want to turn right into Johnston Gate."

Fortunately, my father knew his way around from years past. It only took a few minutes to reach the Yard, though the Cambridge traffic was atrocious far beyond its normal level of atrociousness. I could see why the Admissions Office routed everyone to the mail facility first: the line of cars trying to enter the Yard was absurd, even at 8:00 A.M. Once they passed through the gate, the cars themselves looked funny, as if the machines were too big and shiny to be real. All around them were peaceful trees and old brick buildings. In the center, a large white tent had been erected where keys were being handed out, along with information about how to hook up your computer to the Harvard network.

Through some stroke of unbelievable luck, I had been assigned to Grays M54, one floor above Seth's room from April. Mike and Jenny Armini, my freshman proctors who lived on the first floor, were there to greet us when we pulled up. They were incredibly nice.

There were some other Grays residents who had already moved in waiting around on the steps. One of them offered to help bring my stuff up to my room. Getting everything out of our station wagon was the easy part; it was getting everything up the stairs to the fifth floor that proved difficult.

"Aren't you glad I didn't bring the pretzels?" I asked my mother. She shot me a dirty look.

I was particularly concerned about two boxes: one of them, Think's backup server, and the other, a plastic crate containing all of the company's files. My father went off to see if I could store them somewhere temporarily, since Harvard's regulations frowned upon running a business out of your dorm room. Not that it would have made any difference—Grays M54 was hardly lacking in space.

The common room was large, with a shaded view of the Yard to the north. In the back, the bedrooms overlooked and overheard Harvard Square. An African-American homeless man who I thought might have been on some sort of anti-depressant called out constantly to passers-by, complimenting them on their appearance or otherwise shouting a cheerful greeting as many as twenty times per minute, depending on the number of people outside. He was there every day, chanting in a sing-song voice.

"Good day, sir! How are you!"

"Ma'am you're looking wonderful today!"

Though it was grating to listen to at first, I got used to it over time, just like the screeching instrument of the Asian man outside the Harvard Co-Op. The homeless became a regular presence in everyday life, just like the "Pit People," the sometimes violent Goths who occupied the indented space directly surrounding the Harvard T stop.

Inside our room on the top floor, which for most of the year was considerably warmer and always safer than the rest of Cambridge, the walls sloped inward, compressed between the west side of the roof and the hallway. Bringing up boxes and duffle bags, my father kept telling me not to stress myself too much since he was worried about my lungs, but for once I didn't share his concern. We dumped everything in the middle of the common room for me to sort out later. It was a total mess, and there were still three people who had yet to arrive.

My company's boxes had been deposited safely, for the time being, in the office of Dean Harry Lewis. I recognized the Dean's name because he was also a computer science professor, and because he had written a long essay that had been distributed to every incoming student entitled "SLOW DOWN," referring to our voracious appetites for activities of all kinds.

Before long, I was among the group of students at the bottom of the entry who were waiting around outside for new arrivals. We perked up at the sight of a maroon mini-van when it started heading our way. I noticed that its license plate characters had an unusual syntax. In Ohio, license plates always had three letters on the left followed by three numbers on the right. This plate, from Virginia, had all of the letters grouped together, and then I noticed something else—the word "GOVERNMENT" written in small print above.

When the mini-van pulled directly in front of the dorm so that we could see through the open passenger-side window, everything connected. A blonde-haired woman had her hands on the steering wheel, and a man camouflaged by a thick beard sat beside her. It was the forty-fifth Vice-President of the United States, and the man who had won the popular vote in the 2000 presidential election.

Everyone realized it at once: Al Gore III was going to be in our entryway. The news of the Vice-President's arrival traveled from person to person, entryway to entryway, and then dorm to dorm. Within minutes, the entire Yard knew who had arrived in the maroon van. Then, the man I had seen on television, the man I had desperately hoped would win the presidential election, stepped out, and came right up to me.

"Do you know where there's a bathroom?" he asked with a slight southern drawl I immediately recognized. I let out a huge smile.

"Yeah, I think there's one right up there in each of the rooms," I said, pointing to the open entryway door. "You have your pick." When the Vice-President re-emerged, I joined in the throng of overzealous students who wanted to shake his hand. He kindly obliged us.

My parents had to leave shortly thereafter to avoid the wrath of the Harvard University Police Department, and I said goodbye, giving them both hugs. I saw their Volvo circle the Yard, and then it was out of sight, leaving me surrounded by a steadily growing pool of students, the Arminis, and the belongings of Al Gore.

A Massachusetts native, Nathan was the first of my roommates to arrive. He was exceptionally tall, and his mood was easy to read by one of several grins that frequently crept across his face. There was a grin that meant he saw a girl he liked, a grin that meant he was about to do something mischievous, and a grin that just meant he was happy.

I had always assumed that I would be the token computer nerd in my room, but Nathan instantly rendered that assumption false. He brought at least three giant, black desktop computers with him, several monitors, an assortment of modems, sound cards, USB hubs, and various other gadgets. He explained that even though he'd only be using one computer for his school work, the others were business-related. I was impressed. My business couldn't afford that many computers.

Brian, the football player, was next to arrive. He had already been at Harvard for more than a week for football practice, but had been assigned temporarily to a different dorm. Once he moved his luggage in, he wasted no time getting out. He already had his group of friends, and I guessed that they all weighed about twice what I did. It was clear that we wouldn't be seeing much of Brian.

Wentao, meanwhile, was nowhere to be found. No one, including the Arminis, knew anything about him, except that he was coming from very far away. When it was time to call it a night, Wentao still hadn't arrived. Nathan and I decided to share one of the two bedrooms, leaving Brian by himself.

The next morning, we woke up and headed over to Annenberg for our first breakfast of the school year. Just as it had been in April when I had visited, the hall was packed. Domna was still in the exact same place, swiping cards as if she had never left.

At breakfast alone, I must have met at least ten people. I could scarcely remember a person's name before someone new showed up with a tray full of food. After a while, I started to ignore names completely, just assuming that I would forget them. If I found the person to be interesting, which I almost always did, I simply asked them to remind me of who they were once they were about to leave. I noticed other people doing the same thing.

The Class of 2005 Freshman Register, which I had completely forgotten about until it arrived as a small volume bound in black and gold, proved to be incredibly valuable for finding out more about the legions of students surrounding me. The Register worked just like a yearbook, only temporally in reverse: instead of using it to recall memories of your friends, you used it to select who they might be in the first place. · It indexed students by first name, last name and hometown, and even said which high schools they had attended right next to their home addresses. Some students' photographs were much better than others. At the miniature size it was re-printed in black and white, my own entry made me look life a giraffe. It was still better than being listed in the paper insert of "Faceless Wonders"—students who had failed to turn in a photograph or pay the fee.

Some of students went through the Register, which everyone called the Face Book, from cover to cover, circling the photographs of students of the opposite gender they thought were "hot." I felt the twinge of my conscience when I heard about this explicit highlighting of attractiveness.

"Then again, it's not that different from how we all analyze people face-to-face," I thought. Nonetheless, my Face Book didn't have any circles in it.

Over the two weeks that followed, the logistics of daily life were governed by a small, beige, brochure-sized pamphlet labeled "2001 Calendar of Opening Days for New Students." It contained details on absolutely everything going on at the College, from the Orthodox morning prayer services that I knew I wouldn't be attending, to auditions for music groups I had never even heard of.

I flipped to the first page for September 2nd.

"Students may pick up their trunks and parcels in the Science Center, Room 117 located on the first floor near the Oxford Street entrance," it read, as long as we showed up between 10:00 A.M. and 2:00 P.M. I needed to get my computer, so I decided to head over to the Science Center.

The mail room, located in the basement down a long corridor filled with tiny mailboxes, did indeed have my computer, which had been shipped UPS from Cleveland. The staff lent me a cart to haul my three cow-spotted boxes across the Yard. Unlike most people, I had a desktop with a sixty-pound, nineteen-inch monitor. It was state-of-the-art when I bought it, but not my best decision ever given the lack of elevators. My mother had scribbled all over the boxes to make sure that they got to the right place, and so had someone else, in Arabic.

I checked the monitor box and the third box. I found Arabic on all of them.

"That's a little weird," I thought as my computer bumped along the pavement toward Grays.

By the time I set up my computer and returned the cart back to the mail room, it was almost time for lunch again. Everyone seemed to be motivated by some inner spark, making the process of meeting people as exciting as it was exhausting.

From there, I headed back to the Science Center to set up my e-mail account and check my mailbox. The Faculty of Arts and Sciences Computer Services department, also known as FASCS, instructed everyone to read a set of long and obvious rules about computer use, after which you had to take a quiz to be given the ability to set your account password. My FAS username was "greensp." At first, I thought they had truncated my name at eight letters due to the inherent limitations of older MS-DOS systems, but then I realized that "greensp" only had seven. I felt robbed. With no choice in the matter, I took and passed the quiz on the rules of ethical computer use.

Opening exercises were at 3:15 P.M. in Tercentenary Theatre, which was only a few paces away from Grays. I stood toward the back of the crowd near the towering Widener Library, watching and listening intently. Lawrence Summers, the new president of the University, was to welcome us formally. The man already had rock-star celebrity status among the students, who affectionately called him Larry. The awkwardness he radiated in social settings more than offset his honorific and last name.

"If I may, welcome, fellow members of the class of 2005. Having just returned to Harvard, I think of myself as a member of your class," he began. With those two sentences alone, I knew that he wasn't going to be someone I rushed to hear speak, unless his style underwent a major overhaul. He paused awkwardly between each word and sentence, and he shuffled while he talked. Then, I perked up.

"This class is truly a remarkable group of people. Already...you include professional level musicians and successful Internet entrepreneurs, published scientists and published poets, star athletes and dedicated social service providers, speakers of more than a dozen languages, and experts in countless areas. Every one of you has stood out...and every one of you has great potential."

At least based on his platitudes, President Summers seemed very happy to see us. He then began offering advice.

"First, follow your passion, not your calculation. What you will remember of your time here will be the special experiences, the things that really catch your imagination. Choose courses that cohere. Follow a program towards your objectives. But most importantly, do what catches your imagination. If there is something you really want to do, some curiosity that you want to pursue, make sure that you do it, and don't let anything stand in your way."

"Second, the faculty is here for you. There is no more important responsibility for any of us as members of the faculty than teaching and working with you, the students of Harvard College."

He followed with a vague anecdote about the economics department that I didn't fully comprehend. Then, he started making sense again.

"The last thing I would say is focus on ideas. This is an extraordinary, rich, and diverse community. There are enormous opportunities of all kinds—extracurricular, athletic, social. Those experiences will have a huge impact on many of you. But I hope that none of you will lose sight of how special this time in your life is. It's a time to learn. It's a time to expose yourself, as you likely will only do during this period in your lifetime, to ideas that are completely different from what you have done, what you have seen, perhaps even from what you will see."

After the ceremony was over, I went back to Grays to try to relax and unpack. Wentao, our missing roommate, arrived from China during the middle of the day after battling international airlines and complications with Harvard's own office for international students. He was very down-to-earth, and spoke surprisingly good English. He explained that he had gone to school for several years in Wales. I did my best to explain American idioms to him as fast as I could. He had a penchant for calling everything "bloody."

At 8:00 P.M., everyone in Grays Middle was required to attend an entryway meeting with our new proctors, the Arminis, in the Grays common room. The Arminis started off by introducing themselves once more, and then asked us to memorize five or so facts about the person sitting next to us, which we then had to share out loud. For once, I didn't mind the forced interaction.

Before going to bed, I looked over the schedule for the following day. All freshmen and transfer students were required to take a writing exam for placement into the mandatory Expository Writing class, as well as a mathematics placement exam. I groaned. Fortunately, both tests were scheduled for the afternoon.

I changed into my pajamas, and turned on the small plastic fan that my mother had insisted I take with me. Somewhere between thinking about boxes and Expos, I fell asleep amidst the residual summer heat.

▼

The exams, on which much collective apprehension had been focused, turned out to be reasonable after all. Things were off to a good start.

The number of people I met continued to grow and grow. At the "Ice Cream Bash" (starting at precisely 10:00 P.M. on our schedule), I met an amazingly attractive girl from Greece. I couldn't believe she would even talk to me; in high school, girls had gone out of their way to pretend I didn't exist. Almost as amazing was the sheer volume of ice cream that surrounded everyone. On folding tables positioned in an enormous V shape behind Sever Hall sat large cylindrical containers of every imaginable Ben & Jerry's flavor, waiting for us to sample them.

My social experiment, meanwhile, was proving a miserable failure. Whenever I tried to avoid talking about my interests, conversations just descended into awkwardness. I decided to abandon it once and for all—though I did like my hair better when I didn't look like an extra in an eighties B-movie.

The next few days thrust upon us additional placement tests for various languages and advanced classes, more social events than I had ever attended in my life, and still more people. Out of all of the Asian females in line on registration day, Wentao picked someone who looked like she was ethnically Chinese. Sure enough, she was, and they got to talking right away. It was hardly a rare occurrence—in Annenberg, three times each day, I met a number of people who were insanely bright, but also fun to talk to about virtually any subject.

There were sessions about science classes, sessions about Advanced Standing, lectures about the philosophy of education, advice on how to best utilize different offices in the University—too much for any one person to do on their own. Whenever someone couldn't make it to an event, they asked someone else what had happened there, giving the collective herd of freshmen even more to discuss in Annenberg. The system was positively brilliant, with over-stimulation acting as a catalyst for bonding.

The only thing that struck me in a negative light was the Freshman Seminar registration process. The Freshman Dean's Office had heavily advertised Freshman Seminars as smaller alternatives to standard classes even before anyone arrived. They were conducted on specialized topics, most with no more than twelve students in each. Yet, to get into a seminar, we had to apply all over again, and each application required a separate form and essay.

"Why is it that after completing what's supposed to be the most difficult application process in the world, we have to apply again just to do what we're interested in?" I asked Nathan.

He shrugged. "That's just the way it is, man. It's not so bad." In a way, I knew he was right, but it still bothered me. I was sick of proving myself.

By chance, I also thought I had solved the mystery of the Arabic Gateway boxes. The Crown Prince of Jordan was in our class, living close by in Thayer Hall. Rumor had it that his door was outfitted with a special secure doorknob. I could only guess that his security detail had inspected everything (or at least any suspicious packages, such as those masquerading as cows). I was surprised Harvard hadn't notified us that our parcels would be subject to search, but then again, that might have defeated the purpose of the inspection.

I also learned that a gregarious kid from Cambridge who had shown me around in April, whose last name was Ma, was Yo-Yo Ma's son. So far, I hadn't met a single person that I considered pretentious. I threw my stereotypical views of Harvard out the window.

That Saturday at 10:30 A.M., everyone in Grays Middle grudgingly trekked to Emerson Hall, which I recognized as the same place that our reunion group had used as a home base years before. On the second floor, we found Lecture Hall 201 to have blue carpeting and extremely rickety wooden seats. The thirty of us fit easily into the first four rows of the middle section. We were there to talk about the assigned reading, which had been neatly compiled into a packet with the VERITAS seal on the front and mailed to us in the spring. Like many others, I had done most of the reading the day before. Some of it made sense; other parts were too abstract, which was why, I figured, they wanted us to "discuss."

Our facilitator, a professor of some sort, was only mildly interesting until he deviated from the reading to talk about politeness.

"In Europe, where I used to work," he said without the faintest hint of a European accent, "it was always so, that a man would open a door for a woman. It was just expected. Now, I've watched you, the students here at Harvard, in the ways that you behave, and I've seen that it's quite rare for a gentleman to hold open a door...or carry a girl's books. That was always done, carrying a girl's books. Common courtesy."

"*I doubt that it* always *happened*—," I started to think, but before I could even complete the thought, the professor called on me directly.

"You there!" he said. "What's your name?"

"Aaron," I responded.

"Aaron! Would you carry the books of the beautiful young lady behind you... you, what's your name?" I instinctively turned around and saw that he was picking on Jane Kim, a tall Korean girl who lived two or three floors below me.

"Jane," she said.

"So, Aaron, would you carry Jane's books?"

I started to piece together what we had read with my own personal thoughts on the matter in a rather haphazard fashion, drawing upon a memory from JCWA. "*Women always advocate for equal rights, and that's fine,*" I thought. "*But then doesn't 'equal' mean that everyone should be treated the same? I'd carry Jane's books if she also held the door open for me and carried mine, I suppose...*" Without time to outline my thoughts, I succumbed to the intense gaze of the professor and the silence of everyone else in my entryway, blurting out a single word.

"No!"

The silence continued for a split second, and then the room filled with laughter, including my own, after I realized what I had done.

"I mean, not unless she was also going to carry books for guys, too," I tried to explain, but it was too late. The professor was clearly not expecting my response. Neither was Jane, who looked genuinely insulted. I felt awful.

The episode with Jane was the first real impression of my personality that I'd been able to make, and it was totally wrong. Afraid the entryway might think I was a male chauvinist, I tried to figure out the best way to apologize. Quickly, I designed a gift certificate for a fake book-carrying service, "WE-CARRY-BOOKS-FOR-NOBODY." The certificate went into detail about the origins of the fake service, which were inextricably tied to my equal rights reasoning. Fortunately, Jane liked the certificate, and we assured each other that there were no hard feelings.

That Sunday, our calendars informed us of The President's Barbecue, to be held in the presence of President Summers himself. The President had attended a barbecue on Saturday, too, so that he would have the opportunity to meet more freshmen. We were all very eager to see if the tales of his abrasive personality were actually true. Nathan, Wentao and I walked over to the Sever Hall courtyard, where we eventually settled down at a folding table with a paper tablecloth. Not long after, other students sat down next to us.

"I'm Raluca," said a girl with jet black hair. "Pleased to meet you." As soon as she spoke, she stood out. Her accent placed her origins somewhere in Eastern Europe.

We all introduced ourselves. We learned that Raluca was from Romania, and aside from her hair she had the darkest sense of humor I had ever come across. Raluca's roommate, who I thought I recognized, arrived later on. For a while, I tried to remember her name, until she introduced herself and made it unnecessary. She was a totally different person than the one I had in mind from April. Nonetheless, I liked them both instantly; the food was less impressive.

Wentao based his humor largely on his own misinterpretations, and didn't hesitate to laugh at himself or others. One day over a meal, I had asked him if he found American food tolerable compared to what he was used to at home.

"It's not very good," he said. "Never enough rice or noodles! It's alright though, I can have other things. Chinese eat anything with four legs that is not a table."

The picnic continued, meanwhile, and President Summers was surrounded on all sides by students asking him to sign dollar bills that already bore his signature from his time as Secretary of the Treasury. I looked over. Larry was indeed a little bit chubby, but then again, he had managed to do alright for himself (and the country) despite his appearance.

"I wonder if I should ask him whether or not I'm related to Alan Greenspan..." I said aloud.

"Yeah, definitely, go ask him," everyone encouraged. I tried to resist the peer pressure, which seemed odd given the situation, but eventually I gave in once the mob around the University President subsided.

"Hi, President Summers, it's a pleasure to meet you," I finally said after walking over, guessing it was the three-hundredth time he'd heard the phrase that night.

"Hello," he offered back gruffly with a handshake.

"If you don't mind, I'd like to ask you a quick question," I said. "I've heard that you play tennis with Alan Greenspan, and since my last name is also Greenspan, I was wondering if you might be able to find out if I'm related." He gave me a skeptical glance.

"Well..." he started. There was that awkward pause again, the same kind that had infiltrated each sentence of his opening remarks.

"Chances are, if you don't know...then you're probably *not*." The emphasis he put on the last word struck me, because even though he was right, the way he said it made it sound like he thought I was unequivocally stupid.

"I was also wondering about your thoughts on student entrepreneurship," I tried. Judging from the way the President's jowls were slowly twisting, I couldn't have picked a worse topic.

"Well..." he began again. "Entrepreneurship is great for the economy overall... but you shouldn't really run a company in college. You can run your...little business...for the rest of your life...but you can only study with the greatest minds in the world for four years." I had received an answer, but I didn't like it.

I slept reasonably well on my bed that night and the next. It was just thick enough to be called a bed, and not a plank. My roughly cube-shaped Sony alarm clock, sitting on top of my dresser, was set for 9:00 A.M., and it went off accordingly. One of the advantages of crummy beds, I found, was that you were less likely to want to stay in them.

Wandering into the common room, I found Wentao already awake and at his desk, which was next to mine. I had been wondering how much Communist propaganda he'd been exposed to while in China, since Mr. Burry had given us some vague lessons on Mao Zedong's one-party system in ninth grade. I had no idea how much, if anything, had changed.

Wentao didn't even bother with "good morning."

"Did you hear, they just bombed the Pentagon." His tone was matter-of-fact, and yet what he was telling me sounded ludicrous.

"Maybe they think jokes like these are funny in Communist countries..." I surmised.

"Huh?" I asked, sleepily. "That doesn't make sense..."

I sat down at my desk, turned on my computer, rocked back and forth in my oddly-designed, standard-issue chair as I waited for Windows to start, and then double-clicked on the icon for my web browser. It launched immediately, but the screen remained white. An error appeared. *The New York Times*'s web site wasn't loading for some reason.

"That's weird..." I said. In three years, I had never once had a problem with the *Times*. I typed in "http://www.cnn.com," instead. CNN's page wouldn't load, either.

Immediately, I began analyzing the problem. My company's site appeared fine, indicating that Harvard's the internet connection was still up. The two news sites were on completely different subnets, owned by totally separate companies. A local outage wouldn't make them both go down, and neither would an isolated glitch on Harvard's end. Both sites would have redundant connections in the event of a localized emergency or power failure so that they wouldn't go down no matter what. Still, they were down. Both of them.

"You said what about the Pentagon?" I asked in disbelief.

"They put a bomb! And...the World...Trade...Center," Wentao said, translating in real-time from the Chinese news site on his laptop's screen.

It was 8:47 A.M. Quickly, I took a shower and got dressed, and headed straight to the Science Center since we hadn't bought a television for the room yet. I found the building mostly deserted, except for a few stragglers who were watching something in the lecture halls. I peered inside.

The A-V technicians, using one of the few cable television access points within the entire University, had tuned into CNN and were projecting the cable feed onto the massive, multi-story screens in all of the four main lecture halls. Wentao hadn't been kidding at all. The World Trade Center in New York was on fire.

Both towers now were spewing enormous plumes of thick, black smoke, the camera angle making them look as though they were lilting to the side. A picture-in-picture window as tall as a person appeared, showing grainy footage of an airplane tracking closer and closer to the second tower, and then disappearing. The tower exploded. I stood, transfixed. The first tower looked like it was about to collapse—and within seconds, it did.

I ran to Annenberg, where I was hit by a wall of noise when I opened the door. Everyone there was talking about it.

"Terrorism..."

"They stayed at the Charles Hotel!"

"Do you think Harvard is a target? Would they want to kill all the smart people?"

The same conversation was unfolding at every table. While we ate nervously, students rushed into the dining hall, toting freshly printed copies of a special edition of *The Crimson*. It was one page, front and back, with an usually large headline in bold across the top.

TERRORISTS ATTACK
WORLD TRADE CENTER,
PENTAGON
Planes Hijacked, Steered Into Towers

I finished my meal and headed back to Grays. Some students walking toward the Yard were crying; they were from New York. Back in my room, both news sites were finally loading, but very, very slowly. The sheer amount of internet traffic had crippled every major media site.

I scoffed as I read the *The Crimson* article again, which had highlighted a quote from President Bush: "Today we've had a national tragedy." I was hoping for a more definitive show of leadership than that. I didn't even want to know what would happen next.

An emergency prayer service was hastily scheduled for the afternoon. Programs were distributed in the section of the Yard where opening ceremonies had been held only days before, and the bells of Memorial Church tolled amidst dead silence. President Summers spoke in a manner that was neither pleasant, nor comforting.

The Calendar of Opening Days for New Students couldn't guide us anymore.

▼

Despite the chaos that surrounded us, life had to go on. Events were rescheduled, and a blizzard of e-mails kept everyone on track.

My audition for the Wind Ensemble was positively embarrassing, but my Pops Orchestra audition went well. Another French Horn player handed me a basic arrangement of "Somewhere Over the Rainbow," and told me to improvise. He, one other student and Allen Feinstein, the director, listened. I managed to add a few notes.

Somehow, I was accepted by the Wind Ensemble and listed as an alternate for the Pops—the exact opposite of what I had wanted. I e-mailed Allen Feinstein to plead my case, emphasizing my obsession with Muppets, the fact that I collected soundtracks, and the fact that I didn't particularly care for the Wind Ensemble.

I also checked out the International Relations Council, which I had been curious about since high school. Its offices were located in the basement of Thayer Hall which I recognized from my internship in Cambridge with Carl, but since the steps leading down to the murky entrance ended in front of a card swipe device that had been programmed to deny non-members access, I couldn't get in. It didn't take long before someone exited the building, allowing me to easily defeat Harvard's security.

The IRC was situated right next to the office of the Harvard Computer Society, of which Carl had been President. The doors were all crimson, and though HCS's was locked, the IRC's was not.

I went inside and found myself in another hallway. It was really an extension of the first hallway I had come from, interrupted only by the door. There were old Macintosh computers strewn everywhere. Papers scattered the floor, the trash hadn't been taken out in what looked like a month, and there wasn't a soul in sight. A grid of cardboard mailboxes sat next to a copy machine on my right, behind which there were two doors, one on each side of the hall, leading to what I assumed were more rooms or hallways. I began to wonder if I should leave.

Suddenly, the door to the office opened, and a sullen-looking male with a repulsive green shirt and long hair walked in.

"Can I help you?" he asked, as if I were about to order a hamburger and fries.

"Yeah...I was wondering who I'd talk to about helping with the computers. Is Timothy Li here, or Brian Wong?" I had exchanged e-mails with them when I had been given my free period in high school. They seemed anxious for computer help.

"No, there's no one here," he said. "You should really leave." I was taken aback by his candor.

"Alrighty then," I said. "Thanks."

Classes started a couple of days later. In addition to Math 21a and Expository Writing, I chose to take Computer Science 50, the introductory CS course. I wasn't entirely sure that I was picking the best courses, but the catalog was massive and there was no good way to search through it. The on-line version was almost worthless, with countless links to course names, but no ability to look up courses by keyword or professor.

For my fourth course, I hoped to take a Freshman Seminar on facial recognition with Professor Ken Nakayama, but I had to look for a backup in case I didn't get in. Unable to decide on any one course in particular, I figured I would just choose a Core Curriculum course at random. "The Core," Harvard's set of required courses, was split up into eleven areas, of which students were exempt from three based on their "concentration," which the rest of the world called a major. Harvard's tendency to rename obvious terms left a bitter taste in my mouth.

My interview for Professor Nakayama's seminar took place in an unusual skyscraper called William James Hall. The building was a relic of the 1960s, with weird hexagonal imprints in each one of the massive white tiles that made up the building's exterior, and doors that the wind slammed open and shut.

Professor Nakayama's office was on the seventh floor, providing a gorgeous view of Boston's wide-toothed skyline. The Professor was short and bumbly, with large round eyeglasses. I told him about my general interest in science, and my particular interest in working with computers. He raised his head a little bit when I mentioned imaging technology.

"Well, well, Aaron, I think... I think you're the type of person I'm looking for, but then, so are about, uh, thirty other people."

"How many are you interviewing total?" I asked.

"About sixty applied," he said, making my heart sink in my chest. We spoke for a few more minutes, and then I thanked him for his time. Based on my experience with the music auditions, I figured that I was doomed. The interview had gone well.

Luckily, Professor Nakayama had a soft spot for computer nerds. I was accepted to his seminar, and he immediately sent out an e-mail with instructions for picking up the first set of reading materials. I wasn't accustomed to such dense information, especially coming from psychology journals, but I supposed I would get used to it. As I searched on-line for a place where I could find used books such as "Face and Mind," which Professor Nakayama required for the course, I was surprised to learn that there wasn't one. With no other choice, I bought the book new at an incredibly high price.

I found out that I had been accepted into the Pops Orchestra the day before the first rehearsal in Lowell Lecture Hall, which was also the day before the all-day Model Security Council conference being hosted by the IRC at the Kennedy School of Government. I had been looking forward to the first conference, but I had an obligation to make it to the Pops rehearsal since Allen Feinstein had gone out of his way to let me in. Rather than compromise, I decided to try to do both.

In the morning, I got up early and once more put on my Model U.N. attire. I made my way to the Kennedy School, where I was supposed to represent India. I did my best to figure out the country's policies on the fly, with some help from a friend from Annenberg.

I left early so that I could run back to Grays and grab my French Horn, and from there, I ran to Lowell Lecture Hall, just past the Science Center. I took out my instrument, found a seat next to the other French Horns (including the student who had auditioned me), and tried to blend in behind my blazingly shiny instrument. Allen, a music professor at Northeastern University who was a Harvard graduate himself, didn't seem to care that I was late.

I came to learn that the Pops took almost nothing seriously. There were a few intense violinists who overlapped with the Harvard-Radcliffe Orchestra, but by and large, the students in the Pops were not there because they were virtuosos—they were there because they thought music was fun. I was thrilled to learn that one of our first concerts would feature music from a Muppet movie. The two-hour-long rehearsal took a toll on my jaw muscles, but I had never been so happy to be in an orchestra before.

When I had nothing left to distract me from my upcoming courses, I had to face the fact that all of my textbooks were insanely expensive. I wrote down the ISBN numbers of the ones I needed and bought all except one over the internet, charging everything to my account on my mother's L.L. Bean credit card.

"*I'm getting boot points for this?*" I wondered, bewildered.

After applying for my own credit card, I received a response back from Bank One. Despite the fact that I had run a company with good credit history (and multiple cards) since 1998, I didn't have enough personal credit to get a card of my own. Everything for Think had been done under my father's Social Security number.

"Freaking idiots," I said out loud. Nathan turned to see what I was griping about, laughed to himself, and then turned back to his work.

I had gradually learned more about Nathan's company. From the minute he started telling me about it, any dreams I had of meeting my future business partner in my freshman dorm, as Bill Gates had a few hundred feet away in 1973, vanished. As far as business went, I wanted absolutely nothing to do with him. Nathan was paying his way through college by sending out spam.

His company manufactured custom servers that ran a Linux-Windows hybrid setup that he had designed to maximize the amount of e-mail that each modem could push out per minute. He bought and sold mailing lists of people's e-mail addresses. He wrote programs to automatically guess new ones. He had designed software to scan the internet for vulnerable mail servers, including servers belonging to the Pentagon and the government of the State of Tennessee (though he later filtered them out of the pool). Clients could only view his company's web site on a sporadic basis because at all times, one militant anti-spam agency or another was trying to shut it down. He shuffled internet service providers on a weekly basis. Instead of his own name, he used three different aliases to conduct business.

"Do your e-mails at least let people unsubscribe?" I asked hopefully.

"Well, some of them do, some don't. It's up to the customer to include the link in their e-mail, but half of the problem is that the anti-spammers shut down the removal sites." It was indeed a serious business. He sold his servers for thousands of dollars each. Even though each one had multiple modems and multiple hard drives, they cost him only a couple hundred dollars to build.

"*This is all highly illegal...*" I couldn't stop myself from thinking.

It seemed like a risky way to start off the year. One of the other students in our entryway had already been kicked out of the College. No one would explain why he had suddenly disappeared, but rumor had it that he got so drunk during freshman week that he stumbled into another room, thinking that it was his own—until the female owner of "his" bed arrived and began shrieking.

Nathan wasn't stupid, though. He knew that he would be caught in an instant if he used the Harvard network for business purposes. To avoid detection, he ordered the maximum number of telephone lines allotted to our room. Then, he paid a visit to the girls across the hall to ask them if he could order some of theirs. Much to my surprise, they agreed to help Nathan out. Nathan ran the phone wires across the hall, taping them to the floor underneath our doors. Barely anyone knew, since one had to climb all the way to the fifth floor just to see the wires. Even then, it would have been hard to guess that they were being used to proliferate a global spam network.

CHAPTER 12

The Stick

Once courses began, CS50 started off easy for me. Many of the students had never used a computer for anything beyond word processing. Our professor, Robert Muller, was visiting from Boston University. I e-mailed him soon after the first lecture to set up a time to visit him at "office hours," when he would be free to meet with students. Even though one of my friends who hoped to become a government computer analyst agreed that he was pretty bland, Muller had worked at Apple.

"Section," which was what everyone called the small break-out groups that we were required to attend in addition to class, was taught by a Teaching Fellow, or TF, which almost always meant another student. My assigned TF for CS50 was Karolina, a very attractive sophomore of few words, only a year older than me. She was reputed to be a math genius, justified by the prevailing wisdom that not many sophomores were allowed to teach freshman classes. Sadly, her lectures (about lecture) were impossibly dry.

Professor Muller responded to my office hours inquiry very quickly, informing me that he had time to see me that same afternoon. I stopped by, hoping to chat with him for a while about life in the computer industry. He seemed genuinely uninterested in my presence. After telling him my name, mentioning that I had started my own company, and asking him what life was like at Apple, he nodded, said, "pretty good," and waited. Our conversation lasted three minutes.

"*So much for 'taking the initiative,'*" I thought, walking out.

Meanwhile, in contrast to my high school writing class where Mr. Fox had actually taught us how to write, Harvard's Expository Writing was simply a mild form of torture disguised as busywork. I had been placed into the "Reason and Religion" section, my fourteenth choice. There was no lecture: the class was taught entirely in section, though our teacher was called a "preceptor," and not a "TF" for reasons that I didn't understand.

I assumed that all of our paper topics would be germane to either reason or religion, but the phrase turned out to mean "The Philosophy of Religion," which is exactly what our $75.00 textbook was entitled. While I might have been interested to learn about the philosophy of particular religions, the abstract, over-arching essays our preceptor focused on didn't interest me in the least. One day, during a discussion, a student posed a question.

"What if there's *half* a God?"

As our preceptor pretended that this was a deep and thought-provoking question, I restrained myself from saying anything that might have been construed as insulting. The moment we were allowed to leave, I escaped as fast as I could with my copy of the day's photocopied guide to "good writing."

Math 21a was also taught entirely in section, but there were different sections for different concentrations. The Computer Science section was taught by a quirky old man who seemed like he had been around Harvard for far too long. At least sixty years old, he was almost completely bald except for two rows of white hair along the sides of his head. He tended to look at the ground when he talked, but always in an excited voice, about concepts that were always slightly more complicated than anything I could wrap my head around on the first try. His name was Paul Bamberg.

Professor Bamberg wasn't actually a Professor, but he wasn't just a Teaching Fellow either. His official title, Senior Lecturer, was the highest title that he could earn without being a Professor. Paul, who was on a first name basis with all of his students, had at one time been the chief researcher at a company called Dragon Systems, which marketed the voice recognition software that he had invented in the 1980s. I was awestruck.

"He was my Physics 1a professor," my father said upon learning that Paul Bamberg was teaching me math. "In 1971!"

Paul later explained to us that he had taken several years off from Harvard to work at Dragon. When the company was sold to Lernout & Hauspie, a company he referred to as "the corrupt Belgians," the private sector became less appealing. After the takeover, both Lernout and Hauspie were convicted of fraud and embezzlement.

Everyone in our Math section loved Paul, but it didn't change the fact that I was usually lost. I mentioned my frustration with triple integrals to my father on the telephone.

"I had a horrible experience with Math 21a," my father consoled me. "It was my worst grade ever at Harvard. I got mono midway through."

Luckily, the weekly psychology seminars with Professor Nakayama were fun. They were also long; each lasted three hours, and since there were only nine people in the class, it was unwise to fall asleep.

With my classes and extracurricular activities decided upon, and even a fair bit of free time, life began settling into a routine that I didn't entirely dislike. On October 1st, I received an e-mail informing me that the Technology and Entrepreneurship Center at Harvard would be holding an open house. I found a smattering of students there. Arturo had printed out a packet of available positions in the club that ran several pages long. I chose a title having to do with communications, and spoke to him for a couple of minutes about what I would need to do in order to apply. The conversation didn't seem to go very far; I would say words that I thought made sense, and Arturo would reply as if I had said something completely different. He spoke only using positive, generic terms.

That Friday, we had our first CS50 midterm. I had wondered what tests would be like in college, and I got my answer: Harvard liked "blue books," small lined pamphlets where you wrote your answers separately from the test questions. Then, at the end of the exam, depending on the whim of the professor, the test itself could either be re-collected or stuffed into backpacks as people rushed to leave.

The test—called a "midterm" though it did not take place in, or even near, the middle of the term—was hard. The questions were printed on a pink sheet of a paper that mocked our intelligence. Individually, each question was merely difficult. What made the test truly challenging was that there were so many questions. I panicked, and then wrote as fast as my wrist would let me.

Five minutes into the test, we heard Professor Muller's voice.

"On Part 1, just ignore those directions...about 'potential partial credit'...just ignore that. You don't have to be that specific."

"*Great. Thanks for telling us now,*" I thought. I had already spent five minutes writing a detailed paragraph for Part 1. I skipped to the next part.

Before long, I came to a block of code that had been printed on the pink sheet. Our job was to figure out what was wrong with it.

"The comments are correct," the directions said, referring to casual remarks that programmers often place in their source code to let other programmers know how it works—or in particularly bad cases, to remind themselves later on. We weren't supposed to worry about correcting comments for the purposes of the test, because they were already right. Line 22 had an important comment, denoted by a slash and asterisk.

```
/* void update_previous(int x, int y)
```

I followed the code to find the "update_previous" function somewhere else, and promptly discovered that in order for anything to work, the function had to output an integer. Yet the comment started with "void" instead of "int," meaning that the function would never, under any circumstances, output anything at all.

"*The comments are correct, but if they're correct, the program doesn't work...but the program has to work, we just have to figure out why it isn't working right now. There can't be errors in the comments, since 'the comments are correct', so the program doesn't work. But it has to work!*" The error in the test had put my thinking into an infinite loop, and I was wasting precious time. I decided to skip the question, and then come back to it later.

I never came back; time was up. I grabbed my backpack after turning in the test at the front of the lecture hall, and left the Science Center fuming. I knew I had done horribly.

"*It's not fair,*" I thought. "*Read the directions, and you get screwed. Ignore them, and*" *you do fine. Since when are comments always correct in real life?"*

That afternoon, I had a meeting with Michael, the president of the IRC, and John, its Director of Technology. Unlike TECH, the IRC was so large that the titles actually did seem to mean something.

The club was scheduled to receive a number of new Dell desktops the following day. The problem was that John and I couldn't agree on how to configure them.

"I know you would like to use XP immediately, John," I said, "but I just don't feel that confident that the bugs will have been worked out of the operating system yet." Microsoft had only released Windows XP a few months before, and there was no telling how many updates would be necessary to make it work properly. Windows NT had required no fewer than six "service packs," and Windows 2000 had required four.

"I still think we really should use XP," John urged Michael, in a tone that was amazingly polite no matter how strongly I phrased my arguments. John had been an intern at Microsoft for several summers and was an avid devotee. He had worked specifically on the central bug tracking database, which surprised me, since he seemed to act as if it didn't exist.

Eventually, John won the debate: the computers would have Windows XP installed. He gave me his administrator password so that we could get to work the next day.

Meanwhile, I started up a few projects of my own: making the ancient Macintosh systems in the hallway work on the IRC's network, and untangling the mess of wires that the IRC's offices relied on. I ducked behind every corner, discovering hubs hidden behind couches, Ethernet adapters under books, and cables dropped down from the ceiling to connect to absolutely nothing. It was a complete mess.

The problems I tackled had been neglected for years, so I had no trouble making friends on the IRC staff. As soon as people heard that I was coming, smiles lit up and people's problems came pouring out. Since I had seen almost all of the ailments before in Shaker, I had no trouble doing my job.

There was ample reason to escape to the IRC office, too. CS50 problem sets were getting harder, I dreaded every minute of Expos, and I felt perpetually clueless in Math 21a, even with the help of Wentao and other friends. The only course I really enjoyed was the facial recognition seminar.

On October 10th, there was another TECH meeting for students assigned to communications. Arturo vetoed both of my ideas: re-designing the TECH logo and competing with the Harvard Computer Society to provide web site hosting services to student groups. He spent the remainder of the time talking about Pennsylvania Governor Tom Ridge's upcoming speech at Harvard, which TECH was somehow involved with.

I received a C on my first Expos paper, but I wasn't the only one. Our preceptor tried to soften the blow by handing out his first writing class essay, on which he claimed he received a zero. I didn't doubt it.

What I didn't understand was why he had chosen to propagate the same stupid system of cutting down students to build them up later, instead of actually analyzing each person's work individually. Most of the comments he wrote on my paper implied that he didn't bother to read the entire piece through before commenting on it, since his questions in red ink were often answered in the next sentence.

I tried to coordinate times when I could work in the computer lab on problem sets with friends, since it was always useful to have another pair of eyes to review your code, however tired those eyes were. Working in my dorm was actually more appealing, for the DEC Alpha-based computers in the lab had been outmoded by students' PCs for years, but the CS50 Teaching Fellows hung out in the labs.

Our fifth problem set was complicated by what the TFs kept referring to as "the errata," a web page listing errors in the documentation for ANT, the experimental academic assembly language we were using to build virtual machines. A gruff-looking man with red hair and a beard named Dan Ellard was responsible for the project, and he'd given a correspondingly gruff lecture in class. Like all programmers, he made mistakes, but he hadn't had time to fix them before Professor Muller decided to use his software for our course.

After waiting for twenty minutes, I finally flagged down a TF to help me with the problem I was stuck on.

"Is this right?" I asked, pointing to what looked like a bug in the ANT code.

"All of the errors are already on the errata page," the TF said, looking annoyed.

"No, I know, but I don't think this one is..." He looked for a second or two more, squinting at the screen.

"You're wrong."

"Can you explain why it's returning this value then?" I asked. My being wrong had not helped me solve the problem. He hesitated to look once more, but never finished reviewing the contents of my screen.

"You're just wrong," he repeated. A fairly attractive girl had walked up to him to ask for help.

"I hate this," I grumbled to myself.

At the end of October, I spiked a fever. My first visit to University Health Services yielded an unhelpful diagnosis of "viral infection," and at 2:00 A.M., I woke up shivering with an intense craving for anything at all to drink. I didn't trust the tap water that came out of the sink in our bathroom, but my throat was on fire. The air in the dorms was full of dust, which we knew because it collected in huge piles that constantly rolled around the floor.

The only thing left in our MicroFridge was a bottle of cranapple juice that

Brian had bought to use in mixed drinks. I knew it would be acidic, but I didn't care. I drank all that was left.

"*Serves Brian right*," I thought. He went out of his way never to associate with us. Then, I stumbled back to bed.

So many things were happening at once, it was hard to keep track. The IRC network was making progress. Mike Armini e-mailed me to see if I could fix his Dell laptop's hard drive, which had died. The relentless pace of CS50 was now crushing. Each week brought a new psychology journal article (or two) that we had to read in advance and then discuss in our seminar, whether we knew anything about psychology or not. Pops Orchestra rehearsals were fun, but took up valuable time.

On October 25th, faced with a presentation in Professor Nakayama's seminar and an impossible Math 21a problem set the next day, I stayed up until 4:17 A.M. before giving up, causing me to sleep through half of Math 21a the next morning. The day after, my parents arrived for Freshman Parents Weekend, and the food in Annenberg miraculously tasted better as the kitchen switched into parental mode. Due to a heated argument with my mother about whether I needed a pair of "shoe-boots" to help me through the Cambridge snow ("Everybody has them!" she claimed), I completely forgot about the conference I had scheduled with my Expos preceptor to go over a paper. That night, there were plans to go out to dinner at a restaurant in Chinatown with Metin, another Cleveland freshman in Grays, and his family.

After we had been waiting at the restaurant for an hour, my mother still hadn't arrived. We tried to get in touch with her on her cell phone, but it was turned off. Finally, she called. My grandmother, who was also supposed to meet us, had almost been run over by a car as she was crossing the street. She was in the hospital with a broken hip.

The night after that, Paul Bamberg held a reception in his on-campus apartment for the parents of his Math 21a students. One of the perks of being Paul was that your legendary status as an institution within an institution netted a small apartment in Quincy House, one of the dormitories for upperclassmen near the Charles River.

He stocked his small kitchen table with wine and cheese, and spoke to everyone in the socially awkward but very welcoming manner that was uniquely his. My father made a point of mentioning my dissatisfaction with the incredibly rapid pace of the course's curriculum. I had frequently complained to him that there was so much new material each week, there was hardly any time to absorb, let alone appreciate, any of it. Much to my surprise, Paul agreed completely, but couldn't do anything about it.

With my parents gone and the academic year in full swing by November, I finally had a chance to write a comprehensive e-mail to Professor Muller about my thoughts regarding his first midterm. I had received my grade back, and it wasn't pretty: 24/100. The rest of the class hadn't fared much better, which made me wonder about the test. The curve was simply ridiculous.

The topic of grading served as fodder for numerous conversations in Annenberg. "If you can get three out of four questions wrong on a test," I said, "and that's about average for the entire class, does that mean that the students are really stupid, or that the professor has done a bad job of teaching, or maybe that there's something wrong with the test itself?" I asked two of my close friends. One seemed to give the institution the benefit of the doubt.

"I don't know, just because you did badly doesn't mean it's the test's fault, to be fair," she said. She was right, of course, but she also scored a lot higher than I did on most tests.

"True, but at a place like this there are always going to be geniuses who do really well, no matter how hard the exams are," I replied opaquely, "and then the professors can use those students to justify putting down anything at all on exams."

"Yeah, I don't think they really do that," she said.

"Well, anyway, I don't think it makes a lot of sense to have tests if everyone fails. I think that means that the test is what failed." Ten minutes later, I gave up trying to convince her.

"OK, hun," she said mockingly with a big smile.

CHAPTER 13

The Power of Thought

On November 5th, I received a response from Professor Muller about my e-mail. Weighing in at a single line, it failed to address any of the issues I had raised in my two pages of text.

Thank you for your comments Aaron. We'll keep them in mind as we prepare the second midterm. I'm glad you're getting a lot out of the class.

We were also scheduled to review for our Math 21a midterm that day, which made me incredibly nervous. As if on cue, I began to have chest pain and difficulty breathing while I was studying at night. I wondered if I had finally experienced the third pneumothorax that would mean surgery.

Grabbing onto the railing, I made my way down the stairs to the Arminis' suite. Jenny kindly offered to accompany me to UHS, since I was afraid I might pass out. She hurriedly put on a jacket and walked across a darkened Massachusetts Avenue looking more concerned than I was.

Despite the fact that I was clearly hyperventilating, the person behind the counter at UHS shoved a clipboard at me with four blank forms that I was in no mood to fill out.

"Don't you already have my information in your computer?" I asked between breaths. She didn't even pay attention.

It took over an hour for UHS staff to page an X-ray technician. Jenny, the head speech writer for Massachusetts Governor Jane Swift, had to get back to Grays. I was left alone to wait, wondering how each minute that I was not studying would impact my midterm. Finally, an irritated X-ray technician met me in the basement of UHS, took some films without bothering to affix the lead protective sheet I was used to, and then left me to wait again while they were read by a radiologist.

I didn't have a pneumothorax that anyone could see, but I still couldn't breathe. In a syllogistic fit of anger, I made a decision that changed my life.

"*Computer Science requires Math,*" I thought, since the next CS course was intended to be taken simultaneously with Math 21b. "*I hate Math. Therefore, I hate Computer Science.*"

When I got back to Grays, I e-mailed the CS50 general account, staffed by the TFs, to ask for an extension on my next problem set. They granted me a one-day extension, provided that there was a note from UHS that the TF could see.

"And I bet you've never been sick in your life, either," I thought.

Adding insult to injury, Karolina handed back a problem set two days later. She had removed two points for an issue that actually had been listed on Dan Ellard's errata page. I e-mailed her, asking why I had been penalized. A few days later, she wrote that I was right—so she was giving me one point back.

My anger was growing to a boil. In addition to my daily grading woes, the Math 21a midterm had also been difficult, but not just because it contained challenging material. Almost everyone in the class had missed the same question for the same reason: the directions were poorly-worded. Unfortunately for the students, there were only six questions on the exam, and missing a single one was a big deal.

Not knowing who else to turn to, I fired off an e-mail to the Arminis listing my concerns. I concluded with a paragraph to let them know just how serious I was.

> I don't expect anything to result from my complaints, since no one is going to change an infrastructure based on one student's dissatisfaction. However, right now I am angry enough that if things don't improve after this year, then there's really no reason for me to continue with college. I enjoy teaching myself about computers much more than I enjoy sitting in classes, and I'm clearly not getting enough out of the rest of them to justify $36,000 per year. I don't know that I would necessarily drop out, but I just don't see the point of education when it's presented in this completely stupid and backwards form.

I was talking to my parents, too, voicing my dissatisfaction with increasing frequency. I usually fought with my mother more than I did with my father.

"Why shouldn't I just leave now?" I asked again and again. "What's the point of staying here? They just treat students like crap. Why do I need that right now? Isn't enough wrong with my life already?"

"You need a college education," my mother replied. "How are you going to find a job without one?"

"I'll work for myself!" I said. "I don't need to report to anyone. I've already got plenty of that here. I'm sick of people telling me what to do. I can come up with my own ideas."

"I don't doubt that you can," my father said. "But what happens if your business doesn't work out? Then what? You'll need to find a job then, and if you do, having a diploma helps."

"Thanks for the encouragement," I said bitterly. "Now I want to stay here even more, knowing I'm destined for failure."

The conversation would at that point repeat itself, except louder as I grew increasingly agitated. Nathan raised his eyebrows more than once when I was on the telephone. (Wentao, who worked for the first part of the year in his bedroom, was usually spared.) Nathan didn't seem to be unhappy with his situation at all—but then again, his company was bringing in tens of thousands of dollars each month, he had a girlfriend, and none of my familial problems. I callously figured he would survive my yelling.

Despite our disagreements over what was considered "kosher" in business, Nathan did bring some life to our room. When it was our turn to host the weekly study break, he took charge, making sure that all the refreshments were in order. He was a good-natured kid, and I really liked him, even if I didn't like the way he made his money.

In mid-November, I asked Michael Armini about the possibility of doing a "special concentration," where you could make up your own line of study. Apparently, I had to talk to Dean Deborah Foster about the topic. I made a mental note to get in touch with her when I wasn't studying for my next impending midterm disaster.

November 11, 2001 was the date of the first Harvard Pops concert, and it was a blast. The theme was "Monster Pops," and I volunteered to design the posters that went up all over campus. Pops members were strongly encouraged to deviate from standard attire at concerts, though tuxedos were expected of gentlemen. Accordingly, I went to grab my father's old tuxedo from my half of the bedroom closet that Nathan and I shared. There was an important piece missing.

With exactly thirty minutes to get to Lowell Lecture Hall for the orchestra's call, I had no way to fasten the two halves of my shirt together. I considered using my cufflinks, but decided that they would look fairly odd protruding from my chest.

When a frantic call to my parents yielded no further data on the buttons' location, I hung up and went for the next best option: a plain white shirt, which I hoped no one would notice underneath the tuxedo jacket. I didn't want to give anyone cause to send me back to my status as an alternate. At the last minute, I grabbed a pair of sunglasses, Simon's pair of turtle slippers that I had stolen from his bedroom in Cleveland, and my stuffed spider, Jeepers Creepers. It was the closest thing I had to a monster. From that day forward, I never arrived at a Pops concert without sunglasses and turtles in tow.

Not every note at the concert was perfect, but nobody cared. It was hilarious. For once, I felt like I actually belonged somewhere.

The next night I had dinner with Jenny and Mike Armini in Annenberg, where we talked about my dissatisfaction with academics. Instead of circumventing the core issue, they acknowledged straight away that Harvard was the wrong place for someone with my interests. They also suggested speaking with Jeremy Knowles, but then mentioned that getting on his schedule was a hopeless endeavor. It wasn't exactly what I wanted to hear, but their honesty was refreshing at the very least.

I had e-mailed Carl Sjogreen about my dissatisfaction with the "Harvard experience," and quickly received back a supportive reply. Apparently, I was not the only one who hadn't been in love with coursework. "For me, classes were interesting probably half the time—I can help you pick some good ones once you are out of the requirements phase, but largely 'the price I paid to live at Harvard,'" he wrote.

Depressed, I sent off an e-mail of my own to both of my parents, reporting my Math 21a midterm grade, a 40/60. Later, I pointed out that a 67% once would have been a "D."

On the receiving end of my complaints for three months, my father had finally had enough. I repeatedly told him that I didn't feel like anyone was listening to me about my issues with grading, except perhaps the Arminis.

"Maybe since you've donated money they'll listen to you," I mentioned on the phone one day.

He seemed skeptical. "Well, I'm definitely not one of their biggest donors, but I am an alum...I'll write to them if you want." The next day, he wrote an e-mail to Paul Bamberg, and copied members of the Freshman Dean's Office.

> Aaron informed me yesterday that he received a D on his latest mid-term in Math 21a. As the parent of a college student, I guess I should not be hanging on every grade. I also can easily imagine that you do not have time to correspond with every parent of every student who has a bad test. However, in the present case there are circumstances that lead me to want to check into the matter and to convey my own concerns and opinions.

He repeated much of what I had told him on the phone, and then continued.

> As for my views of the situation, I will now draw on some lessons from my own undergraduate education via Professor Quine. If Aaron, despite putting forth adequate effort, cannot do better than a D on a properly-crafted exam in Math 21a, then either the admissions office and the mathematics placement exam were both shockingly defective, the advising process was deficient, or there is a profound problem (e.g., the pace) with the course. I will admit that I cannot be certain what conclusion is correct, but in light of our earlier conversations I'll bet that you know which way I am leaning. If the last alternative is the most significant, then I would have to voice my strong objection that sorting out students has taken precedence over educating them. Frankly, it makes a mockery of the high-sounding rhetoric about the commitment to undergraduate education that accompanies such events as the installation of new university presidents.

> Let me add that I completed an interview for Harvard College two days ago. Consequently, I had the chance to read the first sentence of the Personal Interview Report form: "Applicants to Harvard College compliment the University by applying, and they deserve our courtesy and respect." I completely concur, but I would add that freshman (and upperclass) students AT Harvard should be also be treated with courtesy and respect. At variance with this wish is the fact that Aaron's lengthy e-mail to his professor for CS50 elicited a one-sentence reply that (at least from Aaron's perspective) addressed none of his concerns. The unwillingness of the course director for Math 21a to acknowledge the flawed wording of the question on the first mid-term that many students answered in the same "incorrect" fashion is another example of

a striking lack of courtesy or respect for the students. I advocate not for excessive concern with grades, but for grades that reflect understanding and, to some extent, effort. Otherwise, the University confirms those students who cynically regard higher education as merely a more expensive game than secondary school.

I am convinced that freshman year does not have to be this inhospitable, this un-welcoming, if the real goal is "the pursuit of truth, insight, and understanding," as President Summers would presumably agree. Yes, students must be channeled into concentrations for which they have the requisite aptitudes and motivation and some sorting must be done, but does it really require this sort of impersonal bashing. As Aaron has found, there is much that is positive, even extraordinary, about Harvard, but the classes should not be, as a friend of Aaron's and recent graduate recently put it, the price to be paid to stay there.

To the Freshman Dean's Office, it was just another routine matter of a parent complaining about grades. Professor Neil Greenspan's message was sent to the Associate Dean of Freshmen, who forwarded it to the Freshman Dean responsible for Grays, who forwarded it to the Office of the Registrar, who dispatched it to a data entry clerk, who quickly read the first and only sentence necessary to update the Harvard Educational Records System.

Aaron...received a D on his latest mid-term in Math 21a.

▼

It was unfortunate for a man named Philip Bean that he decided to become, of all the professions available to him, a college dean. As Raluca, her roommate and I all noted with considerable amusement, Dean Bean's name rhymed. A few days after the Pops concert, an e-mail arrived from him.

I am writing to invite you to pay me a visit so we can chat about how things are going. Your dad sent an e-mail, which I must share with you, that suggests that you are feeling quite adrift and ill-served by the College. At the same time, I got a slightly different impression of the situation from your proctor. I would appreciate hearing what you have to say about your experiences thus far, and to see if I can be of assistance to you as you sort things out.

I knew at once that the meeting would be pointless. I had expressed the exact same sentiments to my father as I had to the Arminis.

"*Adrift?*" I thought after reading Dean Bean's message. "*How about pissed off?*"

On my first day of Thanksgiving break in Cleveland, Karolina sent out our individual exam grades. I earned an 18.5 out of 60. Karolina added in parenthesis, "not too ridiculous, do not worry too much." I disagreed. I thought that it was beyond ridiculous.

At Thanksgiving dinner, I was uniquely thankful for the food in front of me, which was far better than the monotonous selection in Annenberg. I spent most of the break trying not to think about my problem sets or exam grades. Instead, I started to read the first chapter of the kids' book that my mother had been bugging me about, *Harry Potter and the Sorcerer's Stone*. It was surprisingly good. I curled up in my bed and sat there for hours, just reading because I wanted to. I hadn't read on my own—except what teachers wanted me to—in years.

Within three days, I had finished the first three books of the series. I took the fourth with me on the way back to Boston. I could hardly put it down. All I could think about were the creepy similarities between Harry and myself, how much I wanted to go to Hogwarts, and how little I wanted to go back to Harvard.

Back at school, I recounted my simultaneous exhilaration and frustration over *Harry Potter* to one of my friends, who almost jumped out of her skin. A giant poster of Daniel Radcliffe, the British child actor who played Harry in the movies, adorned the space above her desk on the top floor of Massachusetts Hall. It loomed at you when you walked in, as the ceiling jutted into the room, taking Mr. Radcliffe along with it.

"J.K. Rowling is my new hero," I told her. "Not only does she have an iron grip on the press by refusing to divulge any details about the next book, but she gets everything right! Her description of Rita Skeeter is dead on based on the reporters I've talked to, and the fact that Harry isn't perfect in a lot of ways, unlike most 'hero' characters who *are* perfect except for their one 'fatal flaw...' Her writing is actually believable. Except that it's all magic, so it's unbelievable. But you know what I mean."

"Yeah, her characters are definitely multidimensional," she agreed. "I think I'm Hermione." I smiled. It couldn't have been more obvious.

"He has enemies, too, which is so key," I thought aloud. "You rarely read a book where children have real enemies their own age... But there are these people who know about him, but aren't sure what to make of him, and so they just sort of hate him by default. It's just like what I went through—there were all these people who hated me, probably based on what idiot reporters like Rita Skeeter wrote, and there was nothing I could do about it. I don't know how she knows about that particular phenomenon, but it's so true. I felt like she was writing about me as I read that. I mean, fortunately, I'm not an orphan, but I even *look* like the kid!" I said, eyeing the poster.

We proceeded to exchange gossip about the people in our respective hometowns who irritated us, without fear of retribution for being too intolerant or arrogant. We talked until two o'clock in the morning, covering myriad topics from problems with our families, to problems with roommates, to the requisite meaning of life. In the end, we sadly admitted that no matter how hard we tried, we'd probably never make it to Hogwarts.

The next morning, still wishing I could have breakfast in Annenberg along with Harry, Ron and Hermione, I checked my mail in the Science Center to find an official Harvard University envelope from the Freshman Dean's Office. I ripped it open as I walked back, reading until I almost fell up the stairs.

Dear Aaron:

Each semester instructors are asked to report unofficial mid-semester grades to the Registrar to help resident deans identify students who are experiencing difficulty in their coursework. The Freshman Dean's Office has been informed that your standing in MATH 21a is D. This is likely not what you had hoped for in this course. I would like to be of help to you in discerning the source of your difficulties. Instructors often provide suggestions in their reports, and we may be able to identify resources and strategies that you could employ to help you reverse this situation.

Written on the same day that Dean Bean had e-mailed me about my feeling "adrift," the letter went on to suggest that I devise "a good recovery strategy" with my instructor's help. Now, it made sense. I wasn't adrift. I was one step away from failing.

"*Well, I got my wish,*" I thought. "*Now, I'm just like Harry Potter. I suck at classes.*"

Against my better judgment, I scheduled my visit with Dean Bean for the following morning, before Math 21a. As it so happened, I had a review session that afternoon with our Course Assistant, Bill. He was a friendly math nerd who did his best to distill Paul's brilliance into concepts we could actually grasp—except that Bill was a fairly amazing mathematician himself, so his idea of distilling concepts sometimes didn't go far enough.

Our section was on the second floor, and I lazily opted for the nearby elevator. There was one other woman inside who was picking up her child from day-care. The extra-wide freight door closed in front of us. Though the distance we needed to travel was no more than twenty vertical feet, the elevator stopped after about twelve, between the first and second floors. It was stuck.

"*Just my luck,*" I thought. Even though the Cambridge Fire Department was across the street from the Science Center, it took almost forty-five minutes for the firefighters to arrive and manually separate the doors. I arrived more than a half-hour late to section, and not in the mood to learn. Afterward, I approached Bill.

"Am I getting a D?"

"No, I don't think so!" Bill said. "Why would you assume that, may I ask?"

"It's sort of funny, actually. I got a letter in the mail this morning from the Freshman Dean's Office, informing me that I had a D in Math 21a."

"I can double-check for you if you like..." he said, poring over his grade book. "No, it looks like you have a B, maybe B-. Not a D." I thanked Bill and let out a smile through clenched teeth.

Later, I had the opportunity to meet with Dean Bean regarding my grades. Sitting across from his desk, I thought that the Dean was probably one of those kids who got picked on a lot in elementary school. His real hair was slicked across his head with so much gel that it almost looked fake. He spoke impeccable English, so that with each word out of his mouth, you felt progressively stupider, even though nothing he said was actively condescending.

"Your father seemed to indicate when I spoke with him that you were having a less than satisfactory time here at Harvard," he said. "I just wanted to find out what specifically you were finding difficult."

I launched into a politically correct version of the pitch I had given my friends about testing. "Correcting for 'grade inflation' is actually counterproductive when it doesn't exist to start with," I argued. Coming from a student who was earning a D, I could tell he wasn't very impressed. I decided to set things straight.

"I was pretty surprised to get your letter about Math 21a," I told him. "I didn't think I was doing that badly. I mean, I've never liked math that much, but a D is pretty bad. So, I checked, and I'm not getting a D."

"Oh, well, I am pleased to hear that. Even so, Aaron, you know, a lot of students have trouble with their academics during their first year here, so don't feel as that you're that unusual of a case. It's a big change from high school for a lot of people. We'll just have to take care of you and speak with your teachers to make sure that you get back on track."

"Actually, I'm finding Harvard to be easier than high school," I said.

Dean Bean continued his pre-conceived speech. "When I was studying at Oxford, it took me a while to figure out that I was interested in History. When I finally discovered the proper subject for me to be studying, I found that I could do very well at it, as I'm sure you could do if you could find what you are interested in."

"*Is he saying that I'm too stupid to do Math or Computer Science?*" I was having trouble discerning the real meaning of his words.

"Harvard doesn't have a department that lets people study what I'm interested in," I pointed out.

"And what's that?"

"The intersection between entrepreneurship and computer science."

"Well, you should talk to Dean Foster about the possibility of a Special Concentration then. But in the meantime, don't worry so much in general about your grades."

My destiny of "help and hard work" outlined in Dean Bean's letter was at least half fulfilled: I was working plenty hard. The facial recognition seminar seemed like a break by comparison to my other courses. It helped that our professor was enthusiastic, and that I actually liked the material. Of course, Harvard's reward for learning in such a manner was a total of zero credits toward the Core Curriculum or any other discipline.

The first experiment that I conducted along with the other students in the seminar involved figuring out what made faces attractive, and how the brain interpreted the visual data that corresponded to them. I already knew that whatever circuitry was actually involved, it was powerful stuff given the number of freshmen I'd met who obsessed over their paper face books.

My friends in the course and I each cut out thirty-one images of male faces, only some of which were real. The rest were computer-based morphs, or composites, of other faces in the batch. In a ritual familiar to psychology students, each of us brought our stack of face cards home with us and harassed everyone around us until they participated in the experiment. I simply spread out my faces on the floor and asked my roommates, and the girls across the hall, and some other people I knew, and anyone else I could find, to rate them in order of attractiveness. Interestingly enough, the image that was a morph of every real face in the batch—eighteen in all—was rated the most attractive on average.

Then, Professor Nakayama recommended adding a twist: flipping the images upside-down. The expectation was that the orientation of the pictures wouldn't make a difference; after all, the faces hadn't changed at all. Yet, the attractiveness data became completely scrambled.

During class, we were shown images of upside-down faces so that we could test ourselves. Upside-down Margaret Thatcher was completely unrecognizable. Upside-down Bill Clinton was difficult to see. Anyone else was simply impossible to recognize. To the human brain, a mouth, a nose and two eyes were apparently completely different than two eyes, a nose and a mouth.

There was something special about faces.

▼

Two days after I met with Dean Bean, Michael Armini sent out a warning not to smoke marijuana to our entire entryway. I read with a mix of amusement and horror that some of the drugs in the area were being laced with "more dangerous and potentially harmful substances such as cocaine."

I spent most of the afternoon at the IRC office, helping a horde of crazed staffers get ready for the upcoming conference. I left the office thinking about the various problems with the IRC's databases, and went directly to Annenberg for dinner.

When I arrived back at my room in Grays, noticing a chill, my jaw dropped.

Dirt, mud and water covered the ground. My small plastic fan was plugged into one of the wall sockets, spinning as fast as it would go. There was the horrible smell of marijuana, despite the window next to my bed being wide-open. It led outside to the small, metal fire escape balcony that Nathan and I rarely touched for fear it might collapse under our feet. There were muddy footprints on the floor and windowsill, leading in and out. I was furious.

When Nathan arrived home, I was waiting for him. "Nathan! Do you know what happened in our bedroom?"

"No idea," he said, confused. "What are you talking about?"

"Take a look," I suggested.

I checked with Wentao, and he didn't know, either. That left one person.

Brian arrived back just after midnight. I let him settle down at his desk before I walked over, hoping that it wouldn't be the last move I ever made.

"Do you know what happened in my bedroom?" I asked.

"Uhh..." he started.

"Were you smoking pot?" I continued.

"Yeah, me and some football buddies were smoking some earlier... We tried to clean up though."

"Well, you didn't do a very good job!" I almost yelled. "That's *my* fan you used, making it look like *I* was the one doing drugs. Not to mention that it's *my* bedroom, and that I'm worried about my lung collapsing again, which probably isn't helped by marijuana smoke, or whatever else you put into the air." He stared.

"Do not ever do that again."

I went back to my desk and deliberated whether or not to go to the Arminis with my problem. It was ironic that of all of the people in my suite, I was the one who was receiving threatening letters from Deans.

Shortly after midnight, I decided that my lungs failing would be worse than the football team beating me up. I walked out the door, and descended the staircase until I reached the Armini's suite on the first floor. After knocking for several minutes, I gave up. There was no answer.

"*Brian is one lucky bastard*," I thought to myself, and tried to go to sleep without breathing too much.

Chapter 14

The Added Insult

The Harvard Model United Nations 2001 conference was, as always, during the second weekend in December at the Park Plaza. Thankful for the excuse not to work for an extended period of time, I took a trip into Boston with some other IRC members to help move boxes of conference materials.

In addition to sharing my job as Director of Technology for the IRC, John was the Director of Technology for the HMUN conference, as well as the chair of a committee. I didn't see how he could fulfill all three obligations, but as an Assistant Business Director, such matters were none of my concern. My job was to sell T-shirts.

Through Keene Advertising, I had historically taken some interest in designing T-shirts, designing databases for T-shirts, and even marketing T-shirts, but I found out that actually selling T-shirts was not my forte. Around me in the hotel, people buzzed with activity as I sat stupidly in my chair and watched them. If I was lucky, I got to watch high school team advisors bicker about the name badge fees. It was only a matter of time before someone had a computer problem.

"Aaron, can you help me with this laptop projector for NATO?" a passing IRC member asked, whose name I didn't even remember.

"Sure...want to buy a T-shirt?" I asked jokingly, raising a medium in the air to put a price on my services.

One of the concerns that I had mentioned to John was the printer set-up: even though the computers were networked, he had decided not to make use of the networking features built into the printers. Instead, each HP LaserJet 4+ was hooked up directly to one PC. The extra step meant that if the wrong computer went down, no one would be able to print. For a conference whose goal was to emulate the bureaucracy of the United Nations, it made perfect sense.

After the first night, I arrived back home in Grays ready to fall over from exhaustion, even though my job had arguably been one of the least tiring available. I borrowed Nathan's CD writer to create a CD-ROM with the latest printer drivers, so that I could network the printers the next day if necessary.

The following afternoon, every printing device in the building seemed to go haywire, including the copy machines. None of the equipment was very good. The IRC rented it from a local company that appeared to abuse the machines prior to delivery. Knowing this, I had tried in vain to net a sponsor for the conference, but to no avail.

Fortunately, I had my CD-ROM. My first stop was the conference's "Press Corps," where select high school students produced a daily newspaper detailing the goings-on in each committee. I remembered how everyone in JCWA had wished that they could get into the prestigious group, and smiled. Most people in the IRC thought it was a joke.

The Press Corps was using an illegal copy of PageMaker to design its newsletter. I had a better idea.

"I have a legal trial copy of InDesign on my CD if you're interested," I offered the director. She happily agreed.

Installing the new printer drivers seemed to work until the setup program reached the stage of actually creating an icon for the printer, at which point it melted down with a cryptic error message. Technically, I hadn't made the printer problems any worse, but I hadn't solved them, either. I went to look for an internet connection.

Unbeknownst to me, somebody also went to John and pulled him out of his committee session to complain about the printer. He went to the Press Corps office immediately, where he found that everything was suddenly very different.

The hotel had no internet access whatsoever, so I rushed back to Grays where I could use my own computer. The only possible explanation was that I had clicked on the wrong link on HP's web site, downloading the wrong driver.

"*I'm almost positive I chose Windows 95...*" I thought, comparing the two file sizes, but they were different. I burned the second file to the CD and hurried back to Boston.

When I entered the Press Corps office, the director looked noticeably less enthused, the printers had magically reverted back to their previous state, and InDesign was nowhere to be found on any of the computers. Everything bore the mark of John. I went back to sell T-shirts, but before I had gone three steps I almost ran into him.

"Did you change all of this?" he asked, fuming. "Nothing was working when I got here, and it wasn't because I set it up that way!"

"They asked me to fix the printer," I said. "I installed a driver—"

"I'm the Director of Technology here! If they have a problem, they should get me!" he said. "And if they could pull me out of committee, then you could have, too!" He walked away in a huff.

Within minutes, another IRC member came running to my T-shirt table with an urgent request.

"One of the kids got a floppy disk stuck in a computer, and we can't print now! It's stuck in the computer that's connected to the printer!" My prophecy had come true.

"Well, I can't help you. Ask John." I wouldn't overstep my authority twice.

"John is in committee," she said, exasperated.

"Well, he's the Director of Technology. I can't do anything."

"Pleeeeeeeeeease. I know you can fix it."

"Yeah, I can, but I'm not allowed! Ask John." She asked me three more times. "I can't do it! Not unless someone on the Secretariat above John orders me to." The Secretariat members could be easily identified as the only college students with huge staff badges and Motorola radios. The girl ran off, and came back with Catherine, who happened to be in charge of all the Business staff. She looked very stressed.

"Aaron. Fix it." she said. She walked away.

"Okay," I sighed anxiously. I walked over to the computer lab.

Sure enough, there was a badly mangled floppy disk stuck in the computer's floppy drive, and the student who had put it there had tried rebooting the computer to fix it. The machine checked the drive for a boot disk when it turned on, and promptly got stuck because the disk was stuck. Cries of "why can't I print?" could be heard coming from at least ten student delegates in the crowded room.

To remove the disk, the computer needed to be opened, but the only tool I had was the miniature Swiss Army knife on my keychain. Luckily, it had a screwdriver. I managed to set aside the monitor and wrestle off the case after a minute or two of tinkering. Then, I used the knife blade to poke out disk pieces.

"WHAT ARE YOU DOING?" someone behind me bellowed. Temporarily ignoring the person, I did a double-take on the knife to make sure that I wasn't about to stab myself. Of course, it was John.

I couldn't take it anymore. "I'm fixing the network that *originally* went down because you *insisted* on setting it up in a way I *told* you would cause problems, and that *stayed* down because you weren't available!" I shouted back at him. The sudden increase in volume caught the attention of IRC members outside. Within moments, several of the Harvard students who worshipped John for his Microsoft internship were at his side.

John continued to berate me in front of everyone. "Everywhere I go, people are telling me, 'Aaron Greenspan came in, and now the printers don't work anymore.'"

"Well, that's one way of looking at it," I said. "People were coming to me..."

"I thought I told you that we were *not* going to use the JetDirect cards!" he said, referring to the network-ready hardware that came with all of the printers. I was pretty sure we had paid extra for them.

"I had the wrong driver before, but I went back and got the correct one," I said, pulling out my CD.

"No! You are not going to install that. I'm the Director of Technology here. Do you understand?" John seemed both angry and adamant, which was usual given his default state of eerie calm. I didn't put up a fight.

"Okay, do what you want," I said, fuming. "But for now, I'm going to put this computer back together so that people can print again!" I turned my back on him and continued my struggle with the floppy drive, my cheeks bright red.

Finally, with a "cling!" a huge metal fragment popped out of the drive, allowing the eject mechanism to work properly, and I reassembled the case quickly. The computer booted, and paper began to flow again at an astounding rate.

"Aaron, I'd like to have a talk with you," John said afterward, pulling me aside into a brightly-lit closet positioned off of the copying room. He was back in his pacifistic demeanor, and proceeded to tell me that he understood my point of view. I assured him that I saw his, as well, and for the sake of getting out of the small closet, held back just how much I disagreed with it. I didn't like being talked down to by someone who was so controlling that he couldn't accept anyone else's help. I just smiled and nodded, like him.

The next morning, I was so worn out that I overslept and woke up midway through the "thank you" lunch for IRC members. Even after I walked in late, the food took an hour to arrive, and turned out to be merely shell pasta. My friends had already been seated at other tables. The Secretariat thanked everyone but John and I for our work on technology—but John still got thanked for running his committee.

▼

We all knew CS50 was only going to get worse before it was all over. The next and last assignment, Problem Set 9, was notorious for its difficulty. We were instructed to write, using only networking libraries written in C, a fully-functional web browser. As compensation for our pain and suffering, Professor Muller stopped lecturing so as to halt the stream of new material, and turned over his three hours per week to various guest lecturers. Richard Stallman, the head of the Free Software Foundation, came and spoke on what our PowerPoint handouts dubbed "dot-communism." Rebecca Nesson, the daughter of Harvard Law School Professor Charles Nesson and a CS50 TF, talked about some work going on at the Berkman Center. She even invited everyone in the class, comprised almost entirely of freshmen, to take a course being offered at the Law School the following semester on the internet and its impact on society.

My family spent a week of winter vacation in Hawaii, where internet access was spotty. I did manage to connect long enough to check my e-mail and find a page about a course at the Berkman Center offered by Professor Jonathan Zittrain, which I realized was the same course that Rebecca Nesson had invited everyone to sign up for. There was a form to register on-line, something most College professors had never even thought of. The next day, I had a response from Professor Zittrain.

Count yourself in, so long as you can master the cross-reg paperwork. (And surely we can find other courses to suit your interests as well --unless you're saying that you know plenty of interesting courses, but somehow had to take your medicine this year with uninteresting but 'necessary' ones.)

It was the happiest I had been all semester.

Back in Cambridge, as soon as I had unpacked, it was down to business: writing the web browser. It was a truly grueling process, mitigated only by breaks for food and occasional naps. Even when I was desperate to leave Grays, my only alternative was entering the forboding Arctic landscape outdoors. Wentao, who had brought his desk into the common room, could be heard cursing at his "bloody" computer with alarming frequency.

Meanwhile, Nathan flew through the assignment. His browser was crashing just as often as ours, but he had figured out a shortcut. He designed his program so that if the user typed in a web site URL longer than thirty characters, an error would appear.

You have typed in a web address that is too long. Please try again.

By the end of the week, my browser crashed only after the user reloaded CNN's web site ten times in a row. I crossed my fingers, hoping Karolina wasn't a CNN freak.

At 2:00 A.M. on January 4th, I received an urgent e-mail from Mike Armini. He was at a conference in Florida, but Jenny was downstairs on the first floor, trying to write Governor Swift's "State of the State" address, and her computer had crashed. I was thrilled to help, since helping meant doing something other than perfecting memory allocation for a text-based web browser that no one would use. We set up a time in the morning after breakfast for me to come by.

I remembered later on that I wanted to tell the Arminis that I had scheduled an appointment with Dean Foster, who was in charge of special concentrations, as they had suggested. I sent them an e-mail.

I wanted to let you know that I scheduled a meeting with Dean Foster for January 24. Hopefully, I'll be able to figure out what to do about advanced standing paperwork just in the nick of time.

Also, do you have any idea who I would contact at HASCS to let them know that I've solved their web-based e-mail problem? If I don't tell them, they'll probably accuse me of trademark infringement, setting up an unauthorized server (although it's not on their network...), etc.

The "web-based e-mail problem" was that no one at Harvard could check their e-mail over the World Wide Web. The College administration had reportedly been looking for the perfect program for over three years. Meanwhile, most people couldn't check their e-mail unless they were sitting in front of their own personal computer.

In about an hour, I customized a readily-available open-source program called SquirrelMail for Harvard's mail server. Once it was up and running on my own server, I told all of my friends about it so that they could start using it, too. I jokingly named my site FASt Webmail. Just to make sure that I wasn't breaking any rules, I e-mailed the head of Harvard Arts and Sciences Computer Services, a man by the name of Dr. Franklin Steen.

> I am currently an undergraduate at Harvard college. After reading some of the articles on Harvard's need for web-based e-mail, I figured I would try something on my own just to see if I could come up with an adequate solution.
>
> I tailored an open-source IMAP e-mail client written in PHP to the fas.harvard.edu domain, and generated an SSL certificate through my web server to enhance the site's security. The site is not being hosted on Harvard's network, and I am willing to take it down immediately if you or anyone at HASCS perceives it as a threat, along the lines of security, bandwidth, or otherwise. I merely wanted to provide another option for HASCS to consider regarding web-based e-mail. (If the latest Crimson article was accurate, going with Oracle probably be both expensive and difficult to maintain.)
>
> I invite you to take a look at what I have come up with, at https://harvard.thinkcomputer. com. Again, if you would like me to remove the site for any reason at all, I would be more than happy to comply.

Dr. Steen never wrote back.

Final exams took place in mid-January, and proved to be about as boring as final exams had been in high school, only longer. The proctors went through the same mind-numbing routine each time. I left the Math 21a exam feeling more depressed about school than I ever had in my life.

At MIT, my friend Tim from high school wasn't faring much better. With no dining plan, he had been struggling with the simultaneous tasks of cooking whole chickens (or at least trying to), finishing difficult problem sets, and finding normal friends, who seemed to be in short supply down the Charles River. We had been keeping in close touch throughout the year, leaning on each other for support and hoping that it would all magically get better, but it all just kept getting worse.

We were at our lowest point one day after I traveled down Massachusetts Avenue on the #1 bus line to visit. Sitting at a table in the MIT student center, we desperately needed something to cheer us up. Taking the initiative, Tim plunked down $4 on a half-gallon carton of Tropicana orange juice, got us two glasses, and started to drink. I joined in.

"We're so pathetic. Neither of us have girlfriends. We hate school. What's the point?" I said, my glass clanking on the tabletop.

"Yeah, I pretty much hate my life right now," he agreed, taking another long sip.

"Are we that bad? I mean really, look at who the girls choose. The football jocks! Can't they tell they're idiots? I don't get it!"

"I know, it makes no sense," he replied. "Finding a girlfriend seems hopeless... I have no idea what I want to do with my life..."

"These guys have no brains, they're not even sincere... And then the one thing I'm supposed to be good at, computers, isn't even fun anymore. The grading is insane, and the assignments are totally pointless. It all sucks. I should just drop out."

We finished the orange juice, bundled up, and moped back to Tim's creepy dorm, looking forward only to six more bleak months in Cambridge, at least five of them bound to be just as unforgiving as the cruel, sharp air outside.

▼

In mid-January, 2002, I worked furiously to complete my final project for Professor Nakayama's facial recognition seminar. The project agreed upon by the other students in the seminar delved into topics in psychology that I found fascinating. We would measure the general effect of a person's face being visible on his or her ability to tell a compelling lie. Our experiment was based on similar research that had been carried out in 1979. Accordingly, my final paper for the course was titled "The Importance of the Face in Deception."

Working with the other students in the course, we videotaped six student actors and actresses who drank a generic red-colored liquid and proceeded to rave about how much they loved it on camera. Watching the videos felt much like watching commercials for Kool-Aid. The catch was that half of the liquids were very sugary, while half were very salty, and thus almost impossible to drink.

My main job was to take the digital video files and design a database and web-based program around them so that other students could sign on to a web site where they could take our test, and see if they could tell who was lying and who was telling the truth. In some of the videos, faces were visible, but in others, they were not.

The data that emerged from the experiment was inconclusive. "Females appeared to do better at detecting lies when the face was present," I wrote, "while males appeared to do better when the face was cut out." The differences were small, though. What was really apparent was that some people were simply much better at lying than others.

By the time I remembered the experiment years later, it was too late.

All of my CS50 grades came back, and I was not pleased. Even though I had done very well on the final, which was totally inconsistent with my midterm grades, points seemed to have been taken off anywhere and everywhere possible. I wasn't sure if Professor Muller had just ignored what I'd written to him the first time, or if maybe the real target of my message should have been Karolina and the other TFs.

Unafraid of repercussions since the course was over, I decided to write one more e-mail detailing some of the flaws I perceived in the CS50 grading structure. In my view, it made no sense to deduct credit for coding techniques that could be brilliant *or* sloppy, depending upon who you asked. Many such issues in science were controversial, in fact. Penalizing students for actually thinking independently had the opposite effect of teaching.

I made sure that the Dean of Harvard College and the Freshman Dean's Office also received the message. They likely lumped it in with e-mails from other grade-obsessed undergraduates, missing the most important point at the end:

The obvious answer to all of these complaints is the curve. Curving grades instantly compensates for unclear assignment directions, contradictory test directions, tired TFs, and many other anomalies that inevitably surface over a semester. It makes students happy because they get higher grades, and it makes the faculty happy, because students "know the material"--just look at the grades! In reality, the probability of the curve exactly offsetting the course's problems is close to zero, but nobody cares. Nobody, except for the Boston Globe, the New York Times, and apparently, me.

The not-so-obvious answer to my complaints is to actually write tests that test knowledge, actually grade assignments fairly, and actually take students' concerns into account. Then, maybe you'll have a good answer for the reporters when they ask you about grade inflation. Then, maybe you can say that you're actually giving students the grades that they deserve.

I was afraid that I would just receive loud, angered shouting in response to my arguments, but Karolina actually wrote a very thoughtful and reasonable message in reply.

Professor Muller, on the other hand, could not be bothered to address the issues. He wrote back a short message with an extra word for added impact: "Thank you for your *detailed* comments." The rest was just pleasantries.

Paul Bamberg got in touch with his Math 21a section shortly thereafter. "First, the bad news," he wrote. "People did not do well on the final. There were only two scores above 100/120, and only one section averaged 79 or better. Overall, A's were scarcer than the general public believes is the case at Harvard." I knew those weren't mine. I kept reading.

"The good news. Both those scores over 100 were in our section, and the average was 79. Congratulations!" I didn't share his enthusiasm. I ended up with a B- in the course, the lowest grade in Paul's section.

"Better than a 'D,' at least..." I thought to myself.

After intersession, Harvard's break between semesters, I found out that I would have to do some extra work to take Professor Zittrain's course at the Law School. According to the Arminis, the Administrative Board of Harvard College did not let freshmen cross-register at other schools. (Even though the Law School was part of Harvard University, it was still considered a different school.) I wrote a letter petitioning the "Ad" Board to make an exception, and sent it to Dean Bean and Professor Zittrain via e-mail. Professor Zittrain replied immediately: "I'd be delighted to have Aaron in the course."

Several days later, Dean Bean replied, as well, explaining why he needed a full week to forward along my petition. His message concluded ominously with, "By the way, I think you and I should have a little chat sometime about the e-mail you sent out to your instructor." It wasn't until the second semester had already begun, at which point I had been auditing Professor Zittrain's course for two weeks, that the Administrative Board got around to making a decision.

Like every freshman, I had been trying to narrow down my course selection from a wide list. "Fairy Tales" and Pompeii, both Core courses, contained lighthearted and interesting subject matter, respectively, so I left them on the list. Economics 1315 and Engineering Science 51 both seemed good, as well, but I only had three spots to fill. I opted for the economics course since I wouldn't receive credit of any sort for engineering, and I had already sacrificed credit for interesting subject matter by taking two Freshman Seminars.

Fairy Tales, held in the subterranean, windowless auditorium of the Sackler Museum, was stuffed to capacity for the first lecture. The professor, a thin woman who held a position in the Germanic Studies department, announced through her main Teaching Fellow that a lottery would be held; those who won would get to stay in the course. Those who didn't would have to choose another. I still needed a backup.

Pompeii, coincidentally held in the same auditorium, didn't have that problem. The room was two-thirds empty due to the fact that Professor Taylor read verbatim from his 8.5" x 11" papers for one and a half hours, twice weekly. The man was like a zombie, taking my interest in the subject and reducing it to mind–numbing static. Sections for Pompeii, where we analyzed the spatial layouts of ruins with arbitrary indices invented by academics who I assumed would have enjoyed Professor Taylor's company, were especially painful.

"Can you really say for sure that one room is more 'useful' than another, even today?" I asked my TF. She gave me a long explanation, which basically meant "no."

Dean Bean and I had our chat at the Freshman Dean's Office several days before the Administrative Board meeting took place. I bided my time waiting for him downstairs by checking my e-mail on the iMac positioned outside the building's spiral staircase. Many of Harvard's smaller offices were former multi-family homes that the University had purchased, pushing out Cambridge residents so that its Deans would have desks where they could write their letters and generally act like Harvard College officials. My Dean's office was in a cramped attic room upstairs.

The meeting was worthless, much like the one that had preceded it. Dean Bean thanked me for my time by rebuking me for asking my father to help.

My father had indeed sent him a long message, because he was almost as angry as I was about the way that I was being ignored. When I finished reading it, I wanted to cheer the way that most people did at football games.

You suggested that Aaron was perhaps interpreting events in too negative a light, and that this pattern of Aaron's thinking might account for much of his dissatisfaction with aspects of his Harvard experience to date. I was willing to entertain this possibility. However, the (not mutually exclusive) alternative is that his first semester experiences offered several legitimate targets of criticism. I do not see how it makes sense to require a writing course that emphasizes content almost exclusively while ignoring writing, its primary purpose for being. Some of Aaron's criticisms of Math21a and CS50 also seem to me to have some merit. Another problem with the theory that Aaron's negativity is the real problem is that he is quite positive about the friends he has made at Harvard, as well as his extracurricular activities.

Frankly, although you explicitly assured me that you care about Aaron and his fate at Harvard, the implicit message of your collective comments seemed to be much less reassuring. Assuming that you accurately reflect the official position of the Freshman Dean's Office, it would seem to be that if Aaron does not fit in (as determined by the Freshman's Dean's Office), then he is welcome to leave. To the extent that I have correctly inferred the official position, I find it unsatisfactory.

I have thought about your statement that issues of equity must be taken into account in considering Aaron's request to enroll in Professor Zittrain's course on the Internet and Society. My guess is that you and your fellow Deans would have a tough time agreeing among yourselves on the definition of "equity," and an even tougher time convincing anyone else that you had the perfect definition. In my view, if Professor Zittrain honestly believes that Aaron can meaningfully contribute to and succeed in his course, and if you do not have some objective basis for thinking that he cannot succeed, then I think Aaron's request should be honored.

Finally, I would note that Aaron's concerns and requests, are not aimed at altering Harvard's investment policy, or dictating the composition of the faculty, or other issues of grand scale that some students take on, perhaps to the neglect of their studies. He is simply trying to find a way to enjoy learning, which is what he came to Harvard to do and which is one of the chief activities that Harvard professes to value.

This, in turn, elicited an even longer response from Dean Bean, who mistakenly ignored my father's degrees and professorship. He totally misunderstood the reason I had asked my father to intervene. I was merely a freshman (and apparently a "very good man" who was "frittering" away much "psychic energy" by focusing on things that were negative), but my father was an alum, a minor donor to the University, and a university professor himself. If my arguments didn't hold sway because I had not yet achieved the status required for the administration to listen, then I thought that someone in my father's position might be more successful at making my case.

Sensing that the battle might never end, and now further enraged, my father gave his next e-mail the subject, "to be read on weekend or holiday." and hit the Send button.

> I will defer a lengthy response to your e-mail of Feb. 1, encourage you to continue your efforts on Aaron's behalf, hold you and your colleagues to your implied pledge to work for Aaron's best interests, and note that none of your inferences regarding my putative misapprehensions are either logically valid or actually true.

My next chat with Dean Bean, which I guessed that neither of us wanted to attend, took place over lunch at the Harvard Faculty Club. Unlike Annenberg, the Faculty Club spared no expense. There was a long table covered in a forest green tablecloth laden with exquisite food of every sort. Knowing that I wouldn't get a similar opportunity to eat such haute cuisine again anytime soon, I helped myself. Meanwhile, I was checking my watch, because I wanted to shop a core course on the Rome of Augustus. By the time our meeting was over, it was too late; I had to find another course to shop.

The Administrative Board met later that afternoon behind closed doors. Its response to my petition arrived first by e-mail from Dean Bean: "no." I sent him an e-mail in response, asking what I was supposed to do for my fourth course. My top picks were being lotteried, and his last "chat" had eliminated one of my options completely.

Two days later, I found an envelope containing a single manila sheet of Freshman Dean's Office's letterhead in my mailbox.

> On Tuesday, February 5, 2002, the Administrative Board of Harvard College voted to deny your petition to cross register at the Harvard Law School, for the spring term 2002.
>
> If you have any questions, please feel free to contact me, pbean@fas.harvard.edu or at the phone number above.

I had thought Dean Bean's e-mail notification had lacked detail because it was informal. Now, I was holding the real thing in my hands. Not only had "the greatest minds in the world" denied my petition to study something that actually interested me, but they hadn't even been able to come up with a reason why.

"What, do they just assume that anyone who is a freshman will automatically fail any course they try to cross-register in?" I shouted at my father on the phone, who deserved the least blame of any of the parties involved.

"I don't know what they're thinking!" he said. "It makes no sense to me."

Later, I remembered Rebecca Nesson's invitation to CS50. It made no sense. "Do you really think they would have advertised the course to CS50 students because they thought they would FAIL it?" I e-mailed my father after we hung up.

To take my mind off of things, I took a trip over to MIT to visit Tim and attend the introductory assembly for the MIT 50K business plan competition. We'd talked about forming a team to focus on the software we'd spent the previous summer writing. Eventually, we were able to convince two of my friends from TECH and CS50 to join up. Team Think Computer set about writing a business plan for the business I already had going.

The 50K proved to be less of a distraction than I had hoped. I couldn't stop thinking about the injustice of a system that actively worked to prevent me from taking a course I was interested in. It was about more than my unhappiness. I had worked as hard as I could since fifth grade to succeed on society's terms. When I got to college, I found out that my interests didn't fit with the traditional view of computer science—or at least not Harvard's view of it. When I asked to study other topics I thought would be interesting, as an aspiring intellectual and an entrepreneur, the answer was simple, unequivocal, baseless, and stupid: no.

That's when I decided to write a letter to President Summers.

CHAPTER 15

Signs of Impending Entrepreneurship

It was controversial, at least among my friends, from the moment it slipped past my lips. One of my friends and I had lengthy discussions about the meaning of happiness. My extended family thought that the drafts were too poignant. My uncle's father-in-law even offered his own version of my letter, which ended up lacking any point at all. In the end, I took the advice of my parents and the Arminis, toning down the harsh parts, but saying everything that was on my mind, in typical fashion.

On February 13th, I walked the hundred yard distance between Grays Hall and Massachusetts Hall, and politely handed an envelope containing my letter to a secretary. The core of the letter was about the quality of teaching and the uselessness of prohibiting cross-registration, but I soon brought it back to the President's own words.

Incredulous at the short-sightedness of those who you rightfully described as "some of the greatest minds in the world," I thought back to your welcoming speech from September 2, 2001. In it, you stated three main points:

"First, follow your passion, not your calculation...Follow a program towards your objectives...do what catches your imagination...and don't let anything stand in your way. "Second, the faculty is here for you. There is no more important responsibility for any of us as members of the faculty than teaching and working with you, the students of Harvard College...Do not feel that you are ever wasting anyone's time pursuing your curiosity or your interest... "The last thing I would say is focus on ideas...It's a time to learn. It's a time to expose yourself, as you likely will only do during this period in your lifetime, to ideas that are completely different from what you have done, what you have seen, perhaps even from what you will see..."

It is not hard to detect the degree of irony present in my current situation. In trying to follow my passion for technology and business--fields with ideas that are constantly evolving--I have encountered resistance purely for the sake of resistance, and from the Harvard faculty, no less.

Even if you cannot sympathize with my current position, then I hope that you at least take away from this letter the message that Harvard has some very real problems. The University's antiquated and inflexible policies (of which admissions officers are seemingly unaware) have indubitably squelched numerous opportunities for motivated students to learn. That is one problem. The ego of the faculty as a whole is another. I found the ease with which some faculty members dismissed your words to be unsettling. The treatment that I received during the first semester from professors and preceptors was anything but welcoming. Thirdly--and I believe this stems partly from the second problem--faculty members' unwillingness to recognize authority at any of the twelve schools but their own is absurd. Competition between Harvard's schools is not the same as competition in a free market economy. It is detrimental to students, and accordingly, should not be tolerated.

A few days later, my father, who had started to read *The Crimson* on a regular basis partly to see if my eternally pessimistic tone was echoed by anyone else at the College, noticed a paragraph in an article about President Summers visiting the Undergraduate Council. He sent me the relevant text.

"Responding to a question, Summers emphasized the power of advocacy in students' dealings with the administration. 'To make arguments on things they believe in and to engage in thoughtful advocacy is the way students can have the biggest impact,' he said. 'We will always listen, we will always read, and we will always be prepared to defend the positions that we take.'"

I had to laugh. A friend had recently explained to me how the President had missed the pizza party scheduled for the freshman residents of Massachusetts Hall, where his office was located.

"I went down to his office," she said, "and asked as nicely as I could, 'Is President Summers going to be able to make it to the pizza party?' And you know what the lady said, his secretary? She looked around for a second, and then she goes, 'Uhh—I think he had to go—to a...wake. He won't be able to make it.' And then later on I heard them talking about it. There was no wake! He was just too lazy to bring his big butt upstairs!"

Having vented my anger, I went back to plodding through my work. It was as boring and painful as ever, though I did enjoy my economics class with Professor Dwight Perkins. There was something incredible about the fact that the economies of South Korea, Thailand, Taiwan, and Japan had been able to pick themselves up to become industrial powerhouses. We discussed whether or not China would do the same.

I continued to drop in on Professor Zittrain's course at the Law School. It was unlike any course I had ever seen before. Everyone in the room except for me had a laptop computer on their desk; I sat on the floor in the aisle. Zittrain's assistant, a law student named Ben Edelman who had done some impressive work of his own, managed two or three machines at the front of the room, which controlled the course's software. Students could type in questions as Zittrain was speaking, rate their interest in the present topic, and access notes that the course's scribe was taking *for* them.

"*What an idea!*" I thought. "*To actually be able to listen to the lecture and think about it, instead of wasting your time working as a copy machine!"*

Best of all, if a large enough portion of the class thought that Zittrain was droning on a topic or drifting off of one, the overhead speakers emitted a loud snoring sound, which was enough to wake everyone up and crack a few smiles. We rarely heard it though, because Professor Zittrain knew his material.

He knew everyone in the class, too. Zittrain called on students frequently, and they wanted to be heard, straining their arms to get his attention. Going to one of his lectures was so exhilarating, it was exhausting. It made me even angrier that I wasn't allowed to take the course for credit, and that I was stuck with Rabun Taylor in Pompeii, instead.

When I arrived back from class on February 20th, there was an e-mail waiting for me from the President.

> Thank you for your thoughtful letter of February 13. I regret your feeling inhibited from following some of the dicta in my freshman speech. I will find out and ask someone to be in touch with you regarding the rationale for the freshman cross registration policy. IF there is not a rationale, we should change it. But I will reserve judgement until hearing the rationale. It does occur to me that you might be somewhat more generous with the benefit of doubt in complex circumstances. It is at least possible that your computer science professor had considerations in the design of his exams that you might not have been well positioned to evaluate. Harvard certainly does have things that can be improved though I must say your tone with regard to the faculty struck and the issues of governance in the university struck me as disproportionate to the provocation. Larry Summers

I sent the President's reply to Mike Armini and Professor Zittrain. Zittrain, who checked his e-mail even more frequently than I did despite the fact that he had just appeared before the Supreme Court, got back to me incredibly quickly.

"And I'm impressed by his reply. Not a feather-stroker, this one," he wrote.

Still, it was all talk so far. I wondered if he'd really follow up.

I'm still wondering.

▼

It took until late February, when I was ordered to dismantle the Macintosh computers I had spent so much time repairing and to haul them across the Yard for disposal, before I realized that my time might be better spent working on something other than technical support—such as the IRC's magazine, the Harvard International Review. The IR, as everyone called it, was a real publication that actually sat on store shelves in real book stores, such as Barnes and Noble. I had worked with the Editors-in-Chief, Shuko Ogawa and Michael Lopez, on a number of occasions while helping them with their computers.

It was a miracle that they were able to produce anything at all: the magazine's network consisted of two five-year-old PCs that crashed regularly and ran pirated copies of Adobe PageMaker 6.5. No one had the first clue about how to actually use PageMaker, and the web site was never up-to-date. I had suggested, hinted, and strongly insinuated time and again that the magazine should purchase new computers with licenses for InDesign (PageMaker's successor in the Adobe software suite). Each and every time I had been met with considerable resistance. Finally, the magazine's technology was in such a state of disarray that Shuko asked if there was anything I could do to help.

"Sure, I can host the site, and I can even redesign it for you if you want," I said.

Days later, the magazine's outgoing technology guru sent me a request for help with hosting by e-mail. We all arranged for Think to charge the IR half of what Harvard itself had been charging the magazine for the exact same service. I also agreed to redesign the site, just as the IRC held its elections. The new Editors-in-Chief would be Nick Smith and Richard Re.

Meanwhile, the IR was scheduled to print its spring issue in mid-March. Two days before it was supposed to go to press, when the office was always full of panic-stricken copy editors, Shuko almost knocked me over.

"Aaron! Aaron! We need an ad! Can you do an ad?" she asked hopefully with a soft smile.

"What do you mean?" I replied. "I thought you had Harmon Kardon still." The inside front cover of the quarterly magazine had featured an advertisement of a glamorous woman lying atop Harmon Kardon speakers for several issues.

"Yeah—we lost the files when we switched to the new printer."

"Oh, that's no good."

"Can you make an ad for Think Computer?" she asked hopefully. "We'll let you put it in for free!"

"An inside cover color spread for free?" I asked, shocked. "How are you going to make any money?"

"It doesn't matter!" she said. "We just need to fill the space!"

Two days later, the IR had an advertisement for the database software I had written in my spare time in Mrs. Jones's computer lab. Everyone seemed to think that it looked quite nice.

Throughout the rest of March, I wrangled with the IR's web site. I had been working on redesigning Think's web site, as well, trying at last to integrate what I had taught myself about PHP. I was eating dinner in Annenberg one day, when it suddenly occurred to me that with PHP, you could update web sites by making changes in other web sites. I shoved down the rest of my food and ran all the way back to my room in Grays. I had to write down the idea.

I decided to call the program Whiteboard, because it would make it so easy to make and erase changes. Best of all, I had all of spring break to ignore my homework and work on it instead.

♥

The entire freshman class was in fits about "blocking," the housing groups we would spend the next three years with. The College had recently changed its regulations to mandate that we form groups of eight or less, down from the previous limit of sixteen. After considerable agony and intense negotiation with a number of my friends, their friends, Nathan and Wentao, and several people I didn't even know, I found myself included in a perfect group of nine. We had one person too many, and no one would budge. The group fell apart, and we had to start all over again.

Finally, after a second round of agonizing meetings, I got together with Metin, a freshman from Missouri named Elliott, and a friend of Elliott's named Jeff. Together we all formed the core of a blocking group. By the end of the month, many friendships throughout the class had been stretched to the limit, as people were forced by the authorities to enumerate their closest friends and leave the rest feeling as though they had been ditched.

The blocking system didn't guarantee that we would all be roommates, but they did assure us that we would all be placed in the same House together. The twelve residential houses, surrounding Harvard Yard to the south by the Charles River, and to the northwest in the Quad, were where the College's upperclassmen lived. Each had a distinctive character.

Placement in the houses was random thanks to the efforts of Dean Lewis, but it hadn't always been. Adams House was still to some extent the artsy house, the Quad had once been the center for football jocks, and Dunster House was the first house ever built. Its inhabitants were once the wealthy elite among all those at Harvard. Yet Dunster also had tiny rooms, Adams residents had a tradition of smoking cigars, and the Quad's lavish, gigantic rooms were a half-hour away from the Yard on foot. No house was perfect.

My primary concern was getting into the house closest to UHS. If my lung collapsed again, I didn't want to have to walk two miles from the Quad to be able to see a doctor. I called the University Housing Office after the Arminis told me that they gave special consideration to people with disabilities.

The Housing Office referred me to the Disabilities Office, but that office said that I wasn't disabled. "Basically, unless you're in a wheelchair, we can't help you," the unconcerned voice on the other end of the phone said.

"But what if I can't breathe? Literally, not breathing. That doesn't count?" I asked.

"No, I'm sorry. We can't do anything. You'll land up where you land up."

Metin burst into my bedroom at 8:00 A.M. to hand over the computer-generated printout that had been dropped in my door's mailbox. It would determine our fate for the rest of college. Some blocking groups had awoken at dawn.

"Lowell House? Which one is that?" I asked.

"YES!" Metin shouted. "I *love* Lowell House!" Metin loved everything, though. I had never heard of it.

"Great—but where is it?" I asked.

"I'll show you," he said. When I saw it, I had to admit that it did seem nice— and it was the house closest to UHS.

Lowell had a giant sky-blue tower, but I had heard the rooms were fairly cramped. We received a mass e-mail invitation to tea to introduce us to the house. The e-mail was sent by the two professors who ran and lived in the house, Diana Eck and Dorothy Austin.

That day, the entire Class of 2005 received similar invitations to their houses. My friends landed all over: Dunster House, Mather House, and Cabot House in the dreaded Quad, far removed from the rest of campus. It was sad to think that we would all be splitting apart, but there was too much work to worry excessively. We still had through May in the Yard and in Annenberg.

My birthday fell on the very last day of spring vacation, when all of my friends were scattered across the country, waiting to board airplanes or buses back to Cambridge. Vaughn, whom I saw regularly in Annenberg, sent me an e-mail when I tried to schedule a date for us all to get together. I was still trying to wrap my head around his colorful personality and his bizarre sense of humor, which often involved food.

Happy birthday and all
I can't go to your thing cos I'm scheduled to be torn to pieces by beavers this weekend. You'll see me in little shreds on Sunday

Enjoy your breadeating

Having served in the Singaporean military ("Singapore has a military? What on Earth for?" we all asked him), Vaughn was three years older than us. Over dinner one night, he explained how he had arrived at Harvard.

"Well, I applied when I graduated from high school. And I got rejected. So I didn't really have a choice, and I went into the military. And that took about two years. And somewhere in the middle, and I applied again, and by the time I got out of the army, I got in! Now here I am!"

"Wasn't it a pain writing the essays again and again?" I asked.

"Aha!" he exclaimed with a gargantuan smile that became his trademark. "That is the funny thing!" I started laughing just watching him elaborate. "I photocopied the exact same application each and every time! No joke! It was pure luck. They lowered the bar this year!"

Brad, an imposing but quiet boy from Philadelphia with an eclectic taste in film, also belonged to our clan. He was almost literally a genius in the field of chemistry. He barely said anything, but when he did, it tended to be very funny.

Brad had his own personal fan club in a short, ethnically Indian, ultra-liberal, agnostic Catholic who could quote Noam Chomsky off the top of her head in the middle of a hundred-mile-an-hour debate without so much as batting an eyelash. Such vibrant discussions frequently took place over dinner thanks to the presence of Brad's roommate, Kevin, who wrote for the *Salient*, Harvard's conservative newspaper.

Kevin was unlike most Harvard conservatives (a group to which Jeff, Elliott and Metin coincidentally all belonged), who honorably shouldered the task of espousing views that the rest of the campus tended to dismiss consistently and pejoratively. Far from moderate, Kevin was racist, at times vaguely anti-Semitic, and proud of it. At least according to Brad's friend, Kevin chose to sit with a bunch of Jews, a Muslim and two Christians thanks to his hypocritical fetish for non-white women. At first I doubted her account, but after hearing him "talk" with Brad and watching him behave around others, I realized that she had actually hit the nail on the head.

Ben, another friend of Brad's who was as kind as he was tall, was another regular co-conspirator during our Kevin-evasion maneuvers in Annenberg. Ben had a unique sense of humor himself, with a tendency to make Jewish jokes more often that I would have liked, but I enjoyed being around him as his jokes implied an underlying respect for the religion, rather than a distaste. Still, it was hard for me to juxtapose my general fondness for Ben with the unease I felt at being made fun of, even if indirectly. It was the first time I had encountered that particular squeamishness, but I soon learned that it worked both ways. I was shocked to discover that neither Elliott nor Jeff had ever met a Jew before they met me, and where they were from (in completely different parts of the country), "Jew" was considered a bad word. Such personal revelations from each of us, in an unending stream throughout the year, made dinner conversations over the dark wooden tables in Annenberg all the more interesting.

So it was that one night, after enjoying some overpriced ice cream in Harvard Square, one of my friends insisted that I come over to his room so I could watch an episode of the Simpsons.

"I know you're going to love it!" he said excitedly. I was skeptical. The request seemed a little bit too sudden.

I knew something was up, but I went along. "I mean, it's pretty funny, I guess..." I said after watching. We decided to go back to my room in Grays, not more than fifty feet away. When a room full of people shouted, "Surprise!" I knew that my hunch had been correct. The Simpsons episode had been a decoy. It was necessary, too, for I later learned that along with one other friend whose stern motherly manner could have easily instilled fear in grown men, Elliott had taken charge when Brian and his football buddies had decided that our common room would be a good place to hang out for the night. When I arrived, they were nowhere to be found. Elliott was in ROTC, and could apparently herd drunken football players like nobody's business.

Knowing that I loved coffee ice cream, my friends had bought a gorgeous chocolate-and-coffee ice cream cake from a bakery in the Square. I was so amazed by the outpouring of friendship, having never had a surprise birthday party, or a surprise from friends of any sort, that I lapsed into my goofy mindset that had so rarely manifested itself in high school.

"Are you going to cut the cake?" they asked.

"Okay!" I said, and wielded the plastic knife she offered, thinking about the best way to make the first slice. I decided that every birthday cake was the same, so mine would be different. I made it zigzag. The next piece, too, was a zigzag, until the whole cake had been cut at random. Everyone stared on in horror at the destroyed lump of cake, while I grinned wildly. I was having the time of my life.

"Now that the pieces are all random, everyone can help themselves!" I said, not fully realizing that I had made the cake impossible to serve. I struggled with my first piece, while my friends puzzled over what had just happened—except for one, who was laughing hysterically.

Afterward, I opened a few presents, and several of us watched a movie. That night, I went to bed happy.

A few weeks later, the population of Grays M54 increased by two as we received our own set of visiting pre-frosh: Francis and Felix. Both were Asian, both were from California, and both were extremely talented at physics, but in terms of personality, they were polar opposites. Francis was wide-eyed and optimistic, while Felix seemed perpetually depressed and analytical. I enjoyed being around both of them immensely, and did my best to convince them to attend Harvard. The Pops Orchestra had a concert while they were visiting, and I told them all about the International Review.

In the fall of 2002, they both arrived at Johnston Gate.

Simon had made a few friends of his own at Brehm, even earning the affectionate nickname "The Mayor of Brehm" from the staff. The school looked more like a trailer park than the Department of Education Blue-Ribbon School it was billed as. Each gray building was just barely a permanent fixture on the landscape; it looked like you could attach Lego wheels to the bottom of each and watch them roll away with the wind. There was no dining hall and no gymnasium. College students from Southern Illinois University who served as "dorm parents" had the daunting tasks not only of dealing with the children, all of whom were disabled, but also of cooking for them. The entire school seemed to be slightly dysfunctional—even its director boasted that he had learning disabilities—but everyone managed to get along somehow. When they didn't, such as the handful of times that Simon's behavior went beyond unacceptable, they sent children back home to their parents causing even further disruption. It took two hours to reach Brehm by car from St. Louis, and Simon never looked forward to the trip.

When I called my parents from Grays M54 one evening expecting more of the same old news, I was thus shocked to learn that Simon's best friend at Brehm—a girl by the name of Ashley, who I had met and who Simon had apparently taken a romantic interest in—was dead.

On a supervised field trip at a nature preserve in Carbondale, Ashley had lost her balance and fallen off a cliff. The entire school was devastated, and to make matters worse, Ashley's parents had moved from Colorado to be near their daughter.

When Simon lost Ashley, he lost everything he had going for him: a friend, a companion, and perhaps even someone who understood him, even if only a little bit. All I could do was sit in the windowsill and cry.

♥

One week before I had dropped off my resignation letter in the IRC office and turned in my key. A friend who was still involved told me that everyone had been shocked.

My ties weren't completely severed, though. Nick Smith, one of the International Review's new Editors-in-Chief, immediately began pressuring me to join his staff as the webmaster for the magazine, separate from an official role with the IRC. He sent me a long e-mail encouraging me to come back as the IR's Web Editor.

Since I already had plenty of responsibility running the company that hosted the IR web site, I didn't like the idea of getting more involved. I made sure he had my decision in writing a second time to avoid any confusion.

Figuring it would be a good time to transition my main activity outside of coursework, I set up an interview with Harvard Student Agencies, instead, to work as the student-run company's network administrator. After two interviews, one technical and one non-technical, I got the job.

Within a few days, though, I learned that HSA was not quite as entrepreneurial and student-run as it claimed to be. There were several full-time adult staff members who oversaw the organization. With constant turnover every year across a staff of hundreds of students, there was a need for some consistency. One of HSA's biggest divisions was "Let's Go," which made travel guides and flew Harvard students all over the world for free.

With four floors in the HSA building, there were a lot of computers to support. I tried to familiarize myself with their server, which was far more sophisticated and expensive than anything the IRC had ever dreamed about. I was surprised to learn about the software Let's Go was using to create the travel guides.

"We're using FrameMaker. Do you know FrameMaker?" my adult supervisor, Ann, had asked at my interview.

"FrameMaker? I know what it is—but it's used by the FAA to make air traffic controller technical manuals—or at least it was ten years ago. Shouldn't you be using PageMaker or InDesign?" I had read an article that said the company that made the software, Frame, was floundering.

"Well, that's what we're using," she said. "But really, if you have any input at all, I want to hear it. We like people who are open with us."

Two weeks later, Let's Go was having seemingly insurmountable problems coordinating its desktop publishing efforts, which I again traced back to FrameMaker. Once more, I asked if it might be possible to switch to a more modern product. I touched a nerve: the budget.

"You don't know a *thing* about what we do here!" Ann screamed, her eyes wide. Her yelling, more than the insult, kept me thinking about it for the rest of the day. I wasn't getting paid very much, and like the IRC, there were still other highly opinionated, technically-savvy people around whose toes I had to be careful not to step on. I wrote my resignation letter that night.

Once more, I was without a job aside from running Think, but I had been too busy with schoolwork to pay much attention to it. The stress was getting to me; I wasn't even getting along with Nathan that well. On a beautiful spring day, he designed a Visual Basic program that let him control his MP3 playlist from his cell phone. He moved his speakers over to the windows closest to my desk and pointed them outside toward the Yard. Then, he went out to play frisbee, where he could control his music selection remotely. It was clever, but I was stuck inside writing a paper for Pompeii.

Finally, the blasting lyrics and pounding bass of Nathan's playlist were just too much for me to deal with. When he stopped a song for a minute, I switched his speakers off. A few seconds later, my telephone rang.

"Can you turn the music back on?" he asked, calling from his cell phone.

"I'm trying to write an essay," I responded.

"Why can't you write your essay outside?"

"I don't have a laptop. Why don't you bring a Walkman outside?" I added coldly. I apologized, and when Nathan came back in, he put his speakers back.

"*This summer, I'm going to work on Whiteboard,*" I decided at last, giving me something to look forward to.

Within four incredibly hectic weeks, Tim and I worked out living arrangements in a nearby Cambridge apartment and a second employment agreement that would last throughout the summer. I also convinced one of my friends from CS50 to work for Think, so that I would have two programmers in addition to myself making Whiteboard into a usable product.

When classes ended for the year, I realized that Professor Tatar, who taught Fairy Tales, had never handed back my first paper. I was surprised; after visiting her office hours in the spring, she had agreed to examine my first paper personally. She even repeated a point I had raised during my visit in her next lecture.

"I wish more of my teachers were like that," I had told one of my closer friends. Yet I never got the paper back, even after I saw Professor Tatar on the street.

"It's in my kitchen on the table!" she shouted in my direction. I walked over so she wouldn't have to yell. "Actually, I shouldn't tell you this, but I left it there, and my daughter picked it up and started reading it. And you know what she said? 'This is really good! You should have given him a higher grade!' So I'll read it, don't worry!"

That paper had no special significance, but it did demonstrate how subjective the TF-oriented grading system was. Of course, I never got it back.

▼

The summer of 2002 was Boston's hottest on record since 1912. The modern apartment on Banks Street that Tim and I agreed to sublet had one bedroom and a pull-out sofa. What it didn't have was air-conditioning. In the heat, we were miserable.

Tim had several jobs: programming for Think, working in the MIT Undergraduate Research Opportunities Program, and heading a regional conference for Taiwanese students. He was usually exhausted when he got home each night, but it was too hot and humid to relax.

Whiteboard was slowly but steadily turning into a decent program. I used an early version to finish another design of Think's web site, and spent a fair bit of time simply trying to figure out which features to add while my employees were hard at work implementing them.

Getting a telephone installed proved to be more difficult than I had anticipated. I had arranged for Verizon to activate a line on the morning that Tim and I were scheduled to move in, but when I arrived back in Boston from the airport and called Tim in the apartment, no one answered. We had no dial tone.

The following Monday, I used the phone line in the Harvard Property and Real Estate office to call Verizon, but Verizon claimed that we had an inside wiring problem. Talking to a supervisor eventually led to testing on the line that revealed that we, in fact, had an outside wiring problem. Verizon promised to send out a technician the next day who never appeared.

When a technician did finally arrive after several more trips to the Real Estate office, the basement where the interface panel was located was locked. The technician left. For all of June, we didn't have a phone.

One day, Tim and I decided to get some fresh air. In the distance, I spied a Verizon truck on Mt. Auburn Street. I rushed over to the phone technician, halfway inside a manhole.

"Excuse me! We've been trying to get a phone line installed for a full month, and you guys aren't willing to do a thing about it. It doesn't work. There's no dial tone."

"I'm not really supposed to do any inside wiring," he said, looking up.

"This isn't inside wiring," I said. "It's on your end."

"I don't know man, I could get in a lot of trouble..." he began.

"Please! We need a phone!" I said. There was no way to talk to my customers easily, or my parents.

"Alright!" he finally agreed. "Tomorrow at 8:30 A.M. But don't tell no one."

The next day at 8:30 A.M., the technician wasn't there, and the basement was locked. Finally, a Verizon truck pulled up, but there was still no way to get the technician to the access panel. I pleaded with him to wait for the superintendant, who I had paged, and who took an additional half-hour to respond.

With access to the interface panel, the problem was solved in minutes. "Yeah, you were right," he said. "They installed it wrong. Hooked up the copper pair to the wrong pin. There was no voltage on your line."

Once I had a telephone, I tried in vain to figure out how to make Think grow, painfully conscious of the fact that I was roughly the same age as Bill Gates had been when he started working on Microsoft at Harvard—except that I felt like I was getting nowhere.

"You know Java from CS51, right?" I asked one of my employees.

"Sure," she said.

"Okay, can you make a Java applet that uploads multiple files at once?"

"What's an applet?" came her response. When I showed her, she told me that she'd never seen that kind of program in class. My regard for Harvard's Computer Science curriculum plummeted.

Most days, I fell asleep on the couch before I could reach any conclusions about what to do next, until the heat woke me up again. When I got truly desperate, I turned off my monitor, one of four heating up the apartment. By 3:00 P.M. each day when one of my employees ran to catch the bus for her long commute home, I was usually asleep on the couch. My example as a CEO was less than inspiring.

▼

Even without attending classes, I still managed to receive another blow from the University administration. *The Crimson* reported that concentrations would have fewer Core Curriculum requirements in order to simplify the bureaucracy for incoming students. The new rules were to be applied retroactively for one year, so that the Class of 2005 would be the first to be affected by the change. I looked up the new exemptions on-line for economics concentrators. For my exemption, I could choose either Literature & Arts A, or Literature & Arts C: the two Core areas I had fulfilled with Fairy Tales and Pompeii. My blood began to boil.

"Guess what?" I asked my father facetiously the next time I called. "I didn't have to take Pompeii. Or Fairy Tales. Either way, one of them was a complete waste of time."

"What do you mean?" my father asked. "I thought they satisfied the Core."

"They did, until just now," I said. "I've been exempted from one of the two retroactively. Take a look at *The Crimson*."

"What? Retroactively? So you could have taken something else, like Zittrain's course?"

"Well, if they had allowed me to," I said.

"That's unbelievable!" my father exclaimed. "Why couldn't they tell you before?"

I didn't have an answer for him. Still angry about the way I had been treated throughout the year, he wrote an e-mail to Associate Dean of Undergraduate Education Jeffrey Wolcowitz, who also taught the introductory Economics 1010a course for sophomores. Once again, there was no response.

By the end of the summer, though Whiteboard was complete and successfully running Think's web site, Tim and I were barely on speaking terms. The apartment had become a pressure cooker, and the only positive thing to emerge was a computer program that I had no way to actually distribute or sell due to its inherent complexity.

"We need a shopping cart," I lamented a week before the end of August, long after Tim had surmised that no one would ever buy Whiteboard, which hit me hard. We didn't have another normal conversation for eighteen months.

CHAPTER 16

The Comic Tragedy of Robert Neugeboren

In the early fall, Lowell House was truly beautiful. The tower glistened in the sunlight, the trees looked gorgeous in the middle of the House's two rectangular courtyards, and the chandelier hanging from the dining hall's arched yellow ceiling shone brightly. When my uncle helped me move in yet again, he was duly impressed.

"It looks like a castle, not like a dorm," he said.

Elliott, Jeff, Metin and I had been assigned to suite O-31/O-32, separated down the middle by an extremely narrow hallway. Elliott and Jeff imported a couch from a yard sale and took the room on the right facing the street, while Metin and I set up shop on the left with a view of the East courtyard.

There was no orientation as there had been the year before; we were on our own. We were greeted in our new room by a copy of the CUE Guide, a copy of the HSA Unofficial Guide to Life at Harvard, and a large "USE OF THIS FIRE-PLACE IS PROHIBITED" sticker, the subject of much debate on campus since the policy had just been introduced over the summer. I learned by mail that I had been assigned an academic advisor on the faculty, but after I e-mailed him to introduce myself, he never wrote back.

Flipping through the CUE Guide on my desk chair, I realized that the book was of little use. It frequently contained statements to the effect of "43% of students felt that the course was far too slow, while 42% argued that it was much too fast, and 15% said that the professor was confusing." To make matters worse, each factor was ranked on a scale from 1 to 5, but for some factors, 1 was the best score, while for others, it was the worst. What I really wanted to know was what the students had written about their courses in plain English, but as that information was unquantifiable, the CUE Guide quietly omitted it.

Tea took place regularly every Thursday in the Masters' residence, but I found the first sufficiently stuffy to keep me away for most of the year. The bite-sized appetizers were good, but one also had to make polite conversation at all times.

I got to know Metin much better. Like many Harvard students, he seemed fairly normal on the surface, but his zany personality (which I greatly enjoyed) masked an extraordinary intellect with the kind of rigorous focus one typically saw in Harvard's top professors. At the age of twenty, Metin was a soccer player, a good student, and an accomplished archaeologist. He had done field work with the Cleveland Museum of Natural History, was already working on several publishable papers, and had found an encouraging mentor at Harvard's Stone Age Lab.

By our sophomore year, Metin had already been anguishing over his career path for some time. Like many students at Ivy League schools, his parents were well-educated professionals who wanted the best for their child—a justified and well-intentioned sentiment that became the source of excruciating conflict for him. His father, a doctor who ran a private practice, encouraged him to consider medicine, and was understandably surprised when Metin decided that he was more interested in a career as an archaeologist.

Though Metin and I got along well in general, it was this particular quality of independence that I admired most about him. My parents had been flexible about my entrepreneurial ambitions—perhaps more than they should have been—and so starting Think Computer when everyone else was doing homework had cost me relatively little. For Metin, pursuing his interests required winning a personal battle between two good options, and yet it was clear that he was well on his way to being an internationally-renown expert in archaeology. His love for Steven Spielberg's Indiana Jones series was almost tangible, as he did have a fedora. Yet whenever one of our friends made a comparison to Harrison Ford, he was quick to point out all of the inaccuracies in the films and distance himself from the sensationalism they brought upon his field, just as I would have expected of any real scientist. As far as I was concerned, Metin's expertise was just as impressive as a medical doctor's, if not more so, and his father had every reason to be proud of him.

His background before college was equally remarkable. As the only Muslim at St. Ignatius High School, he had been taught Catholic theology for years. The result was a political philosophy all his own, one in which he cared very little for or about Republicans or Democrats. Instead, he gave his vote to Ralph Nader whenever possible, just because he could. (Metin didn't seem to care for Nader that much, either.)

I had known Metin since our senior year of high school, when we sat at the same table at a Harvard Alumni Association dinner for prospective students. It was there that Metin's enthusiasm for everything first manifested itself. Though he didn't show it, he usually ate enough for three people. At first, Metin also seemed far more enthusiastic about being my friend than I did about being his. It was as if I was playing the same game that I had with Adam, but in reverse. Quickly, I told myself to snap out of it; it wasn't every day that someone came along who actively wanted to be my friend.

He was also generally hilarious. Over lunch in downtown Cleveland, I inadvertently introduced Metin to cream soda for the first time in his life. Back in Cambridge, he proceeded to buy not two cans, but two cases worth, which he drank in a period of three days. Our recycling bin overflowed with cans. Before long, our Lowell House dorm room was crawling with fruit flies.

"Did you rinse out those cans?" I asked him, remembering how my father had always instructed me to rinse aluminum cans before leaving them in the sink.

"No, why would I do that? They're trash!" he said.

"I think that's where the fruit flies are coming from," I told him.

"Oh. I did sprinkle some packets of sugar on them..." he said.

"What?" I asked. I thought he was joking.

"You know, like, sugar you put into coffee. I thought it would just be funny, sort of like it was snowing on the cans!"

"No wonder our room is infested!" I exclaimed. "Why do you think fruit flies like *fruit*? BECAUSE OF THE SUGAR!" We quickly removed the cans from the room. To this day, Metin has never had another sip of cream soda.

♦

In a matter of days, we were introduced to Bruce Watson, a fixture of Lowell House. Bruce was the house's economics tutor, one of several who specialized in a particular concentration. The tutors, Masters, and their resident guests made up the Senior Common Room, which was both an actual room and a metaphor used to refer to the people who occasionally inhabited it. The Junior Common Room encompassed the undergraduates who lived there and was a room, too, right across from the dining hall.

While Metin struggled through Physics, Turkish, and some Core courses I wouldn't have touched with a ten-foot pole, I trudged daily to Economics 1010a, Statistics 104, Historical Study B: World War II, and Literature & Arts B: First Nights.

Economics 1010a took place in Emerson Hall, the same building where I had offended Jane and taken many of my final exams the previous semester. The room was filled with 350 students, the only alternative being Economics 1011a, which covered the same material in a more mathematically-intensive manner. I had nothing to prove, so Ec1010a was the course for me and several football players, including my former roommate.

On the first day, it vaguely occurred to me that our professor was not the person my father had e-mailed over the summer about my retroactive exemption. After teaching Ec1010a for ten years, Professor Wolcowitz had stepped down from his position to take on more administrative duties within University Hall. His replacement was a Lecturer in the department who specialized in game theory. His name was Robert Neugeboren.

Professor Neugeboren was a slight man who struck even the nerdiest among us as a nerd. While such telltale characteristics of intelligence were not necessarily a bad thing given the context in this case, his short beard and spastic manner left absolutely no doubt that the man was an academic. He simply didn't fit in anywhere else. Neugeboren launched us into the curriculum by informing us that the course's final would be held on January 18, 2003. I began taking notes.

Right away, he talked about Adam Smith, as most economics professors were wont to do at the beginning of their courses. The lecture concluded with a hurried explanation of the Invisible Hand Theorem, but everything he said sounded hurried. I was free of economics for the rest of the day.

I was far more impressed with my statistics professor. David van Dyk was the head of the Statistics Department, as well as a clear and insightful lecturer. He explained complicated concepts in a manner that I usually understood, much to my own surprise. His only arguably negative trait was the brisk manner that he used with his two Teaching Fellows, Gopi and Hosung. Professor van Dyk had a tendency to become irritated with them during lecture.

"Gopiiiiiiiiiiiiiiiiiii!" he yelled whenever something went wrong. Watching van Dyk yell at the TFs was like watching a more gentrified version of The Three Stooges. It quickly became a running joke amongst our friends.

The lectures for World War II took place in the incredibly uncomfortable auditorium in Sever Hall. The brand new chairs had been constructed to the proportions of midgets. Fortunately, the lectures were interesting. Coincidentally, my TF was a German graduate student with strikingly Aryan features.

My fourth class, about the first nights that five classical music pieces were performed (and thus called "First Nights") was occasionally funny, but I began to realize that the jokes in lecture were the exactly the same as the jokes in the textbook, which Professor Kelly had written and required us to purchase. He had offered the course so many times that he had memorized his book. I amused myself during lecture by watching who laughed at the jokes and who didn't. Anyone laughing hadn't done the reading or was quite easy to amuse.

The second Economics 1010a lecture was horribly boring, and the third started out with still more threats, this time regarding our midterm exam on October 21st, and the first problem set, due on October 4th. Neugeboren seemed to be flying through the material, trying to draw three-dimensional graphs on the chalkboard without much success, throwing equations around that didn't really make sense, and providing hypothetical examples for us to solve. I was having a hard time keeping up, and I didn't seem to be the only one. People were raising their hands to ask questions about the examples on a regular basis.

As I tried to work out an optimization problem in my notes, I kept arriving at

$$2L = 336 + 2L$$

Subtracting 2L from both sides, as we had been taught us to do in fourth grade, yielded the startling result

$$0 = 336$$

I couldn't find the error in my hurried writing, and I wanted to know what was going on. I raised my hand. After calling on someone else, Professor Neugeboren saw it, and called on me.

"Yes," he said.

"I'm trying to work out the example, and I keep getting zero equals three thirty-six," I shouted so that he could hear me all the way at the front of the room.

"Right," he said.

"Can you tell what I'm doing wrong? It's probably something small..." I wasn't sure, but I thought other people might be having the same problem.

Neugeboren turned to the chalkboard to stare at the problem for a minute. "I'm not gonna go through that...here. Take it up... Okay, cause I do want to get onto another problem that has a...funkier, kind of, uh, utility function, which is gonna become quite standard in both ...this form of a function is gonna be...the standard function we're gonna use for...to finish out the theory of the consumer, as well as a function you'll see again in the theory of the firm." He continued with his steadily unraveling lecture.

I was not happy. The reason that people didn't like asking questions in lecture was that there was always the chance that the professor would make them look like complete idiots, and rare though it was, it did happen—as I had just proved in front of three-hundred and fifty people.

I later realized that my plus sign was supposed to be a minus sign, which led to the more logical conclusion that L=84. It didn't take long for me to figure out, and I wondered why Neugeboren couldn't have just taken five seconds to correct my mistake.

"I can't believe he wouldn't answer my question!" I told Jeff at lunch, who had elected to take 1010a despite the fact that he could have handled the harder course.

"Yeah, he's not the best," Jeff admitted, chuckling to himself.

"He's awful!" I fumed. Sophomore year wasn't shaping up to be much better than the year before.

On October 1st, after enduring another lecture full of "inferior goods" and convoluted graphs representing the "income effect," neither of which I understood, I met my TF for Economics 1010a at our first section. A Belgian, he left First Nights as my only course in which I had a TF whose native language was English.

During section, I diligently took notes on the same exact topics that we had already covered in lecture. I wasn't sure if it was my inexperience running Think that led me so far astray when it came to economics, or if I was simply too slow to comprehend the concepts, but they rarely made sense. I couldn't force my mind to work within the sets of assumptions that economists always wanted to use. It was too easy to think of an exception to every rule, based on some interaction with a customer, or something I had once read in a magazine. Programmers thought differently: as soon as you had one exception, the rule was false. You couldn't build a program on rules that didn't work. If you did, it would crash.

I was thus amazed when on October 4th, my self-doubt vanished. Economics 1010a crashed.

It all started with seven graphs. As Professor Neugeboren frantically drew, and erased, and then re-drew, and then re-erased, we all sat in silence. We couldn't start drawing in our notebooks until each graph was finished. Even those with pencils knew enough not to start until Neugeboren was finished unless they wanted to go mad. For those with pens, waiting was simply the logical thing to do. The truly anal-retentive had colored pens, with different colors for each set of curves. They were already mad.

The problem at hand, which Jeff had long since pointed out, was that Robert Neugeboren could not draw. While this ordinarily would not have been a problem, except perhaps for art professors, the kinds of graphs that we were expected to draw required the precise positioning of curved solid lines, straight solid lines, straight dotted lines, and occasional tick marks. If the wrong lines intersected, the graphs suddenly meant something completely different, in which case they might be misinterpreted—which explained a lot about why I never seemed to understand much.

When there wasn't a single person in the packed lecture hall who could answer the Professor when he asked for the proper formula for a straight line on a graph, he turned sarcastic.

"You all worry about calculus..." he chided us, "but you've forgotten your algebra!" I was again incensed by his attempts to make himself feel superior.

"Yeah, that's right Professor Neugeboren," I wrote in my notebook. "This room full of Harvard students has forgotten how to draw a line. Maybe WE HAVE NO IDEA WHAT YOU'RE TALKING ABOUT!"

Yet, much to our collective disbelief, he continued making snide remarks. "You should all just try to plot a line between two points Friday night...when you're hanging around with your friends." We sat.

"Wah-wah-wah," one student mouthed from somewhere in the classroom, spotlighting the Professor's failed punch line.

"That's what *I* do!" Neugeboren said.

The room erupted in laughter. Trying to recover, Professor Neugeboren launched into a new example problem on the proper procedure to calculate aggregate demand. With a sigh, I started taking notes, writing down the two premise equations.

$$Q = 19 - 4P$$
$$P = 20 - 4Q$$

"If *n* is equal to 10, find Q," he said.

"*Where the hell did* n *come from?*" I wondered, looking at the equations. I wasn't even going to bother trying to solve the problem until Neugeboren showed us what he was talking about. It was hopeless, otherwise. Finally, after giving us a few minutes to solve the problem, he set to work himself.

$$Q = 5 - (1/4)P$$
$$10n = 50 - (10/4)P$$

He scribbled out the *n* and wrote Q_i in its place.

$$10Q_i = 50 - (10/4)P$$
$$P = 20 - 4Q$$

We were back at the premise equation. The next line he wrote had me stumped.

$$Q = 10Q$$

"*That could only be true if* Q = 0," I thought. I wrote a large question mark next to the line, so that when I went back to study, I would know not to trust the logic. Not that it was really necessary; I was already at the point of doubting economic logic anyway.

Unable to account for the puzzle of the Qs, Neugeboren frantically moved onto the next example, price elasticity of demand. This one had a graph featuring a single line with a negative slope, in addition to three equations:

$$E_p = \%\Delta Q/\%\Delta P = (\Delta Q/Q) / (\Delta P/P)$$
$$Q_D = a - bP$$
$$E_p = -b(P/Q)$$

At this point, referring to one of the points on the graph, Neugeboren threw out some numbers and scribbled them on the board.

$$E_p = 4(2/11)$$
$$= 8/11$$

A girl raised her hand to ask a question.

"Yes," Neugeboren said, calling on her.

"In that example you just did, you put in some values for the variables for E_p," she said.

"Yes."

"I was just wondering, is b four, or is b negative four?"

"Four. So...here. Four..." Neugebored replied. The girl looked confused.

"But if b is four, then shouldn't E_p be negative eight elevenths?"

"No, no, it's negative b...b, here, is negative four." She was still confused, and now, so was I. He had just directly contradicted himself. Even though I had lost track of what b was, I knew it couldn't be both positive and negative at the same time. Fortunately, she wasn't going to let him get away with it.

"But you just said b was four." Neugeboren stared at the chalkboard for about ten seconds, as he had done after I had asked my question a few weeks before. He let out a gasp of air in exasperation.

"No, because, it's...what I'm saying, bu—" He cut himself off. "No, okay. b is four. b is four, sorry...and everything else is correct." It seemed like he had uttered the last statement more with the hope that by saying it, it would be true, rather than because he knew it for a fact.

The room filled with murmurs as we all did the arithmetic in our heads: -1 x 4 x 2 / 11 = -8 /11, which had the opposite sign of what was written on the chalkboard. The girl pointed out the problem.

"So you want this to be negative and these to be...negative." There was a pause.

"Don't worry about the positive and negatives, okay?!" The man who had only weeks before chastised us for forgetting our algebra had just forgotten it himself.

Over the next few weeks, Economics 1010a continued to deteriorate. Neugeboren sputtered out phrases such as "When we found that, we will have found..." and never went on to specify what "that" was. The problem sets he assigned, which students in previous years had found to be very straightforward, were nearly impossible. Ben and I, along with some other friends in the class, spent late nights in Lowell House and the Dunster House dining hall trying to figure out what it was that the problems were even asking, let alone how to solve them. Nothing made sense, except when Ben gave Neugeboren the finger in a fit of despair.

After the lecture on October 11th, I was so angry at having to endure Neugeboren's lectures three times a week that I wanted to fire off a letter to the administration without any further ado. Doodling was actually more productive than learning. The more I learned, the more confused I became.

In the next lecture, after trying to solve another basic algebraic example on the chalkboard, our professor realized that he had stumbled into another one of his impossible solutions.

"So suppose that we all decide—the thousand of us—to insure each other. We have to pay out a hundred thousand dollars in losses, there are a hu—thousand—of us..." There was another trademark ten-second pause. He had written too many zeroes in the answer scrawled across the board, and we all knew it.

"Nope, sorry, not gonna complete this one. It's not goin' where I want it to go."

The clock struck eleven. People started to get up from their seats.

"I'm gonna...I'm gonna... Wait, wait, wait! Befor— Don't take off!" He let out another desperate gasp. "Instead of finishing this... Because the basic principle is, I suppose, that each of us can decide to insure the other's...loss; r—risk to expos— risk to loss. Ah, can, can you just wait one...one second. Sorry, sorry. I don't want to leave things completely...completely a mess. We will return to, uh, these topics, next time." At this point, I thought he would finally give up, but he didn't.

"I do wanna just say a couple of words before you...rush out of here. Which is...that...at the beginning, we started off with the model of apti—uh, of optimal choice..."

There was no one left in the room except a handful of people. It was awful, both that Neugeboren was so bad, and that the students were so rude. I didn't know what to do when I walked out of Emerson Hall that day, but by the time I crossed Mt. Auburn Street to walk up Lowell House's driveway, it was very clear. Obnoxious as it was for the whole class to get up and leave while the professor was talking, Neugeboren had to go. The people had voted, in a sense, with their feet.

"Okay, you can't do that," two of my closest friends both told me over dinner in Dunster when I brought up the idea of writing a letter once more. "You know the first thing that's going to happen if you want to meet with anyone in the administration is that they're going to ask you if you talked to this guy first. However bad he is."

"Yeah...but he's *so bad*! I don't want to talk to him," I admitted. I knew they were right, though. I had to give Neugeboren a chance. Just after midnight, I wrote him an e-mail, trying to be as polite, but to-the-point, as possible.

By the time I woke up the following morning, I had a response in my mailbox, and much to my surprise, it was the most reasonable response I had ever received from a professor in writing. He was much more coherent than during lecture, and didn't even try to side-step the issue or blame someone else. I was shocked.

The lectures had been horrible, but it was hard to stay angry after reading the e-mail. He knew that there was something wrong, and he was going to try his best to fix it. My friends had been right after all.

Lecture the next day was better than the catastrophe two days before, but it still wasn't coherent. Professor Neugeboren introduced the term "Labor/Hour," which I thought meant labor units per hour. In fact, I realized several minutes later that he really meant "Labor-Hours," which involved multiplication, not division.

I was annoyed by the constant mistakes, and even angry when they wouldn't cease. It took fear to spur me into action. What scared me was the prospect of another test that failed to test anyone's knowledge.

As lecture wore on from 10:00 A.M. to 11:00 A.M. on Wednesday, October 16th, I gave Professor Neugeboren one last chance. If I didn't understand at least half of the material by then, there was no way I thought the midterm, scheduled for the following Monday, could be fair.

At 11:01, I still didn't have a clue. I sat down to write my letter that afternoon. I was sick of being evaluated, sick of being sorted, sick of working so hard, and sick of knowing that my teachers cared so little. I was sick of Harvard's charade. If I was so smart, I wanted to be treated like I was smart. I wanted good teachers and I wanted my grades to actually mean something.

After my roommates helped me tone down several drafts, I had a final copy. Reading it over, I chuckled at two paragraphs that triggered particularly fresh memories.

Professor Neugeboren also consistently appears to be unprepared for lectures. Knowing full well that an example would require taking the natural logarithm of several numbers, he neglected to bring a calculator or even a pre-calculated table of values. He was not sure what to name the equation $U = \ln(W)$; after consulting his notes, he settled on "Von Neumann Utility Index," since none of the teaching fellows knew, either. Later, without explanation, he used the same name to refer to a completely different equation.

Even the most basic and obvious lecturing practices evade Professor Neugeboren. He draws his letter "U"s exactly the same as his letter "V"s, resulting in intriguing, yet wholly inaccurate, recursive mathematical functions. Questions—perhaps the most important learning resource in a confusing lecture—are never repeated, making them impossible to hear in Emerson 105, not to mention forever lost to anyone watching lecture videotapes on-line. The rushed conclusion to the last lecture took place after the Professor sent a clear signal to leave, leaving many students who had to rush to another class extremely irritated.

To the end, I attached a sheet of paper with two columns of densely-packed lines. I tried for several days to get other students in the course to sign the petition, but it proved to be difficult. Almost everyone I spoke with was afraid that signing the letter would affect their grade; they refused to consider the opportunity cost of not signing, and what would happen to their grade then. Or they were merely satisfied with having a curve "fix" everything in the end. That worked for me in CS50 when I nominally understood the concepts being taught, but now that I was an Economics concentrator, I would have to take other courses that depended upon the material in 1010a, about which I was totally clueless. Even the most generous curve wouldn't help me in the long run.

Some people thought I was being mean; others agreed with every word I said, but felt sorry for Neugeboren. One of the people I knew from TECH forwarded me an e-mail that had been going around in opposition to my letter.

> how revolutionary. I think this is WRONG. since when does the hunted shoot the hunter??

> outrageous and terribly lacking in respect..

> just think of how he'll feel...

Another replied:

> I am not in Ec 1010a - but in any case I agree with [the above message]. I think it is disrespectful and inconsiderate to even consider such idea. I am sure this is going to be a miserable failure for the "letter writers".

I explained that I also felt sorry for Neugeboren, but students always seemed to put his welfare ahead of their own. I even resorted to passing the letter around during a lecture, my stomach in knots every time Neugeboren looked up from the lectern.

Out of the three hundred and fifty students taking the course, only thirteen signed. I was bewildered. People seemed to be taking my intentions and putting the worst possible spin on them for no reason at all.

"These are the world's leaders?" I asked a friend at lunch. "They're sheep! I don't really care if Neugeboren is insulted, I tried to let him know what the deal is. It's not *his* education that he's messing up!"

"I dunno man...people are really crazy about their grades," he said.

On the afternoon of October 18th, I sent the letter to Oliver Hart electronically, copying it to a few administrators at University Hall so that they would also be aware of the situation. Then, I waited.

CHAPTER 17

The Substitute

Bruce Watson didn't wait at all. He scheduled a review session for Lowell's 1010a students on the Friday before the midterm so that we wouldn't be doomed to failure.

On Sunday, as I was panicking about indifference curves and equation subscripts, I received an e-mail from Oliver Hart asking to set up a meeting. We arranged for several of the students who had signed my letter to meet with Professor Hart to voice their concerns the next day. There was no chance of meeting before the midterm.

I woke up on Monday morning earlier than usual so that I could make it to Emerson Hall on time. Everyone in Economics 1010a had received an e-mail informing them of a last-minute change. The several hundred students in Statistics 104 who had a midterm immediately following the Economics 1010a midterm could arrive for the 1010a exam a half-hour early and leave a half-hour early, allowing for some transitional time. It applied to me. I knew I would be frazzled following the Economics exam, so I needed the time. I elected to sacrifice sleep, as did many others.

The exam was hard. I knew that we had covered the material in lecture and I tried to recreate the graphs in my mind, but I just couldn't fit it all together. When it was 9:30 A.M., the TFs told us that our time was up if we were in Statistics 104, and we put our pens and pencils down. I left, trying not to think about the exam on my way to Lowell Lecture Hall so that I could prepare for the next one.

The Statistics 104 exam, despite the fact that it was open-book, was also hard. I knew that I wouldn't be entering into a career in either field anytime soon.

It was difficult not to think about the upcoming meeting at 2:00 P.M. After lunch in the Lowell House dining hall with my roommates, I dodged the cars on Mt. Auburn Street and Massachusetts Avenue for the third time that day in order to make it to the Littauer Center, which housed the Economics department. During my father's reunion, I had assumed that the building was a branch of the Massachusetts state government. Its officious exterior didn't fool me anymore. Inside, I met four of the other students who had signed my letter.

Professor Hart welcomed us into his office, and asked the five of us to have a seat in front of his desk. He apologized profusely, and I silently noted that he was one of the first British Harvard professors I had met.

"I must admit, this situation overall sounds very bad," he began. "What I suppose we must figure out is what can be done about it."

We all took turns outlining our concerns, most of which were in the letter, but some of which were so recent, they hadn't yet been mentioned.

"There were people cheating on the midterm today," one student said. "And not just a few. The TFs didn't check to see who was really in Stat 104 and who wasn't. So a lot of students who weren't just came early and took advantage of the extra thirty minutes for the exam, while the rest of us who were actually *in* the class only had the hour."

"Not to mention that there are tons of typos on the problem set answer keys," I said. "It makes it pretty hard to study for a midterm when your lecture notes are worthless because they're wrong, your professor is incoherent, and you can't even be sure what's going on with the problem sets. What else is left?" Everyone voiced murmurs of agreement.

"Well, I was thinking of paying a visit to lecture, today actually...but seeing as how you had a midterm scheduled for this morning, I was unable to do so. So maybe I'll stop by at the next lecture," Professor Hart said. "When would that be?"

"Wednesday," we said, almost in unison.

"Well, I've already spoken to Rob about this," he went on, referring to our Professor, "so he's aware that there's some dissatisfaction with the course."

"We realize he's trying," I said, "but to be blunt, it's just not good enough."

Professor Hart went through a long list of options, which he had clearly put some time into devising.

"There are a few things we can do given the circumstances," he said. "We could replace Friday lectures with review sessions, to be given by another member of the faculty, though we'll have to find one. You know, Rob was not the first person I asked to teach this class. After Jeff Wolcowitz decided not to teach this year, we had a number of people we went through who, for various reasons, did not end up agreeing to take the position. We had one woman secured who I thought was very good, but then she pulled out of the contract at the last minute, and so did the next person..."

"*It's just like CS50*," I thought, reminded of the oddity of a visiting professor in a crucial introductory course. "*It's the course that no one wants to teach*."

"We can also supplement Friday lectures with review sessions, also to be given by another faculty member or a TF."

"I'm not really sure that will be enough," a student said. "I mean, it would be good, but..."

"Well, we can also change the due dates of problem sets, so that your Friday review sessions will be able to cover the relevant material in time." It sounded logical, but it still wasn't really what I was hoping for.

"We could institute some sort of 'team-teaching,' I suppose, with Rob trading off with an experienced lecturer from time to time."

"That sounds like the best option so far," I said.

"Do you have anyone in mind who you'd like to teach?" Professor Hart looked right at me.

"Well, actually..." I thought for a minute, and then realized that it was obvious. "Bruce Watson." Bruce's review session had been excellent, even if I was lousy at economics. Hart wrote his name down on a legal pad.

"I'll have to talk to him, but yes, Bruce would be a good candidate... Alright... A few other options, though. We could make lectures optional and make the tests avoid material only covered in lecture." I knew what that meant: more teaching in section. The other students caught the drift of the suggestion, too.

"Or we could change the purpose of sections entirely, with new TFs as a possibility, as well." That sounded much like the previous suggestion, though I was surprised that he was willing to go so far.

We all agreed that really, the problem wasn't section. It was Professor Neugeboren. Anything he could do to reduce the amount of Neugeboren's lecturing would be a huge improvement.

With that, our meeting ended in a cordial fashion, and we all left, hoping for the best. I sent Professor Hart a thank you e-mail lauding his quick response and flexibility. Once more, it was time to wait.

▼

Our Statistics 104 exam was handed back in class. On the top of mine, one of the TFs had written a huge "69" in a red circle: one of the lowest grades in the class.

"How did I do so badly?" I groused to Metin. "I mean, I know I suck at this stuff, but I didn't think I sucked *that* much." I flopped onto our futon, and browsed through my blue book, which was now full of red pen. When I was done, I looked up. "Hold on a minute."

I added up all of the points I had missed. They totaled 21. I double-checked my arithmetic on a calculator. They totaled 21 again.

"What's one hundred minus twenty-one?" I asked Metin out loud.

"Uh... Seventy-nine?"

"Thought so." I opened the book again, this time comparing my answers to the answers that had already been posted on-line for the previous year's mid-term on the same topic. "It's ten points off!"

The TFs had taken off points for not using the phrase "on average" in one of my answers—but the official answer to the same type of question on the previous exam hadn't used that phrase. They had also taken off points on one question despite the fact that I actually had the correct answer. They had also missed a point on an answer I got wrong.

When I went through each question in as much detail as I could understand, I added up my total score. It was a 92.

"Well that's quite a jump!" I said to myself. I e-mailed my TF with my concerns. Then, after the next lecture, I checked some of my thinking on one particularly tricky problem with Professor van Dyk.

"It's a borderline case…" he said, agreeing that my answer wasn't necessarily incorrect, though it wasn't the only answer possible.

"Then what's it doing on an exam?" I wondered. *"Asking 'borderline' questions doesn't seem like the best way to actually test for knowledge when the test is multiple choice…"*

Gopi ultimately looked at my test the second time around. According to him, my revised score was an 89. I was satisfied. We also learned in lecture that we would be required to do a final project for the course, one that involved a survey of some sort.

A few weeks before, *The Crimson* had published several articles about the college's plans to implement "pre-registration," which students feared would strip them of their shopping period. Instead, so that the College administration could better allocate teaching resources, students would be forced to choose their courses far in advance without knowing much about them, as was the case at most colleges. Under Harvard's existing system, the "shopping" time of one week before each semester gave students a chance to figure out which classes they wanted to take based on their own opinions. With teaching at the level I had witnessed in Economics 1010a, the ensuing uproar over the potential loss in flexibility seemed completely justified.

I knew exactly what I wanted to do.

⛊

When I walked into Emerson Hall with Jeff on Wednesday, I noticed that there was indeed one extra student in the class. Oliver Hart was sitting inconspicuously amongst the students, waiting for Professor Neugeboren to begin his lecture.

He started out with the normal battery of graphs and equations concerning what he referred to as "the theory of the firm," though it was a far cry from Think's checkbook. Suddenly, Professor Neugeboren began writing in extremely large capital letters on the chalkboard. He was clearly trying to emphasize an important point. When he moved away, all of the students, along with Professor Hart, saw what he had written.

PROFIT MAXIMATION

"Take this point to heart," he said sternly. "It's very important."

I laughed out loud as softly as I could. The combination of Neugeboren's haste and nervousness (due to the extraordinary circumstances of his performance review, no doubt) led him to forget a few letters in the second word. He didn't bother correcting what was written on the board, either. Instead, in typical form, he offered an explanation for the new equations he had barely finished writing.

"Hopefully," he said, "that will help the dissonance reduce..." We had no idea what he was talking about, and apparently, he didn't either, because he couldn't find the words to complete his sentence. "Uhh...reduce," he finished.

The rest of the lecture, which left me lost amidst a variety of graphs, was about price takers and price seekers. Professor Hart looked extremely unhappy. Then, with five minutes left in the hour, the lecture ended early.

"We're going to ask you to fill out a mid-semester evaluation, so that we can see how the course is progressing so far," Neugeboren said. "Please take one from the TFs, and pass them around. You can drop them off as you leave."

I took a sheet, which was double-sided and printed on ordinary office paper—not the customary ScanTron that the University used for end-of-semester CUE Guide course evaluations.

"*This was not a planned event,*" I thought to myself, wondering about the role my letter might have played.

A large number of the questions were about the course's instructor. Some asked about the pace of the course, about the TFs and general understanding. I wondered what the other students were writing.

On Friday, Oliver Hart was not there, but Neugeboren still was. He warned us about the date of our next midterm: November 20th. I watched the clock compulsively as he droned on and on. At precisely 10:59 A.M., the lecture was complete. It was just enough time for Neugeboren to leave us with one more incomprehensible assignment.

"As you know, some of my lectures have been...confusing...and I apologize for that, but so that I can get a better handle on teaching, the next few lectures are going to be given by Bruce Watson, so when you come back on Monday, you can expect him here."

It had actually worked. Just like that, the students of Economics 1010a had a new professor, and not just anyone. Bruce was a caring and supremely competent teacher. Much to my amazement, justice had been served.

CHAPTER 18

Round Pegs and Square Holes

The supposedly wealthy Technology and Entrepreneurship Center at Harvard, with its pizza parties and embroidered shirts, did absolutely nothing. The obvious solution as an entrepreneur was to start something new. I tried to get a smattering of friends interested in setting up a club with the same objectives through my non-profit organization, Think Computer Foundation. I had started it in high school as a senior project, and I figured it would make sense to put its tax-exempt status to use.

Nick Smith, who had not let up trying to sidle me into the Webmaster position for the International Review, seemed to be interested in the idea. He even took care of reserving the Lamont Forum Room so that we could have meetings, which I found unusual given how many other things he had to juggle. I e-mailed everyone agendas well before each meeting, trying to improve upon the aimless TECH meetings that took forever and went nowhere. Yet despite all of my efforts, I was lucky if a handful of people showed up. People just didn't seem to care about technology, even though they used it and depended upon it every day.

It didn't take long for Arturo, who was still in charge of TECH, to find out about my plans. They had been outlined in an e-mail with the subject "*Coup d'etat.*" As I expected, he called me a few days later, trying to describe why he wasn't very happy with me. I didn't care.

Meanwhile, Nick was not going to take "no" for an answer, but I was apprehensive that even his organization could become mired in IRC politics. I tried to persuade him to put some pressure on the new IRC President to upgrade the IR's systems first. Nick still wanted to have a meeting.

We talked in the Science Center Greenhouse, which offered snacks and pizza, to discuss exactly what I thought the magazine would need. I stressed that there was no way I would agree to be the webmaster of an organization that forced me to use my home computer to get everything done when it was expected that I would work in the office with everyone else. I wanted the magazine and its web site to be self-sufficient. Nick promised to see what he could do.

Not wanting to bear the burden alone, I also predicated my acceptance of the position on having a staff to work with. Nick assured me that I would have a staff, but having been present at the magazine's chaotic recruiting meeting in the fall, I knew it would never materialize. I explained my plan to him.

Think Computer Foundation needed entrepreneurial, technology-related projects to work on, and the International Review needed a self-sufficient web site. I hoped to have the few students who I had gotten involved with the Foundation help out with the web site, which would ironically teach them more about technology and entrepreneurship than they could learn through TECH. Nick, who was similarly frustrated by TECH's irrelevance on campus, thought it was a good idea.

"So you'll submit a candidacy statement?" Nick said, my system configuration printouts from Dell in his hands.

"Candidacy statement?" I asked. "I have to *run* for this?"

"Oh...yeah," Nick said. "But you'll be running unopposed. And you'll win. I'll make sure of it." I couldn't believe he had left this detail until the last minute, but I grudgingly submitted a short statement for approval.

The night of the elections, everyone—contested or not—felt it necessary to use their full time to explain why they were the best candidate, drawing out what should have been a twenty-minute meeting into a two-and-a-half-hour-long ordeal. I kept my speech short.

"I have a moral obligation to make the following disclaimer: my company, Think Computer Corporation, charges the Harvard International Review $25.00 per month for web site hosting. Any questions?" There were none. It was the shortest speech of the night, and it drew applause. Unfortunately, I hadn't been able to set much of a precedent for later speeches because it was also one of the last. The web site had never been one of the magazine's highest priorities.

During our first general staff meeting I became aware that I had a supervisor, and it wasn't Nick. I reported to the student who oversaw layout for the paper edition of the magazine.

"Why am I reporting to Manik?" I asked Nick.

"That's just the way things are set up," he said. "Don't worry about it, you don't really have to report to him. I'll take care of things for you."

Nevertheless, I received every e-mail from Manik's "media department" requesting my presence at meetings. After attending a few as a courtesy, I stopped going.

Everything needed to be done from scratch. The magazine's e-mail accounts were a mess. There were no databases of photographs, articles, authors, or editors. The paper edition's graphic design was a constant source of infighting, as different staffers had wildly different design abilities. I decided that rather than involve myself in the debate, I would just create a design of my own that worked with the existing one.

Nick and Richard wanted something "different" to make the magazine stand out. I started to put together something attractive but unorthodox for them, wondering about the conditions of our deal the whole time. No one else was doing any work from the Foundation, and the magazine's computers were aging with each passing day.

Meanwhile, the Co-Editors-in-Chief were thoroughly enjoying their new roles. CNN called to interview them, thinking that the magazine was run by professionals who employed full-time journalists. Eventually, CNN retracted its request.

Some of the magazine's student editors were also frustrated. Nick and Richard were adamant that students could not write original content for the publication, even though several were willing and able to write interesting material.

I began working on the databases that would need to be in place for the new web site to function. Nick and I spent hours going over their design, but he barely allowed me any time to train the staff on how to use them.

When I went to the IRC office to begin installing the software I would need on both computers for the site design work, I came across a problem I had never seen before. Clicking on certain menus simply didn't work. Eventually, I figured out that John had locked down the computers so tightly, they were next to impossible to use. Nick sent him an e-mail asking him to lighten the security restrictions so that I could get my work done. John flatly denied Nick's request, calling each program that I wanted to install "antiquated." His own methods were as antiquated as any technology that I knew of—he favored text files to store information so that he was the only one who knew how to format them for his code. John had also used some of the same software programs that I had requested to make the graphic design templates for the IRC sites.

Instead, I worked on the site using my own computer in Lowell House, even though it was exactly what I had hoped to avoid. I didn't want to be the "tech guy" huddled in the corner, working for everyone else's benefit; I wanted my work to have some meaning in the context of the club as a whole. On November 3rd, I hosted a meeting about web site design that Nick and several other Foundation members finally attended.

Nick seemed to enjoy it. "I felt like I learned more useful stuff about computers than I did in a full year of computer science in Switzerland," he wrote to me afterward. "By the end of the year you should easily be able to justify your very own prong of IR-dom." I wondered if he really thought that I was simply lusting for power within the IRC after resisting the job offer for six months.

After the next full IR staff meeting, Nick changed his tune. "I don't think we have the time in the board meeting to actually have people give you ideas," he wrote when I suggested that we discuss how to make the databases most effective.

I kept stressing that the databases were crucial to the club's success, and to the world at large. The IRC, like most organizations on campus, was horribly disorganized. I thought it was patently obvious that relational databases made all the difference between chaos and order, vagueness and precision, lethargy and agility. Whenever something made sense in everyday life, from buying subway tickets to checking movie listings, there was usually a relational database somewhere in the background. They were the single best way to represent information in a concise and completely accurate manner that man had ever devised, and I was growing immensely frustrated that no one—not even people with computer science background like Nick—seemed to understand the importance of what I was talking about.

The next day was worse. "We need to establish some ground rules about which computers you can and cannot use," he said, visibly irritated and clearly not sharing my enthusiasm for progressing with database training for the entire club. I had a flashback to Mrs. Groves's office at Woodbury.

"I'm not going to work with shackles on my arms..." I told him, insulted, but Nick cut me off. I left as soon as I could. What I had come there to say was that the new web site design was almost done.

I had seen posters around campus for a Law School conference titled "Internet & Society Conference 2002: Harvard's Digital Identity," sponsored by the Berkman Center for Internet and Society, with which Professor Zittrain was affiliated. I decided that it was worth checking out, and since I was a Harvard student there was no registration fee.

President Summers was the keynote speaker, and he impressed everyone when he invoked an audio recording that had been prepared for the conference the previous day by his former boss, President Bill Clinton. At the end of the speech, there was time for the audience to ask questions. It suddenly occurred to me that it was the perfect forum to ask the President why it was so important for the Administrative Board to keep freshmen from cross-registering into classes offered in conjunction with the Berkman Center. I raised my hand, and after a couple of other questions had been asked and answered, the microphone was mine.

I rarely got nervous, but with a packed auditorium of Harvard scholars from all across the University and multiple digital video cameras all focusing on me, it was also a rare occasion. I tried to shrug it off.

"As an undergraduate, I've, uh, always been fascinated by topics like thi—" My voice failed and the microphone I was speaking into amplified an embarrassing puff of air. I caught myself and kept going. "...this—uh, with technology—and I've wondered for a long time why something like the Berkman Center, as great as it is, is isolated only to the Law School. And I know a lot of my peers would really like to study topics like this, which are, from my point of view, when you're talking about its impact on society, very much in the realm of liberal arts. So, my question is, is there a day, maybe, that College students will be able to study topics like this, without having to worry about cross-registration and other...impediments."

There was a noticeable pause, and then laughter began to emerge from the front of the room, followed by sporadic applause.

"You know..." the President began, followed by more applause. The ensuing silence lasted a lifetime.

"Harvard is a interesting..." He stopped, the audience unleashing a wave of laughter.

"It's not that often that I'm at a loss for words! Uhh..." He tried once more, finally getting into his bizarre rhythm of short phrases.

"Harvard's an interesting kind of confederation. I think it would be an understatement to say that if anty cent—any center within a single school of the University sought to make its resources available—educationally or intellectually—to other parts of the University, that is something that the central University administration...would not condemn. Indeed, I think it's fair to say that that is something to say that the University administration exhorts...uhhhh, with very considerable, uh, frequency. And, uh, we've seen through the inter-faculty initiatives—other ways—something Neil Rudenstine focused on, uh, very much...I think a considerable coming-together at, uh, Harvard relative to what, uh, existed, eh, fifteen years ago; the university I came back to...after ten years away was a more integrated university...than, uh, the university, uh, that I left. But I think that these kinds of issues should be open, uhhh, much more. They're obviously hard issues of calendars, of budgets, of pre-requisites, that make these things not—make these things a little easier to say than actually to do, but I think the basic thrust of your question is...absolutely right. I hope the administrators at the Berkman Center or Dean Clark will give you a persuasive answer—or if they're unable to give you a persuasive answer, we'll, um, think about how they can adopt their programs to allow a larger role for undergraduates."

I wasn't sure if I followed his response, or if he had even answered my question. It sounded to me like he had delegated it to Dean Clark. I did know one thing, though: based on the audience's response, I wasn't the only one who had been wondering.

After President Summers's speech was finished, I looked around for Professor Zittrain to say hello. Instead, I found Professor Nesson, who quickly introduced me to the Provost of Harvard College, Dr. Steven Hyman.

"Very nice to meet you," I said, shaking his hand. He grumbled something back while avoiding eye contact.

"Meeting a student is far too much of a distraction for someone so important as the Provost," I was left thinking.

The rest of the conference was fairly unremarkable. Many of the law professors seemed downright giddy about distance learning, which I held in much lower esteem. I wondered if they had ever tried to learn anything as described by a two-inch-wide video.

That night, the dinner sponsored by the conference was downright bizarre. One of the attendees gave a Harvard employee at our table a bear hug, started speaking in French about churches in Paris when she was asked to introduce herself, and then left abruptly in the middle of the table's conversation about technology. I assumed that she knew the woman she was hugging and that she had a reason for speaking French when everyone else was speaking English. After she departed, I learned that both of my assumptions were false. She left an entire table of Harvard scholars and employees totally confounded.

From time to time, I noted, Harvard attracted not those who were incredibly gifted, but just incredibly strange.

CHAPTER 19

Finding Critical Mass

We were once more in the middle of midterm season, which never really ended. The stress put everyone on edge. Many of my friends had made it plain that they were sick of my griping about economics and the philosophy of grading. Even those who agreed were having a hard time keeping up with my daily IR reports. Whenever I tried to talk to Tim at MIT, he put the worst possible spin on whatever I was saying, quickly souring and ending the conversation. I finally called Carl, working in Seattle, to ask him for some advice, but this time his sympathy was harder to detect.

"Work on academics, or work on your company. You can't do both." I didn't feel enthusiastic about either.

My frustration rising to new heights, I met with the Allston Burr Senior Tutor of Lowell House, Jay Ellison, telling him that I was considering dropping out. He seemed indifferent. The Economics 1010a situation wasn't helping matters. After the first article about the 1010a debacle surfaced on the front page of *The Crimson* with the headline "Econ Lecturer Removed Amid Complaints," I had been a mini-celebrity for a few days. Everywhere I went, people congratulated me on dethroning a professor. They were taken aback when I expressed minor outrage at having had to write the letter in the first place, expecting instead that I'd be proud of myself.

As if I needed more bad news, on December 3rd, *The Crimson*'s headline read, "Removed Professor Returns to Class." Oliver Hart had decided to bring Neugeboren back. Sure enough, when I trudged through the snow to lecture, there he was, the worst teacher I had ever faced. His power to obliterate understanding and mangle concepts was restored, though he returned with strings attached. He was forbidden from using the chalkboard. All lectures had to be delivered with the aid of Microsoft PowerPoint. TFs were to be given better guidance for sections.

The result was that people simply gave up trying to understand before the slides even hit the screen. There was good reason: while trying to complete one problem set, I realized that of the six lines on a new PowerPoint graph from lecture, none had labels. There were no arrows to indicate progression over time. There were no words—just a bunch of lines—and it was two o'clock in the morning.

▼

At long last, Nick arranged for a meeting in the Leverett House dining hall about the IR web site design, to which he also invited his Co-Editor, Richard Re. I told them that I'd have the web site ready in a week. They didn't seem to comprehend that the only possible way anyone could design an entire site so complex in a week would be if it were mostly done in the first place. Their lack of appreciation made me second-guess the level of effort I was devoting to their cause.

"How's it going with the new equipment?" I asked.

"Look, we'll never get rid of our pirated software," Richard replied, laughing. "That's just how we operate."

"Well, I do run a software company, so I try not to steal things from other software companies..." I responded. They didn't seem phased.

"We probably won't get any new computers, either," Richard laughed again, apparently unaware of my deal with Nick.

One week later, I had the prototype site ready. I put it on-line, securing it so that only Nick and Richard could view it. Then, I decided that I'd had enough of being used. I sent an e-mail to Nick explaining that the public would be able to access the site when he lived up to his end of the deal. I wanted a staff, and I wanted equipment.

The following Friday, Nick and I met in the IRC office. When I arrived, Nick got up from his chair and we went into the "Central Office," a tiny room off the side full of accounting binders. With him sitting on the dilapidated sofa at one end, and me sitting on a swivel chair near the other, the distance between us was real.

He started out relatively calmly, asking about the status of the on-line databases, which I told him had not changed in months; the information I had requested from him in late November was still missing. Then, he got down to business.

"I have to say, Aaron, I'm really angry about that e-mail. To think that you could even send that—it was inappropriate, obnoxious, disrespectful, and really, poorly-thought-out. I still can't believe you did it. That took some nerve."

"Actually, I thought about it quite a bit before sending it," I responded. "But you haven't given me a straight answer about the new equipment, and that's not what we agreed upon."

"I didn't even *ask* about the computers, Aaron," he replied, "because there's no money in the budget for them. You need to change your attitude, because if you continue to act the same way you have been, you're no longer welcome here. You are without question the most difficult member of my staff. Every time something needs to get done, there's a problem, and it's with you. I'm sick and tired of having to deal with it." I continued to listen. "Not only that, but you're undermining the morale of the entire staff!"

"Who brought up the fact that I'm hurting their morale?" I asked.

"Several people..." Nick said, without naming names. "You know, I really think you should quit."

"I'd be reluctant to quit without fulfilling my obligation to create the site," I said. "That was my end of the deal."

"It *would* really be a shame since you've put together so much of the site already. I just don't understand why you're doing this. I have several freshmen who are begging me to work on the site."

"Well by all means, let me talk to them!" I said.

"Absolutely not! I wouldn't want to subject them to your despicable attitude!" Nick shouted, carrying on for several minutes.

"Well, here's how I see it," I said, pausing. "I consider your failing to live up to your word equally disrespectful to whatever disrespect you might have misinterpreted from my e-mail. I view this as a business transaction. We had a verbal agreement, and you failed to live up to it. Not only that, but you knew that I don't tolerate crap from the very beginning; you came to me about this after I resigned from the IRC for that very reason. You knew what you were getting into, and that it would be difficult—and it has been, thanks to John. So this really shouldn't be all that surprising!"

The argument went back and forth for an hour, until I left, my cheeks blazing. I knew I had to sever my ties to the magazine, but I wanted to do it in a way that would reflect the fact that I had at least tried to help. Everyone I talked to thought I was crazy not to quit immediately, but I couldn't go back on my word without stooping to Nick's level. Feeling hopelessly confused, I took the most blatantly magnanimous course of action I could conceive of: Think Computer Foundation purchased two copies of Adobe InDesign and donated them both to the International Review, and then I quit.

"At least now anyone Nick tells I'm 'evil' will at least be confused," I hoped.

I waited several weeks, but neither the IRC nor the magazine acknowledged my donation. The boxes simply went into John's filing cabinet. Francis, who had stayed in our Grays suite as a high school senior one year before and had become an IR editor thanks in part to my sales pitch, informed me that Nick had skewered me personally in front of the everyone at the last general meeting. Apparently, my company was over-charging the IR for web site hosting at the "inflated" price of $25.00 per month. No one remembered Shuko's pleading or my one-sentence disclaimer speech, let alone Harvard's prices.

I had expected the back-stabbing, but what really hurt was the way Francis acted from that point forward. He didn't know who to believe.

My statistics project was due at the end of the semester, and I had spent a long time trying to make it work. My brainchild was a web-based survey of student satisfaction with academics at Harvard. I even found a title for the project in a quote from Professor Hart, buried in the December 3rd *Crimson* article about Economics 1010a.

"If one person complains and no one else does, we're probably not going to respond. There has to be some sort of critical mass," he had told the paper. "That was the case here, but usually, fortunately, it isn't."

CriticalMass became the newest project of Think Computer Foundation. Eventually, the results of the survey produced a few interesting results, which I wrote about in the final paper for Statistics 104. One of my variables, grade inflation, was a hot button issue since *The Boston Globe* had asserted in a number of articles that it was a problem at Harvard. My results indicated that most students didn't agree.

"Only 7.101% of the sample population believed that their own personal grades were inflated, with 72.189% of students seeing no problem and 20.710% under the impression that their grades were actually deflated. This result is surprising, considering the rampant rumors of grade inflation at Harvard that have continued unabated for years," I wrote.

In an ironic twist, the *Globe* ended up covering CriticalMass after *The Crimson* covered it first, due to the connection between my name and Economics 1010a. A month later, *The Crimson* staff even wrote a positive editorial about the site with the by-line, "New website for critiquing teaching and better CUE guide will improve academic life." Unlike the CUE Guide, CriticalMass didn't try to quantify courses in absolute terms. Instead, it allowed students to rank courses on a scale relative to each other. Students could also comment anonymously on a course or its professor, since my letter to Professor Hart had revealed everyone's fear of retribution. As soon as the site guaranteed anonymity, people opened up.

I knew that it was risky shining a bright light on Harvard's teaching, but I didn't care. I was going to school to learn, and if anyone had a problem with that, they could say so.

Eventually, they did.

▼

It was almost spring semester. While everyone studied for final exams, I studied, and scanned in more than 800 pages of documents for Think Computer Corporation's federal trademark opposition before the United States Patent and Trademark Office Trademark Trial and Appeal Board. My company was at risk of losing its name, I was spending all of its cash on lawyers. The stress was incredible. I was fanatical about getting everything done in as efficient a manner as possible.

Purchasing textbooks still took an inordinate amount of time if you wanted to spend your money wisely. Even the cheapest web sites couldn't beat the convenience and low cost of simply buying a book from another student a few hundred feet away—yet there was no way to tell who owned what.

The Undergraduate Council had once sponsored a system called UC Books to facilitate used book sales. As President of the Harvard Computer Society in the late 1990s, Carl had written the system himself, but when he left, it fell into a general state of disrepair. No one had worked on any of the UC's computer systems in ages, which was made evident each time an election took place and they broke down.

With CriticalMass sporting several hundred members, it occurred to me that I already had a captive audience of users. I wasn't doing anything with it, though. *"Why not introduce a book trading site that CriticalMass members can access?"* I thought. No one would be forced to use it, since everyone using CriticalMass had signed up voluntarily in the first place. *"It would save everyone on the system a ton of money."*

I opened Textbook Central, and placed a link on the Foundation's site. People began using it immediately, typing in the details of all of their old textbooks. I was glad, too, because I had plenty of books of my own sitting around.

Then, one night, as I was walking to Mather House to meet several of my friends for dinner, I had a mind-blowing idea. I could hardly contain my excitement. *"If I integrate the two sites,"* I thought, *"you could see which classes you want to take for the next semester based on other people's reviews, and at the same time, see who you needed to e-mail right on campus to get the textbooks!"* It was better than Whiteboard, better than anything I had ever thought of, and I couldn't think of anyone else who was doing it. I hashed over the details in my head, thinking of the best way to merge the database tables as I walked through the street. I spent most of dinner thinking and talking about it as well.

Integration was a foreign concept at Harvard. "Every tub on its own bottom" was a oft-used phrase reflecting the University's predilection for decentralization. Each of its nine schools kept its own books, but the sentiment went far deeper than accounting alone. Each residential house in the College was practically its own fiefdom, with the Masters in absolute control. By not setting up a committee to control the Houses, the College's implied position was that the costs of integrating House life would far outweigh the benefits. I had heard many times from various Senior Common Room members about the importance of each House maintaining its own unique character.

Students, on the other hand, tended to have a different view. Their key cards worked in some houses, but not others. The back and side gates to Lowell House were always kept locked, requiring students to travel all the way around the House to get inside as long as they were coming from any direction except north—and six of the seven nearby houses were east, south, and west. Yet in other houses, the gates were always open.

The differences in room quality from house to house were vast. The first time

I took a shower in Lowell House, I realized that the bathroom had been arranged such that the shower stall was always pitch black, no matter how much light entered the room. The bathroom door also didn't lock. The next time I saw the superintendent, I asked him if there was anything he could do.

"We can't put a light in the shower," he told me, focused on his Solitaire game.

"Really? It seems pretty dangerous right now. I can barely see the ground."

"Yeah, nothing I can do," he said.

"Can you at least replace the doorknob with one that locks?" I asked.

"No."

"Why not?"

"Someone might get hurt in the shower," he said, completely straight-faced. "We'd need to get inside."

Such arbitrary restrictions had crept into the electronic realm, as well. Since each House maintained its own paper face book, the face book web sites were maintained by the House webmasters. Only Winthrop House students could access the information about other students in Winthrop House. Lowell House's face book was accessible to anyone as long as they had a valid Harvard ID. Dunster House required visitors to create a special user account, and restricted access to University computers only. Other Houses restricted access to machines physically within their House alone.

Similarly, some House sites were prettier than others. Living in what was arguably the most gorgeous House of all, the orange, beige and sky-blue Lowell House web site was also the most revolting. Aside from its color scheme, the black and white photographs featured students who had not attended the College for years. The content was nearly worthless for the average user: there were pages and pages about the bell tower's history, but no links to the day's dining hall menu.

Dan Ellard, the same programmer whose ANT errata page had become the source of so much strife in CS50, was the Lowell House webmaster. He lived with his wife and child in the House. I had e-mailed him at the beginning of October to see if he wanted any assistance redesigning the site, but the response I had received back indicated that I had presumed too much in assuming that he wanted it redesigned. Though he seemed perfectly willing to entertain the idea of using volunteers, he didn't want to use any technology that had been developed after the early 1990s to make the site more usable. We exchanged a second round of e-mails, but my suggestions never actually went anywhere.

Despite the success of CriticalMass and Textbook Central, Think Computer

Foundation had not materialized into the proponent of entrepreneurship that I had hoped it would become. On January 21st, I received an e-mail from TECH's faculty advisor, Paul Bottino, that changed everything.

"*This thing is taking forever to load...*" I thought to myself as my e-mail program churned away on the message. After two minutes, it finally appeared.

"Mark your calendars!" it read. "Elections for the Technology and Entrepreneurship Center at Harvard Student Association (TECH SA) are coming up soon!" My jaw dropped.

"Holy crap!" I said out loud.

"What?" Metin asked, working on a problem set a few feet away.

"TECH is finally holding elections for the first time ever..." I replied, still reading.

It was indeed the first time TECH would hold elections since its inception in 2000. One of my chief complaints about TECH had always been that Arturo seemed to have been installed as King of the group for life, with the full backing of the University.

The e-mail went on to list the positions that were available. I intended on running for President. Then, I noticed the reason that the e-mail had taken such an unusually long time to load. Attached to the message was a file nearly nine megabytes in size. I opened it up. In full, glossy detail, there was a giant picture of Arturo, the focus of the latest feature story in Harvard's official mouthpiece for the Division of Engineering and Applied Sciences.

"What the hell?" I exclaimed. "They're calling for open elections, and then sending out propaganda that supports the incumbent?"

I fired off an angry e-mail to Paul Bottino. I didn't understand how he could miss something that was literally so large. A week later, after I talked to him on the telephone, I sent another e-mail summarizing my concerns about the "election" with some proposed changes.

Surprisingly, Paul agreed to almost all of them. On January 30th, he sent out a new announcement about the elections to the TECH mailing list, this time lacking the giant endorsement of Arturo. The date remained the same, set in stone for February 2nd. I nominated myself, and hastily prepared a short speech.

The night of the elections, I put on a new maroon Polo shirt and frantically searched for a tie to match, which Elliott eventually came up with. About twenty people showed up, which was a good turnout according to some long-time TECH members. For years, people had been so unhappy with the club that they had been leaving in droves. I hadn't even noticed, since I had been one of the first to go.

When Paul called my name, I had my note cards ready. "I've done this before," I started off. "The last time I wanted to be President of something, I didn't wait to be elected. The statement on the ballot in front of you is intentionally concise because I don't have to persuade you that I know something about entrepreneurship. I'm already an entrepreneur."

Something that I said must have resonated with those listening, or perhaps my speech was simply less stilted than Arturo's, but either way, I won. My new Executive Board included two elected students I had never met before: Jesus and Anna. My first action as the newly-installed President was to e-mail them a message of congratulations, inviting them to lunch. Neither of them could make it at any of the times I suggested.

"Essentially, the club needs to be completely overhauled," I told them when we finally did meet up. My plan called for a club that looked like a company: it had a number of officers in addition to the overall Vice-President, which was to be Anna's new title, since the "Innovation Network" she was charged with running didn't really exist. In addition to their roles, I wanted a Chairman, a Chief Financial Officer, a Chief Operating Officer to oversee projects, a Chief Information Officer to handle internal technology issues, and a Rotating Spot to provide a mechanism for member feedback. The person filling the Rotating Spot would change every couple of months so that the Board could continue to hear new voices.

Since the club had such a horrible image on campus, literally and figuratively, one of my first suggestions was that we adopt a new logo. I had hated TECH's logo from the start, but Paul Bottino had always been fiercely resistant to change, claiming that the donor's three million dollars came with the stipulation that the club keep its present logo. I doubted that the donor really cared, but I could tell that Paul wasn't going to budge so long as I was just a loud freshman. Now, I was the club's President. I forwarded my logo ideas to my Vice-President of Communications.

Jesse sent back a rambling message that indicated a difference of opinion and a fondness for the caps lock key. He seemed to want a promotion. I wasn't inclined to give him one just yet.

I needed a reliable communications director, I soon realized, because I was getting swamped with the campus's technology-related e-mails. My previous assumption that there was no interest in technology at Harvard was wrong; there *was* interest here and there, but it had all been sucked into the black hole of Arturo's inbox. Now, I had to give it a place to go.

People wanted to know if they could get help setting up companies, how to structure the events the Arturo had put them in charge of months before, where to find money for their businesses, and when meetings were taking place. I felt like it was impossible to respond with anything intelligible until the club actually had some sort of infrastructure. I desperately needed to delegate things, and yet the obvious people to delegate to were positively averse to everything I proposed.

Arturo and Paul had booked Loker Commons, the large room underneath Annenberg, for a general meeting on the 27th of February. I scrambled to put together posters, an agenda, and a consistent message to deliver since I couldn't seem to get help from either of my Board members. I decided to start calling the club by its true name, the TECH Student Association, since Paul had explained to me that TECH was really a "center" at Harvard, which was what had all of the money. The Student Association, of which I was President, was just an offshoot. He wanted to reduce the confusion between the two, which was considerable.

Eventually, Jesse did get back to me with his own logo idea. He drew a picture in Microsoft Paintbrush: a wobbly, red-and-black Gothic shield that had the letters T-E-C-H on it in various places. The colors weren't filled in properly, as if a four-year-old had tried to color between the lines in a coloring book. I hoped he was joking.

I tried to explain to him how hard it would be to print a bitmap logo on T-shirts or other kinds of promotional materials, but he took offense. I informed him that he would have to try again. The result was another Paintbrush creation, this time, with a huge black cross in the center of the shield that looked exactly like the German Iron Cross. Given that Paul was already referring to the club as the TECH "SA," which immediately reminded me of the Nazi *Sturmabteilung* (or Storm Troopers, but abbreviated "SA" in German, as we had learned in World War II), I didn't feel the need to make any more allusions to Hitler's Germany. I rejected his second logo idea. As a compromise, I modified my own designs to include a shield, since many of Harvard's logos were shields of various sorts. Jesse's response was less than accommodating.

I spoke with Paul at great length about the club's identity issues and how to work with Jesse. My preference was to abandon the TECH name and logo completely, and I was surprised to find that he was actually receptive to the idea. He gave me the go-ahead to adopt a new name, and so I did: the Harvard Student Entrepreneurship Council. I figured if there could be a Council on International Relations, there could be one on Student Entrepreneurship too.

I used Whiteboard to make a new site for the club over spring break, building a section where members could upload their résumés to apply for a position on the revamped Board. The club's member database would be built into the web site, so that sending out e-mails to the entire club would not require compiling lists of names based on weekly Microsoft Excel spreadsheets, as had been the case under Arturo's reign. When the first newsletter invited members to submit their résumés on-line, several actually did.

The kinds of people who were interested did not quite fit with my traditional idea of entrepreneurship. One wanted to be a museum curator. Another, named Rodica, had a general interest in business, but was studying to go into medicine. My freshman roommate Wentao and his girlfriend also applied. I knew that both of them were very good at computers, though I wasn't sure how interested they were in business.

I had more meetings with Paul Bottino to figure out a way for TECH to fund several students to go to a Harvard Business School entrepreneurship conference. The SEC was also supposed to be sponsoring a venture capital forum that I was afraid no one would attend, a magazine called "Venture," and something called the "Entrepreneur's Roundtable," where SEC members could gather for free appetizers at local restaurants.

Despite the flurry of activity, I was still concerned that merely asking students to coordinate events missed the point of the club. I wanted people to be able to bounce ideas off of each other, making the SEC an incubator for new student-run businesses. We still had yet to find a project that would teach students all of the skills that they needed in order to be executives in the real world.

The answer came to me in a flash, but this time it was nothing new: integration. One of the many projects I had first outlined over lunch with Jesse and Anna was perfect for the job. At the time, I had called it the "House System," after the residential housing system for upperclassmen. The idea had been to create an attractive template for a standardized set of web sites, one for each house, so that students could actually use the sites to find information. To put the project in motion, though, I still needed people I could rely on, so it had been on the back burner for months. I encouraged more SEC members to submit their résumés on-line so that I would be able to conduct interviews. The new positions I had created would be appointed.

At the beginning of May, I met with my new Executive Board in a conference room in Pierce Hall. It had three new members: Wentao, his girlfriend, and Rodica, the pre-medical student who also conveniently lived in Lowell House. A chemistry student named Philip had been elected to fill in the Rotating Spot. Jesse sent out an e-mail instructing everyone to meet in a location that better suited him, and then did not show up at all. Anna was also missing.

Rodica was the new Secretary. I didn't even need to tell her what to do. She e-mailed me detailed, typed minutes of our meeting almost immediately after it was over. Her first major project was to run the club's name change by Susan Cooke in University Hall, who was responsible for keeping track of all of the student organizations on campus. Within a few days, the change was official: Rodica reported back that the administration had approved the name change from the TECH SA to the SEC.

Wentao's girlfriend was the new CFO. "We need a bank account," I told her. "In order to do any of this stuff, we're going to have to be able to finance it, and right now, Paul doesn't seem to want to give us much of anything unless I go and beg him for it. It's a far cry from three million dollars. That money is tied up in endowment accounts, and Paul gets to spend the interest. There's not much of that, either, because the interest on the account has to pay his salary as well." It was the first anyone had heard of the real setup. "Paul has promised us $2,000 for next year, but in order to accept it, we're going to need our own bank account."

"Are you serious?" our CFO said. "We might be able to use Fleet..."

"I don't know, I think they have a high minimum balance," I thought out loud. "We should definitely compare a bunch and see what's best." After the pitch I'd been given in 2001, I couldn't believe we were worrying about minimum balances.

Wentao was the new CIO, in charge of anything technology-related for the club. His job description was supposed to include management of the computer lab in Pierce Hall that belonged to TECH, but nobody except the Venture Magazine people actually used it on a regular basis. It was simply too far away.

"We also need to get a bunch of databases together right away. I already have a preliminary one now that has all of your résumés in it, but we need to make the front-end easier to use, and integrate it with everything. That sort of ties into what I want to talk about next, which is that I have a bunch of web-based projects floating around that I've been working on, and I'd like the SEC to take them over.

"What I've got is CriticalMass, a site that lets you review courses in plain English on-line, Textbook Central, which lets students buy and sell used textbooks, and FASt Webmail, which is a web-based e-mail program I put together freshman year before the University got around to making an official one—and it *is* still much faster than the official one, as the name implies. I'd also like to make a pre-registration system given all the controversy about pre-registration right now, which would let you map out the classes you want to take during shopping period without being bound to them, and a House System, which would provide consistent, decent-looking web sites for all of the twelve houses, and also one for Harvard Yard.

"Now, the key is that all of the other projects would be encompassed by the House System," I said. "So there would be one place to go for everything. The SEC would be in charge of it, and it would be a pretty substantial task to keep in running. We'll need marketing, programmers, tech support...everything a real start-up would need."

Rodica scribbled notes down. We talked some more about what would be required to get everything set up, and the meeting was over.

In an hour, we had laid the groundwork for a total paradigm shift in the way that people would use the internet.

CHAPTER 20

The Birth of houseSYSTEM

In the short term, we were going to need programmers, but I already knew that the Computer Science department was the last place to look for students with practical skills. I'd have to find the uniquely skilled people to run the SEC's project myself, and if I couldn't find any, I figured I'd just have to create them out of ordinary Classics concentrators.

With Wentao and Rodica's help, the SEC reserved a small computer lab in the Science Center on weekends, where I taught an underground course in the basics of HTML, PHP, and MySQL to about fifty students at time. The main goal was to instill practical technical knowledge in students, and I was pleased to learn that it was knowledge students actually wanted. We called the initiative "! CS50," using the exclamation point to represent the word "not," as it did in the C programming language.

The project had a short life. After a few sessions jammed with students, we had to compete with the World Series, which hurt attendance. Then, word of the operation got out, and the new CS50 professor and one particularly belligerent TF did not appreciate our naming joke. We were forced to succumb to the angry e-mails of CS50 affiliates.

While my extracurricular activities were taking on a life of their own, things were still progressing elsewhere. I was even getting occasional e-mails from Simon at school, sent through my father, since Simon didn't e-mail anyone else and had to be coaxed into sending the few messages that he did. It had taken us years to figure out, as none of more than a dozen psychologists who examined him had ever thought it worth mentioning, but Simon was not just "learning disabled." His sudden obsession with sports statistics, his strange love of calendars, his social ineptitude, his misshapen skull, his slurred speech, his gibberish language, his behavior problems, his eerie independence, his reams of lists... They all added up to something. Simon was autistic. Where he was on the so-called autistic spectrum, we didn't know, but Simon was there.

It wasn't simply a matter of semantics either. To me, the difference between autism and learning disabilities was that Simon was never going to "outgrow" his autism. There was nothing we could do, no magic drug, no cure. Life simply had to go on. I wrote him brief e-mails (since his attention span for reading was limited), and went back to work.

I had cross-registered at the MIT Sloan School of Management for a course officially called "15.394." All of MIT's courses were numbered, as were its buildings. The English title of the course was "Designing and Leading the Entrepreneurial Organization."

The professor, Diane Burton, had previously taught at Harvard Business School, but as I had discovered in the process of formulating my special concentration, it was easier to cross-register at MIT than it was to walk across any of the stone bridges to Harvard Business School. I had never been in a case-method course before, and I found it interesting to watch as fully grown adults were reduced to the mental stature of second-graders. Everyone competed fiercely for the professor's attention to prove that they knew The Answer.

My favorite course by far was a Core course called Foreign Cultures B-48: The Cultural Revolution. Roderick MacFarquhar, our professor, was the real thing. He was the kind of professor that college tour guides talked about when they described what everyone naturally assumed to be every professor at their institution. He had been in China during most of the events he lectured about, reporting as a correspondent for the BBC. Across the board, lectures were captivating. The material was unique, in the sense that one was unlikely to hear it taught anywhere else in such detail—and certainly not in China.

Once, Professor MacFarquhar had his brigade of TFs sit quietly in locations dispersed throughout the classroom for the duration of his lecture. Hardly anyone noticed that they were all wearing red armbands. At the Professor's signal, they jumped into the aisles, running and shouting at the top of their lungs.

"*Mao joo-shee won swei! May Mao live ten thousand years!*" they chanted again and again in unison. Professor MacFarquhar, tying an impressively wide, bright red armband around himself, assumed the role of Mao. After a minute, it was actually frightening, as if mass hysteria had suddenly descended upon the room. There were no more than ten TFs, but they more than sufficed to get the point across. Finally, everyone calmed down.

"You think, just now, that this room was fairly loud," he said in his non-Mao voice to the stunned classroom. "Now imagine Tienenmen Square, full of tens of thousands of people your own age, shouting that in unison, for an hour. Or two hours. That is what it would have been like to be present at one of the Red Guard rallies in Beijing."

The tales of twentieth century back-stabbing and manipulation in Chinese politics were unlike anything I had ever heard. They certainly seemed less drab than the United States History I had been forced to learn from Mrs. Pessel. I was surprised, most of all, at myself; between World War II and the Cultural Revolution, I was gravitating toward history, taught by Harvard's Core Curriculum, as my favorite subject.

The amount of reading we had to do was overwhelming, but I did all of it, underlining each important passage in blue pen. One pattern in particular stood out: when Mao wanted to fire someone, he always got away with it. He would gather all of his top-level officers together for a meeting, inviting the unlucky victim of his wrath a few minutes late. When the victim appeared, he (or she) was already surrounded. It was impossible to win. The lucky ones were deported to far-off regions of southern China. The unlucky ones were executed.

The mere prospect of such a system was horrifying. Mao had been a cruel and unpredictable dictator, but I wondered what would happen if the same system was employed by a benevolent one.

♥

I had been less than successful at convincing University Hall that entrepreneurship was an area worthy of academic study. My meetings with Dean Foster led me on a wild-goose chase in search of the faculty's approval. I travelled to the Law School, the Extension School, to dining halls, and to the Computer Science department. I sent out countless e-mails to professors who I thought might be interested in my ideas. In the end, the only person I was able to relate to was Margo Seltzer, a Computer Science professor who herself had started a business, Sleepycat Software.

Sleepycat distributed a product that Professor Seltzer had invented in graduate school at the University of California, Berkeley, called BerkeleyDB. It was immensely popular among programmers worldwide for its tiny size and flexible use behind the scenes of larger applications. Amazon.com, Google, Netscape, and many other large businesses were her customers.

Margo, as everyone called her, was very receptive to the ideas and frustrations that I spilled out over her small table in Maxwell-Dworkin. I brought an assortment of documents relating to my proposed coursework.

"Well, how about I write this right now so you can give it to the Special Concentration committee," she said, moving over to her UNIX workstation to start typing. She read aloud as she pressed the keys. When she said, "I have reviewed Aaron's statement of purpose and proposed plan of study, and agree with his assessment that the area he targets is both important and underrepresented within current concentrations," I couldn't help but smile. It had taken me nearly two years to do it, but I had finally found someone at Harvard College who understood what I was talking about.

After preparing a General Information form, a revised Statement of Purpose, two Economics Concentration Plans of Study (one three-year with Advanced Standing, and one four-year without), one Special Concentration Plan of Study, a Summary of Course Differences Between Proposed Plan of Study and Alternative Plan of Study, a Statement of Senior Tutor, Professor Seltzer's statement, the Statement of Department(s) Most Closely Related to Proposed Special Concentration, and my Most Recent Grade Report, I had everything I needed to submit to the Committee on Special Concentrations.

"All of this to be able to learn what I want to?" I thought bitterly as I was shuffling the papers I had spent hours writing, fetching, and compiling.

The Committee didn't need long to think about my application. They rejected it immediately. I didn't receive a letter automatically, but instead had to specifically request it from Dean Foster. She e-mailed me a copy.

I regret to tell you that at its meeting of April 25, 2003, the Faculty Committee on Degrees in Special Concentrations voted not to accept your petition for a Special Concentration in :Technology and Entrepreneurship in Society.

As I said to you over the phone, after careful consideration of your application, committee members concluded that the focus of your proposal was too pre-professional for an undergraduate degree in liberal arts. To most members of the committee, your proposal seemed like a petition to concentrate in Business, which, as you know, Harvard does not offer at the undergraduate level. Some committee members expressed their opinion that the premises for rationalizing your proposed study were inadequately articulated in your statement of purpose. Furthermore, they agreed you did not demonstrate convincingly that the coursework you selected would provide the background knowledge necessary for a special concentration in technology and society.
Committee members also felt that your statement of purpose did not demonstrate an understanding of the history of the intersection between technology and society that should be the foundation for a study of this field.

Several committee members volunteered to discuss these issues with you in more detail if you wish clarificaton or guidance toward resubmitting your application next year. I encourage you to contact Professor Claudia Goldin in Economics, Dr. Peter Buck in History of Science, Professor Philip Stone in Psychology and Professor Anthony Oettinger in Applied Mathematics and in Information Resources Policy.

I suspect that this outcome will be disappointing to you. Please do not hesitate to contact me if I can be of any assistance as you think about what to do next.

"I'm flattered that she took such an interest in my case," I thought sarcastically, wishing that I possessed a voodoo doll of Dean Foster. Her specialty was Folklore and Mythology.

Immediately after asking for my letter of rejection, I received an e-mail from Professor Stone, whom Dean Foster had mentioned in her letter. He and a student at the Business School wanted to discuss my point of view on technology, which I had outlined in my Statement of Purpose. Professor Stone seemed doubtful of my assertions.

First, you state that "information technology had a positive economic impact only after 1995" without pointing to the evidence for that.   I'm aware of the writings of Solow and others about the lack of a clear economic impact in the earlier days of computing, but don't know what evidence exists for 1995 being a clear year of transition.   None of the other committee members present knew either. Could you fill me in on that?

"Ha!" I exlaimed, surprising Metin once again. My basis for using the year 1995 had been none other than Harvard's own Economics department. Our Economics 1010b professor, Francesco Caselli, had given several lectures in which he mentioned that it was widely believed that 1995 was the point when information technology began to impact productivity. I wrote back, mentioning Professor Caselli's lecture and my own views on technology and productivity. The fact that Microsoft Windows 95 debuted in 1995 seemed like an obvious data point that economic theory alone couldn't explain.

Professor Caselli, who was Italian, was widely lauded by academics for his work on economic growth, and by students for his sense of humor. When he began writing a formula that involved a function of the variable "U", he got himself into a cultural bind.

"So, $F(U)$," he started out. The class began laughing uproariously.

"What? What?" he said, putting down his chalk. "What is it, what did I say? F-U? So what! F-U! F-U!" We laughed even harder.

Professor Caselli put his hands at his sides. "I am not going to continue this lecture until someone tells me exactly what is going on!" he demanded in accented English. One brave student raised his hand.

Still, the Business School student working with Professor Stone remained unsatisfied. She wanted to know how Professor Caselli had defined the variable g.

I called my parents in a fit of rage. "Why is it that they want to talk to me now? Why couldn't they ask me these questions *before* they made their decision to reject my petition? Do they just want to torture me with it? It's not like I can study it now, anyway! As that freaking woman said, 'I suspect this outcome will be disappointing to you.' It sure as hell is disappointing! Now I have to be stuck with two more years of crap from the Economics department!"

A few weeks later, I met in person with Dean Foster to go over the reasons why my proposal had been rejected in detail. She wasn't willing to offer up much, aside from relaying the accusation that there were "factual errors" in my Statement of Purpose. I e-mailed Professor Seltzer with a summary of our meeting, since as my advisor she had also been interested to learn more.

The other professor Dean Foster had suggested I speak with, Dr. Peter Buck, was even less agreeable than Dean Foster herself.

"Well, for one thing, your Statement of Purpose makes you sound incredibly arrogant," he told me. "It's as if you already know something about the subject."

I held my tongue, trying to be diplomatic. "Well...was there one part or sentence in particular that you took issue with?" I asked.

"No, not really," he said, sitting back in his chair. "It was more...how you used all of these facts. I think you should have asked more rhetorical questions. It projects a more academic feel that way.

"Really, in the context of management, entrepreneurship is almost irrelevant. It's really management that you should be studying." It occurred to me that he was telling me to wait a few years to apply to business school.

"But isn't it sort of ironic that you think I'll be criticized for being *too* specific in what I want to focus on?" I asked.

"Yes. It is," came his response. Professor Buck went on to explain about the Holland Tulip Craze, an incident in the 1600s when the price of tulips in Holland increased sharply due to speculation. I saw the point that he was trying to make: it was just like the dot-com boom.

"Did you know about it?" he asked me.

"No, I didn't," I said.

"Well, that demonstrates perfectly then why your application was rejected. You're not qualified to be studying technology unless you know its history."

I wanted to ask him how he expected me to learn it if I wasn't permitted to study it, but I could see that there was no point. I gave up then and there on the idea of a Special Concentration, and I was one step closer to dropping out.

The semester thankfully came to a close in a burst of final papers and projects. I had made arrangements to live on the Business School campus in an air-conditioned apartment with two other people I had met through the SEC, and I was looking forward to being able to do what I wanted for a change. As an added perk, the next Harry Potter book was due to be released in July, and I was eager to see what my (and the world's) fictional counterpart was up to.

Wentao, who was also in Cambridge for the summer, met with me in Pierce Hall to go over the specifications for what was going to be called "houseSYSTEM." I had decided to make the first word all lowercase and the second completely capitalized simply to catch people's attention. I wanted the site to be a big deal.

"This is going to be like nothing people have seen before," I said excitedly, sketching in dry-erase marker on the whiteboard of the otherwise empty computer lab where we sat. My sketch called for three panes: a photograph in the upper left, and small area to sign in on the upper right, and content below. Instead of separating each pane with a boring line, I used a photograph of ivy leaves that gave the site a refined look.

I had just received a digital camera as a belated birthday gift from my mother and was anxious to put it to use. Over the next week, I walked all around the Harvard campus, taking pictures of every single residential House. I left it up to Wentao to format them appropriately for use on the Web while I went to work trying to integrate all of the code I had written over the prior two years. It would have taken months had it not been for the software toolkit that Think had assembled in order to write Whiteboard.

On June 25th, I appeared for a deposition regarding Think's trademark case, hijacking a conference room at the Business School since I had nowhere else to go. Without anyone present from my Minneapolis-based law firm and left stranded by the Law School's Berkman Center, I spoke very slowly and deliberately the entire time to ensure that I had time to think over what I was saying. A court stenographer captured every word.

By mid-July, I had the majority of the code for houseSYSTEM in place and the photographs dazzled everyone I showed them to, but there was one missing feature: the shopping period scheduling tool. I wanted to be able to select all of the courses I was interested in shopping and then display them on a weekly calendar side-by-side so that any conflicting courses could be highlighted. My plan was to win over both students and faculty with the scheduler, since students clearly needed a more efficient way to research classes, and the faculty needed a more efficient way to allocate professors before each semester began. With houseSYSTEM, students could register their interest for a particular course in a quantifiable database, without actually being committed to the course once the semester began. The College administration would have an easy way to gather its statistics, effectively solving the entire pre-registration problem, which had come up again and again in *The Crimson* throughout 2002 and 2003.

Writing the code for this single feature alone ended up taking another two weeks, during which I slept very little and felt only slightly less like a zombie than I had during the CS50 final project. After working out most of the kinks, the calendar only failed my tests when people chose several hundred courses to shop at once. To keep the system from crashing, I used Nathan's technique from freshman year and capped the number of courses a person could shop at twenty, since I wasn't even sure that it was humanly possible to shop ten. At the top of the course selection form, I made a graphic that read, "HARVARD UNIVERSITY RIDICULOUS FORM NO. 80419884085930000000000000070000000000.6." With such a clear display of sarcasm, I thought it would be impossible to mistake houseSYSTEM for an official site.

By the time houseSYSTEM was ready for testing, students could look up courses, check a calendar of events, buy and sell textbooks, plan their course schedules, and check their e-mail in one centralized location. Each site also featured easy-to-find contact information for house administrators, which was always in a different location on every house's official site, and photos of the respective house, or Harvard Yard.

I had plans for houseSYSTEM's future as well: I wanted students to be able to receive package notifications from their house administrators through the site, and I had some code written to handle room reservations for student groups. I had also talked excitedly to the SEC Board about plans to create an opt-in, university-wide face book that didn't suffer from any of the arcane restrictions imposed by the University. If it caught on, we could even license houseSYSTEM to other schools.

I e-mailed the president of Harvard Student Agencies, Abhishek Gupta, to inquire about setting up a deal that would allow the SEC to use its "Unofficial Guide to Life at Harvard" content on houseSYSTEM, since the Unofficial Guide featured blurbs about each house. The Guide was an extremely useful publication that each undergraduate received at the beginning of each school year, full of restaurant reviews, information about Harvard Square, and general information about places to go and things to do. Abhishek wrote back, and he seemed interested.

I also received an e-mail from the president of the Undergraduate Council, Rohit Chopra, who had been following my progress ever since *The Crimson* had written about CriticalMass. The UC was finally trying to get a site together to allow students to buy and sell used textbooks. Rohit wanted to know if I could help. Ironing out the details of a deal proved difficult, however. Rohit didn't want students to have to sign up for a houseSYSTEM account. I wanted as many members as possible.

At the same time, I was sending out e-mails to all of the big names in technology, trying to get them interested in coming to Harvard to speak. I sent messages to Bill Gates and Steve Ballmer at Microsoft, Mitch Kapor, who had once run Lotus, Jerry Kaplan, the author of the book that Carl had recommended so many years before, and other famous entrepreneurs. No one wanted to come to Harvard.

By the end of July, the centralized calendar, site search, and message board functions were all up and running on houseSYSTEM. In the span of a month and a half, Wentao and I had created a complete student portal that easily rivaled the official "my.harvard" site. The University had been dumping money into it for years, and even included a flyer advertising its address in every student's registration packet each semester. No one used it. It was ugly, it was slow, and it barely worked.

My self-imposed deadline for launching the site was August 1, 2003. I was scheduled to go on vacation in Hilton Head with my family during the first two weeks in August, and I wanted to get everything done ahead of September so that I could relax. I also wanted to give students time to spread the word about the shopping period tool, so that they could use it well before shopping period actually began.

On August 1st, the houseSYSTEM source files went up on Think's server and

I e-mailed an announcement to everyone I could think of at Harvard. I forwarded the SEC's message to the lowell-open mailing list from my personal e-mail account. Through the SSH interface to my server, I could see that all across the world, Harvard students—many of them bored at home as the summer wore on—were signing up.

Felix, my former pre-frosh who I'd coaxed into joining the SEC and the Pops, began work on a Flash animation to market houseSYSTEM on the SEC's web site. I chose a sound clip from the *Spider-Man* theme to accompany the graphics, and made sure to give Sony Records proper credit, along with a reference to the fair use clause in federal copyright law. houseSYSTEM was, after all, an educational endeavor, and we only used part of the CD track. I showed a few of my friends the finished product.

"Wow!" they said. "That is *really* cool."

CHAPTER 21

The Battle of Lowell House

Exactly one day after I sent out the announcement, Dan Ellard, the Lowell House webmaster, sent me an e-mail. His message was polite, but he seemed to be awfully focused on a problem that didn't even exist. He claimed that I had mistakenly typed a comma at the end of houseSYSTEM's address.

In fact, there was a comma after the address, because it came in the middle of a sentence. I had written, "Visit http://www.harvardsec.org/projects/housesystem.html, and see for yourself." This caused the lowell-open mailing list program to incorrectly hyperlink the punctuation as part of the address. It was only a problem, however, if you read lowell-open through Dan Ellard's Lowell House web site. I explained to Dan that it wasn't a mistake in my writing, but rather, a mistake in the mailing list software. Yet he wouldn't back down. Three e-mails later, I gave up, amazed that he had nothing else to say, positive or negative, about something that could fundamentally alter the way students used computers at Harvard.

A more ominous warning came from a friend in Cabot House, who had seen a sneak preview of the site a couple of weeks beforehand. She forwarded me cabot-open's response to my announcement.

Yeah, I feel this web site is partly pretty sketch. Overall legit, but it's ridiculous what they wrongly imply you need to do with your password:

"Please Change Your Password
In order to use houseSYSTEM, your password must be the same as your password for your Harvard FAS network account."

You can change your password to anything, but it makes it sound like you need to use your FAS password, which is only true if you want to get to your e-mail and some other goodies. In fact, to confuse you, even after you change your password, it still says "Please Change Your Password" if you don't match up with your FAS password.

They should change this to say "In order to use e-mail and bluh-bluh, your password must be ... But hey, you don't actually have to have the same password as your FAS password." And they shouldn't keep shouting "Change Your Password."

Also misleading is the copyright notice, which says portions are copyright "The Presidents and Fellows of Harvard College." Which is true, but makes it sound like this web site is really closely affiliated with them, which isn't the case (right?). And then the e-mail they sent introducing the web site doesn't make their disconnect from the college admin. clear either.

I mean, overall it looks like it has some good links and resources, but it is too misleading and needs to make clear that it's independent from the FAS computing services
(esp. re: passwords), the college administration, etc. -- which could be done with a
few simple changes.

Let me know if I'm ranting unjustifiably. Otherwise I'm going to write <info@harvard-
sec.org> an angry e-mail.

Then, my friend forwarded another follow-up from a Cabot resident.

i think the copyright "The Presidents and Fellows of Harvard College." is probably
due to the fact that they're an organization on campus and probably got funding/
grant from some harvard source.

"*I only wish...*" I thought after reading through the message.

In fact, I had attributed the copyright to The President and Fellows of Harvard
College to avoid getting into any legal disputes with Harvard, which was notoriously
picky about copyright attribution. It was simply the right thing to do, since I had
copied some of the content to describe each House from Harvard web sites. Since
the SEC was a student group that was part of the Faculty of Arts and Sciences, which
meant that it was part of Harvard, I didn't think using Harvard's content would be
a problem. Accordingly, I made sure that each page contained a link back to the
original source if it used Harvard's content.

I received yet another forwarded e-mail.

"*Funny, how I can't access these myself because of the Cabot House restrictions...*"

The message was from the same person who had sent the previous one.

the website seems legit enough, although it is student run and thus not affiliated in
any way with FAS coimputing services. the email and password fields on the website
are actually authentication into your houseSYSTEM account, if you have one.

for security purposes, the FASCS do not store your passwords ANYWHERE on the
system. even someone with godlike "root" access to our systems can not retrieve
your password, only change it. However, I don't know how the houseSYSTEM man-
ages their passwords, or whether the administrators of the website can pull up the
passwords you enter when you try to sign up for a houseSYSTEM account. Therefore,
although registering with the houseSYSTEM is not a security risk in itself, i would
probably not give them the same password I use for my FAS email account.

Note further that when you received your FAS account it was explicitly stated and
agreed upon that you may not, for any reason, give your FAS account password to
anyone, not even to your parents, spouses/bfs/gfs, or a staff member of FASCS(we'll
never ask for it). Now all the FASCS sponsored websites (such as webmail) take the
necessary precautions to ensure the safety of your password, and we at FASCS also

make no attempts at hacking your account. However the same can not be said of this website. Until evidence surfaces that proves that the houseSYSTEM does not actually store the passwords of its members, i would say it is technically a breach of your service agreement to give them your FAS account password.

The message was from an Undergraduate Assistant, or UA. UAs were paid by Harvard to help their peers with computer problems, and some of them assumed officious tones when speaking to those they considered less computer literate. house-SYSTEM asked people to verify their FAS passwords so that they could automatically access their Harvard e-mail accounts with one click. The process I had designed was no more or less secure than checking your e-mail from anywhere in the world, including the Harvard campus, which people did thousands of times each day.

"Besides," I thought. *"I'm not even storing the passwords."* I had learned in the process of creating Whiteboard that there was a much better way to authenticate users. When a person typed in their password, it was possible to calculate a unique sequence of characters based upon what had been typed, called a hash. I recalled Mr. Tournoux telling us how some functions would yield a unique result for any variable x that you gave them. Five years later, I was finally putting high school math to practical use—the variable x was the user's password. The key was that no two passwords could ever have the same hash (according to the theory). Hashes also didn't contain any hidden clues about the password; to the human eye, they looked like gibberish. Trying to decrypt them with a special keycode was pointless, because they had never been encrypted with a keycode in the first place. It was the mathematical equivalent of leaving footprints in the snow in order to later match them with the boots that created them.

The best way to verify someone's identity, therefore, was to compare the hash of a user's real password, stored in a database, to the hash of whatever had just been typed. As long as the two hashes matched, the password was correct.

The end result was that houseSYSTEM never stored any passwords at all—nor did any of Think's software. Passwords did pass through the server's Random Access Memory for a infinitesimal fraction of a second, but I had designed Think's toolkit to delete them from memory as soon as they had been hashed.

I sent an e-mail clarifying all of the issues that the Cabot students had raised, and asked my friend to pass it along to the House. Within minutes after forwarding it to cabot-open, she was inundated with more responses, asking about password encryption, Secure Socket Layers, and other miscellaneous security references she didn't understand. She sent them all back to me. There was work to be done convincing the Computer Science concentrators that houseSYSTEM was safe. I wrote up a "Security Statement" explaining hashes, encryption, and databases in detail for those who were interested. It was more comprehensive than anything I'd ever seen on any of Harvard's web sites, which never explained how they stored our IDs or PINs. Everyone simply assumed that they were safe in the hands of University Information Systems.

Before I could even respond to the latest round of questions, Rodica sent me an instant message: lowell-open was going mad. I hadn't even received the latest batch of messages, so I signed in. The first looked alright.

> That new thing at harvardsec.org looks cool...and I want to try it. Why isn't my email registered? Argh. Someone please tell me how to resgister...

And then I saw what had happened. Dan Ellard, still obsessed with the comma, had responded. At best, he was overzealous. At worst, he was paranoid.

> There's a little thing to click on underneath the login thing, titled "New to the SEC HouseSYSTEM?" So if you really want to sign up, that's where you do so.
>
> But, despite the coolness of the web page (it looks pretty nice), maybe you should think twice. They certainly want a lot of information... like your HUID, and your email address. They even suggest that you choose a password that's the same as your FAS password. Hmmm....
>
> Your Name + FAS login + FAS password + HUID = your Harvard identify.
>
> That seems like a bit more than I'd like to give up just to look at a web site that is still mostly "coming soon".
>
> So, who is Harvard SEC anyway? It's not in the list of student organizations. The computer addresses are outside the Harvard domain. In fact, the physical address of the company that manages www.lowell.harvardsec.org is based in Hoboken, New Jersey (datapipe.net), which is even farther away than the Quad.
>
> If you go the HarvardSEC web page, there are lots of familiar names (like our very own Aaron and Rodica). But for all we know, these are just the first people to have their email addresses stolen. After all, the *real* Aaron Greenspan wouldn't botch posting a URL!
>
> It's probably all above board -- I know Aaron's been working on this for a while. However, it still seems like a very bad idea to hand over your HUID and FAS password (and send it over an insecure, unencrypted connection -- even if HarvardSEC is honest, who knows who else is listening or has access to their server logs?) when neither seems related to any functionality of the site and leaves you wide open to a spectrum of mischief.
>
> Thus ends today's lesson in safe surfing.

Then came an e-mail from the same student who had asked about the existence of "half a God" during my Expository Writing course, freshman year.

If you don't use the same password as your FAS account, the site gets a little more insistent the first time you log in:

Please Change Your Password
In order to use houseSYSTEM, your password must be the same as your password for your Harvard FAS network account.

It didn't seem to notice that I gave a phony Harvard ID, though, which is a step.

"*Crap*," I thought. The Harvard ID field was not supposed to have made it into the final version of the site at all, but I hadn't caught the mistake, and none of my friends who had been beta testing the site had recognized it as one either. The code for the houseSYSTEM sign-up form had been copied from the SEC's web site, which had a good reason for asking for prospective members' IDs: every time we wanted to order food through Harvard University Dining Services, we were asked for them. Memories of Domna's incessant card-swiping in Annenberg haunted my thoughts.

Since houseSYSTEM wasn't planning on feeding its members, there was no reason to ask for Harvard IDs. I removed the field from the form in a matter of seconds. Then, I wrote a response for lowell-open, similar to the one I had written for cabot-open. Dan wouldn't give up, though. Minutes later, he wrote to the mailing list again.

Of course, the only way that it could know that you didn't give it your FAS password is by trying to access your FAS account using the password you supplied...

Just say no. Repeat as necessary.

He was distorting the truth to make it sound like my server was attempting some nefarious activity in the background, when it simply wasn't. It took me a minute to realize that his "just say no" directive was in response to the question about how to handle the password prompt. At first, I thought he was telling people not to use the site at all.

Then, another e-mail appeared on the list, this time from a Physics concentrator named Brian Wong. Responding paragraph by paragraph, he addressed each and every point I had made to the mailing list.

Your security statement is, frankly, nonsense. I have strong doubts that you have ever had any formal exposure to cryptography--it reads very much like you read a few web pages on encryption and decided that the more times you encrypt something, so much the better.

You can store a salted hash of the password (which is what most *nixes do). And if you want real security, you would use a protocol like SPEKE or other ZKP password protocols.

> This is a sure sign of someone who doesn't understand cryptography. The number of times something is encrypted does not correlate with security in the least. Also, MD5 does not encrypt, it hashes.

I had tried, in a vain attempt to explain MD-5 to people who had never heard of "hashing" in their lives, to present the technology as something similar to encryption. Though the fundamentals were different, I was confident that more people had heard the word "encrypt" before, and were generally familiar with its meaning as a method to encode a signal. Brian, who had a more finely-honed knowledge of the concepts than the average user, had a great deal to say about my decision.

> 16 bytes, not 32. One does not "decrypt" a hash, one finds a preimage that hashes to the same result. MD5 has sufficient weaknesses in its compression function that its use in newly deployed applications should be discouraged. Use SHA-1 instead.

In response to my explanation that "What matters is that even we can't decrypt it," he went on.

> This is a lie. If you "connect directly to the Harvard IMAP server (imap.fas.harvard. edu) upon login to fetch the number of new messages", you must store passwords in such a form that you can present the same access credential to the FAS server. This means that you store passwords in a way that you can recover.

> So what if the hash of the submitted password matches the stored password hash? You still have the password transmitted in cleartext. Also, that 32 vs. 16 byte mistake is disconcerting. Are you sure you code is well-audited for buffer overflows and other security mistakes? Will your source code be available for people to examine? Why should I (or anyone) trust your site?

> Ever heard of man-in-the-middle attacks? A self-signed certificate means absolutely nothing.

Finally, Brian concluded with a note about my assurance that using FAS passwords with houseSYSTEM was not in violation of any legal agreements.

> This is deceptive. I refer you to http://www.fas.harvard.edu/computing/rules/
> Do you have a written waiver for

> "Consequently, students may not disclose their passwords or otherwise make Harvard's facilities available to unauthorized individuals (including family or friends). Moreover, the possession or collection of others passwords, personal identification numbers (PINs), private digital certificates, or other secure identification information is prohibited. "

> Reading your security statement gives me no confidence in your site's ability to protect confidential information. There are enough omissions, whether deliberate or accidental, and mistakes that I have no reason to believe that any information I submit to your site will be i) used solely for the listed purposes and ii) not improperly disclosed. I suggest that people refrain from giving it such information until the author has demonstrated even a rudimentary understanding of the security issues involved.

By this point, I had lost my patience. "What is wrong with these people?" I asked my parents over dinner in Hilton Head. "I make something useful, and all they can do is complain? There's nothing wrong with the site's security, there's something wrong with them! Dan Ellard is imagining that someone is 'pretending to be Aaron Greenspan,' and Brian Wong is telling people that MD-5 generates 16-byte hashes, when it doesn't! There are 32 characters in all of them! Each ASCII character is one byte! He can count them if he really wants! I don't get it!"

My father had seen Brian's message, and declared him a "moron," which comforted me a little. He was even more incensed at Dan Ellard, who he felt had a responsibility as a member of Lowell House's staff to portray things in an unbiased manner at the very least and to discipline students who were out of line. Yet Dan was going after me as much as anyone, as if it were all a joke.

"People are just mean," my mother said. "They shouldn't be allowed to do that, but they do! They're just mean." For once, I agreed with her.

After we had eaten, one more person wrote to the Lowell House mailing list. This time, the message came from an alum named Isaac Hall who did not even live in the House anymore.

> This is an interesting set of issues. Apparently, Aaron is pursuing a very interesting, ambitious (and, of course, entrepreneurial) project of trying to capture the eyeballs (and passwords) of thousands of Harvard students by providing a sort of private "my.Harvard" for each House and school. (Although the overall goals and purposes of the site are, oddly, not stated.)
>
> His intentions (or those of the SEC) aside......
>
> 1. Although attentive people will notice that that the houseSYSTEM is not an official Harvard initiative, I'd assert that Aaron and co. are under an ethical obligation to state this clearly on the system's homepage.
>
> 2. The idea that, in this day and age, it's reasonable for a private organization to encourage thousands of university students to submit their confidential passwords is, to put it bluntly, crazy. I can't believe Aaron and his colleagues thought this would be uncontroversial. What he promises to do or not do with the information should be irrelevant to a prudent person.
>
> 3. Aaron, your responses to these inquiries about the sytem have done nothing to

inspire my confidence. Instead of openness, clarity, or even a touch of humility in the face of legitimate criticism, you're projecting a sort of weary irritation bordering on arrogance. Even if I were still a Harvard student, there's no way I would subscribe to your system when Lowell's homepage and my.Harvard apparently provide everything you do -- without the apparent problems with security and functionality.

"*'Confidential passwords?' What passwords aren't confidential?*" I immediately thought. I started drafting a response, but decided to wait before sending it. I was too outraged by the whole ordeal, and I wanted to be able think with a level head before pressing the "Send" button. Most of all, I didn't understand why everyone was demanding that houseSYSTEM needed a huge disclaimer about being independent of Harvard, when other student groups (including ones that were separately incorporated) were not required to have such statements on their web sites. It appeared as though my only crime was making the site look too professional.

The next day, there was a new e-mail directed at me on lowell-open. This time, it was from a Computer Science concentrator in the House.

i think that you are missing the point.

the reason that dan and brian brought this to the attention of the house community is because a) you posted it here first and b) to their seasoned,well-trained, computer-science trained eyes this site was not safe for student use.

i'm tempted to concur. why can't this site simply use the mechanism already in place for student authentication, namely the PIN system that we alreadyuse to access grades/portals? now that you can set your PIN to anything (i.e., to be the same as your fas password, not that i'm recommending this), this seems to be a "secure" system that already exists, so why re(miss)invent the wheel? at least then if it's hacked you can blame HASCS.

"*Great idea, then, they can accuse me of stealing PINs, too!*" I thought.

I considered writing back with my views on his concentration and the kind of training it really offered, but decided that it was probably not the best time or place. That a Computer Science student did not see the errors in Brian Wong's logic or understand how closely HASCS held the PIN authentication interface to its chest did not surprise me though.

I wanted to put everyone at ease, but it wasn't clear if it was worth responding to every piece of flame mail that landed in my inbox. Some people were angry, but could be convinced; others were simply irrational. It seemed as though winning over Lowell House was a hopeless endeavor. I had provided a reason for every loudmouth in the place with a speck of technical self-confidence to vent their worries about computer security. While they would probably go away eventually if I ignored them, I then risked confirming Isaac Hall's belief that I was arrogant.

I decided to write back, taking great care to formulate my message. I sent it to Isaac Hall directly, instead of the entire lowell-open mailing list, hoping to avoid adding fuel to the fire.

Though I'm not sure what I can say to convince you that I'm not out to steal the passwords of Harvard students, I do take your suggestions seriously, and I've changed the site slightly to reflect them.

The SEC is a Harvard student group, so houseSYSTEM is not completely unaffiliated with the University, but as you and some others pointed out, it is definitely not endorsed by FAS Computing Services. The site now clearly states that on the bottom of each page. Clicking on the SEC's name in the copyright line also takes you to the club's site, where the visitor can learn more about it and its relationship with the College. The Security Statement has been updated for clarity, as well.

I personally don't think it's crazy to ask college students to use passwords, but that could be a matter of opinion. At the very least, there are plenty of other web sites that college students almost daily use which work almost exactly the same way. Student Advantage, Amazon.com, Orbitz, etc. all require passwords. I'm working on making using the FAS password specifically an optional requirement, but it might take a few days to test the new code.

Also, I never thought the site would be uncontroversial. I expected that a minor uproar along these lines would take place. Major technological changes at traditional institutions usually generate some controversy. It's risky, but then again, that's part of the entrepreneurial angle the SEC is taking.

To address your last point, there's again probably not much I can say, but I think I've been pretty open about the inner workings of the site. I may have been unclear at times, but it wasn't intentional. As far as humility goes, I've done my best. So, even if you don't plan on using the site, I wanted to let you know that your suggestions were appreciated.

Within minutes, as I suspected might happen, I received a new message from Isaac Hall, and it wasn't just to me. He had copied my response to him back to the entire mailing list.

Aaron, I never suggested that you are out to "steal" the passwords of Harvard students. I suggested that it is inappropriate to try to collect them, regardless of the purity of your motives.
I was not pointing out that the site is "not endorsed by FAS Computing Services"; I was pointing out that the site looks like it may have been created by Harvard and that you should make it clear that the site is in no way endorsed by Harvard as an institution, or the Houses, and that you have not been authorized to collect fas passwords so that you can integrate Harvard email into your project.
Aaron, I can only conclude that you are playing dumb. Obviously, I wasn't saying that it's crazy to ask college students to use passwords. I was saying that it's CRAZY TO ASK COLLEGE STUDENTS TO SUBMIT, TO A FELLOW STUDENT, CONFI-

DENTIAL PASSWORDS THAT ARE SET UP TO GIVE THEM ACCESS TO THEIR UNIVERSITY EMAIL AND IN SOME CASES TO THEIR REGISTRAR'S ACCOUNT AND OTHER SENSITIVE INFORMATION! I can't believe you are pretending this is not an issue, but this is exactly the kind of disingenuousness that, in my opinion, has destroyed your credibility.

Aaron, correct me if I'm wrong, but you don't work for Harvard University! This is not a "major technological change at" a traditional institution, initiated by the institution or endorsed by the institution. Rather, this is some kind of guerrilla attempt at a technological coup, wherein you're sneaking in as a subcontractor of students' email and other university information sources.

It was hopeless. He started off by saying that he wasn't accusing me of stealing passwords, and then, in the same message, said that I had launched a "guerrilla attempt at a technological coup...sneaking in as a subcontractor." I wasn't really sure which was worse. Then, the Lowell Computer Science student chimed in about the security statement I had written.

while this is TECHNICALLY (legalistically) accurate, i believe that it's not entirely truthful. even if you use POST, unless it is hashed on the client side (which i doubt) it is _transmitted_ to the server in plain text form. harvard doesn't do this anymore: telnet access to fas server's is disabled and webmail requires SSL, which will encrypt the entire contents of the POST request. the reason is that if your packets were to be sniffed enroute, the contents could be identified, and your username/password stolen.

even if SSL support exists, the fact that non-SSL support exists is a giant leap backwards on houseSYSTEM.

He was right that Harvard had disabled telnet access to its main FAS server (citing telnet's lack of encryption as insecure), but he had missed a crucial fact: aside from web-based e-mail, which everyone hated because it was so slow, Harvard still allowed unencrypted access to e-mail via traditional e-mail programs. Even the official networking CD-ROM provided by HASCS to freshmen at the beginning of each academic year did not enable password encryption by default. Since telnet and e-mail accounts used the exact same password, disabling telnet hadn't really improved the security situation at all. houseSYSTEM was just another e-mail client, behaving the same way as any other. The "giant leap backwards" was purely hypothetical, and the e-mail's author was using faulty assumptions.

A member of the Harvard Computer Society who lived in Lowell House wrote in, extolling the virtues of encryption and recommending that people avoid houseSYSTEM.

"*He's saying that the storage system isn't secure enough without having even seen it.*" I knew the person who had written the message, so I was inclined to believe that he was genuine in his concern, but he certainly wasn't helping the situation. "*Would have been nice of him to e-mail me first..."* I thought.

Finally, a message appeared that, for once, didn't make me feel like I was being punched in the face.

> While I won't be signing up for Harvard HouseSYSTEM based on information from the posts on Lowell-Open from people who know a lot more about computers than I do, can I ask that we send SUGGESTIONS to Aaron, rather than phrasing everything in the form of an attack? Many people seem to be implying that he was knowingly trying to steal the passwords of thousands of Harvard students to use them to some evil purpose. While this might be the case (although I can't see Aaron holed up in some laboratory trying to plot the thousands of ways he can abuse our passwords), I think we should offer him the benefit of the doubt and accept that this is a good idea that is, definitively, a work in progress.
>
> Your resident obnoxiously positive person :-)
> Jody

I e-mailed the rest of the SEC's Board for advice on how to deal with the situation in Lowell House. Some suggested avoiding controversy, but it was too late.

My computer let out a "ding" as I got one more e-mail.

It was from *The Crimson.*

CHAPTER 22

Securitas

Laura Krug, a *Crimson* reporter with the unfortunate job of working on a college newspaper in August, wanted me to give her a call to discuss the debate that had already engulfed two of the house lists. It was one phone call I did not want to make. It didn't matter though: I couldn't use the phone. Simon was on the internet, looking up sports statistics. For him, vacation *meant* another place to look up sports statistics. The beach was totally peripheral. The chances of my father actually having an opportunity to use his own computer for work were low.

"Simon, get off of the internet please," I asked him after delaying as long as possible, knowing that I had to make the call. If I refused to speak to the newspaper, I was afraid they would write the story anyway and just make me look worse. I had to defend myself, since it was clear that no one else was going to. After repeatedly prodding him, Simon finally walked away, muttering.

Due to the Marriott's extraordinarily overpriced long distance rates, I arranged for Laura to call our villa the following night. My family was planning to go mini-golfing, and I didn't feel like sacrificing all of my vacation to the paranoid demons of Lowell House.

The next night, the phone rang a few minutes after nine. "Hi, this is Laura Krug from *The Crimson*," she said by way of introduction, as if I had to be reminded.

"Hi," I responded, trying to sound cheerful.

"So, I just wanted to get a general sense of what you're trying to accomplish with houseSYSTEM, and why there has been this big debate on lowell-open."

"Right. The only guiding idea here is to improve student life," I told her, trying to be as clear as possible from the outset. I didn't want to make it sound like I was side-stepping the issue since I was going to be on the record anyway. "It's not to collect peoples passwords. It's not to abuse information for some evil purpose. It's for students to benefit, however that might take place, whether that means getting a job, or checking your e-mail, or your packages. We're trying to centralize things in a way that FAS should—but does not."

"So you created this because of CriticalMass?"

"Well, it came out of CriticalMass, in a way. There was nowhere to read plain English course reviews, and nowhere to buy and sell used textbooks at Harvard on-line. The second problem was eventually solved by another site I made called Textbook Central."

"So there wasn't a centralized location to do all of these things," she summarized.

"That was my diagnosis of the problem," I replied. "There was nowhere to trade textbooks, the CUE Guide wasn't always as complete as it could have been, and some of the house web sites were...lacking."

"What about the security issues people have brought up... Can you access Harvard student records with the information you have?"

"No, of course not!" I said. "We can't access those and shouldn't access those. Our database is completely separate from that."

"And you encrypt the passwords, you said on the mailing list?"

"Well, let me think of the best way to put it so that it's easy to understand—we don't encrypt passwords, we hash them, but the effect is basically the same. We can't read the passwords, and neither can anyone else, including the server itself."

"A lot of people mentioned that you weren't using...I think it was...SSL, though?"

"No, not initially, but we put up a site on the Harvard Yard portion that lets you use SSL if you're really afraid that someone is monitoring the connection. The main point people should take away is that, yes, it's true that no system is perfectly secure, 'cause that's just impossible, but I don't think the security of houseSYSTEM was ever so bad that anybody's password was in jeopardy. I just wouldn't have released a piece of software like that."

In the interest of covering all my bases, I tried to explain the other issue that Dan Ellard had raised.

"People were also complaining that we were using a self-signed certificate, which isn't really a problem at all. Buying a wildcard certificate, which is what you need for something like houseSYSTEM, would cost almost $1,000, and the SEC just doesn't have that kind of money yet. There are only four companies, really, that web browsers are programmed to 'trust,' VeriSign, Thawte, which I think is a South African company, GeoTrust, which is a division of Equifax, and one other...I think Comodo. Microsoft and Netscape basically have deals with these guys to exclude others from the market, and they all make a fortune as a result. The thing is, going through any of those companies is not technically any more trustworthy than just making your own certificate, which is what we did. You just pay them a lot so that an error message goes away. From a technical perspective, there's absolutely no difference in the encryption."

"What about the MD-5 function? Someone said that wasn't secure?"

"We were using MD-5, but on the advice I received on the list, we're switching everything to SHA-1. MD-5 is widely regarded as being secure, though, based on everything I've read so far."

"How many user accounts are there at this point?"

"About 400," I said, thinking back to the last time I had checked the database.

"All right, those are pretty much all my questions... I'll let you know if I have any others."

"One thing, before you go," I interjected. "Can you send me my quotes to go over before the story runs?"

"We don't usually..." Laura began, but I'd heard that line before.

"I know, but just in case there's anything glaringly obvious that can be fixed."

"OK, I'll try," she said.

"Thanks."

I hung up, and went back to the villa's living room to check my e-mail once more. Then, after watching television for a while, I finally went to bed.

"What would you like for breakfast?" my father asked when I woke up the next morning, reminding me how nice it was to have someone cook meals for you. I had been cooking for myself all summer, with occasionally interesting results.

"A bagel..." I murmured. My mother, who knew that bagels and other assorted foods were hard to find around Hilton Head, had a knack for bargain shopping. Consequently, we brought down a giant box of food from Cleveland with us every year, while most families paid to eat every meal in a restaurant. I personally wasn't sure whether to admire our thriftiness, or curse the sixty-pound box that usually ended up being my responsibility to fit into the station wagon. Either way, we had many bagels.

By the time I was done eating, I had a new message from a fellow SEC Board member. She thanked me for working so hard, and then made a few more observations.

> The controversy is, actually in many ways, good for us, I think... if but for the simple fact that it puts us onto the map for some students. Yet, I still feel taht we shouldn't let anything become potentially liable on us. For all the negative comments people have given us on the Lowell open messages you showed me, most of them are focused on the fact that we collect things that are private for most people. Maybe it'll be easier to make submitting any private information allowing us to identify a Harvard student optional... just to show that we do listen to people's concerns and we are really well-meaning.

> DAN Ellard is, after all, a potential threat... He's on the faculty.. and has quite some prestige in the cs area since, if I remember well, he's still the one working on ANT and stuff for CS classes.

Little did I know that her analysis had already been proven correct. lowell-open arrived on schedule at 11:00 A.M., revealing that Dan Ellard had sent another missive to the list at 5:23 A.M. This time, he was replying to Jody's opinion that it might be better to send me constructive criticism, rather than barbs.

I respectfully disagree.

My first posting on this thread was meant as a general caution about blindly giving information away to web sites that appear out of the blue and ask for all kinds of sensitive stuff. I even mentioned at the end that I thought that this particular organization is probably honest. I have no evidence or cause to believe that they intend to do anything anything evil with the information that they acquire and I am willing to give them the benefit of the doubt. I don't think anyone else has accused them of any particular evil intent, although some of the comments have been a bit strongly worded.

However, while I do not question their intent, I do question their methods. By Aaron's own blase admission, their knowledge of security is sketchy at best. They don't appear to understand the issues, much less how to resolve them, but instead of taking the time to learn, they are rushing to sign up people as quickly as possible.

For example, take the issue of the SSL certificates. An SSL certificate is, at a high level, an identifier issued by a trusted authority to identify an entity and forms a basis for communicating privately with that entity. So, when you connect to a host with an SSL certificate, you can have confidence that it's really them, and not someone masquerading as them. There's also a level of trust that is delegated by the trusted authority; you can't walk in off the street and ask for an SSL certificate that says that you represent Microsoft or IBM or Harvard or whoever. It is the responsibility of the SSL granting authority to ensure that you are who you say you are, and merit being trusted with a certificate.

HarvardSEC does not own a complete SSL certificate. Perhaps they can't get one because they are such a young organization that their constitution doesn't exist and noone will vouch for them. Or perhaps they can't afford one yet (although they're not terribly expensive). This is pardonable. Their solution, however, is not. For their Harvard Yard site, they have a self-signed certificate -- which, as Dev pointed out, is practically meaningless, because it says that you should trust them because they say you should trust them. In fact, when you visit a site with a self-signed certificate, your web browser will probably pop up a warning message telling you that something is very fishy. HarvardSECs instructions say that this is normal and you should ignore this message. It is NOT normal, and you should NOT ignore it. What your browser is telling you is that even if you trust HarvardSEC, you have no way to ensure that who you are communicating with actually is HarvardSEC, nor can you be sure that HarvardSEC is the only entity who is listening. Ignoring these warnings is a bad habit to start.

For the Lowell HarvardSEC site, it's even worse; they don't even bother with a self-signed SSL certificate. Everything is sent in the open. With a self-signed certificate, at least it takes a little work for evil-doers to steal your data. Without any certificate at all, it doesn't take any work whatsoever.

(If my explaination is unclear or inaccurate, I'm sure someone will jump in and correct me.)

This is just one issue, but it illustrates the point. Even if you trust HarvardSECs motivations, you might be a little worried about the careless manner with which they protect your info. To put the icing on the cake, they just don't seem to care, so I don't expect that these problems will be solved any time soon.

Aaron et al may see this as more of an attack than previous posts (because most Harvard students would rather be accused of being evil than of being careless and ignorant), but it's not meant to be personal.

"Not personal?" I thought. *"When someone says, 'I respectfully disagree,' to someone else saying, 'Maybe we should be nicer to them,' that's not meant to be personal?"* I added Dan to my list of people I wished I could punch. I wasn't evil, careless, or ignorant.

"Maybe he'd like to buy the certificate for us," I spat. "A thousand bucks isn't that much to someone like him, I guess. With all of his 'security knowledge' he seems to have forgotten that we need a wildcard certificate, not just a normal one." Dan's e-mail was wholly inaccurate and laced with his usual paranoia, and yet responding to it would only make things worse, as I had already seen. I now knew that *The Crimson* was watching too. I read his latest message out loud to my parents.

"Right, my knowledge of security is 'sketchy,' because I haven't taken four million classes called 'Advanced Cryptography for Advanced Shmucks,' like him. He doesn't know how many computers and networks I've worked on. He doesn't know a thing about me. I could know ten times more or ten times less about security than he does, and he wouldn't have a freaking clue. And in fact, that's what security is all about: not making faulty assumptions, testing everything."

That's when it hit me. Dan Ellard wasn't just out of line—he was a hypocrite.

"And get this! The Lowell House face book, which Dan Ellard *runs*, requires that you sign in with a valid Harvard student ID. It also asks you for your FAS password. But does it encrypt any of it? No! He was too lazy to bother with SSL. It's all submitted in plain-text, just like what he's complaining about on houseSYSTEM. So by his own logic, the whole House should be suffering from massive identity theft right now!"

"This is totally inexcusable," my father said upon hearing my latest rant. "Why doesn't anyone in the administration tell these people to shut up? Don't they think it's inappropriate for a faculty member to beat up on a student? Or for students to beat up on other students?"

"No," I said plainly.

I was nervous about how *The Crimson* was going to portray the situation. Laura had seemed fairly reasonable when I talked to her over the phone, not leaping immediately to conclusions and trying to understand the technical jargon that was inherently tangled in the situation. Nonetheless, I didn't know who else she would be talking to. I hoped not Dan Ellard.

"I guess we'll just have to wait until Friday for *The Crimson* to run, to see what happens," I told my parents. "Maybe people will notice how insane all of this is, then."

"Why Friday?" my mother asked.

"It's the summer; they don't publish every day when no one reads it. Actually, that's my best hope. That no one will read it."

My hope didn't last long.

The next day was a Wednesday. I went to the beach with my family in the morning. When we came back for lunch, I checked lowell-open again. For once, there was no activity. Then, I checked my e-mail.

My heart stopped.

The Dean's office, and the office of computing services for FAS, have asked that I contact you and ask you to immediately stop collecting student email and password information on your HarvardSEC website for security reasons. Any email addresses, passwords, or student information you currently have should not be used or transmitted in any form until this matter is cleared up. Paul Bottino, FAS computing services, and the dean's office, will look into the matter next week (Paul is currently on vacation and has undependable email access only. He will return on Monday).

If you have any questions, please feel free to be in touch with me.

It had only been a semester since I had gone to Jay Ellison with my grievances about academics at Harvard. While I hadn't faulted him any more than anyone else who had done nothing to help, now, everything was different. He was asking me to prevent anyone from signing up for houseSYSTEM until at least Monday, with a potentially positive *Crimson* article running on the Friday before. Either way, the impact was most assuredly going to be negative when people found out that they weren't allowed to sign up, based on the concerns of Harvard's administration.

I told my father. Peering over my shoulder, he read the message, and did not seem pleased. I started drafting a reply.

Before we disable anything, I would like to know precisely what security concerns there are, which Deans or staff members have them, and what they believe can be done to address them. I am sure we can find a solution to whatever concerns have been raised that will allow students to continue using the services on house-SYSTEM.

None of the pieces of member information that are stored in the houseSYSTEM database--information which students volunteer of their own volition--are used or transmitted in any form, with the exception of when we send members a regular newsletter via e-mail. In that particular case, their e-mail address is used in order to send them the e-mail, much as Lowell House sends its occupants e-mail newsletters on a regular basis. Given that we do not store member passwords, but only the their MD5 hashes, there is no risk of passwords being used or transmitted.

I was so anxious that I pressed the Send button without thinking. I kicked myself afterward for including the grammatical gem "the their" in such an important message, but there was nothing I could do.

About an hour later, I had my reply.

There is no way for you to put a condition on this. The security concerns are related to storing student passwords in a server not controlled or administered by Harvard. This is a clear violation of Harvard College rules governing passwords and your site also requires students to violate the rules by giving the passwords to your site.

You must immediately stop collecting student passwords. This is not an option. You do not have to shut down the site, but it must stop collecting this data in any form. Additionally, you must delete any database and record that you have that contains student passwords and send a list to me with all of the user names that were collected by the site since its inception. Those students will be contacted by FAS computer services and told to change their passwords immediately.

The concerns raised by the College will be discussed with Paul when he returns and there will be some attempts to address them with you and the HarvardSEC group. In the meantime, however, I am again instructing you to stop collecting this information, delete what you have collected, and forward the list of all those whose information you have collected.

"What!" I exclaimed after reading it. "Delete the database? That database has all of the course reviews in it! And I can't turn it over! People signed up for CriticalMass *specifically* because it allowed them to be anonymous! I'm not about to say, oh, sorry, what I meant was, anonymous until I hand it over to the same people you're reviewing! It even has people's cell phone numbers in it! What, do they want those, too?"

I picked up the phone and dialed Jay Ellison's direct line in Cambridge. There was no answer. I was furious.

"How can they ask you to delete the database without even hearing your side of the story?" my father said, incredulous. "If everything about the security is how you say it is, then there's nothing wrong..."

"It's more secure than their own damn systems!" I fumed. "If anyone looked at Harvard's IT infrastructure with the same level of scrutiny as what they're doing to me, they'd be absolutely horrified."

Then, I remembered something else.

"You know...what's more, I actually *asked* them about this freshman year! I sent an e-mail to Franklin Steen, the guy who runs HASCS, *asking* him if there was anything wrong with setting up a web-based e-mail system. It wasn't any different. It asked students for their FAS passwords. It was still stored on my server. He didn't even respond! And now, they want me to delete the whole thing? Two years later? It's the same freaking code!

"Elliott, too... He hated the official FAS Webmail so much that he started using some web site that's an outside service to check it. It uses the same kind of technology that houseSYSTEM does to connect to the FAS IMAP server. That's an external site. He, and other students I'm sure, give out their passwords like that all the time! But do those sites get in trouble? Of course not! They aren't doing anything wrong."

I dialed Jay Ellison again. Again, there was no answer. He must have been using his e-mail from somewhere other than his office. Clearly, he didn't care about encrypting his password.

I fired up my web browser to re-read the HASCS usage agreement carefully, which governed student computer use. If I was going to be accused of violating it, I wanted to know why. After looking it over several times, I reached the conclusion that I wasn't actually in violation at all. The University was trying to prevent students from sharing their passwords with other students. Generally, they had reasonable concerns about not wanting people checking each other's e-mail, stealing information electronically, or being generally careless. I wasn't doing any of those things. Due to the way I had programmed houseSYSTEM, I fundamentally didn't have the ability to read passwords. Anyone who saw the code would have had to agree: there was no malicious intent.

"Look," I told my father. "See this column here?" I brought up the database of houseSYSTEM members, narrowing it down to my own record. I pointed to the column labeled "password2," which stored the recently-created SHA-1 password hash.

"This is my password hash." Forty characters of gibberish followed. "I can guarantee you that I do *not* type all of that crap in whenever I want to check my e-mail, either. Between school, the SEC, and my company, I check five accounts every day. My password is only six characters long, but obviously, you couldn't know that unless I told you. Every SHA-1 hash is 40 bytes, regardless of the length of the string you give it."

"Well, maybe if you just explain everything to Jay Ellison as clearly as possible, he'll back off."

I hoped he was right. There wasn't much else I could do, since he wasn't answering his phone. I didn't want to destroy months of work because of a misunderstanding. I sent Jay another e-mail, this time taking care not to miss any details, or to add any extra prepositional phrases.

I am not attempting to put any conditions on your request. From what I can tell, you are under the impression, based only on hearsay, that the site actually collects students' FAS passwords and stores them in a database. This is simply not true. I would be happy to show the database to you or any other concerned parties in order to prove it.

I continued by analyzing the rules of computer use, explaining why I was not in violation of any of them. The message concluded with an admonition.

I would have expected that with allegations this serious, and especially ones with no actual proof, you would have at least asked for my point of view on the matter before leaping to conclusions. I have spent a great deal of time and energy ensuring the security of my software, and I would never have allowed the release of a product which could have jeopardized the privacy of others. houseSYSTEM is, in fact, a great deal more secure than some portions of the actual Lowell House web site--such as the face book, which requires your Harvard ID to be submitted over an unencrypted connection, with no option of using a secure link at all.

I would also have expected that an attempt to improve student life at Harvard at no cost to the University would be met with encouragement and support by its admin-istration, rather than hostility.

That night, it took some time to fall asleep. I was thinking about too many possibilities. Jay Ellison might relent. He might not. I could get in trouble. *The Crimson* could fix everything by just writing something sensible. *The Crimson* could destroy it all. *The Crimson* wouldn't even print a paper copy of the article in the middle of August. The SEC Board would wonder who the hell they had agreed to work for.

No matter what happened, from that moment forward, I would wonder why I ever created houseSYSTEM in the first place.

▼

The next day, I had a response from a kinder, gentler Jay Ellison.

I am sorry that my email appeared hostile, that was not the intent. Because of your response to my first note I felt I had to be clearer in explaining what the College expected of you. My attempt to be clear was evidently too terse and I apologize--harshness and hostility were not my intent.

I would like to address your comments and I want you to understand where I am coming from. I do monitor Lowell-Open so I know what is going on in the House, but I do not respond to posts on the list since I feel it needs to be a forum for students to express their ideas/feelings, etc., without feeling like a dean is going to enter the discussion. I have, on occasion, responded off-line to clarify something (for example, when a student asks about a policy in the college and another student responds incorrectly), but most of the time I remain silent.

When you posted your initial announcement about the houseSystem I visited the site. I was interested in the idea, but was horrified to see that student IDs were requested as were their FAS passwords (I did appreciate your explanation about the IDs and that you fixed that). I also read your security statement and was dissatisfied, feeling that it was deficient, but this is not my area of expertise so this concerned me less. But having FAS passwords was a real problem. BTW: I also went to your home site, Think Computer, which I really enjoyed looking at. I am, as I hope you know (and I hope my last email did not ruin the perception), interested in the students of Lowell House and what they are doing. I am a dean and I work for the dean of the College, not the house, but my area of focus is on the students of Lowell House. My goal, and my job, is to help all of you navigate Harvard successfully, get the most out of it you can, all the while maintaining a healthy balance of work and play. I like nothing more than to see what students are up to, see them succeed, and see them graduate with the course work and experiences they want. Only when things go bad do I get involved in any other capacity.

Others at the university and in the dean's office were also interested in the site and they were concerned as well about the FAS password request. They researched the situation and only this morning contacted me and asked me to contact you and as you to shut off the password portion of the program. I did not, therefore, act on hearsay but I am doing my job as dean. The reason a resident dean is the one who makes contact is because we should have a relationship, you and I that is, where we can communicate reasonably and I think we do have that, thankfully (again, I apologize if my terseness in the last email jeopardized that). I am your dean and my concerns are directed toward your success here. I contacted you as requested and was surprised to see you respond where you stated "Before we disable anything, I would like to know precisely what security concerns there are, which Deans or staff members have them, and what they believe can be done to address them." My initial take on your statement, and the one that still stands out, is that before you were willing to do what was asked you wanted to discuss this with the deans at University Hall. That will come in due course (after Paul returns from vacation and there is more discussion about the whole matter with DEAS and FAS computing services), and I hope that things can be worked out. But the situation of the passwords being asked for, submitted, and retained in any form cannot wait.

My second email came after I had a discussion with the head of FAS computer security. He was adamant about the password file being deleted and the list of those who had sent information being obtained so they could be contacted. Because I assumed, based on your response, that you felt this was optional, I decided to be more direct. Perhaps I should have spent more time on the email since the last thing I want is for you to think I am your enemy or against you and the site. I have no hostility toward your site or you. Nevertheless, I must pass on to you that you must change the site to not request this information, that you must delete the file (even in hash form this file is still a collection of FAS passwords and they cannot be collected in any form), and that you must send me the list.

This whole matter will be addressed soon after Paul returns and he is able to talk to you and everyone else interested. I will continue to be involved since I hope we can still communicate. You will have the opportunity to talk about the project and the situation with others as well but I will stay in the loop so I can assist you in navigating things as they arise and so I can communicate more rapidly, and hopefully with friendly credibility, with you. In the meantime, there is nothing really we can discuss since only after Paul returns will everyone have time to see what can be done to fix this situation.

Now, about the FAS computing rules: students are not to "disclose their passwords or otherwise make Harvard's facilities available to unauthorized individuals (including family or friends)." Even though your program creates as hash and deletes the original password, the fact that the password was ever submitted is a violation of the rules. This is a problem but is not one we need address right now--the problem is not the students but the site asking for the information. Indeed, the bigger problem is in storing anything about the password, even in hash form. As you cited, "Moreover, the possession or collection of others passwords, personal identification numbers (PINs), private digital certificates, or other secure identification information is prohibited," disallows the collection of passwords at all, regardless of whether they are held for a long time, held in another form, or deleted. This is where you are in violation. The College is not out to destroy your site or on a hunt for you. But you must change the program so that it does not require or request the FAS password and you must delete the file that contains anything related to those passwords--no matter what form they are in. And of course, because there are security concerns whenever passwords are transmitted outside the network, each student who provided that information must be contacted by security services so that they can change the password. Only then can the College feel that we can move on to the discussion about the site and how it might work.

I hope that this note at least explains where I am coming from (not a position of hostility but of concern) and that I am not acting on hearsay from students, the Crimson, or anyone else. As the House representative of the College, I am telling you what the College is insisting on so that you can be in compliance with the rules of the College and we can move on to a discussion of the fundamental and underlying ideas involved in the site.

As I said, I will call you later today. Please do respond via email if you have any questions. Please understand also that the requirements of the College are not something that should be delayed.

"Well, that's interesting," I told my father. "He says he didn't act on hearsay, and yet he also cites lowell-open as his source, which is full of...oh, I don't know... hearsay." My father read the message in full.

"I'll say it's not his 'area of expertise...'" he muttered. "What does he do again?"

"Uhhh..." Having forgotten, I looked it up. "Lecturer on Near Eastern Languages and Civilizations," I said. "He studies ancient Hebrew texts. And Aramaic, too, I think. Perfect material for a solid understanding of computer security issues."

The problem, I began to realize, was that Jay Ellison was totally out of his element, just like the members of the Special Concentration committee. Furthermore, he was depending upon the opinions of people who apparently had an ax to grind, despite the fact that I had never met any of them.

"I don't really know what to do, still," I said. "I guess I'll wait until he calls."

The laptop chimed, indicating a new message. At last, Rodica, the SEC's Secretary, had e-mailed me a new draft of the club constitution. Citing the election fiasco as proof of the previous document's worthlessness, I had asked her to start from scratch. As with all of her work, the new draft looked good.

There was a pit in my stomach as I waited for the phone to ring. I couldn't go to the beach. I couldn't go to the pool. I could watch TV, but I didn't want to. I was sick of using the computer. I just wanted the phone to ring.

The phone rang.

"Hi, this is Jay Ellison. Is Aaron there?"

"Hi Jay, this is Aaron," I said. I noticed my father pick up the phone in the bedroom so that he could listen in. I was glad.

"Hi, Aaron. I'm sorry I missed your call yesterday. I was teaching at the Divinity School, like I said in the e-mail." His voice had a southern twang to it, which was consistent with the background the Lowell House Masters had given us at the beginning of the year: Jay Ellison comes to us with his lovely wife, who will also be in the house, from his previous career as a police officer in Atlanta, Georgia. He sounded so jovial, it seemed hard to imagine that I was angry at him.

"No problem. I just want to clear up any misunderstandings there might be about what I'm doing with houseSYSTEM..." I began.

"Well, here's where I'm at," Jay responded. "Now, I'm your Dean. I act as a disciplinarian if I have to, and in this case, Dean Gross's office has asked me to talk to you about getting those passwords taken down. So, I'm really acting on behalf of his office."

"That's the thing—" I said. "I'm not actually storing any passwords. As I tried to explain in the e-mail, I'm storing hashes, but those aren't the same as passwords. I can't do anything with them. No one can. They're just leftover from the password, essentially, to make sure that whatever was just typed in is actually correct. It's not like I can read people's e-mail or anything."

"Well, listen. I saw what you wrote about hashes and encryption and all that, and I'm not a computer person. I don't really understand the technical side of everything here, and I don't *want* to understand."

I was taken aback. It made sense that computers weren't his area of expertise, but if he didn't even want to be able to make sense of all this, then what was the point of talking to him?

"Not to be rude, then," I replied, "but is there someone who *does* have some technical knowledge that I could talk to?"

"No," Jay said. It was that simple. "You have to go through me, that's how it is."

"I mean, I know the people at HASCS are familiar with the kind of work I'm doing. Could I talk to anyone there?"

"No, I can't let you talk to anyone else."

"I'd be even be willing to even show them the source code for the authentication mechanism I'm using so that they can see how I'm deleting the password itself instantaneously after its hash is checked against the hash in the database..."

"We're not really interested in the code, all we want is for you to stop people from using their FAS passwords, and to delete the database."

"Well, that's another issue—do you want me to delete the entire database, or just the password field, because there's a world of difference. If I delete the database then the site will stop working completely. If I delete the password field, the site will continue to work, except that no one will be able to sign in."

"We want the password field gone then."

"OK, I'm glad we cleared that up," I said, relieved. My father was only getting angrier, though.

"But you'll still need to send us a list of everyone who signed up, so that HASCS can reset their passwords on FAS," he said, referring to the College's main server.

"I really don't think I can do that," I said, cautiously. "houseSYSTEM includes CriticalMass, which, as you know, lets students critique their professors. When people signed up for CriticalMass, the site said that their information would be kept anonymous. I can't just hand it over to their professors."

"Well, that's something you're going to have to figure out," Jay said.

"Could I maybe forward an e-mail on behalf of HASCS asking them to reset their FAS passwords? That way, the University wouldn't necessarily know who was reviewing professors, and the same objective would still be achieved."

"I'll look into that for you," Jay said.

"Thanks."

"This is Neil Greenspan, Aaron's father," my father said, cutting in. I didn't mind, since I wanted Jay to hear from someone who wasn't lulled by his accent, and my father most certainly was not.

"Hello, have you been listening the entire time, Mr. Greenspan?"

"Yes, and it's Dr. Greenspan," my father said. "I have three degrees, and one of them is from Harvard, as a matter of fact." He was not happy.

"Well, I have a number, as well," said Jay. "It's Dr. Ellison."

"That's all really besides the point," my father continued. "I've been watching as these people on the mailing list have reacted to Aaron's project, and I must say, I was quite shocked after reading that you continually monitor the list, that you didn't try to put an end to it. Aaron hasn't done anything to hurt anyone. He hasn't publicly insulted anybody. From what Aaron tells me, in fact, he hasn't met any of the people who have been bashing his work before in his life, including Dan Ellard, who seems to have a particularly large need for an attitude adjustment. But what really amazes me is that now you're saying you don't want Aaron to delete the database after all. That's good, but not what you wrote in the first place. And if Aaron had followed your directions, it would have destroyed everything he's been working on, which I happen to think is a very valuable contribution to the Harvard community, having gone to school there myself."

Jay Ellison began to respond.

"Well, Dr. Greenspan, as I've explained to Aaron already, lowell-open was not my only source of information..."

"That's not the issue," my father said. "If Aaron had been berating other students, or other faculty members, in the same manner as other people were berating him, would you have put a stop to it then? It's incredibly inappropriate for Dan Ellard to make the kinds of remarks that he did, when as I recall, he said himself that he had no evidence to back up any of his claims!"

"Well, my main question is how we move forward," I said, trying to steer the conversation back on track. "I can stop people from signing up, but I don't want to, especially since there's nothing wrong with the site's security."

"Well, you're going to have to," Jay replied.

"And just out of curiosity, the consequences otherwise would be..."

"If you don't comply with the request to remove the passwords, then the College may have to take disciplinary action."

I only knew of two things that could mean, but I didn't dare to ask which one he was referring to. The first possibility was that the College would take away my network access at school, which would be disastrous, given that I operated a software company primarily over the internet. It would also be inconvenient when doing my schoolwork, to say the least. The other option was for the College to simply kick me out.

"Well, I'll delete the passwords then, and hopefully put the sign-up page back once that's done."

"Alright. Now about the SEC... Is this something that you did on your own, or were you working with TECH on this? 'Cause we tried to reach Paul Bottino, but he's on vacation, and he didn't seem to know what we were really talking about," Jay said.

"It's a project we did on our own. The SEC is the student group that is affiliated with TECH."

"Alright. Well, we'll get some more input from Paul when he's back next week. They'll be meeting on Monday with him about this. Do you have any other questions for me?"

"No, I think that's it," I said. I wanted to ask who "they" was, but I didn't expect to receive a response.

"Thanks for calling." I didn't mean it.

"No problem, and enjoy your vacation," Jay said.

"*Yeah, this is exactly what I wanted to do on my vacation,*" I thought. "*What a joke.*"

The line disconnected. Now, I had a new problem: 400 Harvard students were about to become very unhappy, specifically, with me.

CHAPTER 23

Authoritas

I e-mailed Jay Ellison a summary of our conversation so that there would be a record in writing.

"Per our conversation," I wrote, "I will make further changes to houseSYSTEM in order to comply with the wishes of the College, though I maintain that none of my actions, nor those of the SEC, ever violated any College policy."

Then, I e-mailed Paul Bottino an update. I didn't want him to have a one-sided view of the story conveyed by Dean Gross's office.

I also bought myself a few days time by pointing out that correcting the alleged problems with houseSYSTEM would be slowed by my dial-up connection. In Hilton Head, my link to the outside world was Keene Advertising's America Online account, which was horribly slow. So long as I could take down the sign-up page after the article ran in *The Crimson*, I thought I could at least try to look moderately competent.

Jay Ellison wrote back in response.

Thanks Aaron. I checked with the dean's office about turning the sign-in back on. The dean who is now over seeing this, Dean Judith Kidd, will be in touch with you early next week. She has asked that you not turn the sign-in back on till she has a chance to personally communicate the College's concerns about the site. In addition to the password issue which you have addressed, I think their are a few more concerns that the College would like clarified. Most importantly though, now that you have addressed the FAS-password seccurity concerns, this can become a discussion about the site and about other matters related to it.

Things are quiet for now so try to enjoy your vacation. The beaches in South Carolina are so nice this time of year (and compared to New England beaches, they are nice every day of the year!)

"*Dean Kidd?*" I thought. "*He said he was representing Dean Gross.*" I looked up Judith Kidd on the internet. She was the director of Phillips Brooks House, the largest social service organization on campus. "*What the hell does she have to do with any of this?*" I wondered. Furthermore, I wasn't sure if it was good or bad that Dean Kidd wanted to have "a discussion about the site and other matters." As far as I could tell, the security problem had been solved in their eyes once I deleted the password field. What other matters were there?

"Do you think I should call Dean Kidd?" I asked my father.

"How should I know! I guess..." He was sore at Harvard for interrupting his vacation, though considerably less than I was.

Since it was Friday, I pulled up the web site of *The Crimson* to see if the article had been posted. Sure enough, one of the headlines was unmistakably about houseSYSTEM. "Student Site Stirs Controversy," it read. The article was factually accurate, but did not rule out the notion that I had some sinister motive, since I was the only one asserting my innocence. It also quoted Kevin Davis, a former Harvard student and a HASCS administrator, in a misleading context about SSL certificates. Nobody seemed willing to admit that SEC was just another student group that didn't have a giant budget to spend on expensive software.

Afraid that Dean Kidd might be basing her plans for further discussion on the article, I grabbed the calling card and placed the call to her office. There was no answer.

▼

The day of the meeting came and went. I spent most of the day and the weekend before it worrying. By the time we had finished dinner, I couldn't stand waiting anymore. I e-mailed Jay Ellison. He wrote back after an hour, which was even more nerve-wracking than the first ten. Jay didn't know what had transpired, and I still couldn't turn the site back on, he said.

I called Dean Kidd's number again on Tuesday to find out why the administration still wanted houseSYSTEM down.

"Hello, who's this?" a woman answered tersely.

"Hi, this is Aaron Greenspan," I responded. "I just spoke with Jay Ellison and he said that you had some concerns about houseSYSTEM that you wanted to discuss."

"Oh, hello, Aaron. I can't talk to you now." Her statement left me holding the receiver to my ear, puzzled.

"You can't—"

"We'll send you a letter. Try next week." The line went dead. I looked at the telephone, my eyebrows raised.

"She hung up on me!" I shouted in disbelief. As I stared at the cheap, beige plastic handset, I wondered how everything had gotten so messed up, and so quickly. It didn't seem right, even from a statistical perspective. There had to be something else going on.

"*I bet whatever it is, they talked about it at that meeting,*" I thought. My next call was to Paul Bottino, whom Jay had mentioned would also be at the meeting.

"Yeah, they had a meeting in University Hall yesterday..." he told me when I asked.

"Can you tell me who was there?"

"Sure, Georgene Herschbach..." I furiously grabbed at a note pad next to the phone, and began writing down names. "Lori Silver from OGC, David Sobel from—"

I cut him off. "OGC?"

"Oh, Office of the General Counsel."

"Great," I said with all the sarcasm I could muster. Harvard had called in its lawyers.

"Sobel from HASCS, Judith Kidd of course...and me. I think that was it." He wouldn't go into much detail about what they had discussed, aside from mentioning that everyone wanted to know if Paul had anything to do with it. We talked in general about what I was trying to accomplish with houseSYSTEM.

"What does Georgene Herschbach do?" I asked, since I had never heard her name before.

"She's a higher-up in University Hall," Paul said. "She's working on the redesign of the College web site."

Everything came into perspective. This administrator was the missing link. The "college.harvard.edu" web site—different from the "my.harvard" portal but arguably more similar to houseSYSTEM in functionality—hadn't been redesigned since the late 1990s when a friend of Carl's had worked on it. It just so happened that I had released houseSYSTEM at the exact same time that the College was planning to re-launch its own site. I was stepping on very large toes, and I hadn't even known that they were there.

"Thanks!" I told Paul gratefully at the end of our conversation. My father, who was standing nearby, had heard me mention Dean Herschbach's name.

"Oh!" he perked up. "That must be Dudley Herschbach's wife," he said.

"Who's that?" I vaguely remembered him talking about a professor named Dudley at some point.

"He's a famous chemist who's at Harvard. I've read some of his papers. I don't understand them all, but he's very well-regarded."

Enough had happened that I figured it was time to update the SEC's Board and my friends. I sent them all a re-cap, asking them to keep everything confidential. In particular, I was worried about what might happen if people heard a rumor that they were going to have to reset their passwords *en masse*.

I knew I could no longer delay the inevitable. I had to start writing a program to change every houseSYSTEM member's password. I was still conflicted about what to do about handing over all of the information to the College. If I backtracked on my promise of anonymity, then I proved that my claims weren't trustworthy. I would be giving people like Dan Ellard all the ammunition to use against me that they ever wanted.

Finally, at 11:24 P.M., the password reset code seemed to be working reliably. I uploaded the final version to my server, watching it crawl across the network at a snail's pace despite the tiny size of the file. Then, I ran it. Within thirty seconds, it reset the passwords of almost 500 people, sending them all e-mails.

My own mailbox dinged, sending a shiver down my spine before I realized that it was my own automated e-mail I had just received.

"Due to a request from Harvard College that we reset your houseSYSTEM password, we have cleared your password from our database. At no time was your plain text password stored on our system, accessed, or compromised in any way. This is simply a precautionary measure. Please be aware that the SEC's FASt Webmail will no longer function as a result of this change, though you can still use standard FAS Webmail," the message began.

I tried signing in. "Your password is incorrect. Please verify that you typed your password correctly, and try again," a houseSYSTEM error message that I had written told me.

I thought I had copied and pasted the password directly from the e-mail, but I tried again nonetheless. The same error message came back.

"Dammit!" I yelled. Quickly, I manually generated the SHA-1 hash of the password that had just arrived in my inbox, and compared it to the one in the database. It didn't take long to figure out the problem. Not only did it not match, but it appeared that every password in the database had the exact same hash. Before, I had been testing the code on only one account—my own—so I hadn't noticed the bug.

"Arrrggh!" I grimaced, furiously fixing the bad database command I had spent all day working on and adding a disclaimer to the e-mail message. I ran the patched program once more, watching 500 more e-mails go out. "Please disregard the previous message. This one contains your correct password," all of the new messages read on top.

Exactly four minutes later, I had my first response. It was from Laura Krug.

Because I'm always curious--how'd the college request that passwords be changed? Who from Harvard made that request? Has everyone's password been changed? Will anyone still be able to access Harvard email through houseSYSTEM?

Then came my friend in Cabot.

What is going on with these new passwords? So the university ultimately triumphed with this FAS (read: SLOOOOW) webmail thing, eh? Oy.

The next morning, Jay Ellison sent me a reminder of what exactly the administration was saying.

In light of our recent email exchange, as well as the phone conversations you have had with me and other members of the College, there appears to be some continuing confusion about the actions you need to take immediately with respect to your requesting FAS passwords on the www.harvardsec.org website. I realize that you have removed the link requesting that students supply their FAS information on the HouseSystem site, but there are still issues that you must address. Many of these issues are best addressed in person when you return to Cambridge later this month, but there are some issues that you must address immediately. In consultation with other members of the College administration, we have determined that you need to take the steps outlined below by 12:00 noon on Friday, August 15:

1.   Ensure that all SEC projects, including HouseSystem and FAStmail, stop asking for, collecting or storing (in any form, encrypted or not) Harvard FAS passwords. HASCS considers the simple fact that your web site asks for FAS passwords to constitute a security breach. Measures that your site may take to protect the security of FAS passwords do not negate this concern, since HASCS has no ability to verify that you have implemented the software the way that you have claimed, that no one else will ever have access to the software, or that the software and the server are and always will be as secure as you assert.

2.   Provide a list of all FAS usernames which you have recorded as having submitted FAS passwords to the SEC web site. HASCS cannot accept your offer to forward a message to users on its behalf. As custodians of the security of FAS computer systems, HASCS must take steps on its own to ensure that students have the opportunity to change their FAS passwords.

3.   Delete all FAS passwords (in any form, encrypted or not) collected from SEC project websites, including HouseSystem and FAStmail. I understand that you agreed in your August 8 email to me that you would take this action for the HouseSystem website. Please confirm that you have taken all steps necessary to ensure that anyone who has access to any and all projects on the SEC site cannot view, retrieve or use FAS passwords in any form, now or in the future.

You have stated that you do not believe that you have violated any Harvard policy. Because of the serious security concerns involved, we need you to comply with these requests, regardless of your personal beliefs. I need to emphasize that this matter may quickly become a disciplinary issue if you do not take immediate action. I also wish to emphasize that I and others want to support you in your work to provide a useful web site for Harvard undergraduates, one that also complies with Harvard policies.

They had backed me into a corner. While the idea of being forced out of Harvard to become a student hero had a certain appeal, it quickly faded as I faced reality. Most of the students who had expressed their views on houseSYSTEM so far saw me as anything but a hero, and there was a good chance no one would even care if I left.

"*What's the point of sacrificing a Harvard diploma to be left with a bunch of enemies?*" I thought. On the other hand, there was the administration's preferred path. "*What's the point of keeping a Harvard diploma to be left with a bunch of enemies?"*

"What am I supposed to do?" I asked my parents. "They want me to betray the trust of all these people, and make all of my critics, most of whom are complete idiots, look like prophets. Watch, they'll just say, 'see, I told you the site was insecure!' Not one person has had their password, or *anything* for that matter, stolen!"

For an hour and a half, I vacillated on what to tell Jay Ellison. Then, I thought back to my original analysis and subtracted "a bunch of enemies" from both sides, making everything clearer.

"*I can either have a Harvard diploma, or not,*" I realized. I thought of all the times I had screamed over the phone freshman year, and even sophomore year, that I wanted to drop out. "*But I'm already halfway through...*"

"*I guess I'll be making a bunch of enemies, then.*" I was going to keep my diploma— if they let me.

I drafted a letter to send to every houseSYSTEM member. If I was going to have to turn over the database, I wasn't going to let it go without a fight. When I ran the new code to send out my third e-mail, I once again received my own personalized copy.

I started CriticalMass about a year ago to try and improve the information available to Harvard College students about courses. My own experience led me to believe that it would be a helpful tool, and my peers confirmed this belief. Aside from Dean Gross's comment in the Crimson that, "Usually bulletin boards of this nature generate more heat than light" (http://www.thecrimson.com/article.aspx?ref=255937), the administration had little to say about it. Nevertheless, I realized that many students, concerned about possible administrative repercussions, would only participate if they could sign up anonymously. This capability was programmed into CriticalMass, and later houseSYSTEM, as well.

Unfortunately, those concerns were not as unfounded as I had once thought. Despite repeated attempts to explain the workings of houseSYSTEM to several administrators, I have been personally threatened with disciplinary action by the Harvard College administration if I do not turn over the e-mail addresses of every houseSYSTEM member, as well as proof that there are no longer any FAS passwords in our database. (The administration refuses accept the argument that there never were.) In other words, I have been asked to disclose the entire table pertaining to members in unaltered form, complete with information about your choice to remain anonymous on houseSYSTEM. My only other option would be deleting houseSYSTEM in its entirety, but that is not an option that I am willing to entertain.

I realize that this is an egregious breach of your privacy. Adding further irony to the situation is the College's claim that it is necessary in order to protect your privacy, and the fact that it has been justified by administrators who actively refuse to understand the technical details necessarily involved. I have done all that I can to avoid this situation, but given that the administration never consulted me or anyone at the SEC about the manner in which the site functions, it has been an uphill battle.

Harvard College has demanded member information by Friday, August 15 at 12:00 noon. If you are dissatisfied with the College's handling of this situation, as I am, or with the idea that the professors whom you rightfully critique on CriticalMass could have your name, cell phone number and e-mail address, please send an e-mail to Dean Gross (gross@math.harvard.edu).

Perhaps if enough students respond with words to enlighten the administration, Harvard will be more inclined to respond to the critical mass.

My next e-mail was to Jay Ellison. I grudgingly pasted the contents of the "members" table in Structured Query Language into the bottom of my message.

Thank you for your latest e-mail. Given that Dean Kidd refused to speak with me on the phone yesterday, I would have to agree that there has been additional confusion as to what the administration actually wants. You already know how I feel about the way I have been treated thus far, so I will address the administration's three points without further ado:

1. This has already been done. I offered to open the code to anyone interested, so I would disagree that "HASCS has no ability to verify that you have implemented the software the way that you have claimed." I cannot guarantee the future security of my servers any more than HASCS can guarantee the future security of theirs.

2. Despite the obvious breach of privacy of 402 students' confidential information, the list has been attached to this message at your request, only in order to avoid disciplinary action for a crime that I did not commit.

3. The attachment, combined with the e-mail that I sent you last night at 12:30 A.M., should verify that there are no FAS passwords, in any form, anywhere in our data-base. More importantly, there never were. There are no databases or permanent password storage file associated with FASt Webmail--which, as you know, Franklin Steen never prohibited after I asked him specifically about it--and all links to it were already removed yesterday.

For the record, my work has always complied with Harvard policies.

If the administration has any actual, founded concerns about houseSYSTEM, I would expect that I will hear about those before the deadline that you have imposed. If not, then I would hope that new members would be allowed to sign up with non-FAS passwords on Friday at noon.

Then, I watched as my inbox became a playpen for the feisty children who comprised the Harvard student body. Felix, who was helping me maintain the SEC's e-mail account separate from my own, set up a system of folders to organize the response. I prayed that the "positive" folder ended up with more messages than the "negative" one.

Laura Krug wrote again.

Not that you don't have plenty of other things on your mind at the moment, but I think I'm writing a follow-up article, chronicling this latest turn of events. If you have some time, it'd be great if we could talk--not that I'm adhering to deadlines, but might sometime tonight be ok? I can call you wherever, or I'll just be around the Crimson and you could call here. Again, sorry to bother you in the midst of everything, but if you could let me know a time that's best for you, I'd appreciate it. Thanks.

I had the same problem as before: I couldn't not respond. Between reading the e-mails that were pouring in, I gave her a call.

Meanwhile, I was receiving an approximately even share of supportive messages and flame mail. Some people copied me on their letters to University Hall.

Dear Dean Gross-

I am writing in support of a student I know named Aaron Greenspan. Aaron and I met in a freshman seminar, and have spoken little since then except for the occasional hello in economics class, however, I know he is a good person and applaud his efforts to offer a forum for discussion.

I am writing to support him because, having heard only his side of the story, it seems as if he is being unfairly required to turn over the members of his site. When I signed up for his site, I did so with the intent that what I said wouldnt be used against me. As it ended up, I am not so concerned about confidentiality because I never wrote anything that criticized any classes, I merely read what others had said. Others, however, might highly value this confidentiality and this issue should not be taken lightly.

When I signed up, I believe the site asked me for my password. It might have even asked me for my FAS password. I can't remember. Since then, I have changed my fas password a number of times, and I imagine most other people have as well.

If you feel the computer system will be compromised unless you compare his database to yours to ensure he hasn't stolen FAS passwords, I support that effort. However, it should be done under the supervision of a third party to ensure the confidentiality of the students who signed up to the site.

Thanks for your time, and I look forward to seeing you this upcoming year!

Another student seemed to have mixed feelings.

Thank you for your e-mail. I think that the idea behind CriticalMass and even the enhanced version in the HouseSystem are interesting and good. However, I have no desire to a)sacrifice any privacy (how, for instance, do you know if I have packages or not?) or b)be a party in this bizarre melodrama that seems to have engulfed the program in recent weeks. Also, the excellence of the idea seems to have been accompanied by poor planning and execution.

I must say that I find this entire situation to be ridiculous. I innocently signed up for this program in its earlier stages, thinking that it was above board. Then, you demand my FAS password, get in trouble with the administration, and decide that you would rather sacrifice the privacy of your trusting members than do the honorable thing and delete the database or, if necessary, the entire system, even if it means that you will take a fall.

Since obviously I cannot compel you to take this course of action, I have instead tried to delete my account. Lo and behold, it seems that there is no "delete account" link on the MyAccount page on the website. This lack of control over my own account simply adds to the questions I have, and to those posted over Lowell-Open, about the legitimacy of this website. I request that you manually remove my information.

The head of the Graduate Student Council wrote in, as well.

Dear Dean Gross-
I have learned that Harvard has demanded the release of private information, including email addresses and passwords, of students who use houseSYSTEM. I have also heard that you plan disciplinary action against the creator of this service unless this private information is released.

It is unacceptable for you to invade user privacy in this way. Additionally, even if Harvard for some reason feels threatened by houseSYSTEM and CriticalMass, it is of course not appropriate for you to lash out against the creator of the service or the service itself.

Furthermore, houseSYSTEM provides services that graduate students have been asking for for years, and that Harvard has been unwilling or unable to provide. Students want a way to anonymously inform each other about the quality of their courses, and houseSYSTEM/CriticalMass enables students to do this. Please realize what a great service houseSYSTEM is to the student community, and please stop undermining this wonderful effort.

Please inform me of any further actions or positions you plan regarding houseSYSTEM so that the issue can be discussed in the Graduate Student Council.

Rebecca Spencer
President 2002-3
Graduate Student Council

Then, she sent me another e-mail that made me smile more than I had in weeks.

Review of courses has been a big issue at the graduate student level for a few years now. It may be useful for you to know that a website (www.teacherreviews.com) is somewhat similar in goal to yours, and I've heard that it has withstood the test of lawsuits. One difference to keep in mind though, is that if a professor or university has a problem with a particular comment and want to sue the author, the website will release contact information, thereby avoiding legal liability and leaving it to the individual to be responsible.

It really is a struggle to work with the Harvard Administration and I sympathize with you. I end up feeling that fostering good education is not a priority on their agenda. I'm hoping you can get a good lawyer and foil the bastards.

The good was, of course, tempered by the bad. Some of the e-mails that Felix had filed away were worse than others.

Exactly what information are you giving to Harvard? Do I need to change my FAS password? What a pain. I wish I'd never signed up for your system.

Others were along the lines of what I had been expecting. Some students simply didn't understand what was going on. In a way, I didn't blame people for being angry, though I usually tried to substantiate my criticism of others, which was a step many of the angry students did not want to be burdened with. One such student was a *Crimson* editor who made it very clear whose side he was on.

I don't intend to be mean when I say this, but I do not support your crusade against the administration.

This is because I _do_ know something about website security. Enough to know that storing passwords on a server accessible from the Internet, even if encrypted, is not perfectly safe. Unless you have professional-grade firewalling and the like (which I doubt), I would not trust my password with you (and I have not).

Additionally, anybody who administers the houseSYSTEM website/database could easily abuse the system (I'm sure you know this is true despite the fact that you would never abuse the system yourself).

As a result, I would much prefer that you find a way to compromise with the administration. I do not think that giving them information that could link students to their anonymous posts is morally acceptable, no matter the circumstances.

That night, I went to bed knowing that if nothing else, I had rocked the boat. The letter from the head of the Graduate Student Council had at least assured me that the issues I was making a fuss about were not trivial ones.

What remained to be determined was whether or not the boat had sunk.

▼

When I woke up on the morning of August 14th, the e-mails were still coming in. More people were taking me up on my call to e-mail Dean Gross than I had anticipated.

Hi Aaron--

I am behind you 100%. This is outrageous. Below is my email to Dean Gross.
~Bird

Dear Dean Gross,

As a member of Harvard college who is dedicated to its improvement, I was very distressed to learn from Aaron Greenspan that by your order, anonymity would be stripped from students contributing to web-sites like Critical Mass or the HouseSYS-TEM, which are designed to allow students a safe venue through which to discuss and try to improve areas of weakness they encounter while at Harvard. By taking away the protection of anonymity, which allows students to question, debate, and try to resolve problems they encounter while at Harvard without fear of unfair retribution, you deny the students their right to demand the best of their (very expensive) educations. How can a student feel able to ask for help regarding a certain professor, for example, if that professor is given access to his/her name, email, and even cell phone number? Critical Mass and its new incarnation in the HouseSYSTEM are designed as forums to improve University life. Why would you, as dean, wish in any way to hinder such an endeavor by making it too risky for students to use? We all only want the best for our school, and as its students, we should not be frightened into silence.

More people were visiting the site, too. My server's logs reflected the heavy volume of traffic, with remote computer's names, dates, times, and requested pages streaming down my father's laptop's screen at a blistering pace. It looked like something out of *The Matrix*.

At 1:32 P.M., a mass e-mail arrived from the "FAS Computer Services Security Group." It was the first time since I had been at Harvard that I had received anything from the Group. I didn't even know if there really was a Group, or if they had made up the name just for this special occasion.

FAS Computer Services has recently received information indicating that your FAS password may have been compromised on a web server located off campus. To protect the security of your FAS account and the privacy of your email and data, we are asking you to change your password at this time.

To reset your password, please visit the FAS Computer Services website at:

    https://www.fas.harvard.edu/computing/utilities/password/

If you need assistance, please visit the Help Desk in Science Center B-13 or contact help@fas.harvard.edu (617-495-9000).

In the future we would also ask, for security reasons, that you never enter your FAS password on any website that is not officially endorsed or operated by FAS Computer Services. If you have concerns about the security of your FAS account, please email us at security@fas.harvard.edu.

Thank you.

I let out a sigh of relief.

"Well, at least they're not forcibly resetting people's passwords. They seem to have made it optional." I was glad that there wouldn't be hundreds of students grousing at me about having made them change their all-important FAS passwords.

My e-mail program dinged again, but this time it wasn't because there was a new message. It was an error. I tried signing into the FAS server through SSH, the more traditional way.

"Welcome. You must change your password," my father's computer displayed across the screen.

"Bastards!" I shouted. They *were* forcing everyone to change their passwords after all! I changed mine as they had asked me to do. Then, I changed it back. Several of my friends did the same.

The next e-mail I received made me laugh out loud. One of my friends had responded to the FAS Computer Services Security Group.

Dear Sir or Madam:

I happen to be aware of the site and server to which you refer and the debate surrounding its security systems. I also happen to know, thanks to my own investigations, that my password has not, in fact, been compromised in any way, shape, or form by this aforementioned website. If require further technical details I suggest you examine the site yourself to see that passwords were NOT collected despite the fears of other members of the Harvard community).

I therefore must decline to change my password at this time.

Thank you for your thoughtful suggestion and your kind concern about the welfare of my computing account.

When I closed the SSH session for Harvard's server, I noticed something odd on my own server. One person in particular visiting houseSYSTEM had a computer name that was slightly different than all of the other visitors' machine names. Of the houseSYSTEM users at Harvard, most of their computers' names ended with "student.harvard.edu." This computer's name was "osterber-nt.fas.harvard.edu."

"*That's odd,*" I thought. "*Student machines never have FAS hostnames. I wonder who this guy is.*"

I ran some tests on the address. It was valid. I searched the houseSYSTEM member database to see who had last signed in from the computer. It was a Graduate School of Arts and Sciences student named Rick Osterberg.

"*Maybe grad students get to use FAS addresses?*" I thought. In some ways, GSAS was a division of the Faculty of Arts and Sciences, but I wasn't really sure. I checked

Rebecca Spencer's member record, since I knew that she was a graduate student. Her address didn't use the fas.harvard.edu domain.

Next, I looked up anyone with the last name Osterberg in the on-line Harvard phone book. Only one result came up: "FAS^FCOR^Computer Svcs - Staff."

"Staff?" I yelled. "This guy works for HASCS, and he's claiming to be a grad student? And they're accusing *me* of breaching privacy? What the hell!"

Having no one else to vent to, I showed my parents. They were infuriated. I kept a closer eye on my log files.

Meanwhile, Rohit Chopra, the President of the Undergraduate Council, wrote to me. His message, at least, contained a bit of good news.

> Sounds like you are being taken for a ride with University Hall. Please let me know if there is anything you think they are overstepping their boundaries on.
>
> As I may have mentioned a while ago, I am looking to buy the "Salesline" software and cut off ties with HCS and our awful Marketplace tool. I think your Student Exchange is fine, and there is no use in me paying some random person and have us steal users from each other.
>
> I have money authorized for this purpose, so I am willing to pay SEC or whatever entity if you can build a form I can embed into the UC website to submit books and items, as well as search for them, without entering passwords...
>
> Let me know if you are interested, otherwise I'll go forward with Salesline.

I wrote back, letting him know that I did indeed believe the administration to be "overstepping." He replied immediately.

> This note concerns me quite a bit. Let's have a phone call when you're back from vacation. Any written correspondence you have that you could share (I can assure you it is for my eyes only) would be helpful.
>
> I can do $750-800, is that fair for creating the features that Student Exchange has for an interface on the UC website?

I smiled ironically at the price tag. It was barely enough money to cover the cost of a wildcard SSL certificate that would work on all twenty-six houseSYSTEM sites.

I had never been so busy on a vacation. Aside from houseSYSTEM, I also had e-mails from the Business School student who was subletting his apartment to us, friends—and Jay Ellison and *The Crimson*. It was unending.

> We do appreciate the measures you have taken and look forward to your return so that any remaining problems can be discussed and addressed. I know this has been

difficult since you are trying to relax and enjoy your vacation.

HASCS has informed me that they are satisfied that you have taken the steps necessary to relieve our immediate concerns. As for your request to turn the sign-in portion
of the site back on for students to register, the SEC site does look like an official
University website and because it gives no indication that it is hosted off campus,
students may be confused or default to using their official information even though
you make it clear on the site that they should not. Because of this, I think there is
a general consensus that you should wait until we have the chance to discuss this
when you return later next week. However, since you do have students wanting to
join, if you would be willing to change the site now so that you ask students to enter
account names that don't correspond to their FAS usernames and passwords that
don't correspond to their FAS passwords, you can go ahead and turn it back on
immediately. This way, students should not be confused and simply use the same
information by default, recognizing instead that the system is separate from their
FAS accounts. This is a small additional step since we have already discussed you
adding a clear statement about not using FAS passwords. By adding a statement
about not using FAS usernames the issue should be clarified.

Please let me know if you do decide to do this and turn the site back on.

In a matter of seconds, I changed the site to ask students specifically not to use
their FAS passwords. Simultaneously, Laura Krug had managed to pick up the
scent of intrigue.

The rumor mill being the odd creature that it is, I heard today via a sketchy network
of sources that there was a concern or possibility that houseSYSTEM itself had been
attacked. Whether by outside hackers or what, I don't know and no one seems to.
Can you tell me if there's any basis for believing this? It's murky but I don't want to
not address it.
Thanks--sorry to grab you again.

I put together a hasty but definitive reply assuring her that no one had broken
into the site. I was so dazed by the week's events, it didn't occur to me that the only
other people I had told about Rick Osterberg's adventure into houseSYSTEM were
my parents, sitting there in the room with me.

Somewhere in the Harvard University administration, there appeared to be a
leak.

▼

I forwarded Laura copies of every e-mail that had been sent to and from the
administration about houseSYSTEM so far. I also told her about Rick Osterberg.
Then, I wrote my next reply to Jay Ellison, asking for clarification on the term "official information" and pointing out that e-mail addresses were public information.

He wrote back alarmingly fast.

I will be glad to attempt to clarify my last message. The status of the SEC web site is actually something that will be discussed when you return. An "official University" site, in this context, means something like the web sites for FAS, Harvard College, GSAS, the Ed School, etc. Your site is not in this category so it is not considered an official University site (again, this will be discussed and clarified when you return). In the meantime, what HASCS and the College are requesting is that if you want to go "live" again immediately, you ask people to give you a unique username and password, both different than their FAS username and password. For example, I have this email address and another, jellison@fas. My username for sites outside of Harvard might be something like jellison2000, or jlellison, or Jayellison, or the like. I do not use my jellison@fas username for anything but my non-Senior Tutor stuff at Harvard proper. It is indeed public information (as you have said), but we are concerned that if students are asked for their FAS username they still might assume the site is part of the official University system (as defined above) and not simply related to it through SEC's relationship. I agree that students are smart enough to follow the directions, but HASCS and the College are requesting that you make the changes if you want open the site up for new sign-in immediately.

Changing to this type of username may require more programing (since, as you said, it cannot currently accept anything but email addresses) and since things are not yet completely clear, you might prefer to wait until you return to discuss the matter. That way, at least the relationship with the site to the University should be clear and then you can program or plan accordingly. Then when you open the site everything should be straightened out.

"Since when is using your Harvard e-mail address on a web site not allowed?" I asked no one in particular. I noticed that Judith Kidd had been copied on the last several e-mails from Jay Ellison, but there was still no hint of Rick Osterberg.

I wrote back again, unwilling to submit to the administration's every whim.

Thanks for the clarification. I think the best solution to potential confusion, which is the only issue here given the lack of actual confusion, would be a disclaimer on each page. It is something that is easy to do, and in fact, something that has already been done, at least in some capacity.

I cannot change the way that houseSYSTEM parses usernames, as you have suggested. houseSYSTEM depends upon Think Computer's shared software libraries for this functionality; many other clients--including Harvard University--depend upon it functioning the way that it currently does, and only that way. I have already changed all of Think Computer's clients' software once, to accommodate the relatively simple change from MD5 to SHA-1 hashing. The change you have suggested would be far more complex, requiring the active participation of every user at every one of Think Computer's clients. Unless Harvard University wants to compensate Think Computer and all of its clients for the significant damage that this change would cause, not to mention to the cost of re-programming a number of complex web sites, this is not an acceptable solution.

More importantly, there seems to be a double standard here. Other student groups are permitted to use student e-mail addresses in conjunction with their web sites. There is no reason why we shouldn't be. Would the administration also argue that by e-mailing students at their Harvard e-mail address, we might be inducing confusion? Frankly, I think this is a non-issue.

It would appear that the administration is digging for random reasons to keep students from signing up for the site. I can assure you that this is not appreciated by me, or based on the number of supportive e-mails the SEC has received, the student body.

Jay responded in turn, telling me to "hold on" while he looking into things. It was driving me crazy that I was not allowed to talk to anyone with technical knowledge. He was the wrong man for the job.

"Does he understand that every time he says 'hold on,' that means 'don't let anyone sign up?' Maybe the man is just dense..."

The next e-mail I received revealed that there were indeed others watching in University Hall.

"It's from Georgene Herschbach," I told my father.

Disclaimers would be good. As for the parsing issue, I don't understand the technical problem. We'll need David Sobel's input here. I know he'll be out of the office today, but may be able to check email.

David Sobel appeared to be another HASCS staff member. My immediate problem was that the administration's deadline was rapidly approaching, and nothing so far had seemed to satisfy their monstrous appetite for petty changes; instead, the number of administrators involved seemed to be growing.

I picked up the telephone to call Dean Kidd once again, who had also been copied on the e-mail. With so many names floating around, I couldn't tell who was really pulling the strings, and I wanted to find out. The venerable Dean sounded just as terse as she had the Friday before, but she thankfully did not hang up.

"Yes, well, aside from the security issues, there are some other problems that you need to fix before you can proceed. The SEC needs to register as an official student group with the College."

"We are an official student group," I said. "We just changed our name. Before it was 'TECH SA.'"

"Not according to what I have here," Dean Kidd responded.

"Susan Cooke approved the change!" I said. "There must be some mistake."

"No. You will need to re-submit your by-laws to the Committee on College Life, which meets in October."

"October!" I jumped. "This site needs to be on-line before shopping period!"

"Well, that's when they meet," she said. "If you're lucky, I can try to move it up somewhat."

"Alright..." I said. "Anything else?"

"Certainly. Actually, I was looking at your...Think Computer...site, and I noticed, you have a press release on there for doing, I don't know what, with the Harvard International Review?"

"*What*?" I thought. I couldn't see how there was any connection to house-SYSTEM.

"Yes, my company hosts the International Review's web site..." I said.

"Right, well, your press release makes it sound as though the Harvard International Review is part of Harvard University. It's not, it's a student group. You need to make that clear. You're also using a photograph the Harvard T stop on your site, I believe. You need to take that down."

"I took that photograph, it's not copyrighted by the College. And the public transit system isn't even College property!"

"It has to come down."

I had no idea why I had to take orders from a Harvard College Dean of Anything when it came to my life outside of school, until I remembered Jay Ellison's threat: disciplinary action. It was all the leverage they needed.

"Okay," I said. "Anything else?"

"Yes, I also noticed that you never registered Think Computer with the Dean's office. All student business activity needs to be registered. You'll need to do that first."

"Actually, I did register with the College, or at least I thought I did. One of the first things that happened when I got to Cambridge freshman year was that my father dropped off one of my servers in Dean Lewis's office. So, Dean Lewis knew about my company...there was never any paperwork to register or anything, though. It was a pretty informal process at the time."

"Well, I'll check on that," she said. With every word, she seemed like she was snapping at me. "We have a new Dean now, as you know. We can discuss more next week, but for now, that's all."

"Alright, thank you," I said.

"Goodbye."

I looked up the list of officially-recognized student groups immediately afterward, and found "TECH Student Association" listed with hundreds of others in the Handbook for Students. I also double-checked with Rodica about Susan Cooke's approval of the change. There had been no problem, but when Rodica asked Susan Cooke to confirm her prior action in writing, she refused. She didn't want to get involved with the mess and risk losing her job.

The next morning, after reading the latest *Crimson* article about houseSYSTEM with a certain mixture of disbelief and apathy, I wrote to Dean Herschbach and Jay Ellison to ask them to explain what they really wanted.

I have less than an hour and a half now to avoid fixing a vague issue which has not been justified in any technical sense, in order to avoid unspecified disciplinary action which has not been justified in any sense at all. Please understand if I feel a little frustrated.

There are already disclaimers on the site, despite the fact that I know of no other student group required to place such disclaimers on their sites. HSA is an entirely separate corporation from the University, and even it is not required to plaster disclaimers all over its web sites. The details of the technical problem with changing usernames are less important than the end result, which is that the usernames for houseSYSTEM must be e-mail addresses. Since every Harvard student is guaranteed to have a Harvard e-mail address, it's the only standardized option available. From a legal standpoint, they are already public information, which means that the University's ability to regulate them is slim to none.

Please inform me whether the administration's issues have been addressed or not. If they have been, I would like to re-open my club's web site to new members.

Jay Ellison's response was swift, but confusing.

The issues that were referenced with the deadline 12:00 today, as I said in my email yesterday, were sufficiently addressed by you. Now we are simply trying to decide about reopening the site so don't feel that the clock is still ticking.

"I could have sworn they told me that if I gave them the member 'database,' they'd let me re-open the site," I told my parents. Now they're trying to decide again? What is their problem? Really? Why won't they tell me what their problem is?"

My father was at a loss. I wrote back again, attempting to extract a list of the remaining unresolved "issues," and a basis for the administration's decision to keep the site down.

"Try Alan Dershowitz," my father suggested. "Maybe he can give you some backing. He knows the law as well as anyone, and he's at Harvard." I sent Dershowitz an e-mail, but never received a response. I also drafted a second reply to Jay's latest e-mail that was more of an ultimatum than a reply, and sent it to Felix to look over from an objective viewpoint. Felix gave it a thumbs-down. It was too harsh.

Brad, my friend who had been following the saga from afar, offered to help when I told him that I was thinking of taking a legal approach.

"My dad's a lawyer. Let me run it by him," he told me. A few hours later, he came back with a name, and suggesting sending his father a written explanation of the situation to look over.

"You should be counseled by professionals in this matter," Brad's father wrote back, along with a friend's name, and his own phone numbers at home and at work. I was especially concerned about the meeting that Jay had implied would be taking place once I returned to Cambridge from vacation.

"I don't want to be sitting alone on one side of the table in a conference room in University Hall, while they've got their legal team, Deans, and computer people on the other," I told my parents. "I'm not going to any meeting like that without a lawyer—or someone."

I e-mailed Rohit and Rebecca, the two most important representatives of the Harvard student body, to see if they could back me up at such a meeting. The timing was unfortunate: they were both going home right before school began. Rohit at least offered to look over the e-mails I had received.

Over the weekend, I flew back to Cambridge. It was a relief to have my own phone line again and a fast internet connection, but I was still a nervous wreck. I didn't want to make use of either medium to let the administration know for certain that I had returned. The last thing that I wanted was a face-to-face meeting that I wasn't ready for.

▼

On Wednesday, August 20th, the administration was willing to play the waiting game no more.

Now that you are back from vacation, I want to sit down with you to discuss some additional issues related to the web site associated with SEC, the HouseSystem site, and some issues related to your own business, Think Computer. I am planning to send a separate email message to the other students involved with SEC, as some of these issues concern them as well.

First, I want to clarify that the College has no desire to shut down the SEC's web sites, or to prevent open dialogue between students. In their current form, however, the SEC web sites raise a number of issues, some of which I've listed in summary form below:
1. The SEC has not yet received approval from the Dean of Harvard College, and therefore at this point is not a recognized undergraduate student group. Until it obtains approval, the SEC does not have permission to use the name "Harvard." (See Harvard College Handbook for Students 2002-2003, pp. 309, 429, 430.)

2. Even if it were an approved undergraduate student group, the SEC would not be permitted to use any of Harvard's trademarks, including the VERITAS shield which currently appears on the SEC's home page without explicit permission. (See Handbook, pp. 309, 432.)

3. Even assuming the SEC becomes a recognized student group, this does not mean that a web site operated by the SEC is an "official" Harvard web site. As I've explained to you before, official Harvard web sites are those operated by the

University itself. Currently, the SEC web site and the houseSYSTEM web site are designed so as to appear to be web sites operated or officially endorsed by the University. The College is concerned that this may create confusion for students accessing or viewing the site.

4. A good deal of the current content of the houseSYSTEM web site constitutes copyright infringement, for example, the long descriptive passages about each of the Houses. You must have permission to use copyrighted material. Providing at-tribution is not sufficient.

5. The SEC's intention to link to House facebooks or otherwise publish identifying information about students raises separate concerns about student privacy.

6. The description of Think Computer as a "Harvard Student-Run Enterprise," which appears on the SEC web site, is unclear and potentially misleading. As currently worded, it sounds as though Think Computer is a Harvard business that is run by students, rather than a business that is run by a student who currently attends Harvard. Students with individual businesses may not use Harvard's name without permission or in any way suggest that their businesses are sponsored or endorsed by Harvard. (See Handbook, pp. 308, 309.)
There are also several serious concerns about your operation of your business, Think Computer. These issues are as follows:
1. You have not registered your intent to operate a business from Harvard property with the Dean of the College and, therefore, have not obtained permission from the College to do so, as the Handbook requires. (See Handbook, p. 308.)

2. The Think Computer web site lists your Harvard mailing address and telephone number as one of your offices, which is prohibited. (See Handbook, p. 308.)

3. The Think Computer web site states that Harvard University is using one of your products. As stated above, students may not in any way suggest that Harvard en-dorses a private business. Nor may Harvard's name be used in connection with any organization without prior permission. (See Handbook, pp. 308, 309.)
I have provided this summary as I wanted you to be aware of the issues in advance of our meeting. All of these issues must be addressed in one way or another. As you know, violations of the College's regulations may lead to disciplinary action.

Please let me know when you are available to meet and discuss this further. Since I am trying to get a little vacation time during the next two weeks, please call my office and set up a time we can meet.

As I marveled at the chutzpah of the Lowell House Senior Tutor, he was busy writing another message, which I received an hour later. This one wasn't addressed to me alone. It was addressed to the entire Executive Board of the SEC.

I wanted to write to you and explain some of the concerns the College has with the SEC web site and the houseSYSTEM site, a number of which I addressed with Aaron Greenspan earlier this month. As you all know, the HouseSystem site went "live" on

August 1. Like many who received this notice, I visited the site and immediately saw two problems: the site asked students to give: (1) their Harvard ID numbers; and (2) their Harvard FAS passwords. Others raised the same concerns and Aaron quickly responded by removing the ID number request. As he explained on the Lowell-Open list, this was simply a programming oversight. The request for FAS passwords was a little more complex. Nevertheless, after some discussion, Aaron shut down the sign-in page and reprogrammed the site to not ask for FAS passwords.

He then re-iterated the message he had just sent me, along with some others.

I emphasize that the College did not ask for personal information about students or your subscribers but only for a list of usernames, so that it could inform those users to change their FAS passwords. Aaron was asked to comply by Friday, August 15, which he did. I note that, in addition to the usernames, Aaron provided information that the College had not requested.

The College has not allowed the site to be turned back on for new sign-in since last Friday because several other issues must be resolved. I do want to clarify that the College has no desire to shut down the SEC's web sites, or to prevent open dialogue between students. In their current form, however, the web sites raise a number of issues, some of which I've listed in summary form below. These issues concern all of you, as members of the SEC with responsibility for its actions. Because Aaron is the primary developer/manager for the sites, I have sent him the same list separately.

All of these issues must be addressed in one way or another. As you know, violations of the College's regulations may lead to disciplinary action. Once you return to campus, I would like to meet with you together to discuss these issues further. In the meantime, I am happy to speak with you should you have any questions.

"*Way to borrow tactics from your police experience, Jay*," I thought. "*Hostage-taking. That is novel.*"

Now they weren't just threatening me with "disciplinary action." They were threatening my friends, as well as two people who had done nothing for house-SYSTEM, let alone the club, in six months.

CHAPTER 24

Veritas

"DO NOT RESPOND to Jay Ellison's e-mail. I am speaking with a number of attorneys right now," I wrote frantically to everyone involved as I looked up the number for the law firm that Brad's father's friend had recommended. After hastily explaining the situation and the time crunch it involved, they agreed to help out on an informal basis free of charge.

"I can't thank you enough," I told them, relieved.

"Well, it seems as though they're a little afraid of the competition you're giving them," one of the lawyers said. "This could be construed as anti-competitive behavior."

"I'm not sure I see it like that," I said, still unsure of Harvard's real motive.

"Well, regardless, that's what it is in a courtroom." Realizing that my opinion really didn't matter, I decided to let the lawyers handle the law.

At noon on Friday, after wrangling over the text of my reply with my three *pro bono* attorneys for two full days, I finally responded to Jay Ellison. Reading it over, I thought I sounded far too friendly. The message went on for pages and responded to Jay's points one-by-one. Then, I attached the e-mails I had exchanged in September of my freshman year regarding my boxes in Dean Lewis's office. It was the only written proof I had that he knew what I was up to—and apparently, didn't care.

Jay Ellison sent a reply. Thankfully, it was brief.

> Thank you for your email message. I appreciate your responding to my earlier email and your willingness to work with the College on all these issues. I will write next week with a more substantive response, once I have some time to consider things again. Perhaps we can meet later in the week to discuss this whole matter.

Over the weekend, I combed through the labyrinth of web sites that fell under the official harvard.edu domain. In a couple of hours, by the standards the administration had been using against me, I found six instances of blatantly insecure systems. I also wrote a query to the Harvard Registrar concerning Rick Osterberg's status as a graduate student.

My father, generally outraged, started drafting another letter to Dean William Kirby, who was Dean Gross's superior. I sent him my list of insecure sites, including Dan Ellard's official Lowell House Face Book, along with proof that I had voluntarily informed the Admissions Office of multiple vulnerabilities in their systems during my freshman year—an odd behavior for a student purportedly abusing the trust of others on-line.

One of my attorneys wrote to me to suggest the next course of action based on the concerns I had expressed to him about having the site down even as shopping period was approaching.

> Write him on Monday a.m. and tell him that you are anxious not to have the site down for new members later than next Thursday because the site has particular functional utility for students at the semester's start. Suggest that your cooperation should be reciprocated with timely approval by then (if not sooner). Reiterate that after making the modifications listed in your email, you can see no basis for any complaint from Harvard nor disciplinary action against anyone if the site resumes resumes accepting new users beginning Thursday. Mention that you think that there are free speech interests at stake that Harvard should take into account in providing a timely and favorable response to your request. He should promptly let you know if there are any remaining issues after making the modifications described in your email.

When he saw the draft of my father's letter, which I wanted him to clear as well, he only wrote back with a single line:

> Hell hath no fury like a father who is also an academic/Harvard alum.

On Monday, the 25th, I followed my lawyer's advice and sent Jay one more e-mail. There was no response. My father sent his letter to Dean Kirby the next day. I wanted to applaud after reading it, but restrained myself so that my summer roommates would not begin questioning my sanity.

It took two more days before I heard anything back from the administration, during which time I was thankful for the reprieve. I had to pack up everything and move yet again, back to Lowell House. It was the last place on Earth I wanted to be.

Jay's new e-mail was short.

> I am in the process of working on a full email response to you. I hope that it will be ready later today. You will not be able to open the site for new students until SEC is approved as a student group by the College. I will explain it all in the email later today.

Sure enough, Jay e-mailed the entire Executive Board that afternoon. He made us aware that we still were not an "approved undergraduate student group," that we could not use the "Harvard" name (but could use "Harvard College"), and that aside from the trademark permission granted to student groups, providing correct copyright attribution without *additional* written permission from each and every House Master was insufficient to use content from any of Harvard's web sites. He also informed us that my opt-in Universal Face Book idea, which I had written to him about before, was specifically forbidden.

> As for the proposed face book, the College will not permit the SEC to post on your site information that it collects or maintains about students. Federal law imposes strict obligations on the College with regard to the dissemination of student information, including names, addresses, phone numbers and photographs. The College therefore will not release information of this kind to you, or to any other student group for that matter, even with students' consent. I should also remind you that it is a violation of College rules to gather such data from a Harvard source and recompile it in any form. You cannot, therefore, simply take information from house facebooks and post it on your site. If you have specific questions about this issue, please feel free to contact me.
>
> To sum up, once SEC has received official approval from the College and you have addressed the above issues, you will be able to reopen the site to new members. As I stated, Dean Kidd has promised to fast-track the approval process, so it is in your interest to get the required information to her as soon as possible. If you have any questions, please feel free to contact me. Again, I would like to have the opportunity to meet with all of you when you return to the Cambridge area.

As I considered how the SEC was outside of the College enough to need Harvard's permission to use copyrighted content, but inside the College enough to be bound by Harvard's student privacy regulations, Jay sent me another e-mail concerning my company. I was to re-register Think Computer with Dean Kidd, as former Dean Lewis's implicit approval was no longer enough, and I was to contact the Provost's office about using Harvard's name. I could also no longer refer to the Harvard International Review as a client.

I felt as though I were going mad, but I sent Dean Kidd an e-mail anyway, requesting whatever forms I needed to re-register my business, which had never yielded a complaint from anyone, with Harvard College.

"And yet Nathan didn't have to register at all?" I laughed, thinking back to the days when his phone lines were running across the corridor of Grays Middle's fifth floor. There seemed to be a double-standard with Dean Kidd's seal of approval on it everywhere I turned.

Venting to Metin, I summarized a trend I had noticed. While he was granted access to every resource he could possibly need to study archaeology, my requests were repeatedly denied. Yet on paper, we were both just Harvard undergraduates.

"It's not as if we're that different," I thought aloud. "We're quite similar, in fact. We both know what we want to do in life, unlike most people. It's just that I don't fit nicely into one of Harvard's little cookie cutters for people, and luckily, you do."

"Yeah, the Peabody Museum has been great for me," Metin replied, referring to the single place where one was guaranteed to find him, whenever he wasn't in class or in our room. "It sucks that you get screwed over so much. You get screwed more than anyone I know!" All I could do was grit my teeth, wondering why.

When I sent an e-mail to the Provost's office requesting permission for Think to use Harvard's name in its list of clients, they seemed confused as to why I would even bother asking. The office quickly granted permission.

Soon enough, my new favorite Dean wrote back, but with no forms attached.

> The regulations for Student Business Activity are on page 303 of the 2003-4 Handbook for Students. We ask that students planning a business send their proposed business plan to my office. The plan is then reviewed by a small advisory group.

"PROPOSED BUSINESS PLAN!" I seethed. "I HAVE BEEN RUNNING THIS COMPANY SINCE I WAS FIFTEEN YEARS OLD! IT ALREADY EXISTS! YOU *KNOW THAT*!"

I also wrote an e-mail to each and every House Master, requesting the permission to use the copyrighted content that had already been properly attributed to them, and that the SEC was already entitled to use as a Harvard College student group. I made sure that Jay Ellison was copied so that he could see I was following his directions. Instead, this only angered my Senior Tutor, who e-mailed me at once.

> I really was surprised to see this since 1) you are not yet approved and therefore cannot use the Harvard name, and 2) you were specifically told in my last email that you had to be approved before contacting the Masters. We should meet as soon as possible.

"What, so you want me to get permission to get permission to get permission? You've got to be out of your mind."

I scheduled the meeting for the next day, Friday, August 29, 2003, at 4:00 P.M. in Jay Ellison's office in Lowell House's "A" entryway. I was ready for him.

▼

Lowell House was once again gorgeous in the summer sun, but I didn't spend much time lingering in the courtyard. I headed straight for "A" entryway.

I waited for a few minutes in the dark Lowell House office outside Jay Ellison's door. I had come prepared with a notebook and some printouts.

I had already responded to Dean Kidd's request for a business plan with exactly what she had asked for: a thirty-three page confidential paper, which just happened to be titled "Extended Business Plan," that I realized I had written for my spring semester course at MIT. I wished I could force her to read every word from cover to cover.

"Hi, Aaron," Jay said, peering out the door. "Come on in. I'm glad we finally got the chance to meet about all of this. I hope you had a good vacation."

Skipping the pleasantries of typical conversation, I didn't respond, and instead busied myself by sitting in one of the two black chairs across from his desk emblazoned with the same VERITAS shield that I had been forbidden to use.

"Now, just to clear something up you mentioned a while ago, I'd like you to use me as a conduit to speak to the rest of the administration."

I let Jay talk, and talk, and talk, re-hashing the same twisted arguments he had put forth over the previous two weeks, which had collectively made my life a living hell. I tried not to scoff or show any hint of emotion. My goal was perfect, icy silence. I would show them how much of a rebel I was.

"...and I'd like you to also know that there's some concern about the copyright notice you have on the houseSYSTEM page," he went on. "Your page says, 'Copyright, with the little copyright sign, 2003 *The* President and Fellows of Harvard College.' The people in the Office of the General Counsel have told me that it should be just, 'President and Fellows of Harvard College.' The 'the' is incorrect."

"No 'the'?" I said sardonically, in utter disbelief that the man's brain had not yet exploded. Someone, whether it was Jay Ellison or one of the Deans he reported to in the mysterious chain of command, had either an obsession with truly inane detail or a real mental disorder.

"Nope, no 'the,'" he replied, clearly oblivious to my sentiment. I made a note.

"Well, I haven't said much," I said after he was done, "so I think I'll reply to some of the points you've made." I spoke slowly so as to give myself time to think, just as I had in the trademark deposition.

"I've done the best that I can, to help students here, and when asked, to comply with your requests—which have been numerous—even when I haven't agreed with them. And, as you know, I still maintain that according to the documents that govern the University, I haven't done a single thing wrong. However, I don't know that the same could really be said for you.

"On August 14th, while I was on vacation, I noticed that someone was accessing houseSYSTEM from the Harvard network, and it didn't look like a student. I looked into it further, and found out that it was a man named Rick Osterberg who worked for HASCS. And when I dug a little further..."

I pulled out the papers I had brought with me. The one on top bore a grainy VERITAS shield that matched the one on the chairs. It was a copy of a fax.

"...I found out that Mr. Osterberg, who wasn't a student, but who claimed to be, had actually signed onto houseSYSTEM not only from his own computer, but from Georgene Herschbach's computer, in University Hall South. Now, I don't know what an average HASCS staffer would be doing logging on there, unless he was showing something to someone."

Jay looked unperturbed. "Yes, there was a meeting where I believe HASCS gave some administrators a tour of your site..."

I cut him off.

"That's not acceptable! I *offered* to show you everything. I *even* offered to show you the source code! You said 'no!' If you didn't want to see it, then why did you have to break in, and instruct someone to sign up under false pretenses?" I was raging mad; my cheeks were on fire.

"Not only that! But you just got finished telling me, for more than thirty minutes, how the club that I was elected President of in February, whatever you'd like to call it, wasn't even a valid student organization! So, if you really believe that, then Rick Osterberg wasn't even breaking into one of Harvard's own servers—he was breaking into MY server! Think Computer Corporation owns that server! Not Harvard! That, Jay, is illegal!"

Before he had time to fully consider the implications of I was driving at, I showed him the document in my hand.

"And this, right here, is proof. Not from some random person. It's a signed letter, from the Harvard Registrar, certifying that Richard Osterberg is *not*, nor has he ever been, a student in the Graduate School of Arts and Sciences."

"You lied! You did this all to find out what was on the site, and you lied to do it! I hope...that I never, ever have to be this disappointed...in my teachers...ever again!"

I couldn't help it; I had let down my guard by revealing my emotions. Fortunately, I had kept it up long enough that it didn't matter. Jay Ellison, for a moment, was speechless. When I left, we both knew who was the adult in the room.

After the meeting, I visited Harvard University's web site as I had once done as a senior in high school. It looked stately and calm. It looked authoritative and fair. I clicked on the link to report copyright infringement, symbolic of the good will the University expected from random strangers. Then, I turned my attention to what I had come for: the page's copyright line.

Copyright © 2003 The President and Fellows of Harvard College

Jay Ellison was a hypocrite.

▼

That night, I spent some time curled up with the Handbook for Students on one of the last remaining pieces of furniture in our summer apartment that wasn't a box. Though I had been directed to the Handbook many times, I had never bothered to read much on the pages that came before the clauses I had been accused of violating. On page 297, I stumbled across a document I found most interesting: a Faculty Resolution on "Rights and Responsibilities" from April 14, 1970. Two particular passages struck a chord.

> ...it is the responsibility of officers of administration and instruction to be alert to the needs of the University community; to give full and fair hearing to reasoned expressions of grievances; and to respond promptly and in good faith to such expressions and to widely expressed needs for change. In making decisions which concern the community as a whole or any part of the community, officers are expected to consult with those affected by the decisions. Failures to meet these responsibilities may be profoundly damaging to the life of the University. Therefore, the University community has the right to establish orderly procedures consistent with imperatives of academic freedom to assess the policies and assure the responsibility of those whose decisions affect the life of the University.

> All members of the community—students and officers alike—should uphold the rights and responsibilities expressed in this Resolution if the University is to be characterized by mutual respect and trust.

Dean Kidd, who had disappeared from my life for a short while during my meeting with Jay Ellison, had sent me yet another e-mail about my business registration in response to an afterthought that I had sent her. In addition to re-re-writing the SEC constitution that Rodica had worked so hard on, I needed to register my other incorporated entity: Think Computer Foundation. In response, I sent her more documents. Her final demand was the most aggravating of all.

"You need to change the club's name again, I'm afraid," she told me. "By just saying 'Harvard' Student Entrepreneurship Council, you make it sound like you encompass the entire University. Your group is only a Harvard College student group."

"But we do encompass the entire University," I said. "A lot of our members are graduate students!"

"Well, that's irrelevant. You operate out of the College."

"What about 'Harvard' Student Agencies?" I asked.

"We would like all groups to change their names, if possible," she responded. It was like some sort of cruel joke. "HSA" had been "HSA" since the 1950s. It would never change its name.

"So, what would you like the new name to be?"

"Harvard *College* Student Entrepreneurship Council," she responded.

"Well, that really flows off the tongue," I thought.

"Okay." I asked Rodica to make the change in our constitution and set about updating hundreds of documents on-line and in print.

By the last day of August, with houseSYSTEM still closed to new members, I thought I saw the light at the end of the tunnel. I received another e-mail from Dean Kidd.

> Thank you for making the changes requested in your by-laws and for your willingness to change the name to Harvard College SEC. Is my reading of the document correct in that Corporate Members do not have a vote?
>
> Has the membership ratified the By-Laws?
>
> My final step would be to meet with you and at least two other officers of Harvard College SEC. When would that be possible?

I e-mailed the Executive Board to find out when it would be possible to arrange the meeting. Almost everyone was still out of town. Anna sent me a message saying something other than "I can't make the meeting" for the first time since March—but it still indirectly meant that she couldn't make it.

Even though Rodica and I had been working on the new constitution for weeks, without Dean Kidd's approval, we would not be permitted to recruit new members for the club at all. I sent her another draft, and she wrote back.

> Thank you for making the suggested final change to the constitution of Harvard College SEC. The organization may recruit at the Activity Fairs. You need to contact Jay Ellison for permission to turn on houseSYSTEM.
>
> I would like to meet with you and at least two of the other Harvard College SEC officers on Monday, Sept. 8th at 2 p.m. in my office, first floor, University Hall. Please let me know if this is possible.

I did as I was told. I e-mailed Jay Ellison a quick note, forwarding Dean Kidd's message to him as proof that she wanted me to ask. His reply was equally brief.

> You may open the houseSYSTEM sign up for new members.

It was the third day of September, 2003, and only one thought crossed my mind.

"*I win.*"

CHAPTER 25

The Decision

With the semester starting and houseSYSTEM open to Harvard College at last, I was trying desperately to get back into the normal swing of things. I arranged for the SEC to have a spot in HSA's massive tent in Harvard Yard, so that when freshmen arrived to pick up their keys they would find out about our site. Meanwhile, the version of Textbook Central designed for the Undergraduate Council's web site was almost done. We decided to rename it "Student Exchange" when I added features to buy and sell more than just textbooks.

I had signed up for HSA's Business Leadership Program the previous spring on the recommendation of some former TECH members. The idea of the session was to introduce College students to the case method of teaching at Harvard Business School, but I had long since grown weary of discussing business cases, thanks to my MIT class.

I also began to notice a pattern. Huge corporations such as Bear Stearns came to recruit the members every night and had representatives deliver lectures on their companies' brilliant strategies during the day. One strategy we learned about was the grouping of poorly-rated debt obligations and mortgages into practically risk-free financial instruments. However much money they were making, it sounded deadly boring.

"How can HSA's 'Center for Enterprise' run an event that just supports big business?" I asked the other attendees.

"At least there's free food," people replied, referring to the extravagant recruiting dinners at locales such as the Charles Hotel. I realized that they were not going to see my point of view. It all made me want to gag.

A couple of days later, the stress of moving, worrying about the SEC, making repeated trips to and from the Business School in formal attire, and setting up my new dorm room in the same entryway as Jay Ellison's office became too much to bear. I started having intense chest pain, and I was afraid my lung might collapse again, if it hadn't already.

"I'm quitting," I told the student in charge of the Center for Enterprise. It was one of her club's two big events each year, and students had to be invited to attend. I had put it off for days, since quitting was a "big deal," as we had been reminded repeatedly at each recruiting dinner. They didn't want students to eat and run.

"I know it's wrong of me to prevent someone else from having received my spot, but I don't care. It's affecting my health; I can't do it. I'm sorry."

"Okay," she said, and I left.

With half my luggage locked away under Lowell House, I made my way back to my dishevelled room on the fourth floor to send out an e-mail to the SEC's Executive Board begging for help at the activity fairs, and for help with the meeting with Dean Kidd, which she had inexplicably scheduled simultaneously.

By September 9th, both the UC and HSA were completely tied into house-SYSTEM so that students could search the Unofficial Guide and the UC's book database (which was really houseSYSTEM) all in one location. It had required winning the approval of both Rohit and Abhishek, but in the end, it was worth it.

The night before the activity fair and our meeting with Dean Kidd, the Dean switched the location and time from University Hall to Philips Brooks House, and from 10:00 A.M. to 10:15 A.M.

"Please excuse this late switch in plans," she wrote.

In the morning, I did all of the printing, cutting, taping, and hauling I was supposed to, according to the plan I had put together to get our activity fair table set up while three of us would be absent, and left the rest to Felix, who was as competent as anyone I would ever find.

We arrived in the Philips Brooks House office to find Dean Kidd: a thin, white-haired woman who was at least in her sixties. She seemed, to my great surprise, remarkably cordial.

"Nice to finally meet you," she said, holding out her hand in a very businesslike manner. I instantly recognized the terse voice.

We discussed the constitution, and the club's general aims, and what could be done to better foster entrepreneurship on campus. It was as if nothing had ever happened. Rodica was silent most of the time, but I could tell that she was as amazed as I was.

To get the issue out of the way, I decided to bring it up outright. "You know, these past few weeks were fairly difficult for me," I said. "I never expected to meet this much resistance for trying to do something decent for students." I hesitated. "I even had to hire lawyers."

Dean Kidd's warm, welcoming composure disappeared, leaving a cold stare behind.

"I know *all* about it," she said.

Walking down the stairs, Rodica came alive again. I always enjoyed listening to her speak, thanks to her slight Romanian accent.

"*What* was *that*?" she said, laughing.

"Well, given that I never told her about the lawyers, I guess they've been reading my e-mail," I surmised. "It's the only explanation I can think of that makes sense."

"Whaaaaa?" Wentao exclaimed. "They can do that?"

"Yeah, actually, someone warned me about it back when I was involved with the whole Economics 1010a fiasco... She said that she had friends who were members of the PSLM back when we were pre-frosh. When the students staged the sit-in of Mass Hall, the way the administration found out how to disrupt their plans was by reading their e-mail. It makes sense—legally, all of our e-mail belongs to the University. It happens in the workplace all the time, employers reading employees' e-mail..."

I kicked myself for not being more careful. I knew that there had been a risk to e-mailing my lawyers from my Harvard address, and I'd even warned them about it on a couple of occasions, but I had been so stressed that I'd occasionally forgotten to use my Think e-mail account, which was hosted on my own server—not that the administration had bothered to respect that boundary anyway.

"Or maybe I'm just being paranoid," I said. "I did tell Jay Ellison about the lawyers, and we all know that they talk plenty... But still, the way she said it."

"Oh, yeah. She definitely knows more than she should have," Rodica agreed.

And for the rest of the day, we took turns standing behind a beat-up wooden table in the middle of Harvard Yard, advertising our club and its new web site, called houseSYSTEM, to incoming freshmen.

○ ▌

With the activity fair behind us, I decided to follow up with Jay Ellison. I wasn't worried that Dean Kidd was about to cut him out of the loop on our meeting, but I did want to let some people know that I was, to say the least, unhappy.

It occurred to me that the only way that the SEC could have suddenly stopped being recognized as a valid student group was if someone had intentionally disbanded the TECH Student Association before it. Such an action would have required an instigator, who didn't exist so far as I could tell. I gave my e-mail the subject line, "Who disbanded the TECH SA?" and addressed it to Jay Ellison and a number of his colleagues: Dean Herschbach, Dean Kidd, Dean Gross, Dean Kirby, David Sobel and Rick Osterberg at HASCS, Paul Bottino at TECH, Lori Silver and Heather Quay in the Office of the General Counsel, Susan Cooke, and President Summers. I also added in Laura Krug's name after debating about whether or not it made sense to invite more criticism again. I simply wanted her to know the truth. I made sure that my parents and my lawyers received a blind CC, as well, because the most important part of the message was the summary of the paper trail I had compiled, proving that Rick Osterberg had deliberately signed in as a student, when he was actually a staff member giving administrators an inside view.

According to the Harvard ph directory, Rich Osterberg is an employee of FAS Computer Services.

name: Rick Osterberg
department: FAS^FCOR^Computer Svcs - Staff
email: osterber@fas.harvard.edu

Rick Osterberg signed up from his own computer, with hostname osterber-nt.fas. harvard.edu, on August 3, 2003, at 1:20.06 P.M. He was assigned unique member ID number 366. He signed up as a GSAS student, since houseSYSTEM is currently only open to students to protect student privacy. His password was never stored--only its MD5 hash, which was later removed from the password2 field, and converted to an SHA-1 hash, stored in the password field.

366 Rick   Osterberg   999   29   9   9   9
617-493-1000   osterber@fas.harvard.edu   dc724af18fbd-
d4e59189f5fe768a5f8311527050   M   GSAS   1   0
1   Y   4   osterber-nt.fas.harvard.edu   2   5
20030820094006   20030803132006   0

Later, unique member ID 366, Rick Osterberg, signed into houseSYSTEM from a different computer, with IP address 140.247.70.245, on August 18, 2003 at 11:18.48 A.M.

af3115e13937642d84be071e549ab019   366   houseSYSTEM   1.00   www.
currier.harvardsec.org 140.247.70.245   Mozilla/4.0 (compatible; MSIE 6.0; Windows NT 5.0)   20030818111848

Since IP addresses are themselves unique identifiers, there is only one computer on the internet with the IP address 140.247.70.245. It has the hostname herschba. fas.harvard.edu.

C:\WINDOWS>ping herschba.fas.harvard.edu

Pinging herschba.fas.harvard.edu [140.247.70.245] with 32 bytes of data...

"herschba" is an FAS username that corresponds to Associate Dean Georgene Herschbach. Therefore, Rick Osterberg signed into houseSYSTEM in University Hall 1st Floor South for Dean Herschbach while claiming to be a GSAS student. According to the University Registrar, Rick Osterberg is not a GSAS student, and never was. Instead of accepting Aaron Greenspan's offer to show the administration houseSYSTEM, the administration instead chose to have a HASCS employee show it to them. That employee lied in order to do it, while violating students' privacy.

name: Georgene B. Herschbach (Assc Dean)
department: FAS^FCOL^Clg Lif+Stdnt Svc-Stf
email: herschba@fas.harvard.edu

By the time I was finished writing the e-mail, there was no doubt in my mind that just like the men and women of every other large, imperfect institution I had come across, the men and women of Harvard University, sitting below their vaunted shield, on occasion, and when they deemed it necessary, lied.

▼

Five days later, Jay wrote back in reply to my message. He copied everyone that I had. I laughed out loud at his response.

> Sorry it has taken me so long to respond--as you can imagine things are quite busy. Thank you for this letter. I am sorry that you have felt unsupported by the College. As I made clear from the outset, the College had no desire to shut down the house-SYSTEM site. However, we did have important and immediate concerns about security and about copyright issues that needed to be addressed.
>
> I gather from your email that you continue to disagree with the College's concerns, and that you feel aggrieved by the mention of potential disciplinary action over what you term "imaginary trespasses." But as you and I have discussed over the phone and by email, your actions in fact violated a number of rules set forth in the Student Handbook. You have responded to the issues that were raised, which the College acknowledges. That you may now be in compliance with the College's rules does not, however, mean that the College's concerns were "unfounded," "mistaken," or "irrelevant."
>
> As for your question about the disbanding of TECH SA, my understanding (based in part on your own earlier correspondence) is that once you and the rest of the governing board decided to change the name and write a new constitution, it became a new organization. As such, it needed official approval from the Dean's office. That the College continued to reserve space for TECH SA at the activities fair in anticipation of the new group's taking over TECH SA's spot does not contradict this point.
>
> Finally, I must emphasize that I never asked that you communicate only with me. As your Senior Tutor I have tried, and continue to try, to have a relationship with you so that I can assist you in your time here. For that reason, I wanted to be in direct contact with you during this period. I never suggested, however, that you could not be in touch with other administrators. I simply asked that you copy me on your correspondence.
>
> I hope the beginning of the semester is going well for you. Please feel free to stop by the office and talk sometime.

"If this man thinks I'm going to stop by his office and have a little chat, he's got another thing coming." It was almost beyond belief that he had written it, aside from the blatant falsehood about who he had permitted me to speak with.

"Part of the problem," I told my friends, recounting the e-mail, "is that with the system here, your resident strict disciplinarian is also supposed to be your friend!

Somehow, that just doesn't work."

I tried to put the SEC out of my mind to focus on school—I was taking two Core courses and two economics courses—but I couldn't escape from its grasp no matter how hard I tried. I was still trying to get houseSYSTEM's Universal Face Book up and running.

Unlike the traditional face books, in print and on-line, houseSYSTEM's Face Book let students post their AOL Instant Messenger screennames, cell phone numbers and color photographs, but only if they chose to. Since it was updated on demand, rather than once per year, the information was much more useful than content on the official house sites. Only a few weeks after launching on September 19, 2003, there were over 100 houseSYSTEM members participating.

Then, one night, at 1:30 A.M., the phone rang.

"Hey, Aaron?" I didn't recognize the voice at all.

"Who's this?" I asked.

"It's Jesse," the voice said.

"Oh. Hi." Sometimes, my friends called late, but very rarely; we usually talked on-line. Since I hadn't heard from Jesse in months, I figured he was having some sort of emergency.

"What's going on?" I asked.

"Uh, I just wanted to get a sense of what the club is up to," Jesse replied. I was taken aback.

"Jesse, it's one-thirty in the morning. I'm about to go to bed. Can we talk about this some other time?"

"Not really, I need to sort of know now. It won't take long," Jesse said.

"OK, well, I almost got kicked out of school over the summer, we're running a site called houseSYSTEM that you were supposed to do marketing for, and...that's it. Why do you need to know?" I was extremely irritated.

"Oh, well, recruiting is coming up for i-banking and consulting jobs, and I listed TECH on my résumé. I just want to be prepared if they ask me any questions about it." I had to stop myself from hanging up the phone right then and there.

"Good night, Jesse," I said, breathless at his raw nerve. I put down the receiver. He stood for everything that the SEC stood against. He was enthusiastic about working as a cog in the large machine of big business. He seemed almost incapable of thinking for himself. He was rude. He didn't follow through.

"*He's fired*," I thought. Then, I remembered what Roderick MacFarquhar had taught us about the Cultural Revolution in China.

I set up our next Board meeting for Sunday, September 21st at 1:15 P.M. in Pierce Hall, where the TECH computer lab was located, and explained to everyone what would be taking place. I e-mailed Jesse a separate invitation for 1:30.

When he walked through the doors to the conference room that Sunday, the entire Board of the SEC was waiting for him, already seated, and absolutely silent.

"Glad you could make it," I said. "We asked you here because I'm relieving you of all of your duties as Vice-President of Communications. I'm sorry." He had barely had enough time to saunter into his seat.

"Wha—what are you talking about? You don't think I did a good enough job?" The room stared at him.

"No, actually, I don't," I said. "I think you did a really awful job, in fact. And everyone here agrees." The room remained silent. The effect was chilling.

"You're fired, Jesse." After a few seconds, he figured out that I was serious.

"Fine," he scowled. On the way out, we heard him let out a sarcastic, "Bye."

"Well, I'm glad that's taken care of!" I smiled. People resumed their normal composures.

"Very nicely done," said Rodica.

"Now, I just have to find a new Vice-President of Communications." Fortunately, I had a friend in mind. His full name was Piriya Tantrativud, but everyone called him by his Thai nickname, Tum. He was a friend of both Rodica and myself, he lived in Lowell, and most importantly, he knew how to make posters.

Tum attacked his new job with a ferocity and enthusiasm that was at first totally undetectable but very real. While he was reserved and shy if you didn't know him, he had a tendency to voice strong and remarkably well-informed opinions if you did. I took great pleasure in my new appointee's work. Best of all, he brought an entire contingent of Thai students into the club.

At the beginning of October, I ran into Rodica at breakfast in the dining hall. I scoffed when she pointed out an advertisement in the corner of one of *The Crimson*'s middle sections.

"See that?" she asked with a smile. I looked over.

Office of the President

**President Lawrence H. Summers
will hold office hours in his
Massachusetts Hall office
for students from 3:30 to 4:30 p.m.
Thursday, October 2.**

(sign-up begins at 2:30 p.m.)

"It's his hour-a-month special!" I said.

"Are you gonna go?" Rodica asked.

"I don't know, maybe I should," I thought out loud. "But there will probably be a thousand people there, there's so little time for everyone." The more I thought about it though, the more I convinced myself that I had a good reason to speak to the President. I still felt that the College had violated its own policies in the 1970 resolution, and I hadn't been satisfied with Jay Ellison's response to my question about who disbanded the club.

Slightly after 2:30 P.M., I arrived in Massachusetts Hall. The waiting list only had a handful of names on it, so I added mine to the bottom in print, and signed my name next to it. Then, I waited.

After thirty minutes of observation, I concluded that not a lot happened in Massachusetts Hall. It was warm and quiet, and the President's secretary spent a lot of time sending Instant Messages instead of working.

"I wonder how they can consider technology and entrepreneurship's effects on society so unimportant that they don't even merit study, when they've shaped everything around us," I wondered, watching the secretary type. *"That's AIM running on Windows 98. That's Gates. That's Harvard, playing a role in everyone's lives. If Gates hadn't gotten pissed off and left, maybe she wouldn't be using Windows; maybe someone else would have come along. How can they be so ignorant?"*

Bored of reading my coursepacks for class after another twenty minutes had passed, I overheard the conversation that two formally dressed gentlemen, apparently graduate students, were having a few feet away. The issue they wanted to talk to President Summers about sounded like it was pretty standard: fund-raising. They were eventually called into his office, and later disgorged out another exit, since I didn't see them leave.

"Aaron Greenspan?" an office worker called out some time later. At last, it was my turn.

I put my books in my backpack, and followed her through a maze of short corridors on the first floor. "Right this way," she said.

"Who paints all of their walls red?" I wondered in disbelief as I entered the President's office. I had read about the psychological effects that different colored-environments could have on people. *"Maybe that's why he's always angry..."*

"The President will see you in a moment," the woman smiled. "Have a seat." She motioned to a small sofa that was positioned across from a giant armchair. There was another chair beside the larger one, more expensive-looking than the standard-issue chairs I had seen in other Deans' offices. I glanced at my watch. It was twenty minutes until five o'clock.

"No wonder it seems like I've been waiting forever," I thought. *"I have."*

A minute or two later, the President himself walked into the room, followed by an African-American woman. I didn't catch her name, but President Summers needed no introduction. When the conversation began, there was still a faint glimmer of hope left that I could make it through Harvard.

By the time it reached its end, it had been extinguished, thoroughly and completely.

CHAPTER 26

The Dawn of the Facebook Era

The Harvard College Student Entrepreneurship Council had a lively year. After the houseSYSTEM affair, Paul Bottino promptly withdrew his offer of supporting the club with $2,000. The club's CFO dutifully tried to convince me to bargain with him, but I couldn't stand the thought of even seeing him. I had finally created a truly entrepreneurial project that improved student life, and all he could do was run and hide. Instead, I found the SEC two new faculty advisors: Professor Margo Seltzer, and my former Math 21a TF, Paul Bamberg. I funded the club's new bank account with a fresh check signed by Rohit Chopra, which went unreported in the press. Rohit knew that the Undergraduate Council would never have let him make the deal had anyone known about it.

Once houseSYSTEM was re-opened, hundreds, and then thousands of students, staff, faculty, and alumni used it to make their lives slightly easier in a variety of different ways. The Undergraduate Council's version of Student Exchange flourished, with more than seven hundred listings. CriticalMass had numerous course reviews for all sorts of different departments, and it was thrilling to watch traffic surge at the beginning of every semester. Still, I wanted the site to be a staple of student life—something that people had a reason to use every day. Initially, the ability to check your e-mail had been intended to draw people in and keep them coming back, but without the ability to relay FAS passwords through to Harvard's server, we were back to square one.

It had occurred to me throughout the fall that I had built houseSYSTEM around things—books, reviews, and courses—rather than people. I toyed with the idea of making a profile page for each houseSYSTEM user beyond what was already available on the Universal Face Book, but with Brian Wong, Dan Ellard and *The Crimson* looking for any reason to smear houseSYSTEM, I thought better of it. I could wait until after I graduated to try something else new and controversial—or so I thought. My Face Book already provided a great deal of information.

"Can we get *The Crimson* to give us any decent coverage at all?" I kept asking my Board, week after week. The answer was almost always silence. No matter which connections we tried, we could never seem to get anyone at the newspaper interested. *The Crimson's* official policy on houseSYSTEM seemed to have been set in stone from the moment I first picked up the phone to talk to Laura Krug. I suspected that even if she had mixed or even positive feelings about the site, her editors probably disagreed with her.

Once, I tried simply walking into the newspaper's offices, hoping to find someone I recognized and could talk to. The plan didn't work; a horde of student reporters wanted to know who I was and why I was there the instant they saw me. I explained that I had been in an article about Economics 1010a a while back, and that I had created a new web site they might be interested in seeing or writing about. One reporter took a look. I might as well have been showing him Think's sales tax returns; there wasn't even a spark of interest.

On October 23rd, an article appeared in the newspaper's weekly magazine, *Fifteen Minutes*, that caught my eye. It was about a freshman named Mark Zuckerberg who had created an MP3 player called Synapse in high school. He sounded like the perfect kind of person to join the SEC—and, I hoped, to help out with houseSYSTEM. A few days later, I remembered that I needed to e-mail him.

> I saw the article in FM about Synapse, and wanted offer my congratulations. It's not easy to attract that kind of industry attention. If you don't already know about it, you should take a look at the Student Entrepreneurship Council, a club here on campus. We'd love to have you as a member.
>
> If you have any questions, feel free to let me know.

In early November, he wrote back at 3:03 in the morning, which didn't surprise me at all. Programming was always easiest for me late at night, when there were no distractions and it was easy to focus.

> I'd definitely be interested in checking out SEC. When and where do you guys meet? I'll try to make the next meeting...

He didn't appear at the next meeting, or the following one, but I did eventually figure out that he was the same person who had created the "Course Match" system that had circulated on several open lists about a month before. It let students see who else was in their courses, and it reminded me a great deal of CriticalMass. The user interface wasn't nearly as polished though. The welcome message I had received had been signed "team zuckerberg."

It was only two days later that I heard Mark's name again, once more in print. He had created another small project called "facemash" that allowed students to choose the more attractive of their peers from photographs collected from the official face book web sites. *The Crimson* had written an astonishingly two-faced editorial about the site, glowing about its "possibilities" for two paragraphs, before pointing out that the site was "hurtful and demeaning." I was stunned, both that Mark would be callous enough to make such a site, and that *The Crimson* would even come close to endorsing it. Coverage of Mark's travails with the Harvard College Administrative Board followed for several days, though his eventual punishment was never specified.

A month later, another *Crimson* editorial followed about Mark's facemash project, beginning with, "After the ill-fated 'facemash' debacle—where, for a few short-lived hours, students perused their peers' often-unbecoming likenesses online—it seemed that Harvard students' hopes of a campus-wide, electronic facebook had been dashed." The piece went on to talk about the distant possibility of a college-wide face book site, possibly maintained by HASCS. They had again neglected to mention that the College already had such a site on houseSYSTEM. Almost two thousand students had already signed up, though most had not opted into the Face Book. The most likely reason was that they didn't know it was there.

On January 6th, I received an e-mail from Mark.

> I was thinking of making a web app that would use the Harvard course catalog, but I'm a little worried about the university getting upset after the whole facemash episode. I know you used info from the catalog in your shopping list scheduler in housesystem (which is awesome by the way), so I was wondering if you had to get permission to use that material and if so, whom you contacted. Or maybe if you didn't ask permission but you think I should for extra precaution, do you have any idea whom I could ask?
> Thanks a lot!

My instinct was not to show him how to re-invent a wheel that had destroyed a month of my life. I wrote back.

> What kind of app were you thinking of? Maybe we could integrate it into house-SYSTEM.

The discussion continued immediately, as if we were talking in real time.

> I actually did think about integrating it into houseSYSTEM before you even suggested it, but I decided that it's probably best to keep them separated at least for now. I really like the houseSYSTEM app, but this app requires a lot of user participation, and I'm worried that a) many of the people who have registered for houseSYSTEM in the past don't really go to the site anymore, and b) the vast number of features offered by houseSYSTEM might intimidate someone just looking for my app. That said, once it's off the ground, I think it could be mutually beneficial to integrate the two, but we can speak about that then.
>
> For now I'm trying to keep the project on the dl, so I'd rather not discuss the details, but we can definitely speak about it once I am ready to release it.
>
> Yea so I don't know if you'd be willing to help me out by telling me what processes you've gone through in the past to avoid getting ad boarded and such, but if you can tell me anything I would appreciate it greatly.
> Thanks!

I sensed the tension that he was under, guessing that the timing was about right for the Administrative Board to be meeting about his facemash creation. I wrote back, feeling some pity.

I had to enlist the assistance of three lawyers in order to avoid Harvard following through on its repeated threats of "disciplinary action," but those threats didn't relate to the course list at all. It seemed as if they could have cared less about that. I just imported the list from the registrar's site and put it into a table after some crazy string parsing. I'm sure you'd have no trouble doing the same, but you'll quickly find that Harvard's Oracle backend for courses is really a piece of crap. It takes some effort to work around it and turn the data into something sensible.

I'll look out for your project. Be careful, though...

Mark was clearly still sitting in front of his computer.

Thanks for the info. That's really intense that you had to get lawyers to fend them off. What exactly were they claiming you were doing wrong? And was this in connection to houseSYSTEM or just some personal work you were doing?

I actually already have all that stuff parsed, and if you ever need it just let me know. I know you have a version of it since you're using it for houseSYSTEM, but if you need one with course descriptions and prereqs I can give that to you if you're interested and don't already have those fields.

I responded.

Very interesting. That might actually be useful. You know we could definitely use someone like you to keep houseSYSTEM going, especially since I'll be graduating soon... You sure you don't want to work on it? Seems like you're doing similar work anyway... :)

For me, accusations included, but were not limited to, trademark infringment, copyright infringement, violation of network policies, violation of security policies, and possible future security breaches. Maybe we should meet for dinner sometime or something and I can tell you the whole story, or what I can remember of it. I'd be interested to hear yours, as well.

The next message confirmed bits of what I'd guessed about his personality. Even though he was clearly smart, he seemed like he had the capacity to go off in a zany direction at any point in time, totally unconcerned about the consequences of his actions. I couldn't figure out any other scenario that would have allowed for the creation of the facemash site.

I've definitely considered joining SEC and I still want to come to a meeting sometime when I get a chance. The general problem I have with these things is I don't usually

have a long attention span for lots of coding. I like coming up with ideas and implementing them quickly, which is why I've stuck to mostly web development recently. So rather than join the houseSYSTEM team, I'd probably rather do development independently and then just intregrate stuff when it makes sense to do so.
I'm still interested in checking out SEC and seeing the other stuff you guys are into though.

And yea, we should totally meet up sometime. I'm busy tomorrow night, but how about Thursday? Let me know.

On Thursday, January 8th, 2004, at 6:45 P.M., I met Mark for dinner in Kirkland House, where he lived. It was only a few hundred feet from my dorm room. He looked and sounded fairly nerdy, but with a level of self-confidence that took me aback. It was out of line with the way he acted, which was anything but professional. Alarm bells went off in my head as I thought of Cameron Johnson.

"So I'm working on this site," he said. "And I think it's gonna be really cool."

"OK..." I said. "Can you tell me what it is?" I was used to entrepreneurs being overprotective of their usually uninspiring ideas.

"I'd really rather not..." he said. "I want to keep this on the d-l, but it has something to do with graph theory." I didn't know much about graph theory, but I thought it involved the paths between nodes in a network, and the challenge of finding the quickest route from point A to point B. It made perfect sense in the context of what I already knew Mark was interested in.

"Is it a Friendster for Harvard?" I asked. It was my best guess based on his *modus operandi* thus far. He seemed to be awfully interested in my course database, and it made sense to try to combine it with a more upstanding version of the facemash site, despite the fact that he had already faced the Administrative Board once.

"I can't say," he replied.

"I don't know about a site like that. It seems like if people started posting the wrong kind of information—which I think a lot of students wouldn't think twice about—it would be a privacy nightmare."

"I don't think privacy is that big of a deal," Mark replied. "I mean, we can always improve the controls, and we just want to make something that will get as many people as possible involved."

"Well, still, whatever it is, why don't you consider making it part of house-SYSTEM? We already have 1,200 members who use it regularly..."

"I dunno," he said. "houseSYSTEM, it's really nice, and I like it a lot, but it's just too...useful."

"Too useful?" I asked. "That's a problem?" He explained.

"It just does too much stuff. Like, it's almost overwhelming how useful it is. I want my thing to stay separate for now."

"Okay..." I conceded. "But then why bother talking to me? I mean, it's pretty obvious that I have a vested interest in sticking with this thing I've built already."

"Yeah, I know," he admitted. "But I thought you'd be a good guy to talk to in order to see if you wanted to work on this project with me. My roommates are already helping me out, and I'd like you to, as well." His roommate Dustin Moskovitz, sitting next to him, nodded.

Something stuck me as being off about the situation. I didn't like the idea of working for someone who had just been disciplined for ignoring privacy rights on a massive scale. I also had no idea if I was facing another Cameron, though I was beginning to sense that Mark was not nearly as smooth, regardless of his similar ability to overlook ethical issues.

I could picture the FBI agent standing in my living room in Cleveland once again, and I knew that any site with thousands of profiles would be attracting the attention of law enforcement and attorneys at one point or another. After my first experience with SurfingPrizes being the token "mature" founder, I didn't feel like I needed a repeat experience.

"And why me?" I asked, entertaining the notion for a split second.

"I think you have good ideas," Mark said. It was a revealing statement, but I wasn't persuaded.

"Well, thanks," I replied. "But I don't think I'd do very well working for someone. I'm a pretty independent kind of guy," I responded.

"That's okay, we can still exchange ideas and stuff," Mark said. We had a pleasant enough dinner, exchanged AOL Instant Messenger screennames, and I left to go back to Lowell House.

As of 6:22 P.M. that night, I noticed that Mark Zuckerberg had been a house-SYSTEM member for thirty-six hours.

Mark's roommates, Dustin Moskovitz and Chris Hughes, had been signed up for houseSYSTEM almost since the first days of its launch in the fall, but it wasn't until January 4th, two days before Mark e-mailed me about his "web app," that I noticed him spending a lot of time on houseSYSTEM and browsing the Universal Face Book in particular. I could tell just from watching the server logs fly by on my screen. After logging on intermittently before and after our January 8th dinner meeting, on the 10th, he spent considerable time re-loading the same Face Book pages. On the 11th, he was back again.

What my server didn't show was that same day, January 11th, Mark registered the domain name "thefacebook.com" within hours of using The Universal Face Book at http://www.kirkland.harvardsec.org/facebook. Since we had called the houseSYSTEM feature both the "Facebook" and the "Universal Face Book" in e-mails and on Tum's posters that were visible all around Harvard's campus and beyond, I was keenly aware that Mark was infringing on what I considered to be my own trademark in the electronic realm. The fact that "face book" was a generic term used for many years before my birth (or Mark's) made me reluctant to spend any money attempting to enforce it, however. In theory, one couldn't trademark a generic term.

In short order, Mark's roommate, Dustin, sent out an e-mail to the Harvard User Assistants who helped students with technology, informing them that Mark's site was already lined up to get coverage in *The Crimson*.

On February 4th, within an hour after it launched, I became member ID 82 of Mark's site: The Facebook. As I had surmised, it was a copy of Friendster for use at Harvard, and I guessed it would have a run similar to CriticalMass or Textbook Central, with a few hundred students signing up. What I didn't expect was that the *The Crimson* would run a front-page article on Mark and his site with the angle of "student-rebel-hero" almost ten times throughout the semester. The coverage was always the same and unequivocally positive. When students in the Quad sued Mark for neglecting to finish work on their dating site, *The Crimson* took Mark's side in an unbelievable editorial because he was "better looking." It was as if 14-year-old girls (with bad vision, given the plaintiffs' Brooks Brothers catalog-style glamour shots in the papers) had taken over the newspaper on Plympton Street.

Given that I thought Mark and I both looked and sounded relatively dorky, I couldn't figure out why *The Crimson* appeared to like Mark's work so much more than mine. His site's membership figures went through the roof as people listed each other as friends and posted information about themselves, while the free press lived up to its name, acting more as Mark's personal public relations firm than an objective observer of campus events. If there was a privacy backlash on the house lists, I failed to notice.

"He must have a friend or two, or like twenty, there," I told the stymied Board of the SEC. I kept pushing my Board and the club's members to devise ways to make houseSYSTEM more attractive to users.

"Competition is healthy," I told them. "This is what entrepreneurship is really like." Inside, I was fuming.

"Did I really suffer through all of this so that Mark could stab me in the back?" I kept thinking. Facebook's popularity largely revolved around the Friendster-like ability to make a list of one's friends. When I saw Mark in person, we treated each other as friends might, saying hello and sitting next to each other in class. Yet on Facebook, he never made the effort to reach out. I couldn't imagine one of my other real friends coincidentally launching a site to compete with one I had made. I wondered if he knew the meaning of the word.

A few weeks after The Facebook launched, the SEC had elections once again, and my roommate Wentao and his girlfriend were elected co-Presidents. In short order, Mark sent me a message informing me that I was infringing on his copyright. I was flabbergast. Trying to remain calm and diplomatic for the sake of appearance, I pointed out that I wasn't even in control of the club anymore, and that despite a screenshot of The Facebook appearing on a poster contrasting it with houseSYSTEM, which had more features overall, no one really thought that I or the SEC had created both sites. He seemed appeased when I pointed out that the Yard Operations staff would tear the posters down anyway.

Everyone I talked to seemed to agree that houseSYSTEM's Universal Face Book desperately needed social networking features—the ability to explicitly list other people as friends. I had considered creating detailed user profile pages at houseSYSTEM's inception in August, but it seemed like the worst idea possible when students began to worry loudly about privacy.

"I'm going to need help with this," I told our CFO. Since she had taken CS51 and I hadn't, she knew how to program Dijsktra's algorithm—a computer's way of finding the shortest path between point A and point B. I could only guess at what needed to be done. It was necessary to display people's relationships to one another on the screen. Alas, she was too busy with schoolwork to handle yet another side project.

"I don't have a lot of time to do extra coding," she said, "but I can look over what you've got." I continued pleading for help with everyone I knew who had ever expressed a remote interest in computers. At each Pops rehearsal, I asked Francis, who had once told me how cool he thought Think Computer was, if he might have changed his mind about helping out. Each time, he gracefully declined my request.

When the SEC met in March, I somehow had a social networking code infrastructure put together. I began to realize what people meant when they said that some students went to Harvard and ended up majoring in *Crimson*, spending all of their time in the newspaper's office. I had spent more time working on house-SYSTEM, usually until 2:00 A.M. or later each morning, than I had on economics problem sets by far.

Now that there were two campus-wide "Face Books," with the Undergraduate Council mulling over the creation of a third (as it had already rejected my offer to use houseSYSTEM's), the name issue was becoming a real problem. Mark hadn't asked me for permission before going ahead with his project, and I didn't think he'd take me seriously if I asked him to stop. My legal bills from Think Computer's trademark opposition were piling up, and I couldn't imagine enduring—let alone being able to afford—another similar confrontation.

In an effort to solve the problem elegantly, I decided to call my improved houseSYSTEM module FaceNet, adding a few more features that Mark's site lacked. FaceNet let you note where you met your friends, so that you could search for everyone you had met in Annenberg, or through an extracurricular activity, or on the street. It was also designed to tie into the next feature I was working on: a centralized site for student groups. Dean Kidd, in her capacity as the head of student activities, lacked any database of the College's 300 groups. We already had a database and the ability to let students upload digital posters to advertise their group's events, which in turn integrated with the houseSYSTEM event calendar and pinpointed the exact location of the event on the interactive Harvard campus map.

"And all thanks to bugs in Harvard's code," I pointed out gleefully to my Board. "'Insecurities,' even!" Sure enough, searching for a space character on the Harvard Map revealed the entire campus location database, and searching for "%" on the official course catalog revealed all six thousand Harvard courses offered at every single one of Harvard's schools. What I really wanted to implement was a private message board for each student group that helped coordinate and schedule activities, but without anyone to help program the feature, I put it on the back burner.

Tum picked up on my call for ideas immediately, and made a suggestion. "I don't know about Americans, but to Thai people, birthdays are really, really important," he said during one meeting in the Lamont Forum Room. "I saw this birthday reminder site, and it was really cool; you could type in your friends' birthdays and it would remind you of them, so that you never forgot. A lot of Thai people use it."

"Oh, well, that's easy," I said. "We capture people's birthday information when they sign up, I think. Let's just send them e-mails when their friends have birthdays coming up. We already know who their friends are."

A few nights later, houseSYSTEM began automatically e-mailing its members to remind them about their friends' upcoming birthdays. A few nights after that, I saw that thefacebook.com started keeping track of birthdays too.

I began to think increasingly about an exit strategy. I didn't want to worry about houseSYSTEM forever, but I didn't want it to die after everything I'd invested either. I continued my search for a successor to run the site, asking anyone and everyone who had ever mentioned to me that they also "liked computers" for help. Felix and Francis were both too busy, and didn't know PHP. A few programmers I tried talking to didn't have the resolve to work on it non-stop. In the end, the only one with enough drive and programming knowledge to run the site was Mark Zuckerberg.

Instead of running it, Mark ran it into the ground.

▼

Spring semester ended up being much more enjoyable than usual thanks to Paul

Bamberg. He offered to teach an independent study course about voice recognition to a group of about ten students. Mark and I were both in it, as well as the president of the Harvard Computer Society.

"Aaron, I know you've run software projects before," Paul said, looking down at the ground in his typically awkward but lovable manner. "You're going to be the Project Manager for this."

I could see some of the other faces in the room looking less-than-pleased, but most people seemed not to mind. I found it ironic that I had the least amount of formal Computer Science training of anyone in the room, and yet Paul still trusted me enough to review and integrate everyone's code.

"We'll need a version tracking system," someone said.

"I can write that," I offered, not wanting to be the only one without code to write, and so I became the hub for the entire project. Some of the other students who gathered with me in Paul's apartment every week were positively brilliant.

After class one day I decided that avoiding a confrontation with Mark was not going to get me anywhere. I asked him point-blank the question that was on my mind.

"Are you copying my work? The Facebook is exactly the same as house-SYSTEM in a lot of ways."

"No!" he responded strongly, looking offended. "I'm not copying anything. I can't believe you'd think that."

"Okay," I said, taking him at his word, but still feeling uncomfortable. I couldn't believe that he had acted so surprised, with all of the similarities between our projects.

As time wore on, Mark began to show up to class less and less frequently. Since the seminar involved so few people, his attendance was sorely missed.

"We need those fast Fourier transforms right now!" Paul remarked each week throughout the semester. "Where is he? Running his company, I suppose? Well, he won't be getting a fantastic grade from me..." The algorithms necessary to decode voice signals had been assigned to Mark, and without them, our product wouldn't work. Finally, at the very last minute, Paul had no choice. Another student took Mark's job.

Mark sent me an AOL Instant Message, furious, and looking for sympathy. I tried to keep him calm, while also explaining how we couldn't use code if it didn't work—or exist. I had seen what he had written, and it fundamentally looked awful. I had seen the same consistently lazy shortcuts in the code of The Facebook, as well. I didn't let him know how angry the entire class was, since I figured that was Paul's job.

"Mark is going to the marketing department!" Paul proclaimed gleefully. We all knew what that meant: Mark was getting a C or worse in CS91r. Marketing was an engineer's worst nightmare, and Paul's grading scale functioned accordingly.

On the day of our final demonstration in front of one of the independent study's Computer Science department sponsors, Mark finally did show up, but it was too late. Our product didn't work as planned. Everyone went home disappointed.

I was disappointed about the course but happy overall. Thanks to another arcane regulation passed by the Faculty of Arts and Sciences, I had managed to win back the Advanced Standing status I had previously abandoned. My A.P. test scores from high school were still enough to give me senior standing, with one less Core Curriculum requirement than the typical student. As soon as finals were over, I would be a college graduate one year early.

On the day of my last final, I woke up apprehensive, excited, and since it was a morning exam, earlier than usual. After carefully selecting my courses since freshman year so that none ever started before 10:00 A.M., getting out of bed before 9:00 made me feel like a seventy-year-old with arthritis. My comforter defied physics, enhancing the force of gravity.

Fortunately, I hadn't overslept, and it was sunny and amazingly temperate for New England. In other places across the country, weather forecasters were worthless because they were wrong. In Cambridge they were worthless because for nine months out of the year, the weather never changed. Seeing the sun outside was a pleasure.

Once I had showered, dressed, and grabbed breakfast from the dining hall, the walk over to Divinity Avenue went quicker than I had expected. This had the disadvantage of bringing me face-to-face with the exam room on an accelerated schedule, and once I was there, Jeff and Elliott, who were both in American Economic Policy as well, wouldn't be able to help me anymore. We'd spent at least two hours the previous night going over graphs and formulas in our room, spending more time laughing at each other's bizarre explanations of economic phenomena than actually committing anything to memory.

When I walked into the room, I saw one student in the corner suffering through a cold with a large box of tissue on his desk, and hundreds more waiting for the test to begin. I resigned myself to a chair.

The proctor spoke.

"You may begin."

Three hours later, I was free. My education was over.

CHAPTER 27

Denial

It was that summer, with all of my friends engrossed in deep contemplation about what to write their respective theses on (which made me feel awful about my intentional dodging of the bullet) that I decided to write something of my own. I began writing in longhand on an airplane before realizing that it was a rather unsustainable endeavor and that my computer skills might actually provide a solution to the problem of recording a large number of words for later redistribution.

Simon's graduation from Brehm took place immediately after finals in May, and I went to Carbondale straight from Boston to meet my parents. As usual, Simon was in a foul mood. When it actually came time to prepare for walking across the stage, he was yelling at us bitterly in his cap and gown. His temperament improved noticeably after everyone was seated and he won an award. Yet the one student he cared about most was not there, and the unfortunate metaphors chosen during a horribly awkward (though well-intentioned) memorial for Ashley during the graduation ceremony did not help to put anyone's mind at ease about her conspicuous absence.

By way of our hotel business center's internet connection, I found out the same day that Simon received his high school diploma that I had won my three-year-long legal battle concerning the Think Computer trademark. My grand prize was the satisfaction of knowing that I had been right all along. No monetary rewards existed in the United States Patent and Trademark Office's Trademark Trial and Appeal Board dispute resolution system. Nevertheless, the case had still cost my company almost half of a year's tuition at Harvard, and had I not convinced my law firm to consider the fact that Think Computer Foundation shared the same name and therefore indirectly benefited from the same trademark's protection, the price would have been double. I was incredibly relieved to be free of the burden of legal proceedings.

Once I returned to Boston, I sublet an apartment (as I had the previous summer) on the gorgeous campus of Harvard Business School. It was nestled across the winding Charles River from the College—so winding, in fact, that it had taken me several years to figure out just how Harvard could be both parallel and perpendicular to itself. On the eleventh floor of the brand new One Western Avenue graduate student dormitory, I had an excellent view of the campus that allowed me to put my geometric concerns at ease. It also provided me with a literal window for reflection, as I looked at Harvard with a mixture of longing and disgust, remembering the events of three relatively long years.

My Lowell House roommate Jeff was my roommate once more, and we spent a considerable amount of time sparring about politics as the Democratic National Convention was in Boston that summer. Jeff was as much a Republican as ever. Our only dispute aside from political philosophy concerned food shopping: I would frequently walk a mile down Western Avenue in the blistering heat with my grandmother's rusty metal laundry cart to get groceries from Star Market. Jeff was (rightly) embarrassed to be seen with such a contraption.

During the day, I worked for myself in the downtown office of Keene Promotions, my uncle's renamed company, a block away from South Station. Keene was in dire need of technical support, and without many other prospects for Think at the time, I was willing and able to provide it.

The eleven months that followed my move out of One Western Avenue in August 2004 comprised of a distinct brand of misery. The problems started out relatively minor and accelerated at what seemed to be an exponential pace.

Even with the help of a realtor who dragged me along on pointless excursions that I loathed for much of the summer, I was unable to locate affordable housing in Boston that met my own standards (clean, modern, and close to a subway stop), not to mention my mother's exacting criteria (impossibly inexpensive). The city was in the midst of a real estate boom that my realtor claimed would never end. My economics background told me otherwise, lessening the sense of urgency to buy that she was trying to instill. When I expressed my opinion on market bubbles to her, she dismissed my arguments with a wave of her hand, insisting that Boston was immune from cyclical economic phenomena.

The unfortunate reality was that for the time being, she was right. There was nowhere I could live in Boston for a price my mother was willing to spend, which was already higher than I expected. Since I wanted to remain close to my college friends for as long as possible and needed a place to live in short order, I moved in with Nana, who resided in Brookline relatively nearby Cambridge. This was a mistake.

As I came to realize, Nana was remarkably similar to another member of my family who I had largely been spared while both of us had been away at our respective schools. The parallels between her behavior and Simon's were at times uncanny. Both of them were beyond stubborn, craved social contact to an unhealthy extreme, and still could barely maintain a long-lasting friendship. Though Nana was quite intelligent, having graduated early from Boston University before becoming a reporter for the United Press (similar to today's Associated Press)—three unusual feats for a woman in the 1940s—her understanding of the world was truly limited, just as was the case with my brother.

Their areas of deficiency were different but equally pronounced. Simon couldn't make change for a dollar or tie his shoes. In Nana's case, screen doors and alarm clocks presented insurmountable technological challenges, and the items in her refrigerator were, without fail, as organized and appealing as her garbage bin. She knew how to use a typewriter from her days as a reporter. For a while I was able to get her to use e-mail, but the phase only lasted a few weeks.

The fact that Nana's health was beginning to deteriorate at age eighty-two did not help matters. Macular degeneration made it difficult for her to see clearly, and her driver's license was revoked over her shrill protests (every other day) that she could still drive because she could see "large objects." I was deathly afraid that she might actually try, and so I held onto her car keys closely.

She was even dangerous as a passenger. On those occasions when I was driving, she slammed her foot on an imaginary passenger-side break pedal with alarming frequency, almost causing a number of accidents. No matter what speed I was going, she never hesitated to criticize me for it.

Nana's inability to see was likely related to her diabetes, which had never been kept well under control, for she refused to try to comprehend the concept of carbohydrates that my mother had attempted to teach her. Decades earlier, smoking had taken its toll on her voice—raspy and harsh as ever—and probably on her lungs as well. Her muscles constantly ached and she had trouble sleeping. On the plus side, she did attempt to exercise at her condominium's gym, more than I did. Whenever I attempted to give her advice on her health, it meant that I had to endure a speech about why I should give up on computers and be a doctor.

Like Simon, Nana did occasionally crack a joke in spite of herself. "You can't trust the weather these days," was one of her favorite lines. She was generous but simply unable to relate to others in person.

With all of Nana's children busy with their own families or careers, it quickly fell to me to serve as her caretaker. None of the tasks I was expected to perform were onerous on their own. I was capable of filling insulin syringes, going grocery shopping, banking, setting up books on tape, preventing her refrigerator from turning into a dumpster, paying stacks of bills, taking her car in for service, cooking, and sending out her mail at the Post Office just as well as about anyone. The problem was that in each case, Nana had something to say about it.

In one instance, when I signed up for high-speed internet service, Nana roared that her phone bill was too high, and insinuated that I would never pay her back for the extra cost of the internet connection. This took place every week for months on end, despite my being entrusted with all of her finances, which were worth considerably more than her phone bill. After a while, it was insulting. When I complained that she was letting vast quantities of food rot in her refrigerator, she yelled at me for criticizing her. When my uncle offered to simply purchase prepared meals for both of us so that I wouldn't have to cook (in addition to providing his company with round-the-clock technical support), Nana insisted that the meals were far too expensive but ate them anyway. Sometimes, his wife was also nice enough to cook for us. No matter who had prepared the food, I was merely thankful that I didn't have to.

Then, there were the discussions, mostly between Nana and her three children, about her living in an "assisted living" community. They did not go well.

I was finding it difficult to lead a life of my own. For the first time in years, I had enough time to think about what I wanted to do with myself, instead of what some professor thought I should do. Aside from working on software, one of the things I wanted to do was date girls. Yet the one person I was interested in, and whom I could muster the courage to ask out to dinner, was understandably horrified at my living situation. Taking a girl home to watch a movie at "Nana's house" was about as far from romance as you could get (and so I never did). Not to mention that Nana refused to purchase a VCR or DVD player, or that her television's default volume level induced hearing damage in those who did not already suffer from it.

I attempted a few dates with that same girl. Boring as they must have been for her, they were thrilling for me, but I quickly realized that I was essentially unfit for any type of relationship. It had been my fear since high school. I worried incessantly about my family, and didn't try to hide it whenever I was asked what was on my mind. Simon was back home from Brehm and home was arguably the worst place for him, making his and my parents' life a living nightmare once more. In a bizarre manner he would repeatedly rub my mother's arms or massage my father's shoulders at inappropriate times, sometimes hurting them, despite being asked not to do so in as clear a tone as possible. He would sit in my mother's lap like a four-year-old, despite being twenty and weighing close to two hundred pounds. He would throw violent tantrums that left both of my parents bruised and exhausted. The police were regular visitors to our house. Who wanted to date someone with such problems? These were the signs of a stable life ahead? I didn't blame anyone for wanting to stay away, and it was exhausting to explain it all.

There was never a break. When I tried talking to Mark on-line to find out about the direction he was headed with The Facebook, I was interrupted by Nana exclaiming something about her tape player being broken. True to form, she had taken what had once been a perfectly good audiobook casette and spilled the magnetic tape into a mangled mess all over the floor.

My plan for Think after graduation had been to sell houseSYSTEM as a whole or on an *à la carte* basis, with the Universal Face Book, CriticalMass, Student Exchange, Posters, and Jobs being some of the many software modules I could offer to universities across the country. Little did I know that over the summer, Mark had beat me to the punch by attracting the venture capital I distrusted so much after reading Jerry Kaplan's book. Instead of selling to administrators, he opted to market directly to students for free, hoping to make money on advertising.

I was still upset that Mark had denied copying my features when I had asked him point-blank months before, since it was quite obvious that our software applications did the exact same thing. Foolishly, I thought that perhaps there was still a slim chance that he was telling the truth. I decided that it would be most prudent to maintain the limited friendship we had left, and so we kept in touch, usually over AOL Instant Messenger. Mark had been asking me for technical advice on and off for months.

Still, the more I thought about it, and the more I saw Facebook in the press, the more Mark's plan didn't make sense to me on any level. Of all of the ideas I had coded and saved away on my hard drive, my on-line Face Book seemed like it had the least profit potential of them all. Making money off of advertising seemed downright boring compared to the things I wanted to work on. True to form, Mark had grown bored with it too. He started working on a program called Wirehog that facilitated illegal music sharing between students. I advised him in the strongest terms possible to kill the product if he wanted Facebook to survive. Eventually, he did.

In late September of 2004, I was reading *The Crimson* when I came across an article lauding Mark for his genius and likely similarities to Bill Gates. I didn't see any similarities between Mark and Bill Gates. Mark was inarticulate and naïve; Gates was shrewd, calculating, and insanely competitive, bordering on autistic.

When Gates had given a speech at Harvard encouraging students to study computer science on a tour of many colleges, I had asked him a loaded question: "Will there be a next Microsoft, and if not, will the reason be Microsoft?" His answer was that there was no reason why there couldn't be, and that in fact, it was almost guaranteed that there would be a successor to his company's legacy. He emphasized that all one needed was "the right idea." It was exactly the kind of answer I was hoping for, and it reflected well on him for telling the truth.

His particular brand of insight came through in his answer to another question, when a student asked why Microsoft PowerPoint had become more difficult to use over the years. Gates thought for a moment before responding.

"You know, what we should really do is bring back PowerPoint 3.0 and sell it for more!" he said to a great deal of laughter.

Knowing that Gates's aggressive personality differed greatly from Mark's carefree approach to life, I wrote an editorial in response to the *Crimson* article. Like every other editorial I had ever sent in, it was never published. The fact was that Mark had the press in a frenzy, and I didn't—I had to give him credit for at least that much.

I felt lost, and I couldn't decide whether I had been wronged, or whether Mark was simply smarter than I was. My only consolation was that the press wasn't only in love with Mark. As an avid reader of multiple newspapers, I knew the press sometimes acted just as obsessively as Simon's classmates at Brehm, unable to let go of a particular individual or concept even when more important events were taking shape. Paris Hilton came to mind.

Since the site's first days, the phrase "A Mark Zuckerberg production" appeared at the bottom of every page on Facebook. I was sure that it would disappear once Mark's funding came through and his investors gave the site a once-over. It didn't. My former classmate's antics were beginning to grate on me.

By December, I figured that I might be able to salvage all of those hours of work if I simply admitted defeat and got in with Facebook, Inc. on the ground floor. I gave Mark a call in Palo Alto and asked if they were still looking for someone for their Vice-President of Engineering position, which was advertised as being open on their web site.

"We're looking for someone with more engineering experience, like, ten to fifteen years," he told me. Knowing what kind of engineering experience Mark had, I bit my tongue, hard. I had one more idea.

"I heard about your lawsuit," I told him, referring to the suit that had been filed by Divya Narenda and Cameron and Tyler Winklevoss, twins who had lived near my friend in Cabot House. I didn't know any of them, but I knew about their web site, ConnectU. Word had it that they had hired Mark to write the initial site, which they alleged Mark had finished right around the time that we had dinner in the Kirkland dining hall—only Mark never delivered the product.

"You know, houseSYSTEM came before Facebook *and* ConnectU, and they both have features that look remarkably similar to mine. I have grounds to sue both of you," I told him.

Mark remained silent.

"If we teamed up then ConnectU would have no case; with Facebook owning the rights to houseSYSTEM, ConnectU couldn't claim that you had copied off of them. It would be the other way around."

"I'll have to run it by my legal team," Mark responded. We chatted for a few more minutes, and I said hello to Sean Parker of Napster fame, who Mark had apparently run into on the street. Parker was serving as Facebook's President.

When I hung up the phone, I felt like I had exhausted my options. If Mark didn't want to cooperate with me, there was always the possibility that I could sue him myself. I knew something about intellectual property law from my trademark dispute, however, and there was one question that kept running through my mind.

"*Maybe I could sue him, but what for?*"

Whether or not a lawsuit was the right choice wasn't the only question that was looping through my brain on a daily basis. Why couldn't he have told me that he was going to seek funding? What did he have to lose by offering me a job?

The answer, of course, was that he had a lot to lose. We probably wouldn't have gotten along in a working environment with Mark owning the majority of the company's stock, since I naturally felt entitled to the proceeds of my own idea. I would have been a threat. Still, when I had rejected his informal employment offer in Kirkland, he had been talking about a side-project like hundreds I had seen before at Harvard—not a venture-backed corporation. Would it have really taken that much time to make a phone call before taking the plunge, if only to ask my permission?

I had questions about Mark's business model too. Sites that relied purely on advertising for growth reminded me of SurfingPrizes, and SurfingPrizes was emblematic of the mass hysteria of 1999 that I wanted to avoid at all costs. From everything I read in the press about Facebook, however, mass hysteria was as much Mark's strategy as anything. Everyone was talking about Facebook—CNN ran an article saying that most college students thought it was "cooler than beer"—but what was it actually doing? Turning a profit did not appear to be high on the list in the short-term, and I hadn't entirely figured out what the long-term strategy was either.

I wanted Think to make a profit, and a large one, so I considered another approach: selling my database software to the government, the way Larry Ellison had when he started Oracle in the 1970s. I wrote a proposal involving the use of open source software for the FBI's case management system, on which the government had already wasted hundreds of millions of dollars for proprietary systems that simply didn't work at all. I thought about ways to re-write code Think already had, to make it more generic, and therefore more applicable to different situations that might exist in a large bureaucracy. I tried to think about the big problems that needed to be solved in society, and how I could get by in life contributing at least some part of a solution.

It didn't take long to find an issue that needed attention. I had been commuting from Nana's stuffy condominium in Brookline to downtown Boston every day by way of South Station, which connected Amtrak with the subway's Red Line. I had never actually bothered to stop in the train station on my two minute walk, until one day when I had to wait for a friend's Amtrak train to arrive. It was late.

Sitting in the plaza with my laptop, I found a wireless internet signal that advertised it was worth my paying $6.95 to access what I could get for free a block away. I had just come from the office, though, and had a while to wait. I wondered how hard it would be to get around the fee-based system.

About twenty minutes later, suddenly terrified by the presence of MBTA police who had been standing around the train station all day, and giddy with success, I had my answer. It wasn't difficult to get around at all, and in fact, by reverse engineering South Station's system, I had stumbled upon flaws that affected several dozen companies all across Massachusetts. Once my friend arrived, I told him about the problem I had discovered (much to his horror), and we discussed the best way to handle it. Soon after, I wrote a "white paper," the commercial equivalent of an academic journal article, and posted it on the internet. My career as a so-called security expert had begun.

Naturally, I had been keeping tabs on The Facebook, and quickly uncovered a serious problem. Mark and his team had designed a feature to list all of your friends in a text file that you could then import into contact management programs, such as Microsoft Outlook. Their algorithm worked so well that it littered their server's hard drive with the files so that anyone could access them. With the right web address, which was easy to guess, one could download the names, home addresses, birthdates, cell phone numbers and e-mail addresses of several thousand Harvard students at once. I told Mark immediately, but he ignored me for weeks until I told the *Yale Daily News*. *The Crimson* picked up the story from there, and only then did a none-too-pleased Mark finally fix the problem.

It was only a few days after the South Station incident that I received an e-mail from the company I had contracted to do Think's payroll regarding my W-2 tax form for the end of the 2004 fiscal year. I had chosen PayMaxx as Think's payroll processor in 1999 because my prior payroll providers had been horrible, and the sponsor of the Junior Achievement contest I had won, BrightLane.com, resold PayMaxx services at the time. I felt like I owed something back to them for giving me the award.

There was a link in the e-mail directing customers to download their personalized W-2 forms. With one click, I knew the PayMaxx system was potentially vulnerable to the same flaw I had found at South Station, and with two more keystrokes, I confirmed that the flaw actually existed. The W-2s of tens of thousands of PayMaxx customers, including my own, were publicly available on-line, and it didn't take a degree in particle physics to find them all. Once you knew where one was located, the only skill required to get the rest was the ability to count. I could flip through the salaries of CEOs, the home addresses of competitors, and the Social Security Numbers of complete strangers with the greatest of ease. PayMaxx had no idea.

I saved three random W-2s to my hard drive to prove the existence of the flaw. Then, I considered what to do next. It was clear at least that I wouldn't be using PayMaxx much longer.

When I told my PayMaxx sales representative about the problem, he ignored me, largely because I offered to fix it for my standard hourly rate, and PayMaxx wasn't about to hire a random computer consultant talking about supposed security flaws. I wasn't about to volunteer a complete solution for free, however. Without my base of reliable consulting clients far away in Shaker Heights, I needed a way to make a living. PayMaxx had certainly not shown me any favors over the years; the price of cutting one check was ludicrous.

I was careful to word an e-mail to PayMaxx in such a way that they wouldn't think that I was attempting to extort money from them. After all, I had been a paying customer for more than five years, even though according to my records, they hadn't exactly done a perfect job. I simply wanted to help solve a problem and to receive appropriate compensation for my services and expertise.

In retrospect, the reaction from PayMaxx was predictable: they continued to ignore me until a white paper, this time about their flaw, appeared on Think's web site. An article also appeared on c|net *news.com*, a popular computer news site. PayMaxx and its law firm began bombarding Think's web site with hits, trying desperately to figure out who this annoying customer was and what "flaw" he was talking about.

Not too long after, I began receiving calls from PayMaxx's lawyers, vaguely informing me that I had made their client unhappy. After the first flaw, I had un-covered two more serious problems in different systems at PayMaxx. My birthday passed in a blur of anxiety, and potential lawsuits were all I could think about on the subway to and from work, passing through South Station each and every time.

Had the press coverage continued unabated, PayMaxx might have sued. Luckily, divine intervention saved Think Computer Corporation from what would undoubt-edly have been a most unhappy fate of bankruptcy by legal fees.

First, Terry Schiavo died. Then, so did the Pope. The press was so distracted that it took ten extra days before my interview from Boston about PayMaxx aired on CNN.

That's when disaster really struck.

■

While PayMaxx had been figuring out what to do about my unfortunate dis-covery of their unfortunate programming errors, I had been figuring out what to do about the fact that I no longer had a mechanism by which I could pay myself a salary. Simply writing myself a check from Think's bank account, simple though it was, didn't work; I also had to file appropriate forms with the plethora of tax agencies PayMaxx had once handled for me, and I had no idea how. By the end of April, which was inconveniently also tax season for personal returns, I had prepared thirteen returns ranging in complexity from moderate to extraordinary difficult for various federal, state and local agencies. I scrambled to integrate payroll functionality into the accounting software I had been working on for months by ordering equipment that I could use to reverse engineer the U.S. banking system.

Stupidly, I updated Think's web site to reflect the new and improved features of my software, and PayMaxx went into a frenzy, possibly thinking that I was out to destroy them with a new killer technology. In reality, I had spent $45.00 total on eBay for some magnetic toner that would fit into my nine-year-old laser printer, and the same Magtek scanning equipment that banks used to read checks. Within only a few sleep-deprived days, I was printing and scanning my own checks, with Think's logo printed neatly on top of each one. The bank teller didn't even blink when I presented the first one for deposit.

The CNN segment appeared on televisions scattered across the country on the evening of April 12th, which is precisely when hackers from a chat room in Romania began testing the news network's implicitly exaggerated claims of my security prowess. It took the hackers' automated scripts a few minutes to find that one of my clients had set his password to the same four characters as his first name. That was all they needed to gain access to Think's main server, which they summarily destroyed.

Servers that run web sites are fundamentally just like any other computer. They have hard drives, memory, sometimes monitors, and always at least one "network card" to communicate with the outside world. The major difference is typically that they are located in data centers with extraordinarily fast internet connections so that the world's requests for information can reach them quickly. That night, the Romanians sent my server some truly interesting requests, and it responded as instructed, downloading a Linux-based virus called RST.B that in turn required my staying awake for the next 24 hours in order to salvage whatever data I could.

It happened again the next night, this time exploiting a different flaw in a popular message board program. By the third night, when other hackers in Asia decided to use my server as a high-speed relay for illegal movie sharing (which was fortunately easier to clean up), I had really had enough.

I was a complete wreck. I was angry, I needed sleep, and I had been given the run-around by the FBI and the Secret Service, the two federal agencies responsible for handling "cybercrime," who I had dutifully reported each of the attacks to. Ironically, none of the flaws that had been exploited were in Think's software—they were in open-source programs that my clients used on their web sites. I was furious at the open-source zealots who bleated about the superiority of their code, and who had just cost me three nights worth of sleep.

Since the original hard drive was barely salvageable, but contained evidence of the perpetrators' actions from afar, I had my data center's staff in New Jersey remove the drive and send it to the Secret Service for processing. The FBI arrived at Keene's offices a few days later to interview me.

"We weren't going to come initially, but once you called the third time, your name stuck and we decided to pay a visit," one of the two agents said, notebook in hand. The other remained silent and stony-faced. "Can we ask some questions about your server?"

"Sure, go ahead." We discussed the hacking incidents for about ten minutes before the talkative agent cut me off.

"Actually, we're not really here about your server. We figure that you might... know some people...who we're interested in." The FBI apparently thought I had connections with criminal masterminds.

"OK..." I said.

"We were wondering if you might be able to give us information on them."

"Are you asking me to spy on people?" I said, alarmed.

"No, nothing like that. You see, the FBI's mission has changed considerably over the years," the agent responded quickly. "Where we used to be focused only on CI, now we're doing more DI." The silent agent nodded. I had no idea what he was talking about. Later I looked up what the abbreviations stood for: Counterintelligence and Domestic Intelligence, respectively.

"So you're asking me to spy on people," I repeated.

"No, just to tell us what you know," the agent responded.

"Any...people...in particular?" I asked, now curious.

"People." The agent said it definitively, with a half-smile.

Some of my best friends were Muslim, and the Bush administration had not exactly been friendly toward Muslim-Americans based on what I read in the news. Others I knew were merely interesting people. I couldn't imagine who they were interested in.

"I don't think I'd feel comfortable doing that," I said, slightly nervous at the turn our meeting had taken.

"Would you say you are a supporter of the Administration?" came the next question. I felt trapped. I knew Hoover's FBI had asked politically-charged questions, but I thought Hoover had been dead for years.

"I'm not sure how I should answer that..." I said carefully. Soon, I signaled that it was a good time for the agents to leave, and followed up with an e-mail offering to sell the FBI software, not information. They promised they would follow up with a phone call, which fortunately, I never received.

What followed then was a seemingly apocalyptic series of events that I don't remember in any particular order. The father of one of my roommates passed away; another friend's father had died in a plane crash only three months before. I discovered a mistake in Think's tax returns that carried through all the way to my personal returns, themselves at least twenty pages long. I decided to launch a project I had been working on for a while called Inbox Island, which was a short-lived spam-free e-mail system. I told Mark Zuckerberg that he should advertise Facebook the same way; he told me he didn't want to compete with Microsoft, which confused me. My mother fought with me over whether or not I should assume ownership of Nana's 1991 Toyota, which I could barely coax into accelerating past 25 miles per hour, and which had no alert feature when you left the lights on, causing the battery to die routinely. Nana herself was unbearable. The seventh anniversary of Think's founding took place on April 29th, a symbolic date important in my own mind because each year I marveled that my side-project had lasted at all, and because it was the day before April 30th.

I spent April 30th in the hospital.

■

There's a certain kind of strangling terror that comes over a person when, during the routine process of using the bathroom just after waking up, quarts of blood begin pouring out of one's body. Perhaps it's the red color that makes it so terrifying, or perhaps it's the fact that you don't know if it will ever stop. In my case, I thought it was entirely possible that my lungs hadn't just collapsed, but that they had somehow ceased to function entirely, and were now just one large, bloody, liquid mass, meaning that I only had a few moments to live. I rushed to the telephone and called my doctor. Aware that somehow I could still breathe, and doubly aware of the dull pain that flanked both sides of my torso, I felt almost as if someone had pounded on my back and my sides with a hammer while I slept.

I wasn't sure how I had managed to acquire two kidney stones by the age of twenty-two, but I had, and they were large. The first doctor I saw at Massachusetts General Hospital told me that lithotripsy, a noninvasive operation involving the use of ultrasound waves to break up stones, was no longer performed anywhere. He prescribed me a medication that carried with it a high risk of fainting. The side-effect so scared me that I refused to take it, which turned out to be fortunate because the next thing that happened was that the hospital scheduled me to have a lithotripsy operation—an operation for which you were specifically forbidden from taking any prescription medications beforehand that might affect circulation, such as medications that might make you faint.

A few days after my initial visit to the emergency room, I was sitting on the MBTA Red Line in pain, hoping to reach the Charles/MGH stop without passing out. From there, I walked the three blocks in the rain so that I could have the operation. I wanted to know what kind of drugs I would receive for the anesthesia because I didn't like the idea of being on narcotics, but it was too late. Before I knew it I had already blacked out. Afterward, someone had to be available to pick me up, since patients were forbidden to leave on their own. At some point, my uncle arrived and I was free to go.

I tried calling MGH that night to find out the results of the lithotripsy procedure. The nurse asked for my medical record number and name, and then told me that although she had the information I was asking for in front of her, she would not repeat it over the phone.

"Why not? I asked, incensed, and in pain.

"Due to HIPAA," she said. "We can't give out any information over the phone."

"But it's about *me*!" I screamed. "I need to know if I should go back to the hospital! I'm not some cousin's roommate's brother calling. That's *my* information!"

"The only way you can find that out is by coming back to the hospital," she insisted.

The next day I called my doctor, who (while abiding by the same law) promptly told me that the first lithotripsy didn't work. I had another identical operation a few days later.

Suddenly, I understood what health insurance was for. The hospital sent me a bill for $20,000, which somehow, Think Computer Corporation had already paid via Blue Cross Blue Shield of Massachusetts. While I had earlier cursed myself for the decision to digitize seven years of invoices and receipts one by one, I was now glad I had paid so much attention to my company's accounting records.

June 2005 was the light at the end of the tunnel, the time when I would walk across the improvised stage in the Lowell House courtyard and receive my symbolic diploma along with my friends. My entire family had been waiting for my graduation from Harvard for years. In some sense, I had been waiting for years too, but by June I was worn out and depressed. All I wanted to do was sleep.

The night before commencement, the majority of my headstrong and some-times-autistic family had converged upon Nana's small condominium in Brookline with a tempestuous wrath that I had only witnessed in fragments before. To make matters worse, inwardly, I was terrified of losing my friends to the unpredictable meandering of life the minute we exited Harvard Yard the next morning. I was sure my father and mother had made mutual assurances to stay in touch with their college friends, but I only rarely heard about them.

Outwardly, there was a more immediate situation to deal with. Simon wanted to watch baseball on Nana's television.

Nana disapproved of Simon watching so much television, of Simon watch-ing baseball, and of Simon profoundly ignoring her disapproval (in the exact same way she ignored his). In turn, my mother screamed at her mother, my father at his mother-in-law, my grandmother at both my father and mother for "failing" as Simon's parents, I at my grandmother for being clueless, insulting, inflexible and belligerent, and my mother's sister at everyone including me for being ungrateful.

I was more depressed than I had ever been in my life, with the crowded room full of sheer human noise without end. It continued in this way for hours. The intractable and yet completely unnecessary nature of the argument made me want to punch a hole through the wall; this was no way to celebrate anyone's graduation. But I couldn't punch a hole through the wall, so I again locked myself in my bedroom, which was, after all, still my bedroom, and I wrapped a cord around my neck as tightly as I could three times in succession. It hurt.

Just as in high school, each time I failed to achieve the desired result. Instead, I quietly cried myself to sleep, with Simon banging on the door the whole time since my locking myself in my room had angered him even more. Eventually, some hours later, I had to get up and let him in so that he could sleep too. Simon was always better asleep.

The next morning, I graduated from Harvard College without anyone knowing what had transpired the night before. During the various ceremonies, and while talking with my friends and their families, I even forgot about it myself. Our commencement speaker, Tim Russert, was notable only because a muffled shout emerged during the middle of his canned speech. Later, we learned that bingo cards had been distributed in the back corner of the crowd to mark off the clichés Russert used each time he imparted his wisdom. The shout had been someone yelling, "Bingo!"

The ceremony in Lowell House was anti-climactic. I was forced to be around my family, and most of my friends were in Mather House. Worst of all, on the stage I had to shake Jay Ellison's hand as part of the proper procedure.

On July 11, 2005, ignoring my family's protests, I left Boston, never looking back.

∎

When I stepped off the plane, I was in Dallas, Texas. It was a New Englander's nightmare, but having had my fill of New England, that was fine with me. My first impression of the city was that it was dusty, and that it had too many highways given the number of people who actually needed to be transported. One of my close college friends originally from Dallas picked me up, and I stayed with her family for some time until Metin arrived for archaeology graduate school at Southern Methodist University. Shortly thereafter, we moved into our apartment close to campus and Interstate 75.

About a month later, I was in the emergency room again, this time without anything but a temporary insurance plan. The reason was a spasm of pain so intense that it left me on the floor of my apartment, thinking only about how much my abdomen hurt, and how Harry Potter must have felt when he was being tortured by the human embodiment of evil. No one else was home. Eventually, I crawled to the cordless phone base and dialed my friend, who took a detour with her family to bring me to the nearest hospital.

My visit only lasted twenty minutes, but my bills totaled over $1,500: fees to imaging specialists, a radiology office I'd never been to, nurses, one doctor, and the hospital itself. After the visit, I tried to download my recent films from MGH's highly-touted digital medical record system in time for another doctor's appointment in Dallas and found that I couldn't. Instead, I had to fill out a web-based form requesting that a CD-ROM be mailed to me for a fee, payable by credit card. The only other alternative was to have a relative pick up the disc in person.

I asked Vaughn, temporarily in Boston, to pick up the disc for me, and signed and faxed a letter to MGH that granted him permission to do so. We joked about the implication that he, a Singaporean, was my Jewish uncle. After Vaughn had the disc, he put it in his laptop and uploaded the contents to my company's server. According to MGH, this method was more secure than a direct encrypted download.

I simultaneously noticed that the web-based film request form was exposing patients' medical histories and credit card numbers. The hospital president's secretary hung up on me when I called to notify him. It was only at the request of my father's brother's colleague, who happened to be the head of MGH Radiology, that the site was eventually shut down.

It wasn't until I had been in Dallas for several months that the events which had transpired since August 2003 really hit me. I was walking around SMU's campus, thinking that it was almost a carbon copy of the University of Virginia's, except for the fact that it was in Texas. It was beautiful. The undergraduates there had the benefit of a brand new student union, complete with outdoor pools that Harvard students would never have even thought to ask for. I remember being alone, though Metin must have been somewhere nearby, when I saw her.

I don't know who she was, and I had probably seen students like her a thousand times before, but she is the one who sticks out in my mind. She was an undergraduate I had never met and had no connection to whatsoever—not through friends, not through family, not through roommates, not even through my temple in Cleveland—standing there in the sparkling student center before a public computer terminal, completely engrossed in the screen before her. It took only a moment to recognize the pale blue streaks and blocks of text on the screen that were apparently so intriguing. She was looking at The Facebook.

I was standing alone at the dead-end of a maze of dead-ends, watching from a distance as others reaped the rewards of my creation in which my participation was forbidden. Something had gone horribly wrong.

That's when I had to admit the truth that for so long I had suspected, but hadn't wanted to believe.

"He really did steal it from me after all."

CHAPTER 28

"Five Years" to the Offer of a Life

Think was not doing very well. I had written a monumental amount of code, but it was all sitting on my hard drive where it didn't do much good. The cost of living in Dallas was low, but I still wasn't paying myself anything close to a reasonable salary. I needed to make a change, and fast.

The next part of my plan to sell software to the government market involved applying for a General Services Administration schedule, which would allow Think to sell to all branches of the federal bureaucracy through a centralized depot, the equivalent of Sam's Club for government agencies.

The GSA made it notoriously difficult to obtain a schedule. Expensive private seminars helped small business owners navigate through the process, which typically involved 200 or more pages of completely opaque contract verbiage in eight-point type. I thought my computer skills might lend me an advantage. The process for Information Technology contractors had recently been digitized. Think could apply on-line.

I filled out the paperwork to receive a special digital encryption program from AT&T that I would need to install in my web browser in order to access the GSA's site. In a few weeks, I had what I needed.

I also had to hire a company called Open Ratings, Inc. to send out a survey to my clients asking them to rate my performance as a contractor. The responses were generally good, mostly 9 and 10 out of 10, with and 7 or 8 here and there.

The most difficult part of the process was simply figuring out how much to charge. When I started Think, I had observed that Bill Gates was the richest man in the world for no other reason that it was impossible to truly value software as an intangible good. Now I realized that this presented a challenging problem. The only rate I was sure of was my hourly consulting rate. It was $125.00 per hour, but I planned on raising it to $150.00 by the beginning of 2006. Knowing how long the application process would take, I wrote $150.00 on my pricing spreadsheet, yielding a final price of $127.50 per hour after the government's 15% discount.

I spoke with my case representative at the GSA on the phone for months. There were some fundamental problems with my application. I had left the spreadsheet of material costs blank, since there were none for my products. Explaining this to the GSA was difficult.

"Don't you need to buy steel, or paper, or anything to make your product?" my representative asked.

"I'm writing software. You just need labor," I replied, aghast. *"She couldn't have asked about this in September?"*

"Well, you can't leave it blank," she said.

"I really have nothing to put on it!"

Discussions like this continued for much longer than they should have. I was at some point asked to write a pricing memo to myself, informing myself of the prices I had just set so that there would be a record of my having set them—never mind that the memo was completely bogus.

"I'm a one-person company," I objected. "This makes no sense."

"Are you saying that you would like to withdraw your application?" came the response. I wrote the memo.

In December, I received a letter from the GSA informing me that my application for a government contract schedule had been rejected. The reason was quite simple: I was over-charging the government. One of my documents discussed my hourly consulting rate as presently being $125.00 per hour. My pricing spreadsheet, calculated to account for the gap of many months between the beginning and the end of the process, stated a price two dollars and fifty cents higher. (My completely arbitrary software prices were, of course, perfectly acceptable, as were Halliburton's astronomical prices for services rendered in Iraq.)

I was furious. I told the representative, and then her boss, that I was writing a letter to Senator Cornyn of Texas. The letter was half-completed on the screen in front of me. Then her boss offered a compromise.

"You can apply again and because we know who you are now, and about all of this...software...we'll be able to fast track you." I reined in some of my anger.

"Are you sure? I will be able to do this without going through all of the paperwork I just did?"

"Yes, we'll make sure we get it done."

"Okay." I told her. "I'll do it."

◼

The second attempt started off easier than the first. I already had my digital certificate, my client survey, and a decent understanding of the entire process. I just needed to make sure that there were absolutely no discrepancies in any of the documents of any kind. That meant no typographical errors, no misplaced decimal points, no rounded numbers—none at all.

I uploaded the client survey. Without thinking, I typed in the name of the report as "OpenRatings Report," leaving out the space between "Open" and "Ratings." After I had already uploaded the document, I realized my mistake, double-checking the company's web site (whose address actually lacked a space, explaining my confusion). Strangely, the GSA's system did not offer a way to edit the entry; I had to delete it. I clicked on the "Delete" link and a new screen appeared.

CONFIRM DELETE

Are you sure you want to delete this file?

YES   NO

The message seemed clear to me, and I was certain I wanted to delete the file. I clicked "YES," and re-uploaded the Open Ratings Report with the space properly inserted in the file's description. I clicked on the new link that had been created to ensure that my file was there.

The link ended with a unique identifier that corresponded to my document's row in the GSA system's table of documents. Curious, I wondered if I could still access the document I had just deleted. Sure enough, changing the identifier in the web address demonstrated that I could. South Station, PayMaxx and MGH came to mind.

"*Do you think...*" I wondered. I changed the identifier to a random number. Random data appeared before me—some company's pricing list. Some company's *confidential* pricing list.

"*Not again!*" I thought. I called my father at work, explaining the situation. He was understandably angry, both at me for testing the system and at the government for undoubtedly spending millions of dollars on a broken application. When I pointed out that in addition to my own records, more than 400,000 other companies' records were being exposed, he softened. In the end, he recommended that I call the GSA's Inspector General.

What followed was a fascinating lesson in government, commerce, national security, and politics. It took me to the nation's capital, where with the invaluable assistance of Brad's father, I once again found a lawyer. This time, I needed one who was available to practice criminal technology law in the Alexandria, Virginia district immediately, leaving me very few options. The cost was steep, both in terms of my finances and my health. When I was able to sleep, I woke up each morning to find that more of my hair had actually fallen out; my parents, still in Cleveland, were paralyzed with fear. With the NSA spying scandal in the news, I had good reason to worry that my phone might be tapped.

In the end, in a flagrant violation of my first amendment right to freedom of speech, a Bush administration official told me that if I ever repeated the latter half of this story in a manner that might attract the attention of the press, I could find myself facing criminal charges that automatically carried with them five years in prison as a penalty.

All that matters for you, the reader, is that in this way, I learned not to trust my government, I learned not to disclose security flaws no matter the danger to society, and I was introduced to a *New York Times* reporter named John Markoff.

◼

In April, 2006, I had completely abandoned my plans to sell software to the government, and was trying to figure out how to attract new commercial clients for Think once more. I had landed a handful of large accounts, but I was still effectively overworked and underpaid, working out of my bedroom in Dallas. My social life was fairly limited, and though I enjoyed Metin's company thoroughly, I was beginning to grow bored.

When I saw the March 28, 2006 edition of *BusinessWeek* on-line several weeks after its release, I was bored no longer. The same Mark I had gone to class with for so many months was touting my idea, and not just my idea, but the fundamentals of my work, the code I had written, as being worth $2 billion. Worst of all, people were taking him somewhat seriously, or at least seriously enough to write an article repeating the grandiose claim in writing.

"If Mark can get $2 billion for my ideas, I should at least be able to get a couple million!" I told Metin. Against my better judgment, I had already been in touch with some venture capitalists, so I confirmed their availability for meetings and booked my first flight to Silicon Valley as soon as I could.

It just so happened that Nana's brother lived in San Mateo, California, essentially across the street from Oracle's shimmering cylindrical headquarters. Being from Ohio, I had never known that San Mateo was anywhere close to the Valley. As soon as he picked me up at the San Francisco airport, my education in the lay of the land began. I was thrilled to see so many of the companies I had read about all my life in one place.

With the exception of my first face-to-face meeting with John Markoff, who was based in San Francisco, my meetings did not go so well. One venture capitalist laughed me out of the room, telling me that it was impossible that I had written all the code I had claimed to. When I showed it to him in its operational form on my laptop, he had an answer for that too.

"It could just be a Flash demo. How am I supposed to know it's real? You should have come to me with a pitch for something real, like an operating system."

"I do want to make an operating system, in fact!" I told him.

"What, are you on crack?" he then mocked. It wasn't the first time he had used the phrase. I left his office with a huge smirk on my face, knowing that to have elicited a response so extreme, either he or I was a complete idiot—and I had the code.

The other venture capitalist I met with had a more whimsical approach. He was older, had the calm air of someone who had nothing left to prove, and spun around in his chair while I talked.

"When are you going to give up?" he exclaimed after hearing my story and seeing my software.

I was taken aback. People weren't supposed to encourage you to give up.

"I don't really plan to, actually...as long as I can eat, I suppose, I'll just keep going."

"Well, you're certainly an oddball." I had already gathered that he did not want to invest. "But we like oddballs here." I sat, puzzled.

"Why don't you come work for us?" he asked. This surprised me even more.

"I mean...I'd consider it if it were an option," I told him.

"Let me talk to some people," he said. "I might get back to you and say, yeah, you should come back out and we'll chat, or I might get back to you and say, no it won't work out. And it will take me a little while. But I'll check." I thanked him and left. It was just in the nick of time. There was little more than a month left on my lease in Dallas.

I got my answer with surprising haste. About two weeks later, I was back in the offices of the same venture capital firm, one of the most prominent in the Valley. My friends told me that I was most certainly going to be rich.

"Yeah, right. I'll believe it when I see it," I told them with healthy skepticism.

I was scheduled to meet with two more partners during my interview. I met with one of them, as well as the firm's CFO and technical staff person. The second partner never showed up. Everything seemed to be going well, and the firm was paying for everything. I wasn't used to such lavish accommodations. Unlike most of my friends at Harvard, I had never been recruited for anything before.

"We have very deep pockets," the CFO assured me. I believed her.

When I arrived home, all I could do was sit and wait. Eventually, I received an e-mail informing me that the last partner still wanted to talk, but had been busy when I had been in town. Was it alright to set up a phone call?

I responded as quickly as I could, offering to be free whenever I was needed. Finally, the call took place. The partner asked questions that seemed fairly typical of the others I had heard and answered, except for two.

"Have you ever done something without trying to invent it yourself?"

"Can you tell me how you were involved with Facebook again?"

On Simon's birthday, I received a call from the first partner I had met on my most recent trip.

"Congratulations, you got the job!" he told me. I was ecstatic; it would be my first real job ever. "Now for the details: what are your financial requirements?"

"Financial requirements?" I asked. I wasn't sure what he meant. To me, requirements and desires were completely different.

"How much do you think you'll need to make?" he clarified.

"Oh," I stammered, uncomfortable. "Just more than I make now, I suppose."

"How much is that?" he asked. I told him. He sounded like he'd been caught off-guard.

"Oh! Well..." There was a pause. "I don't think you could even *live* on that salary here. I'll make sure we put something together good for you. We'll send you the written offer tonight—tomorrow at the very latest."

I thanked him and hung up.

I would be proud to state that I am the technological guru behind what is typically regarded as the most successful venture capital firm in the world, except that the written offer never came.

The last partner to interview me had just left his job a month or two before at another Palo Alto venture capital firm that had invested in a number of successful startups. Foremost among their portfolio companies was a small enterprise started by a Harvard dropout named Mark Zuckerberg.

■

I had less than two weeks to move. I considered my options. Staying in Dallas meant at least one more year of sheer boredom, and not very many business opportunities unless I wanted Think Computer Corporation to diversify into oil holdings. Leaving Dallas meant finding a moving company that could transport all of my belongings to some unknown destination in a short time frame, aside from the separate problems of figuring out how to transport myself and how to pay for it all. I had been counting on my supposed employer to reimburse me for the move.

Ultimately, I decided to leave Dallas for Silicon Valley even without the job. I spent several days straight combing Craigslist for a stable place to live, sight unseen. Finally, on the third day, I found what looked like a white mansion in a place called Atherton, available for sublet from a student at the Stanford Graduate School of Business. Subletting from business school students was something I could handle. Finding a moving company and driving from Texas to California proved to be more of a challenge, but with my father's help, it worked out at the last second. He flew to Dallas and we started driving west the minute I picked him up at the airport.

During my two months in Atherton, where I really *was* living in a miniature mansion (in the dining room, to be precise), I got my bearings and tried to adapt to life surrounded by ostentatious displays of wealth. Unfortunately for me, the only thing more prominent in the Valley's mindset than Google's stock price was the startup of the decade: Facebook.

The constant talking, writing, gossiping and droning about Facebook put me into a kind of semi-amnesic state. Some days, I would wonder if I had merely imagined the whole thing; it all seemed so surreal. I still was making barely enough to get by, especially with my new rent being almost double what it had been in Dallas, and I found myself looking for jobs. If I mentioned my role in Facebook's creation during interviews, people would give me strange looks and accuse me of lying, as if I were psychotic. Others would wait for the punch line to the joke, in which case they were left hanging. Everyone knew that Mark Zuckerberg started Facebook. Yet if I didn't mention it, as became the case more and more often, then I was nothing special; just one more engineer in a sea of engineers with Ivy League degrees, most far more impressive than my own.

The only thing that could prove my case, I realized, was evidence. I already had the e-mails, the houseSYSTEM code, the database, and some of the IM conversations, but they only said so much. What I really wanted were the server logs, but they were long gone.

"*Unless...*" I thought. "*Unless the government is as incompetent as I think it is.*"

I e-mailed the Secret Service agent I had worked with in the chaotic weeks of April 2005 concerning the hacking incidents. Sure enough, my untouched hard drive was still sitting in a lab at the Department of Homeland Security, which had absorbed the Secret Service. The Secret Service was more than willing to have one fewer case to worry about. The agent put the drive on a FedEx truck, and I had it in Atherton in a few days.

When I put the hard drive into my trusty desktop computer and turned it on, my heart sunk. Instead of the familiar Gateway logo, all I saw was a totally blank screen. The drive appeared to be in such bad shape that there was nothing that could be done with it, so long as it prevented my computer from even turning on.

In a last-ditch attempt to salvage the only remaining proof of Mark repeatedly scanning through houseSYSTEM's Face Book in the days before he created his copy, I took the drive out and turned my computer back on, combing the internet for tips on how to repair broken hard drives. Quickly, I acted on the best one I could find: "put the hard drive in the freezer."

It actually made sense. If the drive's platters (on which bits of data are physically stored) were not damaged, but some other physical defect was stopping the drive from "spinning up," then the drop in temperature might force the metal moving parts inside to contract without affecting the plastic ones as much, possibly solving what could only be an unbelievably esoteric problem. It was a long shot, but I had nothing else left to do. I put the drive in a plastic bag so that I didn't introduce ice into the equation.

After about fifteen minutes, I removed my frozen hard drive from its place next to the chicken stir fry, hoping my roommates weren't around to ask exactly what I was doing. Then, I reconnected it to my desktop computer's ribbon cable. The Gateway logo appeared, along with two lines of text: one for each hard drive connected to the system's IDE bus. The trick worked.

I was delighted to find that my hacked server had intact archived logs for house-SYSTEM going all the way back to September 2003—more than enough time to prove what I had been saying all along. Indeed, every one of Mark Zuckerberg's visits to houseSYSTEM was logged in excruciating detail. I wasn't imagining after all.

■

In August 2006, I moved again to Mountain View, where rent was slightly cheaper. Passing Facebook's headquarters on the way, I met John Markoff for breakfast in Palo Alto one morning at *Il Fornaio*, an Italian restaurant that was a frequent hangout for venture capitalists. At the time, I was trying to make something useful out of the houseSYSTEM code, which had been comatose for two years. I told him the full story of Facebook.

"Hmm, maybe I'll write something," he said. "Maybe for September."

September 2006 came and went, and no story appeared. I figured I'd missed my opportunity and didn't think much of it after that. Widely regarded as the top technology columnist for the *Times*, I knew John Markoff had better things to do. He had broken the story of the first computer virus in the *Times* before I knew what a virus was, and he had been covering the World Economic Forum in Davos, Switzerland when the GSA episode took place. (The next year, Mark was asked to speak there.)

A year passed, with my projects going mostly nowhere and my self-esteem at its usual low. Then, I received an instant message from John, asking what I thought of the ConnectU lawsuit.

We had one more meeting in a coffee shop in Palo Alto, and on September 1, 2007, the front page of the *Times* Business section posed the question, "Who Found the Bright Idea?" with my picture blanketing the page. Though the picture was the worst of the batch the photographer had shown me, the article was everything I could have asked for and more. It put to rest years of intense frustration and brought to light a transgression that arguably changed the world, and that up until then only a select few had even known about. Much to my surprise, Mark didn't dispute any of it.

I didn't invent social networking. I didn't invent the concept of the yearbook. I didn't invent digital photographs. I didn't invent a lot of things, and I never claimed to have created any such generic concepts that everyone knows have been around for ages. The one thing I did invent as a student at Harvard University in 2003, the one idea that has everyone talking for now, and the one thing I'm actually quite proud of, is the component of houseSYSTEM that allowed students to communicate easier than they ever had before: the Universal Face Book.

CHAPTER 29

Lessons for Tomorrow

It would be an understatement to say that the site that grew out of my work on houseSYSTEM is now immensely popular. Ask any college student, and even if they're not on the network (and they probably have been at least once at some point in time), they've heard of it. This used to be true only in the United States of America; now, it's likely to be true many other places in the world, from the United Kingdom to Germany to Australia. There are Facebook clones, sites that look and work identical to Mark Zuckerberg's version, in a number of countries including Russia and China. I've been asked to help write some of them, though I've never been enthusiastic about working on copies of ideas, let alone copies of copies.

"To Facebook" has been introduced into the vernacular as a verb, with a definition meaning something between researching and stalking a given person, who is typically the subject of the same sentence. Facebook is frequently the topic of lunch and dinner conversations, which for years were excruciatingly painful for me to endure, as people generally had no idea of my connection to its roots. (Fortunately, that's not as much the case now; it's merely funny to me.) It's the main subject of Silicon Valley news articles and blog posts, and on the tip of every software engineer's and reporter's tongue.

We've witnessed what seems to be a notable change in the way communication works for an entire generation of people thanks to Facebook, and a lot of the people it hasn't reached yet have legitimate questions about what that means. Will we continue to see an unending stream of social networks until people can't even keep track anymore? Will Facebook be the next Microsoft? Could it be the next Google? Will it change how adults communicate with one another and not just students? Is Facebook really worth the many billions of dollars that people think it is? What does this say about the next thirty years of computer software? I'm no better at predicting the future than anyone else, but these are all questions I've spent a considerable about of time thinking about.

The phrase "social networking" seems to me now reminiscent of the phrase "CD-ROM" in 1993. When I would work in the library at Woodbury in fifth and sixth grade, the main attraction was the single computer with a CD-ROM encyclopedia. It could hold vastly more information than a traditional floppy disk, and we were told that the difference in capacity was going to transform the way computers worked. Sure enough, it did: the distribution of desktop software took place for a decade thereafter on CD-ROM, and still does today (though newer formats have been introduced, such as DVD-ROM and Sony Blu-ray, but they are backward-compatible, meaning that you can put a CD-ROM in a DVD-ROM drive). The CD-ROM craze was extended far past its prime when hardware manufacturers released 2X, then 3X, then 4X, then 6X drives. Now, every CD-ROM drive in existence is at least twenty-four times as fast as the first one ever released—and nobody cares at all.

In this context, what does social networking mean? It will not increase information storage capacity the way CD-ROM did, but it is a more efficient way to store information in the first place. Computers, being digital machines—or said another way, machines that process digits—have a much easier time handling numbers than they do words. Numbers generally take up fewer bits of storage in databases, are faster to process, and never repeat so that you can use them anywhere in a system without worrying about running into one record when you've asked to view information about another. The technological leap inherent in social networks is that each person with a profile is really just a number. The genius of it is that so far, these people-numbering systems have lacked the cultural stigmata that usually come with images of barcodes on people's foreheads, or the iconic tattoos that were forced upon prisoners of Nazi concentration camps (which were "necessary" so that IBM Hollerith machines could record them on punch cards). Quite the opposite: people are very enthusiastic about social networks, which just goes to show that a database's moral worth is determined entirely by its creator.

The truth is that we could have had social networking software much earlier than 1997, when Six Degrees was released (the first modern-day social network that I know of), had we only asked for it. The privacy concerns surrounding the public availability of information are so profound, however, that it took a critical mass of millions of individuals deciding in unison to buck the *status quo* in order to change the prevailing mindset on whether we should ask at all. After all, houseSYSTEM's Face Book was remarkably similar to Mark's Facebook, but enthusiasm among the exact same individuals at Harvard was completely different before and after February 4, 2004: the day Mark's site launched. It's worth asking, why?

Certainly, it is possible that I am simply wrong in my accounting of the similarities and differences between the sites; that houseSYSTEM's Face Book was "bad" software and Mark's Facebook was "good" software, and as a result people decided to change their personal views on privacy. That explanation is too simple for me to believe, however. Just using one software application that is simpler or better-looking than another should not make people alter their personal philosophy on privacy, religion, or anything at all. Something else had to be involved.

The phrase "viral growth" is kicked around Silicon Valley quite a bit these days, to the point where it has become a meaningless buzzword along with many others like "Web 2.0." Most people who talk about it don't understand the first thing about viral behavior in either a biological or a mathematical sense. My own understanding of the way biological viruses behave is limited at best, but I do have some sense of the math, and a third aspect which I think is often overlooked. According to conventional wisdom, on February 4th when Facebook went on-line, friends began referring friends, who in turn referred their friends, who referred more, and so on. There are two fundamental problems with this view. First, your friends already had to be signed up for The Facebook in order to connect with them, meaning that the site initially had to spread off-line. Second, as houseSYSTEM's debut clearly demonstrated, *everyone started out afraid.*

This fear was a serious issue, and I almost lost my college degree over it. Even after students knew that I had only the best of intentions, almost no one wanted to volunteer their information to be posted on houseSYSTEM. Out of almost two thousand members, only a hundred or so ended up on the Universal Face Book (though everyone received multiple e-mails about it). Some of them had undoubtedly been pointed there by their friends, though perhaps not as many as on Mark's site, since he let people explicitly define who their friends were much like Friendster. Yet, a few months after houseSYSTEM's Face Book launched, the prevailing attitude was completely different with regard to serving up personal information. "Viral growth" had nothing to do with that transformation.

The contrast between most college students' view of privacy in 2003 compared to today could not be more pronounced. While I attended Harvard, a man known only as "The Whisperer" terrified scores of female undergraduates by calling them and whispering obscenities over the phone. My friend Raluca, with her dark sense of humor, probably handled his call better than anyone because she mistakenly thought it was her boyfriend.

"What are you wearing?" The Whisperer whispered.

"No! What are *you* wearing?" she countered loudly.

Eventually, a man in Florida was arrested in connection with the calls. Students were more vigilant than ever about guarding access to their personal information. After Facebook launched, the opposite was true: students happily posted their home address, telephone number, cell phone number, sexual orientation, and eventually, photographs in all states of dress and sobriety.

Years later, the headlines that ensued caught the attention of the Attorneys General of several states, who began a 50-state investigation of Facebook's privacy policies in September 2007. As I warned Mark almost four years prior, his hazy ideas amounted to a privacy nightmare without proper controls, and the legal system was sure to get involved.

I saw the impact of this cultural shift best when I asked my own friends for permission to use their names in this book. Most of them politely declined, citing personal privacy as the reason why. I suspect a few were worried about how being associated with a so-called troublemaker might affect their careers—a legitimate, if unfortunate, concern. The rest are simply private individuals and I felt as though I had to respect their right to restrict the flow of information about themselves. Yet all of my friends, who are intelligent people, have profiles on Facebook, and those pages alone tell you more about them than I probably could here.

Until I was locked out of the site, my Facebook profile, however, was blank. Not having one at all would have left me locked out (as I am now); having one just as complete as the next user's would have meant that I endorsed intellectual property theft. Privacy is a complicated and not completely logical business.

There's also the issue of privacy beyond what the public can see. Recent news stories have finally uncovered something that was obvious to me all along: He Who Controls The Database, Knows All. Facebook employees are human beings (many, in fact, are members of Harvard's Class of 2005), and it came as no surprise to me that several had abused their abilities to monitor site activity, sometimes even going so far as to modify user profiles without consent. When I monitored users on houseSYSTEM, I did so to ensure that the site *wasn't* tampered with.

Sadly, this should not surprise anyone familiar with Facebook's top management. As soon as I heard about "facemash" years ago I knew what lay ahead. It was one thing to compare facial attractiveness amongst anonymous volunteers in an academic setting such as Professor Nakayama's course, but quite another to use the names and pictures of the students next door without their permission. (Mark's on-line journal from that time has since revealed that he initially set out to compare his peers to farm animals, not each other, making his drunken creation that much more horrific. A new slogan along the lines of "never drink and develop" may be in order.)

How is it that such irresponsible people land in positions of such power? Unlike politics, where this question is also frequently applicable, there is no election process to puzzle over here, only market forces. In business, people vote with their dollars. In Silicon Valley (where the rules of economics are slightly bent every few years), people vote with their clicks but also by proxy through investors.

The part of venture capital that Jerry Kaplan never had the chance to write about was the best case scenario: what happens when it works. What happened for Mark was the perfect storm of press coverage, the kind that really does only hit once a decade. I contend that the press is the key ingredient which every startup you've never heard of has overlooked in their quest for "viral growth," and which Facebook unintentionally mastered from day one.

The press doesn't tell you merely what sites are out there; it tells you what to think about them. The *Crimson* told students to avoid houseSYSTEM, and avoid it they did. When the same trusted and respected newspaper told them to flock to Facebook because of its revolutionary "new" features, they flocked, even though houseSYSTEM had them for months. When Mark Zuckerberg used his limited knowledge of graph theory to create incentives to spread the word, he helped not only to accelerate the growth of his project, but simultaneously to accelerate the growth of *The Crimson*'s rosy (and rather naïve) mindset about it. Each successive student who signed up was faced with an ever-increasing amount of peer pressure from an ever-increasing number of peers to post information when only days before, probably little or no information would have been posted at all.

This helps answer the question of how many social networking sites we will ultimately see. If my theory is right, the ones that the press supports will succeed, and the rest you will probably never hear about. Reporters are human beings too, hopefully with some desire for diversity in life, and when they get sick of writing about social networks, we will all probably stop hearing about them in favor of the next big thing.

It's also worth noting that since reporters love to copy one another, there are exponential growth phenomena at work within the media as well. For a business, netting a single news story can end up meaning ten stories in the end. This all, of course, is nothing new. The press has always been crucial to commerce, but part of the legend that reporters have engendered about Facebook in their writing is that Mark Zuckerberg somehow hit upon a magic formula that led to his web site's ultimate success. On the contrary, reporters simply capitalized on the "Harvard dropout" template that Bill Gates had written for him thirty years prior, except that unlike Bill Gates, Mark didn't actually know how to turn a profit.

Facebook, Inc. has inspired many startup founders to ignore everything necessary to run a profitable business, searching instead for a way to replicate this formula of chance. The fact that not a single social network has turned into a profitable industry force without significant quantities of outside investment lends credence to the argument that there is no formula—or if there is, it's not a very good one. This is not to say that social networks aren't useful, because they are; they're simply not good businesses. In my mind, for the profit-driven entrepreneur, the business case to study is still Microsoft circa 1985.

As for Facebook becoming the next Google or Microsoft, I have yet to be convinced. Taking into account developments such as Microsoft's investment of $240 million for 1.6% of the company, it's hard to imagine that Facebook will simply sit on the capital without turning it into something that generates revenue. Nonetheless, I think my initial judgment of the idea was correct. If you look at the Face Book component of houseSYSTEM as a stand-alone business, there are easier things to monetize. What that inevitably means is that Facebook, Inc. will have to branch out, because the real money to be made exists in other markets.

The recent addition of "Social Ads" (also known as "Beacon"), is a case in point. It represents a massive departure from the site's original goal of making student life better (my view), or more fun (Mark's). The advertising system, which puts members' faces next to advertisements of products they have purchased elsewhere on the internet, along with claims of "endorsement," has students and consumers furious. Some have inadvertently advertised their Christmas gifts to their peers well ahead of time. Others have ended up endorsing products they didn't mean to. Facebook resisted making any changes to the system, until organized protests began and advertisers such as Coca-Cola started questioning whether they really wanted to be associated with such a controversial (read "irresponsible"), Orwellian idea. It is not the first time Facebook, Inc. has made its users upset. It probably won't be the last.

Careless management decisions aside, I have a hard time imagining that Facebook will become the pervasive force amongst baby boomers that it has become amongst their children, because their children hate the fact that their parents are on the same web sites as they are. Dismissing this argument as essentially cultural and lacking any quantitative basis is perilous, in my opinion, because Facebook got its start on the equally cultural and difficult-to-quantify basis of making voyeurism cool. Yet, as any college student will attest, voyeurism is considerably less cool when your own parents are the voyeurs.

The fundamental truth that there *should* be limits to openness should in turn impact the worth that people attribute to Facebook and sites like it. Mark Zuckerberg claims that he is making the world more open and seems to genuinely believe that doing so is always a good thing. Yet anyone with any understanding of the world's complexity knows that it is not always the case that complete transparency is good. Even Facebook, Inc. as a company disproves its own mantra. If openness is universally good, then Facebook's accounting department should have no problem telling the world how much money the company actually makes, without the involvement of subpoenas. Similarly, its founder should have no problem with reporters (or classmates) writing about his past.

■

Mark has succeeded in enlisting an entire generation of youth, but without profit, he can't stop there. MySpace, the competing site which is more popular among younger high school students, is where Mark set his sights as early as 2004 according to my conversations with him. Facebook is making good progress catching up. However, just as I correctly told my realtor around the same time, no one can escape the force of equilibrium. Facebook will not maintain its torrential growth rates forever, and when they begin to slip, the company will have a serious problem.

As it is, the Microsoft investment, indirectly valuing Facebook at $15 billion, or approximately $375 per user, yields some strange numbers. Advertisers are seeing banner advertisement click-through rates of 0.02%, or sometimes less. (This is consistent with my own usage of the site, as well as my friends'. If anyone clicks on the advertisements, it is usually by mistake.) I have yet to meet anyone who purchased a product thanks to Facebook. So, unless advertisers are marketing big-ticket items such as cruises, pianos, and diamonds—things your average student would never buy—there is almost no possible way that they are making up for their advertising expenses on Facebook in terms of product sales. That fact alone makes me think that the valuation is severely inflated.

The more likely explanation for Facebook's astronomical valuation is that very few people, not even wealthy people who run software companies, know what the future holds. Microsoft placed a bet on Facebook as insurance against the future, and as insurance against Google posing a threat to its monopolies in the consumer and enterprise software markets. We'll see if the bet pays off. My guess is that it won't, but that won't hurt Microsoft, which has billions of dollars of cash on hand.

Venture capital-backed companies come and go. Napster had a precipitous rise and fall in 2000; Friendster, which was even in the same industry as Facebook, followed soon after. In the grand scheme of things, all of the social networking hype of the past several years will be reduced to the simple insight that people are the most important entity to consider when designing software. The robots of the future will seem a lot more intelligent if they can keep track of who they're talking to or about, instead of shouting a person's first name and last name in all capital letters as most of today's UNIX-based database applications do.

There are more immediate implications for the future of software too. They'll dwarf today's Facebook in significance once they're more fully developed in a few years' time.

If you ever visit Palo Alto, three blocks from the intersection of Harvard and California, that's what you'll find me working on.

Epilogue

I received my Harvard College diploma shortly after completing final exams in the spring of 2004. It came inside a large crimson folder, which the Registrar's Office placed inside a Harvard Co-Op plastic bag. It looked as if I'd made a five-dollar purchase.

After Rohit Chopra's term as the President of the Undergraduate Council expired, Student Exchange was removed from the UC's web site. Shortly thereafter, the SEC's new leadership presented houseSYSTEM to the UC's new leadership, hoping to gain official backing from the student government. Despite calls from *The Crimson*, the general student populace, and the UC itself for a site containing the same features as houseSYSTEM, the UC's new president and vice-president had no interest.

Except for the table demanded by University Hall containing 402 private student records, no personal information of any sort stored in houseSYSTEM was ever compromised. I attempted to sell the rights to the site, owned by Think Computer Corporation, to HASCS. Though Dr. Steen and his associates agreed that houseSYSTEM was both useful and well-designed, they refused to consider using it, even at no cost, on "technical grounds." A meeting with the Harvard University Registrar yielded further positive feedback and no subsequent action. In the fall of 2004, a shopping period scheduling tool, remarkably similar to the one found on houseSYSTEM, appeared on HASCS's "my.harvard" portal. The Mather House web team took one of my photographs from houseSYSTEM and placed it on the official Mather House home page; it was only removed after I pointed out the blatant copyright infringement, but the irony was lost on them. In the fall of 2005, the Registrar announced the creation of an information technology fellowship to digitize the course feedback process, which CriticalMass had already done.

Without anyone to run or provide backing for houseSYSTEM, I opted to shut it down myself, rather than allow it to decay. I posted two quotes from Ayn Rand's *Atlas Shrugged* in its place on the internet, one of which can be found at beginning of this book. The quotes eventually disappeared as well, when the SEC failed to renew its domain name and the club effectively dissolved. In place of houseSYSTEM, several small sites have sprung up at Harvard to provide the same types of services. None of them have lasted long, however, and none of them offered even a fraction of houseSYSTEM's features.

Overnight, thefacebook.com turned into a huge hit as Mark Zuckerberg expanded its reach to colleges across the country. He was placed on probation by the Administrative Board during the latter part of his sophomore year, after which he voluntarily left Harvard College. *The Crimson*'s relentlessly positive coverage either directly or indirectly attracted the attention of a Stanford Graduate School of Business student who had plans to work for Accel Partners, which later offered Mark $12.7 million in venture capital financing when Mark finally returned their calls. Facebook, Inc. raised $25 million more after that from various venture capitalists, and eventually accepted a $240 million investment from Microsoft for 1.6% of the company. Other wealthy investors have since flocked to the company.

houseSYSTEM's friend classification, campus postering, message board, photo album, item exchange, user profile and group profile features all progressively appeared in barely altered forms on the Facebook web site. I had the opportunity to discuss the similarities between the two sites in detail when I received a subpoena in the ConnectU, Inc. vs. Facebook, Inc. lawsuit, and was forced to present evidence of my involvement with Facebook at a videotaped legal deposition. Facebook, Inc. paid for my lawyer's time, a quick lunch, and nothing more.

Before it became a shell corporation for the lawsuit, ConnectU diversified, branching into the used textbook exchange marketplace with a web page form whose user interface exactly matched houseSYSTEM's. One of ConnectU's three founders, as well as several of its programmers, were houseSYSTEM members.

Months after the fact, Nick Smith apologized via e-mail for his conduct during his term as Editor-in-Chief of the Harvard International Review, citing an unspecified life-changing event that had re-shaped his outlook on life. I accepted his apology, wondering how many people aside from Francis still believed the lies he had spread about Think Computer Corporation and myself.

Dean Herschbach, Dean Kidd and Senior Tutor Jay Ellison are still employed by Harvard University. (Jay Ellison even received a promotion.) Their conduct was never called into question at any official level. Dean Bean, possibly feeling adrift, left after my freshman year. Susan Cooke was right to fear for her job; Dean Gross eliminated her as part of a re-organization in September 2003, and eventually gave up his own position. President Summers, who received a vote of no confidence from the Faculty of Arts and Sciences in early 2005, was accused of conspiring to fire Dean William Kirby and subsequently agreed to resign, rather than face a second vote of no confidence.

Bruce Watson, the TF who replaced Robert Neugeboren in Economics 1010a during the fall of 2002, was forced out of Harvard College for reaching the six-year time limit imposed on teaching assistants. Despite having the support of prominent faculty members, not to mention a petition signed by almost one thousand students, the College administration denied his request to stay, forcibly ending the tenure of one of the best instructors the Economics department has ever known. Professor

Robert Neugeboren still teaches at Harvard. His courses are considerably smaller in size.

Former Dean Harry Lewis, still a professor at Harvard College, went on to teach a Core Curriculum course called "Bits," which focused on information technology. Dean Lewis has also written a book, in part about his tenure as Dean of Harvard College. A Curricular Review resulted in the downfall of the Core Curriculum, and in March 2008, *The Crimson* reported that the College would introduce a new major "combining the study of technology and society" through the recently re-named School of Engineering and Applied Sciences.

Adrienne Geszler and Dr. James Paces are still employed by the Shaker Heights City School District. Mrs. Groves earned her doctorate in educational administration from the University of Akron, and retired from her role as principal of Woodbury Elementary School. Treasurer Daniel Wilson left the District a couple of years after the Technology Committee stopped meeting. The District ordered its first shipment of Dell personal computers to replace hundreds of broken MTI machines the day after I completed my high school senior project in 2001.

Cameron Johnson, who avoided being sued for his instrumental role in the demise of SurfingPrizes.com, was invited back to Japan a second time for a public-ity tour that he used to promote his Japanese-language biography. He had granted interviews to a writer on his first tour, who had used recorded material to produce the book. Today, Cameron is a used car salesman at Magic City Ford, a car dealership run by his father in Roanoke, Virginia. He is one of a select number of car salesmen who employs his own public relations firm, which netted his English book deal.

During my freshman year at Harvard, I realized what "Scalable Techniques for Mining Causal Structures" meant while reading a transcribed interview on the internet with a person whose name rang a bell: Craig Silverstein. After he gradu-ated from Stanford, Craig took a full-time job as the Chief Technology Officer of a start-up called Google, Inc. Carl Sjogreen later defected to Google with a number of his co-workers. Google hired my friend Vaughn in 2005.

Brad went on to study chemistry at the University of Pennsylvania in his home town of Philadelphia, where his father still practices law. After MIT, Tim entered the Mechanical Engineering graduate program at the University of California, Berkeley. After Princeton, my high school friend Adam took a position with Hu-man Rights Watch in Chile, and later entered law school at Berkeley as well. Philip left his adolescent persona behind (as many high school students fortunately do), attended Wesleyan University, and was later accepted to Princeton to pursue a Ph.D. in politics. His work is sure to be influential.

My roommate Metin chose Southern Methodist University, and then The Uni-versity of Exeter in England, to continue his study of archaeology. He has published papers in the top journals in his field (including one that I had the honor of helping him write), and eventually earned the whole-hearted support and pride of both of his parents. Jeff accepted a job at the White House's Council of Economic Advisers and later went back to Harvard, while Elliott went off to U.S. Army Ranger School for training from which he graduated, unlike most of the cadets who entered. He plans to attend Harvard Law School after his tours of duty in Afghanistan. Nathan eventually shut down his spam distribution business on his own, and now works in Silicon Valley.

After my brother, Simon, graduated from the Brehm Preparatory School the weekend after I picked up my diploma, he returned home where my both my parents assumed the additional full-time jobs of looking after him. My mother found him work with Cleveland sports teams and large companies—jobs that he was sadly unable to hold. The State of Ohio often seemed to go out of its way to introduce obstacles into his path, paying only for part of his treatment plan at the Cleveland Clinic and not paying his part-time providers at all. Some Shaker residents were no better, leading to charges being filed against Simon for making a single phone call late at night. (The neighbors later apologized, but Shaker refused to drop the charges.) Simon's autistic tendencies continue to worsen, putting enormous strain on my family. He is the epitome of the Child Left Behind.

Still, Simon does have flashes of brilliance from time to time. At the Lowell House Master's reception for Class of 2005 graduates, Simon refused to eat any of the appetizers.

"This isn't real food. This is Ivy League food," he reasoned bitterly in front of one of the House Masters, to everyone else's amusement.

When I suggested that Simon might sign up for The Facebook in order to meet new friends, he also had an answer for that.

"No. It's not safe," he said, eliciting my and my mother's shock.

"How do you know?" I asked.

"It's on the *news*," he said. I couldn't help but laugh.

I no longer tell anyone about the security flaws I find, save my parents and close friends. It is amusing, however, that of all the sites that I discovered with serious security issues in 2005, several belonged to Harvard University. To this day, despite repeated efforts to warn both HASCS and University Hall, Harvard's official sites are plagued with numerous and extremely serious vulnerabilities, some of which hackers have already exploited in highly-publicized breaches affecting thousands of people, some of which *The Crimson* has uncovered, and most of which it has not.

■

In the end, everyone mentioned in this book, except perhaps Simon and my family, will live comfortably enough. There is no immediate, dire threat to speak of. The threat is more subtle, more long-term, and it holds vast implications for our society. That is to say, we are failing our students at every point along the educational spectrum from grade school through college. Most of them don't even know it; their troubles are just attributed to teenage angst, or drugs, or alcohol, or any number of common scapegoats. Sometimes those problems are indeed real, but more often than we'd like to think, the root cause can be found somewhere in a classroom.

While my own turbulent and mostly unhappy experience of going from a public school to Harvard College—the dream that families around the globe hope for—may not be the "average" student's experience, there is no such thing as the average student. The fact that the events in my story even took place disturbs me deeply, not only because they affected me, but because already, I've seen them happen in bits and pieces to others I know.

With the correct checks and balances in place, whether in eighth grade before the Technology Committee, or in tenth grade while I slaved away at meaningless homework, or during my freshman year of college with Harvard's Administrative Board, or during my junior year involving University Hall, my life might have been different. It might have been better, and I might have learned more. Yet in each case, educators appeared to go out of their way to do more harm than good.

In short, if you demand that a child who wants to teach himself learn only in lock-step with "the A.P. curriculum" or "the SAT study guide" (or any number of accepted, conventional methods), you'll do more than fail him; you'll crush him. Conversely, ignore the needs of an autistic or otherwise disabled child who craves structure simply to make it through the day, and you may very well end up destroying not only the entire day for that child, but his family's day as well. The American educational system drove me to the verge of suicide. It did the same for my brother. Our educational system is not flexible, it is not logically structured, and it is not working.

What makes me truly sick is that I bought into it all, filling out the Common Application as a senior in high school, worrying about where to write the next extra-curricular activity in the blank after I had already run out of room. While Dean Lewis encouraged us so strongly to slow down, the Harvard Admissions Office couldn't seem to work the controls on the treadmill that it helped set in motion years ago. This monster of a system is no one's fault but our own, for we created it, and though we may critique it, we still deem it acceptable. It isn't.

If I ever have children, I dread the day that they will ask me if they should apply to Harvard College. I cannot separate my own negative experience from the multiple, positive facets of the institution. I will be guilty of turning the next generation away from wonderful people, or I will be guilty of exposing it to irreversible harm at the hands of belligerent tyrants posing as wise-men. It is a difficult choice, and not one that can be solved merely by increasing the number of stops on a high school college tour. Our educational system requires fundamental change. It requires more than the dregs of society interspersed with the occasional few who care. It requires the best.

After all, there is a difference between the enforcement of structure for learning's sake, and the exertion of authority for its own sake. Education should be a result of the former, but only tyranny stems from the latter. Making the distinction in practice requires some modicum of intelligence, and if our nation's teachers are unable to, then our prospects for the future will most certainly be ruined. Only that mythical average student will survive such a conformist environment, as the rest are driven off a mental cliff.

The consequences of such conflation have already begun to manifest themselves in unexpected ways. At our nation's greatest institutions of learning, independent thinkers are punished and not praised, while plagiarists and thieves are praised and not punished. The whole world now accepts the whim of one such individual as technological "genius." Unless corrected, we will all be in danger, for what happens in our classrooms today—and especially Harvard's classrooms—affects the world tomorrow.

Acknowledgments

There are many people to whom I owe a deep debt of gratitude. The most obvious two are my parents, who nurtured me, supported me, and listened to me throughout the lightest and darkest of times, often while under unimaginable stress themselves. My love for them goes far beyond what words can express.

My aunt, Leila, and uncle, Michael, for their support of Simon and me in so many ways over the years, from gifts of software to last-minute flights to Cleveland.

My friends deserve my eternal thanks. Throughout much of my life I was sure that my bar for friendship was so high as to be unrealistic, but you have all proven that notion wrong. In no particular order, K.S.A.J.R. (we always joked about your initials, and this is why: there are far too many of them), S.K.M., R.J.S., A.K.K., B.A.F., T.C.N., Meredith Reiches, Metin Eren, Elliott Neal, Jeff Clemens, Tim Suen, Brad Rosen, Vaughn Tan, Wentao Mo, Josh Weinstein, Jonathan Leong, Jini Kim, Melissa Sconyers, Joshua Go, John Lynch, Brookes Brown, Schuyler Brown, Rodica, Felix and surely others I have left out but who know me well—I feel honored to have enjoyed your companionship.

Ronald Rosen and Andrew Good, who kept me out of jail and who I could always turn to in a time of crisis (which turned out to be often). I have encountered few people so caring, so enthusiastic, so generous, and so committed.

Jerry Kaplan, J.K. Rowling, and the late Richard Feynman, who influenced me through their writing more than anyone else.

Carl Sjogreen, who proved that success as an entrepreneur is possible.

Over the years, I have had a few stellar teachers. Some may not even know that I was their student, but others definitely do: Robert Morgan at University School, Dianne Derrick at Woodbury Elementary, Diana Jones and Eileen Blattner at Shaker Heights High School, and at Harvard University, Margo Seltzer, Paul Bamberg, Harry Lewis, Roderick MacFarquhar, Jonathan Zittrain, James Medoff, Dwight Perkins and Bruce Watson. May the world's teachers aspire to your example.

Thanks to Jonathon Lazear, and his staff, Darrick Kline and Christi Cardenas, for hearing me out when hundreds of others would not.

I can never thank John Markoff at *The New York Times* enough for writing about parts of my tale in an accurate (and still engaging) manner.

Thanks lastly to the many curious individuals who found my manuscript on a corner of the internet, read it in its infancy, and wrote encouraging words of support.

About the Author

Aaron Greenspan started Think Computer Corporation from his bedroom in Shaker Heights, Ohio at the age of 15. While he attended high school, Aaron grew Think to support more than 150 businesses, individuals and schools across the United States and Canada. He subsequently changed the focus of the company from IT consulting to software development. In October of 2000, Aaron spearheaded the creation of Think Computer Foundation, a 501(c)3 non-profit organization with the goal of helping children through technology. Aaron invented The Facebook while attending Harvard College in September 2003 and graduated *cum laude* with an A.B. in Economics in 2004. He lives in Palo Alto, California.